Leading Product Innovation

ACCELERATING GROWTH IN A PRODUCT–BASED BUSINESS

Marvin L. Patterson
with
John A. Fenoglio

JOHN WILEY & SONS, INC.

New York ➤ Chichester ➤ Weinheim ➤ Brisbane ➤ Singapore ➤ Toronto

Published by John Wiley & Sons, Inc.

Published simultaneously in Canada.

This publication is designed to provide accurate and authoritative information in regard to the subject matter covered. It is sold with the understanding that the publisher is not engaged in rendering professional services. If professional advice or other expert assistance is required, the services of a competent professional person should be sought.

Library of Congress Cataloging-in-Publication Data:

Patterson, Marvin L.
    Leading product innovation : accelerating growth in a
product-based business / Marvin L. Patterson with John A.
Fenoglio.
        p.   cm.
    Includes index.
    ISBN 0-471-34517-2 (cloth : alk. paper)
    1. New products—Management.   I. Fenoglio, John A.   II.
Title.
HD69.N4P34   1999
658.5′75—dc21   99-15417

To product innovators everywhere.
May your efforts always stimulate growth.
May your lives have balance—
as professionals, as spouses, as parents, as citizens,
and as individuals. May you always have fun at work.

Contents

Preface

This book describes how to strengthen product innovation efforts in a business enterprise, thereby improving its long-term financial performance. The central premise is that the creation and introduction of new products is accomplished by a key business process that spans most of the functions in an enterprise. The top-level management team in the business unit owns this process by virtue of being the only group with control over the entire product innovation system. This team sets long-term strategic directions, selects new product investments, and then applies due diligence to these investments as each project unfolds. The team members ensure that the performance of this enterprisewide business process is competitive. Thus high-level managers, in guiding and directing product innovation efforts, greatly influence the long-term financial success of their business enterprise.

These high-level managers in an enterprise comprise the primary target audience for this book and include at least the president or general manager of a strategic business unit and every staff member who reports to that person. Middle managers may also gain significant value from this work. A common understanding of the material presented here will equip management teams with a consistent mental framework and a common vocabulary for discussing performance issues and conceptualizing solutions.

The audience for this book also includes both graduate students in business and individual business managers who may be participating in a university executive program. The perspective on product innovation provided by this book—particularly in Chapters 2 through 6, Chapter 8, and Chapter 12—provides mental models and fundamental principles that are essential to any career in business management.

This book is based largely on the experience of both authors who were involved in product innovation for the Hewlett-Packard Company (HP) from 1973 through 1993. Early in this period, they were new product engineers. Then they managed new product efforts in a variety of functional departments, including both R&D and marketing. Toward the end of this period, the authors were responsible for improving the overall effectiveness of product innovation as a business process. In 1988, Marv Patterson became the Director of Corporate Engineering for HP and was responsible for companywide improvements to new product development processes and tools. John Fenoglio joined Corporate Engineering shortly thereafter and took charge of improving R&D management skills and processes throughout the company.

While in Corporate Engineering, the authors broadened their perspective to encompass HP's new product activities worldwide. In addition, the authors often were able to exchange information about product innovation issues and best practices with representatives from other companies. Executive seminars that HP provided for its customers frequently highlighted Corporate Engineering's improvement efforts and allowed the authors to compare notes on product innovation issues with HP's visitors. The Hewlett-Packard Company was a popular target for benchmarking efforts by other firms, and Corporate Engineering hosted these visits. In return for sharing our expertise, we asked each visiting team to teach us as much as possible about their experience, performance issues, and best practices.

These interactions demonstrated a pervasive need for improving the effectiveness of new product efforts. With CEO Lew Platt's blessing, the authors left HP in 1993 to launch Innovation Resultants International (IRI), a firm dedicated to helping client companies achieve greater business success through more effective product innovation. Since then, IRI has worked with dozens of companies in industries ranging from semiconductors to heavy equipment, and from home entertainment to office products.

While the authors are proud to describe themselves as "HP alumni," serving as consultants to other firms has provided new learning and a broader perspective than would have been possible at HP. This most recent experience has enabled the authors to generalize their learning into the useful mental models and fundamental principles described in this book.

Many stories, drawn from the authors' experiences, are included in this work to both illustrate leadership principles and highlight common pitfalls. As a rule throughout, companies and individuals associated with a positive experience are named whereas the identities of companies and persons associated with negative examples are disguised. The experience that the authors gained at HP, the lessons learned, and the role models that they encountered there were generally positive so that company and people who worked there are mentioned frequently. This tends to inject an HP-centric tone to this work that is difficult to avoid. The intended focus of this book is on product innovation leadership principles, not HP. The HP stories, though, reflect the knowledge and experience the authors gained there and are thus essential to this work.

MARVIN L. PATTERSON
JOHN A. FENOGLIO

Acknowledgments

If I have seen farther . . . it is by standing upon the shoulders of Giants.

Sir Isaac Newton
1642–1727

John and I have enjoyed careers with extraordinary opportunities to learn about product innovation. The situations that we have encountered as well as the people with whom we have worked have shaped our understanding of this important business process. On occasion, both of us have had to present our product development work to Bill Hewlett, the late Dave Packard, and the late Barney Oliver. These people scared us to death at times, but they asked tough questions and held us accountable for knowing our customer, our competition, and our contribution. More importantly, they created an excellent working environment in which we, like our peers throughout the Hewlett-Packard Company (HP), were able to do our very best work. So, to begin, we want to acknowledge the incredible gifts that we have received from these three people over the years.

John Young, retired CEO of HP, provided leadership to our efforts in Corporate Engineering while we were with HP, and has been our role model over the years as a visionary and results-oriented business leader. John too scared us at times. He also asked difficult questions and had the unsettling habit of never forgetting anything to which we might have committed. He always held us accountable for good solutions and excellent results in our efforts to serve HP.

We appreciate the leadership, trust, and support that we have received from Lew Platt, current Chairman, CEO, and President of HP. In 1988, Lew gave me the opportunity to lead the Corporate Engineering group and develop it into an effective agent of change in HP's product development community. This assignment gave John and me irreplaceable experience in evaluating and improving product innovation performance and ultimately launched us on our current career path.

Tom Vos, retired Vice President of HP, probably taught us more about managing both people and product development than any other individual. His leadership, and the role model he provided during our years at HP's San Diego division, provided us with lessons that we still draw on today. Tom created the environment in which we first experienced the incredible joy and sense of accomplishment that comes with introducing an excellent new product. Because of Tom, we know how good product innovation can be when it is managed well.

John Doyle, retired Executive Vice President of HP, was also a strong influence. John guided and supported us during our Corporate Engineering experience and infused us with his passion for an imaginative understanding of customer needs. At first we didn't get it, and wondered about this man's zealotry. Over time, though, he infected us with the fundamental importance of this concept; now our clients wonder why we are always uttering these same strange incantations.

We also need to thank Al Bagley, the business group R&D manager who tracked our product development efforts in San Diego. Al taught us many important lessons about product portfolio management. He has been my mentor throughout much of my career and has shaped and guided it in many ways.

John and I have learned much about managing the product development process from Norm Johnson, retired HP R&D manager, and our good friend. Norm hired both John and me into HP so many years ago, and since we founded IRI, he has participated in many of our diagnostic efforts at client companies. Most recently, he helped us with our retrospective analysis of product portfolio leadership practices, both at HP and at other companies with which we have had experience. Norm provided invaluable assistance in articulating the key leadership roles covered in Chapter 8.

Finally, my wife, Mary Lou Simmermacher, has contributed ongoing help and support to this work. My partnership with Mary

Lou has provided an essential foundation for this book, and her unwavering belief in the project's worth has kept me hard at work at my laptop computer. Our conversations have nurtured into being many of the ideas presented here. In particular, our dialogue has helped shape the discussion of the human elements in product creation presented in Chapter 11.

M.L.P
J.A.F.

Chapter 1

Introduction

Most kinds of power require a substantial sacrifice ... There is an apprenticeship, a discipline lasting many years. ... Whatever it is you seek, you have to put in the time, the practice, the effort. You must give up a lot to get it. It has to be very important to you. And once you have attained it, it is your power. It can't be given away: It resides in you. It is literally the result of your discipline.

Michael Crichton
Jurassic Park

Sometimes businesses lose their power. Perhaps they have experienced the birth process of being a start-up operation with an exciting new product concept, launched their product line, and succeeded in becoming powerful—even dominant—in their marketplace. But now, for some reason, the rapid and exhilarating growth has stopped. Revenues have flattened, profits are plummeting. The original product line is losing its luster. Recent product introductions have been clumsy, and sales have been disappointing. The competition is making significant inroads into a market that was once the company's home turf.

In many respects, the early phase of corporate development follows the same pattern as human growth from infancy through the teenage years. As the body and intellect develop, so does a young person's sense of power grow into the wonderful arrogance of adolescence. At this time in life, teenagers tend to believe that this incredible progress will simply continue forever, without effort. Adulthood, however, provides a rude wake-up call. Progress in adulthood requires investment, focus, hard work, and discipline.

Sometimes even a very large company that is well into "adulthood" loses its power. It has paid its dues. It is multinational and in diverse businesses. The company name is a catchword throughout the world. The enterprise has adopted excellent business processes, has invested in quality management skills, and has world-class plants and equipment. And this has all paid off—for a while. Returns on shareholder investment, while traditionally excellent, have been disappointing in the past few years. Remedies that have worked in the past—sales promotions, cost cutting, quality improvement—no longer restore financial performance to desired levels. Revenue growth has flattened, with earnings consistently coming in below expectations. The company is losing significant customer accounts to upstart competitors that didn't even exist five years earlier.

This phase in corporate development parallels that of an adult who learned a trade when young and for years has earned a good living applying those skills. But the world has changed. Shifts in technology and markets have systematically eliminated jobs that require this person's expertise. Making a living is becoming more and more difficult. Younger people with new and different skills are somehow able to succeed where the older worker is failing. They are passing him by.

■ THE VALUE PROPOSITION OF THIS BOOK

This book is about regaining the power to compete and to restore healthy business performance and growth. It does not offer any "silver bullets"—there are none. Instead, the perspective it provides on industry best practices in product innovation is unparalleled in both breadth and depth. Decades of collective experience in product innovation shaped this perspective; doing it, managing it, improving it. Although the authors gained much of this experience with the Hewlett-Packard Company (HP), they have expanded their understanding through helping client companies more effectively create new products. The many opportunities to compare and contrast various business approaches to product innovation—those that work well and others that work poorly—have deepened the authors' understanding. As a result, the general principles, conceptual models, and real-life stories presented here will provide the reader with new tools for dealing with business performance issues.

Executives who are at least partially responsible for restoring and maintaining desired business performance comprise the target audience for this book. The discussion presumes that the reader's business generates revenue through the sale and support of specific products. While the subject matter is often applicable in service industries, such companies are outside the primary focus of this book.

A prevalent misconception among business leaders is that product innovation is the sole purview and concern of the engineering department. The perspective here is that new products are an enterprisewide responsibility. Engineering alone cannot make the new product program competitive.

In many companies, executives categorize product innovation as an expense, to be minimized whenever possible just like other expenses. The perspective here is that new product operations are an investment. With proper placement and management, the investment yields a high rate of growth in both revenue and profit.

Product innovation is one of the most important business processes in the enterprise and should be under the management control of the executive leadership team. Because the competitive success of this critical activity is ultimately their responsibility, the executive team must understand how product innovation is supposed to work, identify flaws in its operation, and implement improvements to restore it to competitive levels of performance. Some executive team members may be familiar with new product operations, whereas others may have little knowledge in this area. To work effectively as a team, business leaders must develop a common understanding of product innovation concepts and share a common vocabulary.

The concise treatment of product innovation in this book is expressed in plain language as well as insightful graphics, and reaches just the breadth and depth needed at the executive level. For the reader who is familiar with the generation of new products, this work will provide a useful review with valuable new insights. The executive who has less experience with product innovation will find a thorough remedial treatment of the subject.

Executives are busy people, and time is usually their most precious resource. Reading this book thus represents a considerable investment that should yield the following worthwhile return:

➤ New mental models that embody the relationships between new product operations and healthy business growth.

➤ A working knowledge of industry best practices in bringing new products to market.

➤ An understanding of how executives can support and lead new product processes.

➤ Insight into how to launch and manage successful new product operations.

➤ Awareness of how the working environment contributes to successful new product programs.

➤ Information about the best ways to measure the performance of new product initiatives.

The material in the following chapters covers the fundamentals of product innovation as a business process and emphasizes general principles that are applicable across a broad range of technologies and business arenas; the information is generic and relatively timeless. Since executives seldom have as much familiarity with the product innovation process as with other business processes, they should receive a high return on the time invested in reading this book.

This work also can serve as a basis of communication for entire executive teams by providing a framework of useful concepts along with a common vocabulary. In this capacity, it can (1) help focus the business team on critical issues that limit successful performance and (2) help them identify strategies for improving the competitiveness of their enterprise.

■ MASTERING THE PRODUCT INNOVATION PROCESS

The quotation from *Jurassic Park* at the beginning of this chapter is about mastering a particular skill or practice. A key premise of this book is that long-term success is only possible when businesses strive for mastery in their new product operations. This activity is the primary means for creating new value for customers and shareholders. The most competitive companies approach this level of performance and create a steady stream of outstanding new products that sustains their growth and financial success. With tireless energy, they identify new opportunities in the high-growth segments of their businesses. An ongoing search for new and better methods and tools for product innovation keeps them among the top competitors in each market that they serve. The only way to compete with such companies is to attain equal mastery in the innovation of new products and services for your customers.

As the quotation suggests, achieving mastery takes much time and investment. To persevere in achieving this goal, executives must deem it to be very important indeed. Companies who master new product innovation exhibit the following success factors:

➤ Executive leaders translate business performance issues into specific strategic objectives for improving new product operations.

➤ Root causes for important product innovation performance issues are well understood and prioritized.

➤ The business leadership team invests substantially in specific improvement projects and tracks and supports these efforts.

➤ Key practitioners at the grassroots level in the company are involved in defining and implementing solutions.

➤ Maintaining new product operations at competitive levels is a high priority and is viewed as an essential, ongoing investment.

Achieving mastery in product innovation can indeed require much time and a large investment. This does not mean, however, that years must pass before the investment can yield significant benefits. Benefits can start almost immediately. In fact, simply by paying attention to key performance issues, the business leadership team can initiate improvements. Like students in school, product innovators respond to expectations. When someone who understands is watching and caring about their performance, they tend to work more effectively. The willingness of executives to invest in specific improvement projects sends strong signals throughout the organization communicating the importance of competitive performance in product innovation. Benefits become evident as soon as the participants start looking around for better ways of working and discover the so-called low-hanging fruit—obvious improvements that require little investment and can be implemented almost immediately.

■ OVERVIEW

This book is organized into five interrelated sections, as outlined in Figure 1.1. Each section is essential to the whole. Together, they provide a thorough discussion of the total system necessary to achieve competitive new product operations. Part I establishes the relationship between product innovation and business success and provides useful mental models for business leaders. Parts II, III, and IV describe key system components that are critical in building a competitive capacity to create new products and services. The final part describes methods for measuring successful implementation of the processes and behaviors presented in earlier sections.

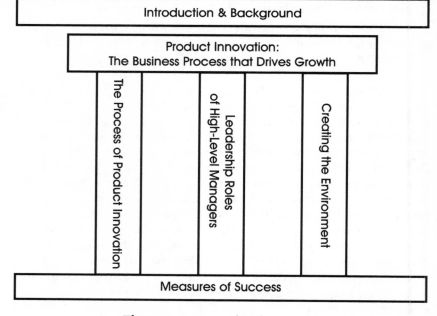

Figure 1.1 A graphical overview.

➤ Part I. Product Innovation—The Business Process That Drives Growth

This section describes relationships between new product innovation and business success. New product innovation is not about technology or engineering. It is fundamentally a business process and it should be measured and managed as such. Part I establishes this fundamental principle up front to serve as a backdrop throughout the book.

Part I first discusses product innovation and its relationship to the enterprise revenue stream. Product innovation is a key element in a closed-loop system that includes both the flow of value to customers and the flow of revenues back to the enterprise. Product innovation is the engine that drives exponential growth, not only in revenues and profits but in shareholder value as well. Relationships between investments in product innovation and rates of revenue growth for various types of businesses are established.

Product innovation is viewed first as a collective, enterprisewide business process and then from the perspective of a single development project. Critical success factors that affect business performance are identified and discussed. In Chapter 4, the time dynamics of product innovation are explored, and the impact of innovation system response time on business decisions and results is examined.

➤ Part II. The Process of Product Innovation

Many business leaders with career experience in areas such as sales or perhaps operations may have little working knowledge of how new products and services come into being. Others with experience in this area may be unaware of recently proven best practices that leading companies have adopted. Part II provides a high-level summary of how product innovation works in the ideal case to create a vision of desired performance.

Product innovation is an enterprisewide system whose primary purpose is to methodically add value to an information set until it describes how to manufacture, use, sell, and support an exciting new product. This information set not only enables the company to create revenue with a new product but also contributes to the pool of knowledge and know-how that distinguishes the company from its competitors. This focus on adding value to information helps describe product innovation as a process and provides a framework for process-quality improvements. The material in Part II offers insight into many ways to improve the performance of the innovation engine.

➤ Part III. Leading Product Innovation — Upper Management Roles

While excellent new product processes and tools are essential, the business leadership team must become actively involved with the new product program to achieve the full potential for competitive performance. Part III outlines key leadership roles and responsibilities that are essential to a first-rate new product program.

High-level executives must set strategic directions for new product activity, oversee specific new product investments, and build the competitive capacity of new product operations. New product activities rank among the largest and most important expenditures that a business incurs. This section outlines key points of focus for high-quality tracking and management of new product investments.

➤ Part IV. Creating the Environment

In addition to excellent processes and strong executive leadership, the working environment—the social and professional climate— can have tremendous impact on competitive performance in a new product program. In a start-up company, motivated employees may create an exciting and successful product, despite haphazard processes and tools. In another company, tremendous investment in processes and tools and the best efforts of business leaders may fail to substantially improve the performance of the new product team. The difference is likely to be the effect of the working environment on individual behavior. Part IV discusses the importance of the working environment as a competitive business asset and explains how executive leaders can, either intentionally or unconsciously, influence the performance of the product-innovation workforce.

➤ Part V. Measures of Success

This final section discusses fundamental principles in the measurement of product-innovation performance. Performance measures are a double-edged sword. They are powerful agents for changing behavior, but emphasizing the wrong measures can actually damage long-term business performance. The relationship between performance measures and desired business behaviors is described. Performance measures that relate to the processes and behaviors recommended in earlier sections of the book are then discussed. While Part V cannot provide a fully detailed description of product-innovation performance measurement, it offers guidance and insight that will help executives avoid most of the common performance-measurement pitfalls.

■ A FOCUS ON BUSINESS BEHAVIOR

This book provides fundamental principles and mental models that a business leader needs to effectively manage product innovation. Business performance, though, depends not so much on what we know as on what we do—our work-related behavior. In view of this, a common practice throughout this work is to end each chapter with suggested upper-management actions that are implied by the chapter content. Tables listing these desired behaviors are included at the end of Chapters 2 through 11. The information in these tables is then used in Chapter 12 to establish effective measures for evaluating the overall performance of business leaders in their management of new product efforts.

Part I

Product Innovation—
The Business Process
That Drives Growth

Chapter 2

Linking Product Innovation with Business Growth

in–vest (in vest′) v. l. to put (money) to use, by purchase or expenditure, in something offering potential profitable returns.

Random House Dictionary of the English Language

New products and services are the lifeblood of an enterprise that fuels business growth. During our years with HP, almost everyone understood this principle, regardless of background—engineering, marketing, sales, or finance. It was a common point of focus at all levels in the company, from top executive to individual contributor.

Our experience since leaving HP, though, leads us to believe that business leaders in other companies often pay surprisingly little attention to their firm's product innovation efforts. Instead, they focus on other matters—manufacturing operations, sales and distribution challenges, or perhaps financial issues. Often the aspects of the enterprise that receive the greatest mind-share from an executive tend to reflect that person's own training and vocational background. For example, business leaders with sales background pay the most attention to business operations in that arena. When performance falls off, they often focus improvement efforts on aspects of the business that they know best and relegate new product matters to the engineering department with the assumption that engineering will do whatever needs to be done.

The purpose of this chapter is to position product innovation as a critical business process that drives growth in both revenues and profits. The competitive performance of product innovation activities should be of central importance to business leaders in every enterprise. The innovation of new products and services, which is described here as a proprietary investment option open only to executives who control the expenditure of available funds, can potentially create a greater financial return than any other investment alternative. The level of performance inherent in a firm's product innovation activities sets the rate of return on these investments. The product innovation process is crucial to business success and thus deserves the highest quality attention, leadership, and support from business leaders at all levels.

This chapter develops a useful conceptual model that quantifies the relationship between product innovation investments and business growth. This discussion begins with a description of the business enterprise as a closed-loop system with product innovation acting as the engine that drives revenue growth. Next, three factors key to revenue growth are described. These factors are linked by a set of useful mathematical relationships that can be presented in the form of growth tables that are unique to each particular enterprise. In deference to the nonmathematical reader, the derivation of these relationships is shown in the Appendix. Revenue growth versus product innovation investment is analyzed for three types of enterprises: (1) businesses with short market windows such as personal computers, (2) businesses with long market windows such as agricultural products, and (3) a middle case. Finally, some implications of this business model on the management of new product-related investments and business processes are outlined.

■ THE INNOVATION ENGINE IN THE REVENUE LOOP

Figure 2.1 depicts graphically the exchange of value between a company and its customers.[1] A company's operational efforts convert parts, materials, and labor into products and services that are delivered to customers. In return for the value they receive, customers pay the company money and thereby create the revenue stream. Part of that cash is used to pay for the cost of operations,

---

[1] Patterson, Marvin L. "From Experience: Linking Product Innovation to Business Growth," *Journal of Product Innovation Management (JPIM)*, Vol. 15, No. 5, September 1998, 390–402.

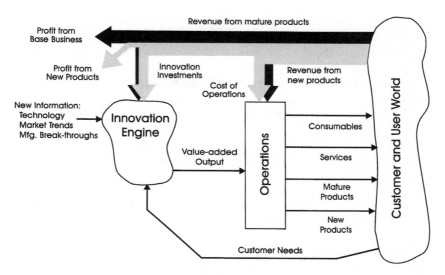

Figure 2.1   The innovation engine—A key business process.

and the rest is used to fund other parts of the business and to provide profit. In this diagram, the cost of operations includes not only the expense of assembling the products and services delivered but also all general, administrative, and selling expenses—everything except investments in product innovation. As long as the company has products and services that customers want, this revenue stream continues, fluctuating up and down a bit as market conditions vary. If left alone, though, over time this revenue stream will decline to nothing as the competition has their way in the marketplace and an ever-aging product line becomes less and less attractive to the customer community.

To counteract this decline, some of the money from the revenue stream that is left over after the cost of operations has been paid must be invested in a critical business process—labeled here *the innovation engine*—that is responsible for the creation and introduction of new products and services. The innovation engine symbolizes all the enterprisewide resources—the people, the business processes and tools, the plants and equipment—that are devoted to creating competitive new products and services and bringing them to market. From a broad perspective, the work of the innovation engine is to gather information that might have business value (market information, customer needs, new technologies) and systematically add value to this information until it describes how to manufacture, use, sell, and support exciting new products and services. This growing pool of proprietary product knowledge is one of the most valuable assets that a business owns. When effectively transferred to operations, it enables delivery of an ongoing stream of new value for the customer.

While more will be said about this in Part II, for the purposes of this discussion, "adding value to information" means answering questions and removing uncertainty. Key questions and uncertainties addressed as the innovation engine performs its function include the following:

➤ What product strategies will best address market opportunities and create competitive advantage?

➤ How can we best use our core competencies? What new competencies do we need?

➤ What strategic partners do we need to supplement our core competencies?

➤ What families of products and services will best achieve our strategic objectives?

➤ What features are needed in each product to best attract customer interest?

➤ Which new technologies will be needed to make our products and services competitive in the future?

➤ What design approaches will most effectively implement key product features?

➤ What manufacturing methods and tools will be needed to fabricate a given new product design in a reliable and cost-effective manner?

➤ How can we best communicate the value of each new product and service to its intended customers?

➤ How can we educate users of each new product in how to apply it most effectively in their work?

➤ What support issues will each new product raise? How can we address them to enhance customer loyalty?

When the investment in the innovation engine is large enough and effectively applied, the resulting transfer of information to operations results in a stream of new products that more than replaces the revenue lost as old products become obsolete. This contest between new product introductions and product obsolescence goes on all the time in most businesses. When the balance tips in favor of new products, revenue grows exponentially. But how much investment in new products and services is enough? How does this amount vary from company to company? How can a company get more out of its product innovation investment? The discussion that follows provides answers to these important questions.

■ THE HP VINTAGE CHART

How new products contribute to exponential revenue growth is best illustrated by the product vintage chart published by HP in its annual report each year. (HP first published the vintage chart in its annual report in about 1979 and included one in its annual report each year through 1996. The vintage chart was omitted in the 1997 annual report.) A version of this graph, compiled from several annual reports, is shown in Figure 2.2. Total revenues for each fiscal year are shown as the sum of revenues contributed by products

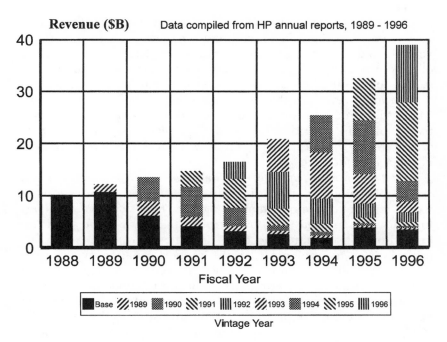

Figure 2.2 The Hewlett-Packard vintage chart.

introduced in that year and in each preceding year. To display the impact of each vintage year on future revenues, product revenues are coded by vintage year (the year in which the products were introduced). Like fine wines, new HP products apparently have great vintage years and other years that are not so great. For example, the revenues contributed by vintage years 1993 and 1995 are strong; whereas 1989 seems to have been a fairly weak vintage year.

The pattern of revenue growth followed by obsolescence is apparent in Figure 2.2. Revenue contributed by new products is modest in their year of introduction and then peaks dramatically in the following year. By the third year, revenues have begun to decline; they are quite small in the fourth year and continue to decline exponentially after that. For simplicity, the small fraction of revenues that occurs beyond the eighth year in a vintage series has been included in the baseline revenue segment. This rise and fall of revenues for each vintage year is characteristic of the products that HP develops and of HP's tendency to render obsolete its own products with new versions. Other companies in other industries will, in general, exhibit different patterns of revenue versus time for a given vintage year.

The vintage chart also illustrates the ongoing contest: new products and services versus obsolescence. As revenues for a given vintage year in Figure 2.2 decline after their peak in the second year, the only thing that keeps overall revenue growing is the surge of new revenues created by products and services introduced in subsequent years. Revenue growth results from wave after wave of new product revenues that build on a declining base of revenues from older products. If new products and services are not competitive, their contributions to the overall revenue picture can decrease. When this happens, revenues will grow at a slower rate and perhaps even decline.

The innovation engine must always remain adaptable and ready to change to stay competitive because the conditions in which it operates are not stable. Customer needs change. Competitors alter the ground rules by introducing new products that are better and earlier than expected. The structure of the marketplace evolves. New technologies destabilize performance expectations and price structures. Someone once offered an analogy between sailing and managing a company: "You can tell good sailors by the straightness of their wake. Likewise you can tell good managers by how well they execute proven methods and stick to the plan." This straight-wake theory of management rarely works with product innovation. Instead of focusing on where you've been, you have to look forward, see the obstacles, and plan ahead to outmaneuver the competition. As with sailing, if you steer to keep the wake ever-straight, you will eventually end up on the rocks.

■ THE LINK BETWEEN NEW PRODUCT INVESTMENT AND REVENUE GROWTH

Three factors determine the growth of revenues in response to investments in product innovation: (1) the fraction of revenues invested in product innovation, (2) an attribute of the new product program labeled *new product revenue gain,* and (3) the dynamics of product revenue versus time typical to a particular business. The first factor is under management control and is established each fiscal year as business leaders decide where to spend available funds. The second factor is determined by a combination of influences that all relate to the excellence of the new product program and the ability of the enterprise to distribute and sell its products. The behavior of revenue over time is established by market dynamics and by the nature of the technology and products introduced. For a large company such as HP, the dynamic performance of revenue for each vintage year tends to stabilize into fairly regular patterns.

➤ Vintage-Year Revenue Dynamic

The dynamic relationship between new product revenue and time for HP is easily seen in Figure 2.2. An average vintage-year revenue dynamic, typical of HP's operations, was derived by analyzing the revenue data used to plot Figure 2.2. Table 2.1 contains the data used to create this graph. These data were gathered by physically measuring graphs printed in HP annual reports, so they are approximate. Percentage changes in revenue from one year to the next were analyzed for each vintage-year data set. These changes were then averaged to create a typical year-to-year revenue dynamic. For example, the revenue increase from the year of introduction to the second year for vintage year 1989 is 83 percent. The average value of this initial increase is 68.9 percent over vintage years 1989 through 1995. The typical revenue dynamic was thus adjusted to exhibit a 68.9 percent revenue increase between the year of introduction and the second year.

Table 2.1 HP Vintage-Year Revenue Data ($B)

Vintage Year	Intro	Year 2	Year 3	Year 4	Year 5	Year 6
1989	1.51	2.76	1.79	0.95	0.66	0.46
1990	4.61	5.81	3.55	1.01	0.72	
1991	3.02	5.54	3.23	1.57		
1992	3.24	7.06	4.83	2.66		
1993	6.25	8.81	5.62	2.12		
1994	7.12	10.34	3.89			
1995	8.13	15.10				
1996	11.10					

Figure 2.3 shows the prototypical revenue dynamic derived from the HP vintage chart. The data have been normalized so that the sum of all annual revenue contributions is 1.0. The meaning of the data presented in Figure 2.3 is that, for a typical HP vintage year, about 20 percent of its total revenue will occur in the initial year of introduction. A little over 34 percent of the total revenue will be received in the second year and about 20 percent in the third. The fourth year will yield 9 percent and annual contributions will taper off after that to a final installment of a little over 2

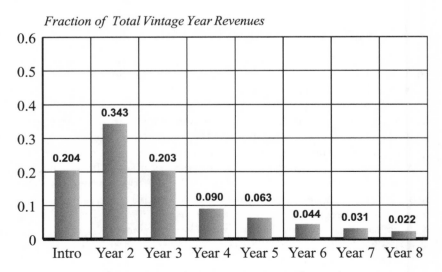

Figure 2.3 Vintage-year revenue dynamic.

percent in the eighth year. The revenue is assumed to drop to zero after the eighth year.

The revenue dynamic typical to HP's new product operations has changed over the years. Vintage chart data from 1979 through 1996 were analyzed by plotting the wave of revenues created by each vintage year. Market window trends were then estimated by measuring the width of each wave at 50 percent of its peak amplitude. These data are plotted in Figure 2.4. Figure 2.4 indicates that market windows for HP's products declined dramatically in the years after 1979 and then stabilized in about 1988. During these years, the HP product line was in transition, going from mostly test and measurement products in 1979 to a heavy emphasis on workstations, personal computers, and desktop printers in 1996. As Figure 2.4 shows, the data used to create Figure 2.3 comes from a period in which the shape of the revenue dynamic was relatively stable.

➤ New Product Revenue Gain

Until now, this discussion has emphasized product innovation as an enterprisewide activity, not just the function of engineering

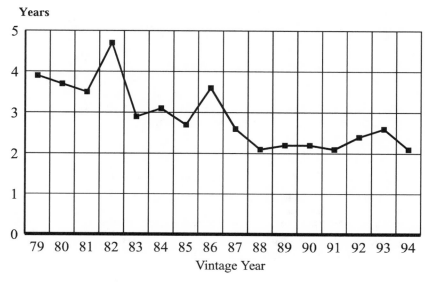

Figure 2.4 Hewlett-Packard market window trend (width of vintage-year revenue envelope at 50% of peak).

operations. Ideally, corporations should keep track of all expenses associated with product innovation whether they occur in engineering operations, manufacturing, marketing, or elsewhere. Typically, however, the only relevant number that is reported in external financial reports is total annual expenditures for R&D. The discussion in the remainder of this section will thus focus on that number as a measure of total investment in product innovation.

New product revenue gain is defined here as the total nondiscounted revenue generated by products introduced in a given vintage year divided by the total investment in product innovation in that vintage year. Referring to Figure 2.2, revenue gain is calculated by adding up the revenue segments associated with a given vintage year and then dividing that number by the R&D investment made in that year. Table 2.2 provides estimated revenue gain information derived from HP financial data. Since there are eight annual installments to the revenue created by products introduced in a given HP vintage year, the full revenues returned by vintage years 1990 through 1996 had not occurred by 1996. In view of this, the totals for these years were estimated by weighting the revenue returned through 1996 with the appropriate segments from Figure 2.3. The average value of new product revenue gain calculated for vintage years 1990 to 1993 is 13.07. This means that, on average, HP has created or will create over time about $13.07 in revenue for each dollar invested in R&D during those years.

► Revenue Growth Relationships

Mathematical relationships for revenue growth as a function of product innovation investment rate and new product revenue gain are derived in the Appendix. For simplicity, this derivation

Table 2.2 Estimated HP Revenue Gain Performance

Vintage Year	Total Vintage Revenue ($B)	R&D ($B)	R&D as a % of Revenue	Revenue Gain
1989	8.69	1.27	10.7	6.85
1990	16.94*	1.37	10.3	12.39
1991	16.10*	1.46	10.1	11.00
1992	21.79*	1.62	9.9	13.45
1993	27.18*	1.76	8.7	15.43

* Estimated from incomplete vintage-year returns.

assumes that, over the analysis period, both revenue growth rate and a factor used in the derivation, labeled K, are constant. This second factor, K, is equal to product innovation investment rate (IR) times new product revenue gain. The relationship between K and revenue growth rate is unique for a given shape of the revenue versus time graph. Many combinations of product innovation investment rate and new product revenue gain, however, will yield a given value of K. To make these relationships more tangible for the reader, revenue growth is given here as a tabular function of both product innovation investment rate and revenue gain.

The relationships derived from the HP data with these assumptions in mind are summarized in Table 2.3. The investment rate shown in the left-hand column of this table is the fraction of current revenues expended on current R&D operations, since this is the only quantitative information available on HP product innovation. To use the table, pick the row in the table that corresponds to the R&D investment rate and then read the revenue growth at the intersection of that row with the column corresponding to the estimated value of new product revenue gain. For example, an R&D investment rate of 10.0 percent (0.100) combined with a new product revenue gain of 11.5 yields a revenue growth of 1.085. Under these conditions, revenues for a given year will always be 1.085 times the revenues of the previous year. While the derivation given in the Appendix can be adapted to any time dynamic for vintage-year

Table 2.3 Revenue Growth Relationships
(Growth = 1 + AGR)

IR	New Product Revenue Gain											
	9.0	9.5	10.0	10.5	11.0	11.5	12.0	12.5	13.0	13.5	14.0	14.5
0.070	0.811	0.828	0.845	0.862	0.880	0.898	0.915	0.934	0.952	0.971	0.989	1.008
0.075	0.833	0.851	0.870	0.889	0.908	0.927	0.947	0.967	0.987	1.007	1.028	1.049
0.080	0.855	0.875	0.895	0.915	0.937	0.958	0.979	1.000	1.022	1.044	1.067	1.091
0.085	0.877	0.899	0.921	0.943	0.965	0.988	1.011	1.035	1.059	1.083	1.108	1.134
0.090	0.900	0.923	0.947	0.971	0.995	1.019	1.044	1.070	1.097	1.123	1.151	1.179
0.095	0.923	0.948	0.973	0.999	1.025	1.051	1.079	1.107	1.135	1.165	1.195	1.225
0.100	0.947	0.973	1.000	1.028	1.056	1.085	1.114	1.144	1.176	1.207	1.241	1.274
0.105	0.971	0.999	1.028	1.057	1.088	1.119	1.151	1.183	1.217	1.252	1.288	1.325
0.110	0.995	1.025	1.056	1.088	1.120	1.154	1.188	1.224	1.261	1.298	1.338	1.378
0.115	1.019	1.051	1.085	1.119	1.154	1.190	1.227	1.266	1.305	1.347	1.389	1.433

revenues, Table 2.3 provides the growth factors representative of HP's revenue dynamics in recent years. Tables for other types of business dynamics are given in the next section.

Figure 2.5 illustrates the relationships between R&D investment, new product revenue gain, and revenue growth that are implied by Table 2.3. For an R&D investment of 0.100 and a revenue gain value of 12.5, Table 2.3 indicates that revenue growth should be about 1.144 from year to year, for an annual growth rate of 14.4 percent. In this example, the revenue for fiscal year 1992 was picked as $200M and the revenue contributions generated by each vintage product set were calculated by multiplying the fractional revenue elements in Figure 2.3 by the R&D investment in that vintage year times the assumed revenue gain of 12.5. Figure 2.5, the graphical result of those calculations, indeed reflects an annual revenue growth rate of a little over 14 percent.

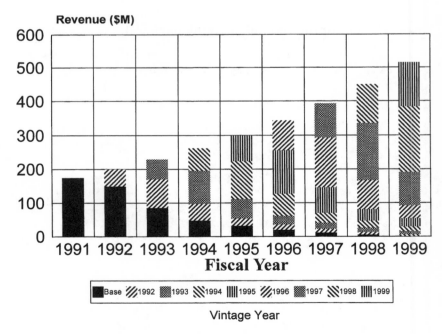

Figure 2.5 A simulated vintage chart
(Investment Rate = 0.100; Revenue Gain = 12.5).

■ GROWTH MODELS FOR OTHER BUSINESSES

The derivation of growth relationships in the Appendix is applied here to two other types of enterprises, both quite different from the preceding case. The intent is to bracket the revenue behavior of a company like HP so that the reader can see how these relationships may vary over a range of revenue dynamics. Readers also can compare these three different cases with their own operation as an aid in understanding the fundamentals of their own revenue growth.

The products of the first company have a long market life, typical of the paper industry, perhaps, or maybe an agricultural products operation. The revenue for a vintage product set from this company increases during the first year, remains level at a mature sales volume for the next nine years and then declines toward zero in the eleventh year.

Products from the second enterprise have a very short market window, typical of the personal computer industry or perhaps a toy manufacturer. The revenue profile assumed for this business has 60 percent of the revenue arriving during the year each vintage product set is introduced. In the second year, 35 percent of total vintage revenues are received; revenues then rapidly fall to zero with only the remaining 5 percent occurring the final year of the market window.

Table 2.4 gives growth relationships for the long market-life case. Again, revenue growth rate and the value of new product investment times new product revenue gain are assumed to be constant throughout the analysis period. A vintage chart typical of this business type is presented as Figure 2.6. As in the previous example, values of product innovation investment rate and revenue gain are picked that produce a revenue annual growth rate near 14 percent and the level of revenue for 1992 is set to $200M. The long product life and stable level of mature revenues for each vintage year are evident in this graph. While the internal structure of revenues is quite different from that of Figure 2.5, total revenues for corresponding years is much the same and the revenue growth from year to year is nearly identical.

Growth relationships for the short product life case are presented in Table 2.5, and the corresponding vintage chart is shown in Figure 2.7. Again, values of product innovation investment rate and revenue gain are picked for a revenue growth rate near 14 percent

Table 2.4 Growth Relationships for Products with Long Life
(Growth = 1 + AGR)

IR	New Product Revenue Gain												
	10.5	11.0	11.5	12.0	12.5	13.0	13.5	14.0	14.5	15.0	15.5	16.0	16.5
0.070	0.943	0.951	0.959	0.967	0.974	0.982	0.989	0.996	1.003	1.010	1.017	1.023	1.030
0.075	0.955	0.964	0.972	0.980	0.987	0.995	1.003	1.010	1.017	1.024	1.032	1.038	1.045
0.080	0.967	0.975	0.984	0.992	1.000	1.008	1.016	1.023	1.031	1.038	1.046	1.053	1.060
0.085	0.978	0.987	0.996	1.004	1.012	1.021	1.029	1.037	1.044	1.052	1.060	1.067	1.075
0.090	0.989	0.998	1.007	1.016	1.024	1.033	1.041	1.049	1.058	1.066	1.073	1.081	1.089
0.095	1.000	1.009	1.018	1.027	1.036	1.045	1.053	1.062	1.070	1.079	1.087	1.095	1.103
0.100	1.010	1.020	1.029	1.038	1.048	1.057	1.066	1.074	1.083	1.092	1.100	1.108	1.117
0.105	1.020	1.030	1.040	1.049	1.059	1.068	1.077	1.086	1.095	1.104	1.113	1.122	1.130
0.110	1.030	1.040	1.050	1.060	1.070	1.079	1.089	1.098	1.108	1.117	1.126	1.135	1.144
0.115	1.040	1.050	1.061	1.071	1.081	1.091	1.100	1.110	1.120	1.129	1.139	1.148	1.157
0.120	1.049	1.060	1.071	1.081	1.092	1.102	1.112	1.122	1.132	1.141	1.151	1.161	1.170
0.125	1.059	1.070	1.081	1.092	1.102	1.113	1.123	1.133	1.143	1.153	1.163	1.173	1.183
0.130	1.068	1.079	1.091	1.102	1.113	1.123	1.134	1.145	1.155	1.165	1.176	1.186	1.196
0.135	1.077	1.089	1.100	1.112	1.123	1.134	1.145	1.156	1.167	1.177	1.188	1.199	1.209
0.140	1.086	1.098	1.110	1.122	1.133	1.145	1.156	1.167	1.178	1.189	1.200	1.211	1.222

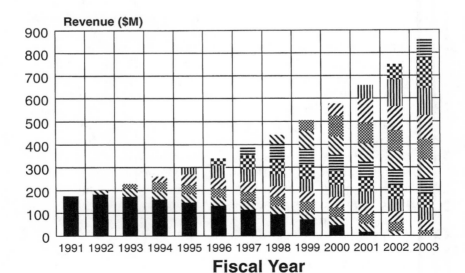

Figure 2.6 Vintage chart—Long product life
(Investment Rate = 0.12; Revenue Gain = 15.0).

Table 2.5 Growth Relationship for Products with Short Market Life
(Growth = 1 + AGR)

IR	\multicolumn{10}{c}{New Product Revenue Gain}
	9.0	9.5	10.0	10.5	11.0	11.5	12.0	12.5	13.0	13.5
0.070	0.465	0.500	0.536	0.575	0.617	0.663	0.712	0.767	0.825	0.888
0.075	0.510	0.550	0.593	0.640	0.690	0.748	0.808	0.874	0.947	1.029
0.080	0.558	0.605	0.656	0.712	0.775	0.842	0.917	1.000	1.095	1.203
0.085	0.611	0.666	0.727	0.795	0.869	0.952	1.046	1.153	1.277	1.419
0.090	0.669	0.734	0.808	0.888	0.978	1.082	1.203	1.341	1.505	1.702
0.095	0.734	0.812	0.897	0.995	1.107	1.240	1.393	1.577	1.802	
0.100	0.808	0.897	1.000	1.120	1.262	1.429	1.631	1.883		
0.105	0.888	0.995	1.120	1.270	1.447	1.667	1.941			
0.110	0.978	1.107	1.262	1.447	1.679	1.970				
0.115	1.082	1.240	1.429	1.667	1.970					

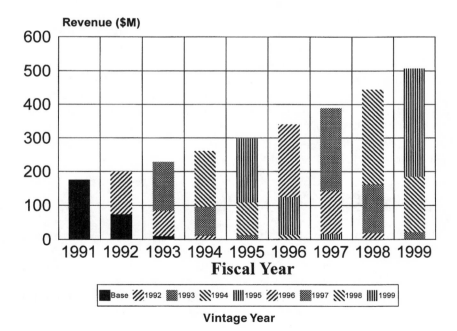

Figure 2.7 Vintage chart—Short product life
(Investment Rate = 0.085; Revenue Gain = 12.45).

and the level of revenues in 1992 was set to \$200M. This graph provides a third example, unlike the first two in its internal vintage structure, that exhibits nearly identical revenue growth performance.

Moving from shortest vintage-year revenue life to the longest reveals a trend in the value of K that corresponds to an annual revenue growth rate of 14 percent. In Figure 2.7, the revenue window is short, beginning and ending within three years. The value of K used to generate Figure 2.7 was 1.058. The HP-like example in Figure 2.5 has a longer revenue window and required a value for K of 1.25 to achieve similar growth rates. The revenue window in Figure 2.6 is eleven years, much longer than the other two, and requires a value for K of 1.80 to produce a 14 percent annual growth in revenues.

Looking at this trend another way, if new product revenue gain is held constant for all three cases, then longer revenue market windows will require higher R&D investment rates to maintain the 14 percent revenue growth rate. Assuming a constant value for revenue gain of 13.0 implies product innovation investment rates of 8.14 percent, 9.63 percent, and 13.85 percent, respectively, for the three cases with increasing revenue windows. This makes sense since revenue gain is computed from the total revenues created by a given vintage-year product set. As revenue windows get longer, this total revenue is spread over a longer time period so that year-to-year revenue growth will be lower. In Figure 2.6, revenues are spread over a window of eleven years so only about 10 percent of the revenue from any given vintage year is available in a single fiscal year. Higher product innovation investment rates are thus required to maintain a given growth rate.

■ DISCUSSION OF ASSUMPTIONS

The derivation of the growth tables presented here presumes that a number of business parameters remain constant although, in many businesses, these are rarely stable for long. The derivation of these tables assumes a stable vintage-year revenue dynamic, a constant annual revenue growth rate, and a stable value for K, the value of product innovation investment rate times revenue gain. The HP performance data presented in Figures 2.2 and 2.4 and in Table 2.2 show that HP's performance in these areas is not constant, but in fact, varies considerably. Nonetheless, the understanding of fundamentals has to start somewhere. The temporary assumption of stability is necessary to the derivation of the under-lying relationships illustrated by the tables.

If these assumptions are valid, then the tables will accurately predict revenue growth rate. Nevertheless, variations from year to year in product innovation investment rate, revenue gain, or revenue dynamic may cause actual revenue growth performance to differ from predictions. The usefulness of the numbers published in the tables depends on the validity of the underlying assumptions for a given business, so the quantitative information published here should thus be applied with considerable suspicion.

The qualitative information provided by the model, however, is more robust. More investment in product innovation, for example, will always increase revenue growth rate for a given level of revenue gain. Increasing revenue gain will always create more revenue growth for a given level of product innovation investment. Short product market windows will always make revenue growth rate more sensitive to changes in revenue gain. The value of the model developed here is more in the structuring of these fundamental interdependencies than its quantitative data.

Finally, there is an implicit assumption here that the product innovation investment made in a given vintage year *causes* a corresponding wave of revenue to occur. Revenue gain for a vintage year is calculated using only the product innovation investment made in that year. In reality, the wave of revenue launched in a given vintage year is caused by new product activity not only in that year, but perhaps in the preceding one, two, or more years as well. Nonetheless, for simplicity, the vintage-year product innovation investment is used here as a surrogate for value creation activities that may have occurred much earlier and that are, at least partially, responsible for the wave of new revenue.

■ THE INNOVATION ENGINE AS AN INVESTMENT

One of the fundamental reasons that businesses exist is that they make more money for investors than other alternatives. If this ceases to be true, investors will inevitably move their money elsewhere. Business leaders in a well-run company thus strive to manage the resources at their disposal in ways that lead to excellent financial growth and return for investors. When the firm's innovation engine is operating effectively, it offers the best available growth opportunity to corporate leaders. Funds invested here will generate growth—in revenue, in profit, and in capital gains—that provides an overall rate of return greater than any other available option. Furthermore, this investment opportunity is completely proprietary, available exclusively to the business leadership team and under their management control. If the innovation engine is not performing as well as they would like, they can work to improve this vital business process.

The financial yield on the product innovation investment is the incremental profit that it creates. The analysis presented in the preceding sections has only addressed the essential drivers of revenue growth. Whether profits grow in step with revenues depends on many attributes of the particular business situation including competitive pressures, product pricing, distribution channel discounts, unit manufacturing cost, and internal expense structures. Growth rates for profits will match revenue growth rates only if the new products introduced have gross margins and expense structures that are similar to those of the existing product base. In fact, profit growth rates can be either less than or greater than the revenue growth rate depending on (1) the markets addressed by the resulting stream of new products, and (2) the level of contribution that new products make to the customer.

A suitable return for shareholders is anything greater than the return they can get by investing similar amounts of money in other alternatives that have similar levels of risk. Investors care about the rate of return that their investments earn but they also care about the risk associated with those investments. The financial world offers a standard for comparison, the cost of capital, that sets the rate of return on business investments at various levels of risk. Shareholders can always get the cost of capital as a rate of return on their money so, to compete as an investment, a business must offer a rate of return greater than the current cost of capital.

Increases in the value of their stock holdings generally provide more return to investors than they get from the distribution of dividends. The stock price per share will roughly track the shareholder value of the company divided by the number of outstanding shares.[2] Shareholder value is, in turn, related to the present value of expected cash flow from operations, discounted by the current cost of capital for the firm. The value of expected cash flow has two components: (1) the present value of cash flow from operations throughout the current forecast period; and (2) a residual

---

[2] McTaggart, James M., Kontes, Peter W., and Mankins, Michael C. *The Value Imperative: Managing for Superior Shareholder Return.* New York: Free Press, 1994.

value, which is the present value of cash flow that is expected to occur beyond the current forecast. Of these two components, the second is generally, by far, the most important determinant of shareholder value.[3]

Residual value is difficult to calculate with precision. It is determined by, among other things, the competitive position of the firm at the end of its forecast period. Residual value thus depends on the current new product strategy of the firm, actions taken within the innovation engine in response to that strategy, actions taken by the competition and the current and future core competencies of the enterprise. Even though residual value is less objective and precise than other business measures, it serves to focus attention on aspects of current operations that are critical to future success. In particular, it highlights the importance of the innovation engine in growing the value of the corporation. The return that a business can expect to provide to its investors is therefore, to a large degree, determined by the performance and ongoing growth in capability of its innovation engine.

Product innovation investments have a strategic payoff as well. They set the strategic direction for an enterprise and move it toward its future. Judicious placement of product innovation investments can move a firm out of one business arena that has stopped providing growth and into another that holds greater promise. HP's history illustrates how this can happen:

> In the late 1970s, HP was concerned that the electronic test and measurement business had matured to a point that limited future growth potential. The firm's strategic sights were thus aimed at the computer industry, and under John Young's leadership, the company began to emphasize R&D investments in computer technologies and products. The 1980s were a time of transition as HP learned how to compete in this dynamic new business arena. Revenue and profit growth were problematic at times and the stock price dropped to half of its peak value at one point. John occasionally endured severe criticism for leading the company into such difficult waters. Discount structures and sales costs for computer products proved to be quite different and operating profit margins were driven to much lower levels than the company had learned to expect in the electronic instrument business.

---

[3] Rappaport, Alfred. *Creating Shareholder Value: The New Standard for Business Performance* (chap. 3). New York: Free Press, 1986.

*John persevered, though, and by the early 1990s, HP had be-
come the second largest computer company in the world.
Today HP's growth in revenues and profits is among the
healthiest in the industry. The company still produces test
and measurement equipment, but these products create a
fairly small fraction of the company's annual revenues. While
HP's profit growth has not kept pace with revenue growth
rates, annual earnings are vastly greater now than they were
when this transition began. This increase in earnings is, in
part, a long-term yield on product innovation investments
that were made almost two decades ago.*

■ INSTRUCTIVE "CORNER CASES"

A couple of interesting real-life examples from industry will highlight the relationships in this growth model more completely.[4]
First, in the personal computer (PC) industry, R&D investment
rates are traditionally low, on the order of 3 percent of revenues,
while revenue growth rates are high. This implies a very high revenue gain if R&D is the only form of product innovation investment that is considered. In learning this business, HP found that a
higher rate of R&D spending did not necessarily cause revenues to
grow faster. In fact, there were indications that more investment
in R&D might actually cause revenue growth to decline. Doesn't
the model presented earlier predict that larger R&D investments
will always produce an increase in revenue growth? How can the
growth model possibly explain this effect?

The most common measure of product innovation investment
rate is the fraction of revenues spent on R&D, but engineering new
products is only one of many ways that an enterprise can create
new value for customers. The product innovation model presented
here includes not only R&D investments but spans all functions in
the business enterprise that might play a role in generating new
value for the customer. In the PC industry, most players realize that
they can't do much inventing and stay within industry standards
and constraints, so R&D budgets remain small. Operating systems,
data buses, back planes, and even the internal physical configura-
tion of PCs must remain standard so that third-party software and

---

[4]This discussion resulted from feedback provided by John Young after his review of
the *JPIM* article.

plug-in modules can be utilized. An R&D budget that is too large can encourage engineering to implement "improvements" that actually reduce overall customer value. In this industry, the revenue gain created by R&D investments is very high for small investments but will decline sharply as R&D investments grow too large.

As an alternative to R&D investment, though, a PC company may decide to invest in other ways, such as providing improved customer support with dramatically faster repair turnaround time. This would provide their customers with terrific new value and thus help increase their market share. If their sales and distribution operation takes full advantage of this market differentiator, this enterprise should enjoy revenue growth rates higher than those of their competitors and higher than the current average market growth rate. In the growth model presented here, this kind of investment is included within the innovation engine. The revenue gain for this form of investment would be relatively high and would, therefore, create a higher growth rate than, say, adding the same amount of money to the R&D budget.

The trick is knowing where in your total enterprise you should invest to create the highest possible revenue gain performance. The revenue gain will be greatest in those departments that currently have the most leverage on increasing the total customer value offered. The product marketing effort must thus consider all areas in the company where new value can be created, not just R&D. The search for new business opportunities must consider the entire customer experience, not just new products.

This strategy for increasing revenue growth works as long as there is headroom over the company's market share. As a company reaches a dominant position where further growth in market share becomes increasingly difficult, their revenue growth rate must approach that of the overall market. As this happens, the difficulty of capturing further market share will force revenue gain on incremental product innovation investments down to the value needed to sustain market growth rates. At this point, the investment strategy should change to a defensive one—how little can we invest and still maintain market share in this business?

At this point, the only way out of this "market growth rate" box is to punt—the company must launch an entirely new business effort in a higher growth industry, as John Young did by guiding HP toward the computer business. The Beretta Corporation has done this repeatedly, over hundreds of years. Their current focus is on firearms but several hundred years ago they were primarily in the horse-drawn carriage business. Each time their growth has flattened, they have launched some new business enterprises. When one of these businesses shows rapid growth, they transfer the family name to that firm and continue on into the next generation. They have reinvented themselves in this way many times to become the oldest family-owned business in the world.

In the second corner case, HP's instrument group tried to invent its way out of revenue growth doldrums in the early 1980s. R&D budgets were increased and product development processes were improved. The result was reduced new product cycle times and more new product introductions than ever before. Revenue growth, however, did not increase as expected. Instead, each new HP product simply made its predecessor obsolete and replaced it in the marketplace, with little impact on overall revenues. Faster new product cycle time and more R&D investment are both good, right? So how does the model explain this example?

The answers to these question are much like those in the previous example. The instrument market that HP was addressing at that time was a mature, slow-growth market, and HP's market share was about as high as it was going to get with their current approach to providing customer value. As HP introduced new products, they simply cannibalized revenue from older HP products, thus lowering the revenue gain for those earlier investments. Here the magnitude of K, product innovation investment rate times new product revenue gain, had leveled off to a constant value (the value required to achieve revenue growth at the market average rate). When R&D investments went up, revenue gain decreased accordingly to maintain the same value for K. And vice versa. HP could have had essentially the same revenue growth rate in that business with a much lower R&D investment.

In this example as well, the paths to increased revenue gain and higher revenue growth rates include finding new ways to create value for the customer, other than engineering new products; and launching new product efforts in higher growth markets. About a year ago, one of the authors paid a little over $300 for a very nice dual-channel oscilloscope produced by a Korean electronics firm. Products like this were nonexistent at the time HP was struggling to renew its revenue growth in the electronic instruments market. Perhaps the untapped opportunity to provide low-cost electronics instruments for the hobbyist would have been an alternative solution for HP's revenue growth problems. As it is, other firms have taken the high ground in this arena.

■ IMPLICATIONS FOR BUSINESS LEADERS

This conceptual model for business growth has important implications for the business leader who is responsible for keeping shareholders happy. Some of these implications are obvious, some are more subtle. This section summarizes key insights that can be drawn from this work.

➤ Product Innovation Drives Growth

The growth tables in this chapter show that the fraction of revenues invested in product innovation directly impacts revenue growth rate. For a given level of performance in revenue gain and vintage-year revenue dynamic, more product innovation investment will yield a greater revenue growth rate, regardless of short- or long-term product life. This is true, however, only so long as incremental increases in product innovation spending can be effectively utilized. A point will inevitably be reached where the revenue gain declines because the new product organization has reached its limits and can no longer create additional development projects that have the same level of "bang per buck." In the authors' experience, however, most enterprises traditionally operate far short of this point.

The right level of product innovation investment depends, though, on the profit picture as well. Increasing the investment in new products decreases current profit from operations by an equal amount. The right level of product innovation investment for an enterprise will thus strike a suitable balance between revenue growth rate and current profit levels.

➤ Vintage-Year Revenue Dynamics Establish Growth Relationships

The answer to the question, "How much product innovation is enough?" depends on the shape of the vintage-year revenue dynamic that is typical to a given enterprise. Each collection of products introduced in a given vintage year will create a bow wave of revenue that begins at the time of introduction and extends into the future. The shape and extent of this wave is an important characteristic of each particular business and establishes the relationships between product innovation investment and revenue growth rate. Yet, businesses often have no idea what their typical revenue wave looks like (with the notable exception of HP). An important step for any enterprise is to characterize both its typical vintage-year revenue dynamic and its new product revenue gain performance. With these in hand, an enterprise can (1) begin to understand the fundamental relationships that drive its own revenue growth, and (2) develop its own revenue growth tables. These growth tables will enable business leaders to set realistic targets for both revenue growth rate and product innovation investment level that are based on a solid understanding of underlying business principles.

➤ New Product Revenue Gain Is Key to Business Success

The business purpose of new product efforts is to convert the fraction of revenues that they consume into growth in revenue and profits for the enterprise. This is done best by creating new value for customers. As the tables in this chapter illustrate, increasing revenue gain has an immense impact on the level of revenue growth created by a given product innovation investment rate. For example, in a business with short product life, the sensitivity of revenue growth to changes in revenue gain is a little scary. Table 2.5 indicates that, at an investment rate of 0.09, a change in revenue gain from 11.0 to 12.0 means the difference between a 2.2 percent annual decline in revenue and a 20.3 percent annual revenue growth rate.

The revenue gain that results from new product efforts is a function of the opportunities addressed and the company's productivity in creating new products and services. The four fundamental drivers of revenue gain performance are:

1. Effectiveness of distribution and sales operations.
2. The quality of new product-related business processes.
3. Effective leadership from high-level business managers.
4. The creativity and productivity of employees working on new product efforts.

Each of these drivers is essential, and they work together to create an effective innovation engine. Management and improvement of performance in distribution and sales operations is beyond the scope of this book. The management and improvement of the other three drivers are addressed in Parts II, III, and IV of this book, respectively.

➤ Manage Product Innovation as the Solution, Not the Problem

In times of financial stress, business leaders often cut spending on new products along with other expenses. When revenue growth softens and profits decline, the natural reflex is to control expenses to minimize the damage. Across-the-board cuts are typical: "All expense areas will hereby run at 85 percent of targeted levels until further notice." Most often, such policies include R&D and all other areas involved in getting new products out.

The impact on the bottom line is immediate. Every dollar saved is a dollar added to operating profits in the current accounting period. But the impact on revenue growth is more obscure. A cut in new product investment rate will move the operating position of the enterprise on its revenue growth table. Referring to Table 2.3, if the firm had been operating at a revenue gain of 12.5 and an investment rate of 0.10, a 15 percent cut in spending rate will change revenue growth in the future from 14.4 percent to 3.5 percent. If this change were permanent, revenue growth rates would eventually stabilize at the new value. Usually, though, these cuts are temporary so the result is simply a transitory weakening of revenue growth at some point in the future. The financial impact of this cut in new product investment rate is, in fact, usually so far removed in time that it is never connected with the original cause.

➤ Inertia in the Revenue Loop Can Hide a Multitude of Sins

The revenue loop depicted in Figure 2.1 has a built-in inertia related to the new product-development cycle time and the vintage-year revenue dynamic. The delay between a good decision on where to invest new product resources and its impact on business success includes the time-to-market typical of new product operations and the ramp-up time inherent in the vintage-year revenue dynamic. The business impact of a good decision thus may not be felt for several years.

Likewise, damage to an effective new product program caused by bad decisions takes a long time to be reflected in business results. New products that have just been introduced will create their revenue wave, regardless of what happens to future new product efforts. Likewise, new products that are well along in the innovation cycle will be introduced more or less on time unless something truly drastic happens. The impact of bad decisions on revenue growth cannot occur until these products have run their course in the marketplace.

To visualize this revenue loop inertia, refer to the vintage chart in Figure 2.6. Suppose that, for some odd reason, this company decided in 1998 to scrap the new product program altogether so that no further products were introduced after this year. The resulting future revenues for this company beyond 1998 are easy to visualize by simply ignoring the revenue contributions from vintage years beginning with 1999. The inertia built into this revenue loop is so strong that, even with no new products, revenues would actually grow from 1998 to 1999. In the year 2000, they would be only slightly lower than the 1998 level. Beyond 2000, revenues would begin a steady decline at roughly 9 percent per year.

Chapter 4 will illustrate more completely the impact of revenue loop inertia and expense controls on long-term business performance.

■ CONCLUSION

This chapter has positioned the innovation engine as a vital business process essential to the future growth and vitality of a company. Because of its unique relationship in the revenue loop, the innovation engine is a primary driving force for both revenue growth and profitability. The proprietary knowledge that the innovation engine accumulates over time represents an important competitive asset for the company that helps determine its future competitive stature and, hence, its current shareholder value.

The conceptual model developed here links product innovation to the financial growth of the enterprise. The vintage chart was highlighted to explain the dynamic relationships between the introduction of new products and revenue growth. Three critical factors that drive revenue growth were identified and a method for deriving quantitative relationships between these growth drivers and revenue growth rate was described. This conceptual model was applied to three different hypothetical business cases to demonstrate the validity and utility of the model and to highlight fundamental relationships.

Finally, the conceptual model presented here highlights business fundamentals and interrelationships in a new way that has important implications for business leaders. It provides them with important new ways to understand their business and better manage its financial performance. It offers new ways to anticipate the long-term financial impact of expense control measures. Further, it emphasizes new points of focus for improving the business effectiveness of product innovation activities.

This chapter has raised some questions that business leaders may want to address in their own enterprise. How much should we be investing in product innovation? What does our revenue growth table look like? What new product revenue gain do we typically create and what determines that value? How do we know if our innovation engine is as competitive as it can be? What actions are needed to increase the performance of our innovation engine to competitive levels? The principles conveyed in the remaining chapters address these questions and, if applied well, will help ensure that the innovation engine in an enterprise always offers the best possible investment opportunity to business leaders.

The material presented in this chapter must be translated into action in order to have any impact at all on business results. What steps, then, might the reader take in applying these ideas to his or her own enterprise? Table 2.6 begins a practice that will be repeated in each chapter that follows. It summarizes desired work-related behaviors for upper level managers that are implied by the ideas and principles presented earlier. This and similar tables at the end of Chapters 3 through 11 are then used in Chapter 12 to design a set of performance measures for assessing the overall effectiveness of product innovation leadership.

Table 2.6 Desired Upper Management Behaviors:
Linking Product Innovation to Business Growth

➤ View costs associated with new product innovation as investments, not expenses, and manage them accordingly.

➤ Get curious about your innovation engine. Expect excellence, but be willing deal with reality and improve it.

➤ Request product vintage charts for recent years. Expect them in the future.

➤ Understand your baseline performance:

New product investment rate, enterprisewide.

New product revenue gain.

Revenue versus time for each vintage year.

Chapter 3

Business Considerations
for a Single Product

> Now there are three ways in which a ruler can bring misfortune upon his
> army:
>
> > When ignorant that the army should not advance, to order an advance ...
> >
> > When ignorant of military affairs, to participate in their administration ...
> >
> > When ignorant of command problems, to share in the exercise of responsibilities ...
>
> Sun Tzu
> *The Art of War*

A business enterprise is much like a sovereign nation in the days of Sun Tzu. Each nation was surrounded by other countries. Some were allies and some were hostile. The nation strove to protect its territory and even expand it, for the land was what fed the nation and allowed it to prosper. In business, a company is surrounded by other companies. Some are strategic partners and some are competitors for market share. The business strives to protect its share of the market and even expand it, for the market provides a reliable revenue stream and profit that keeps the company prosperous.

A sovereign nation was not usually embroiled in outright war. There were times of peace when the borders remained well defined and stable. And sometimes military action was limited to border skirmishes. But the land that a nation possessed was a valuable asset and would be taken by others if left unprotected. So the ruler had to nurture the capacities to both till the soil and exercise military force against aggressors. Likewise, business leaders must nurture the capacity to serve the markets that the company owns as well as protect those markets against invaders, and enter new markets where competitors may currently prevail.

The processes that kept the sovereign nation prosperous and protected were executed by individuals working at the local level using the methods and tools at their disposal. Local decisions and actions determined, to a large degree, the future of the nation. What crops should they plant, how should they best till the soil? What weapons should they construct? Should they invade a neighbor or retaliate against an aggressor? Even in a centrally planned economy, people at the local level have always had the power to decide how hard they will work, how vigorously they will defend their land, and whether they will support or undermine directives from the central government.

In business, local decisions and actions also determine the future of the company. What products should be developed for our existing markets? What new markets should we enter, and what products will provide an edge against competitors there? How should we respond to a new competitor in a market that we have dominated for years? Again, individuals working at the local level decide how hard to work, how vigorously to defend the company, and whether to support or undermine central policy.

The challenge for both rulers of nations and business leaders is similar. They must somehow understand how things work at the local level and influence these efforts to align them and cause collective progress in desired directions. Their goal is success and prosperity for the entire nation or enterprise and their only means of achieving this is through effective and productive local efforts.

The revenue stream of a business, as illustrated in Figure 2.1, is usually made up of contributions over time from many individual products. Just as the success of a nation is created by behavior at the local level, the strength and success of a business is determined by the market performance of individual products. The revenue stream over time created by a particular vintage year is an aggregate of the performance of the dozens or, perhaps, hundreds of products that happen to be bundled into that group. For healthy, profitable revenue growth to occur and for the company to advance in desired strategic directions, each one of these products, on average, must do its part.

In this chapter, the focus shifts from an enterprisewide perspective down to the world of the individual new product. The influence of business leaders at this level is crucial in controlling the strategic direction of the business, the profitability of the revenue stream, and the growth in shareholder value. Without effective high-level leadership, local action can become disjointed, pulling the company in many directions at once. As the quotation from Sun Tzu implies, however, business leaders should avoid meddling in local new product activities unless they understand how things are supposed to work. The goal of this chapter is to continue development of effective mental models for the reader by reviewing fundamental principles that govern how each new product effort contributes to the success of the overall business.

■ THE SINGLE PRODUCT LIFE CYCLE

Individual products share a common cash flow life cycle that begins with the emergence of a market opportunity and ends when product sales drop to zero. This cash flow cycle is shown in Figure 3.1. While the cash flow waveform in Figure 3.1 is idealized, it suffices to illustrate some important principles that establish the contribution that a product makes to the overall success of the business.

The new product cycle begins when an opportunity for a new product occurs. This is a conceptual point in time, not usually discernible: the moment when a technology overlays a customer

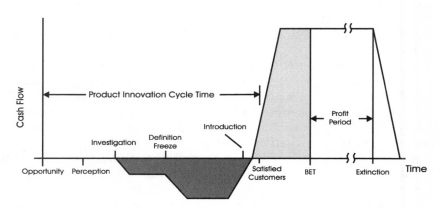

Figure 3.1 Single product cash flow cycle.

need in a manner that makes a new product possible. Circumstances around the moment of opportunity vary. Often an emerging technology provides new ways of addressing existing customer needs. Frequently, however, new customer needs arise that can be addressed by existing technology. Almost never, though, is anyone standing by when this moment occurs, ready to start the clock on the new product life cycle.

In general, time will pass before the new opportunity is even perceived. The length of this delay will depend on how diligently a business is searching for new product possibilities. Some enterprises latch on to new product ideas very early. Others may not recognize an opportunity until a competitor introduces an exciting new product that captures a large share of their market and sends them scrambling to catch up.

Once the company perceives the opportunity, there is generally more delay before it begins to take action. Then the initial response is most often some form of investigation. At this point, the cash flow goes negative, but usually at a fairly low level as a few people work to answer some fundamental questions. What is this new technology and what can we do with it? What is this new customer need? Who are these customers and what kind of product would attract their attention? How might this product fit into our business strategy? How big is the potential market? Is this business that we want? Once the investigation has provided satisfactory answers, product definition and product plans are frozen and the investment level gets more serious as a team is assembled and begins in earnest to work on the new product.

Eventually, the business introduces the product, and cash flow ramps upward and becomes positive. At some point after the introduction, customers actually get the product in their hands and attempt to apply it to their needs. When they find that it provides good value and they are satisfied, innovation is complete and the product is ready to realize its market potential. Sales volume then ramps up to mature levels.

The product innovation cycle time defined in Figure 3.1 is extremely demanding and is nearly impossible to measure. Even so, it focuses attention on some key opportunities for improving the business impact of product innovation efforts. The clock starts at the first moment an opportunity exists and doesn't stop until customers are satisfied with the new product. Most measures of time-to-market start at definition freeze and stop when the product is released for shipment. The definition offered here, on the other hand, acknowledges that the time to perceive an opportunity and then to start a suitable business response is important, too. Furthermore, this definition emphasizes customer satisfaction as the goal, not simply the manufacturing release of the product.

The positive part of the cash flow waveform is determined by the gross profit margin on revenues generated by the product. At some point in time, usually after mature sales volumes have been reached, net positive cash flow is just equal to the total amount invested to get the product to market. This is the so-called breakeven time (BET). Beyond this point, sales of the product begin to provide a positive return on the investment made in the product. The amount of positive return received depends on two factors: (1) the levels of gross margin per month associated with product revenues, and (2) the length of the profit period—the time between BET and the end of the product cash flow cycle.

■ FUNDAMENTAL PRODUCT CASH FLOW RELATIONSHIPS

Financial success for the enterprise depends, in part, on effectively engineering the cash flow waveform for each new product. To manage this, executives must understand some underlying relationships that influence the shape of the waveform in Figure 3.1.[1]

The total gross margin returned by each new product investment is the area under the positive part of the waveform. The project return on investment (ROI) is thus depicted graphically in the diagram as the ratio of the area under the positive part of the waveform to the area of the negative part. Raising ROI thus means increasing the height and width of the positive part of the waveform while shortening and reducing the amplitude of the investment part.

For example, in a typical product innovation project that, at its peak level, involves 20 people, the magnitude of the investment cash flow might reach $400,000 per month, including labor, overhead, and investments in production tooling and materials. The total cost of an 18-month-long project would be roughly $6 million to $7 million. At mature sales levels, the gross margin returned by a successful product resulting from this effort might be somewhere

---

[1] Patterson, Marvin L. *Accelerating Innovation: Improving the Process of Product Development* (chap. 1). New York: Van Nostrand Reinhold, 1993.

around $1.5 million per month. The amplitude of the positive part of the cash flow waveform may thus be three or four times that of the investment part. A successful product thus has the potential of returning its original development investment in perhaps 4 or 5 months, at mature sales volumes. With a 3-year market window, this product would create a gross-margin return on investment (ROI) of perhaps eight to nine.

Increasing the total positive cash flow received over the life of a product means increasing the positive cash flow received per month from product sales while making the market window as long as possible. The following business performance factors are important in doing this.

➤ Increasing the Positive Cash Flow Rate

Making the monthly gross margin larger means selling more product and keeping the cost-of-goods-sold as low as possible. Monthly sales over the life of the product are determined by the effectiveness of the sales effort and the value that the product provides to the customer, relative to that of other solutions that they might choose. The size of the opportunity offered by the product also determines sales volume. The value of the product to the customer depends on how well the product innovation team matched the product definition to customer needs and how well they implemented the product. Cost-of-goods-sold is established by the product design, by the manufacturing methods and tools selected, by the sales volume, and by the yield and quality realized in the manufacturing process.

➤ Increasing Market Window

The market window, as depicted in Figure 3.1, is the period between product introduction and its extinction at the end of the cash flow cycle. The market window is obviously improved by getting the product to market early while extending the extinction time as far into the future as possible. This section discusses both options for improving market window.

Moving extinction time as far into the future as possible is an important step in improving ROI. Knowing when a product will become extinct, though, and controlling this point in time are often difficult. The decisions that establish product extinction are made very early in the product life cycle, between the beginning of the investigation and the point at which product definition and project plans are frozen. During this time, features and design approaches are discussed and selected. The system design is established, including the selection of important alternatives for the product implementation. These choices will have a major impact on the performance, functionality, and cost of the eventual product. Manufacturing plans are discussed. Decisions are made about how to position the product in the marketplace.

As management considers each decision, one can imagine the product extinction time moving around at some unknowable point in the future. "Should we use the next-generation memory chips? They are supposed to be on the market in nine months." The extinction time moves further out into the future. "No, they might slip and not be ready in time for our introduction. Let's use what's on the shelf." The extinction time moves back in.

Once the product definition and the plans for its implementation have been frozen, the extinction time is also frozen at some obscure, but fixed, point in the future. What will cause sales to cease cannot be known for sure ahead of time. Perhaps a competitor will introduce a better, more cost-effective solution. Perhaps customer needs will change. Perhaps the company will introduce new models that obsolete its own products. Whatever these opposing forces may be, the defenses that the current product has against them are established very early in its life cycle and, from that point forward, these defenses do not change. When extinction time comes, by definition, market forces will be strong enough to collapse sales of this product to zero.

The decisions made early in the product's life cycle are thus crucial to its ultimate business success. They deserve the best resources that the company can bring to bear on them. They deserve executive attention. In many cases, though, executives do not get interested in new product matters until a product gets into trouble late in development. When the introduction of a product is threatened with delays, the senior management team often gets embroiled in the fire fighting needed to get the project back on track. The good news is that, in companies where senior management involvement is concentrated at the tail end of the product innovation cycle, major opportunities usually exist for improving overall business performance. Methods for defining and implementing these improvements are presented in the following chapters.

Another important step in improving project ROI is moving the product introduction as far forward in time as possible. The first approach to this always seems to be an effort to remove time from product development activities. This is indeed important and is discussed later in the next section. Reviewing the product innovation cycle time defined in Figure 3.1, however, highlights other approaches to earlier product introduction that are often overlooked.

Product innovation cycle time includes not only the time to develop the product but also the time to perceive the opportunity, the delay before an investigation starts, and the time taken by the investigation. Product introduction can be moved forward in time by shortening any of these four elements. Usually time can be removed from the front end of the innovation cycle much more easily and inexpensively than it can be taken out of development activities. And a month saved leads to a one-month earlier product introduction, regardless of where that month was removed from the cycle. Improving the way the business searches for new opportunities, focusing attention on how new opportunities become new investments, and getting serious about product investigation as a business process all represent tremendous opportunities for improving performance.

➤ Improving the "Bang per Buck" for New Product Investments

Taking cost and time out of the product innovation investment involves optimizing both the number of people on the innovation team and their productivity. This section discusses factors that are important in improving performance during the investment phase of the new product cycle.

Product innovation often takes longer than necessary because new product teams are staffed below the level that will achieve minimum time-to-market. Adding more people to the team, up to a point, will not significantly increase the total cost of product innovation. Getting a particular product out requires a set amount of work. With the right skills, more people can generally finish that work sooner. Total investment, however, does not change much—the total number of people on the team multiplied by the time they are involved stays constant—but time-to-market improves. Every project has an optimum staffing level, however. Adding people to the project beyond this point adds cost to the project, but will not significantly improve the rate of progress.

Assembling an optimum team for a given project is a skill that executives learn through experience. The optimum staffing level varies from project to project and from business to business. The mix of skills needed on a project team varies as well. Most businesses attempt to spread their resources too thinly across too many projects. Every project is then understaffed and takes longer than necessary to complete.

Staffing product innovation teams to achieve best time-to-market can significantly increase the market window and, hence, the total financial return without significantly increasing the total investment. Figure 3.2 illustrates this benefit. In Figure 3.2a, two projects are executed concurrently, each with a staff of seven people. Both products are released after a development time of four years, and the revenue stream begins. Extinction time for both products is the same and determines the limit of the future revenue stream. In Figure 3.2b, the same two products are developed and both are completed in four years. The difference is that the staffing level on each project is doubled to fourteen people and the time-to-market is reduced by a factor of two. The first project is completed in two years, and its revenue stream starts at that point. The second product also takes two years and is introduced at four years, just as it was in Figure 3.2a. Its revenue stream starts at exactly the same time as before. Revenue for both products stops at the same time as before since nothing has been done that affects extinction time. The advantage of staffing these projects for minimum TTM is that the market window of the first product is dramatically increased,

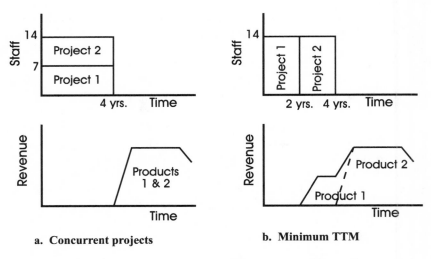

a. Concurrent projects   b. Minimum TTM

Figure 3.2 Advantages of optimizing project staff.

and total revenues generated by the two products are thus much higher than in the previous case.

The rate of progress toward completion also depends, however, on the productivity of each individual on the team. Productivity depends on the skills and motivation of the people involved, the processes that they use as they work, and the tools that support those processes. Hiring the best people and keeping their skills up to date is important to overall productivity. Establishing a competitive product-innovation process and then providing the training and support needed to keep it effective is important. Once the process is in place, the best tools to support it can be acquired and installed. Again, providing the training and support that people need to use these tools effectively is crucial.

Rework often reduces productivity and increases time in product innovation. Lack of timely information or other communication flaws from the early phases of product innovation activity may mean redoing designs because the product definition changed late in the product development cycle. Or product documentation may have to be rewritten because data about product features and performance were inaccurate. The early phases in the process offer significant opportunities for improvement in overall business performance. Understanding how this process occasionally creates flaws that lead to rework is a key step in improving productivity. These issues are examined in detail in Part II.

■ THE COST OF TIME

The premise that the extinction time becomes frozen early in the product innovation cycle has major implications for the financial impact of project delays. How much does a one-month slip in the introduction of a new product cost the business? Many people will calculate the monthly running costs of the new product team and offer that number as the answer. In view of the preceding market window discussion, the actual cost of a project delay is clearly much greater.

The primary cost of a one-month delay is the lost gross margin due to the shortened market window.[2] Since extinction time does not move when product introduction slips, a one-month slip in

---

[2] Smith, Preston G., and Reinertsen, Donald G. *Developing Products in Half the Time* (chap. 2). New York: Van Nostrand Reinhold, 1992.

product introduction means a market window that is one month shorter. The profit period shown in Figure 3.1 is thus one month shorter, and the total return is reduced by the gross margin that would have been collected in the lost month—figured at mature sales volumes. In effect, project delays squeeze the profit period against an unyielding extinction time. The impact of this loss in return is usually somewhere between 3 and 10 times that of the increase in product innovation expense. Estimated costs for a one-month introduction slip calculated for various client companies have ranged from as little as $500,000 to as much as $30 million, depending on the business arena.

Figure 3.3 illustrates the effect of a one-month slip in product introduction for three different types of products. In the first case, Figure 3.3b concerning space shuttles, little impact is felt in total return. The contract calls for six space shuttles and that doesn't change if the introduction is delayed a month. The cost of the

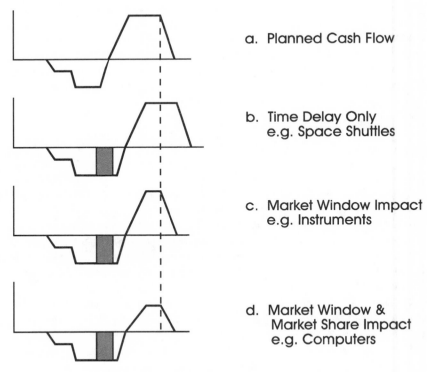

a. Planned Cash Flow

b. Time Delay Only
   e.g. Space Shuttles

c. Market Window Impact
   e.g. Instruments

d. Market Window &
   Market Share Impact
   e.g. Computers

Figure 3.3 Impact of project slip on return.

extra time is felt primarily in the added project team expenses. The time value of money on delayed revenues, however, does add a further cost.

Figure 3.3c illustrates the situation described earlier in this section. This case is typical for products such as electronic instruments where mature sales volumes remain unaffected by a one-month delay. Only the market window changes.

For products in other businesses, however, both market window and market share can be reduced by a delay in product introduction. Market share for personal computers and peripherals can depend critically on getting the right product on the market in time to introduce it at a key trade show. Buyers for distributors make decisions based on what they see at the show. The next opportunity to get their attention will occur in six months. Missing that show by a month can have a drastic effect on both market window and market share. Figure 3.3c shows the impact of an introduction slip of this type. The market window is again squeezed against an unyielding extinction time, but mature monthly gross margins are also dramatically reduced.

Because the cost of project delays is so high, even drastic measures to keep projects on schedule often make good business sense. Executives often judge the actions needed to keep projects on schedule simply by their immediate impact on the current budget. More often than not, the answer comes back, "We can't afford that." When compared with the gross margin lost through reduced market window, though, the cost of corrective measures begins to look like a bargain. Shareholders hope for insightful leadership that can correctly evaluate these circumstances and make the best decisions for overall gain in business value.

■ CRITICAL SUCCESS FACTORS FOR A SINGLE PRODUCT

Chapter 2 established three business factors that impact revenue growth: (1) the fraction of revenues that the enterprise invests in product innovation, (2) the new product revenue gain, and (3) the vintage year revenue dynamic. Individual projects have no influence on the first growth driver and only a little influence on the third. The performance of individual product innovation projects, though, greatly impacts on new product revenue gain. In fact, once executives have established the investment rate, the company's revenue dynamic will establish a value for new product revenue gain that is required to meet revenue growth targets. Once this value for revenue gain has been established, it should be adopted as a target by each product innovation project.

To make this more clear with numbers, suppose that an agricultural products enterprise, represented by the vintage chart in Figure 2.6, wants to increase its annual growth rate from its current value of 14 percent to something over 18 percent. The executives are willing to increase spending on product innovation from 12 percent of revenues to 12.5 percent, but no further. Shareholders will only tolerate a limited amount of additional pressure on earnings. The rest will have to come from improved performance by new product efforts. Table 2.4 shows that, at this investment rate, a revenue gain of 16.5 will be required to achieve a sustained annual growth rate of 18.3 percent. The average revenue gain performance for the enterprise will thus have to increase from its current level of 15.0 to at least 16.5. This means that, on average, each product innovation project must create $16.50 in new revenue for each dollar spent on bringing its product to market. To achieve the more aggressive revenue growth target, this expectation for revenue gain performance should be used as an acceptance criterion imposed on each new project proposal.

Where then should improvement efforts focus to bring about these increases in revenue gain performance? While numerical values are difficult to find for its terms, the quasi-equation presented in Figure 3.4 highlights project performance factors for a single product effort that impact its revenue gain performance, and outlines their relationships and interdependencies. More a conceptual tool than an mathematical truth, this equation implies that good scores on four parameters will ensure good new product

New Product Revenue Gain ≅

Opportunity Size x Implementation Excellence x Market Window

Project Investment Level

Figure 3.4 Critical success factors for a single product.

revenue gain performance for each new product. These success factors are:

1. The size of the market opportunity addressed.
2. The excellence of the product implementation.
3. The market window.
4. The level of effort invested in the project.

This equation for new product revenue gain is much like return-on-investment in that the terms in the numerator all relate to the financial return of the product in some way and the denominator reflects the business investment. This section describes these four important aspects of a product innovation effort and outlines important interrelationships.

➤ Opportunity Size

Different opportunities that emerge offer different levels of potential financial reward to a business. The first step in ensuring a good business return from a new product effort is to focus that investment on an opportunity that offers excellent sales volume and profit potential. The work done by a product innovation team generates a financial return that is directly proportional to the size of the opportunity addressed. If the opportunity picked is large, financial returns can be substantial. If the opportunity is small, even an outstanding effort by the product innovation team will generate little financial return. This is another way of saying that no amount of excellent effort will turn a sow's ear into a silk purse. If you want a silk purse, you have to start with silk.

The size of an opportunity is determined by four attributes: (1) the magnitude of customer need; (2) the pricing and profit structure that the market will tolerate; (3) technical, market, and manufacturing feasibility; and (4) ability to establish a sustainable competitive advantage. The magnitude of customer need depends on how many customers there are who will buy a new product and how intensely they need the value that it provides. The profit potential of a new product is very much a function of how valuable the new product is to the customer, relative to other solutions that they might buy. A product that offers great differential value can command a high profit margin.

Product feasibility is an important component of a major business opportunity. Every businessperson has heard horror stories in which an exciting opportunity triggers a new product effort that soaks up a large investment of both money and time. But the project simply grinds to a halt, never providing any financial return at all. The technology failed to support a workable design, or manufacturing methods could not be found that would meet unit cost targets. Or perhaps a product was introduced that was too new and too radical for the marketplace. Customers were not ready to understand or trust its value. In such cases, the opportunity may be exciting but questionable product feasibility limits its size.

The final component of opportunity size is the ability to create a sustainable competitive advantage in the marketplace. For an opportunity to be large, its attributes must allow a business to establish and maintain a substantial advantage over competitors. This advantage may take the form of patent protection, trade secrets, product know-how or, perhaps, special skills or business processes that are difficult to duplicate. Without a sustainable competitive advantage, introduction of a new product can simply alert the competition to the opportunity and lead to a market free-for-all that erodes market share and profit margins for everyone. When this happens, it greatly reduces the value of the opportunity to any single business.

The external nostril dilator is a real-world example of a currently available product that illustrates these four elements of opportunity size. The dilator consists of a springy plastic strip with adhesive on one side and a smooth, flesh-colored plastic coating on the other. These devices are worn on the outside of the nose and pull the sides of the nostrils out to expand the nasal air passages. Athletes use these devices to help them breathe more effectively. A more prevalent application, however, is to improve nighttime breathing for people who snore or suffer from sleep apnea.

The size of the market opportunity is large. Probably 50 million people or more in the United States alone fall into at least one of these categories and could receive value from this product. Most customers in this population could potentially use 365 of these devices per year for a total potential market on the order of 18 billion devices per year. The value to the customer includes either improved athletic performance or better sleep for both the user and his or her spouse. The magnitude of customer need seems large indeed.

The current market price of these devices is currently about $0.43 per device and, since the cost-of-goods-sold (COGS) must be below a penny each, they command a terrific gross-profit margin. Assuming a 1 percent market penetration, an annual gross-margin of around $77 million per year seems like a reasonable expectation. The market seems willing to tolerate an attractive profit margin.

While technical and manufacturing issues undoubtedly existed during development of this product, the technologies involved seem similar to those used successfully in small, adhesive bandages—no feasibility issues here. Market feasibility, on the other hand, seems less certain. Nothing like this product existed before its introduction. Customers must first be introduced to the product and then be educated in its use and the value that it provides. Those who might use this product at night must first be convinced that they can sleep with one of these devices on their nose. Market penetration will depend on how effectively the public can be reached and educated. The ultimate size of this opportunity will depend directly on how well this can be done.

Sustaining a competitive advantage may also prove to be a challenge. A patent on the product concept and, perhaps, on unique manufacturing processes may create enough advantage to discourage competitors. Once the market for these dilators has been developed and the profits are rolling in, though, competitors will be strongly motivated to find other solutions that circumvent any patents that may exist. Perhaps a plastic-insert device that will hold the nostrils open will do it. The size of the opportunity for the original product will depend on whether these competitors are successful in penetrating the market with alternative products that provide similar value.

➤ Implementation Excellence

To fully exploit a particular opportunity, the product response must be implemented with performance, quality, and unit manufacturing costs that leave little on the table for competitors. If the competition can find a weakness in your product offering, they can take advantage of it and tear away at your competitive position. On the other hand, a high-quality product that outperforms competing alternatives and provides much better value for the price is downright discouraging to competitors. They must invent a breakthrough of their own before they can attract customer attention and enter the market. This takes time and investment on their part, which leaves you with a substantial market window and a good profit margin.

➤ Market Window

Project factors that affect market window were discussed earlier. Often the characteristics of a particular opportunity also have implications for the available market window. An opportunity to introduce a new line of Christmas ornaments has an inherently different market window characteristic than the opportunity to create a new brand of toothpaste. To be substantial, an opportunity must offer enough time before product extinction to allow completion of a reasonable product effort and enough time in the market for the business to reap its financial return.

➤ Project Investment Level

The size of the investment that a business makes in a particular opportunity is important in determining the business value of the effort. One of the first principles of war (and business competition) is that, if you decide to engage the enemy, you had better have enough resources on your side to win.[3] The measure of your resources may simply be the head count of your army, or it might include strategy and proprietary knowledge that you have managed to accumulate. Before you decide to compete in the business world, assess the strength of your competitors and make sure you will be able to invest at a level of competitive intensity sufficient to gain a market advantage. Otherwise you just might lose your entire investment with no gain at all. A better strategy is to move investments into an arena where your investments *can* create competitive results. Just as a general must choose battles wisely, a business must also place its new product investments with care.

➤ Interrelationships and Dependencies

The terms in the numerator of the new product revenue gain equation are shown as multiplied together because they are all essential to the financial return from a single product effort. All three terms must be healthy to create a large financial gain. A low score in any one of these terms can cripple the financial viability of the project. The following examples illustrate how this works.

---

[3]Tzu, Sun. *The Art of War* (chap. III. Offensive Strategy), Samuel B. Griffin, trans. New York: Oxford University Press, 1963.

Low Opportunity Size

A computer peripheral company invested over $10M and several years to create a printer that used special thermal paper. The product implementation was excellent, with characteristically high quality and robust performance. The product was introduced early enough to provide a substantial market window. The target price and special paper requirements, though, were not attractive to the customer base, and sales were extremely disappointing. Thus, the opportunity selected for this investment was a poor one. After a short time, the company pulled the product from the market. The few units that had been sold, however, required support for several years into the future at significant cost to the company. This product effort resulted in a terrific loss.

Poor Product Implementation

An extremely clever product was created to measure mechanical motion with almost no effect on the performance of the mechanical system. An electro-optical device simply tracked a black-white target painted on the mechanism under test and generated electrical signals that corresponded to target motion. Nothing else was available that could perform such measurements. While the instrument was very expensive, its utility made it worth the price. The market window for the product was wide open, seemingly limitless. Implementation of the product, however, was extremely poor. The product was unreliable and needed frequent factory repairs. Examination revealed that design and fabrication techniques used in this device were far below current industry standards. The unit manufacturing cost was obviously much higher than necessary. Marketing and distribution of the product were poorly executed, and sales were far below what they could have been. Warrantee costs were high. The fledgling company struggled, despite having an uncontested product positioned squarely on a viable market opportunity.

Short Market Window

A personal computer company invested in a next-generation family of products with the latest microprocessor and memory chips. A huge opportunity for this product line was identified in southeast Asia. This market would, however, require extra

investment in special keyboards and screen character generation. Management decided to delay this work until the company finished U.S. versions of the product. As planned, work
began on the Asian product line immediately after the U.S. introduction. The Asian version of the product line was introduced six months later, just as new products were being
introduced by competitors that contained even newer microprocessor and memory chips. The market window for the
Asian version had just vanished, and sales were nonexistent.
Even though the opportunity was large and the product engineering was solid, return on investment for the project was
zero.

These examples illustrate how poor performance with respect
to each of the terms in the numerator of the equation in Figure 3.4
can dramatically reduce the business value of the product. The
business impact of the denominator, project investment level, will
now be examined. To achieve and maintain business success, the
project investment for each new product effort must accomplish
two things simultaneously. First, the investment must yield a high
return per dollar of investment. In addition, though, the project
investment level must provide a sufficient measure of competitive
intensity in the marketplace to place the company among the
leaders. The following example illustrates the importance of this
factor.

An electronic workstation company decided to launch a new
line of engineering-design software products. At that time, this
line of products clearly addressed a large and growing opportunity with an excellent market window. The new product
team was outstanding and was able to implement excellent
products. Each product created a good return on investment.
The company only invested a team of perhaps 15 people at any
one time in this product line, however, while the toughest competitors had development teams of 60 people or more in place.
Over time, the company had increasing difficulty attracting attention to its new software products. Customers expected more
breadth and depth in the product line than the company could
achieve. The competitors who, for years, had been investing at
levels of competitive intensity several times higher now dominated the market and established customer expectations. Eventually the workstation company had to withdraw from the
business.

■ CONCLUSION

This chapter described principles important to the financial success of individual product efforts. The cash flow generated by a single product was discussed and effects of project activity and decisions on the shape of the cash flow versus time waveform were outlined. Conditions for profitability and healthy project ROI were described.

An important outcome of this discussion is an understanding of the factors that establish the cost to the business of a delay in new product activities. The cost of a one-month delay is much more serious than most would expect. A clear understanding of these costs fundamentally changes the decision criteria that executives should use when dealing with project delays. Keeping projects on schedule deserves a much higher priority than it is often given.

The financial success of a new product effort is directly proportional to the size of the opportunity addressed by the project. An excellent project effort aimed at a mediocre opportunity will create a limited financial return, whereas the same effort focused on a large opportunity will result in major financial success. Four factors establish the size of a new product opportunity and can be used to test each proposed new product effort and ensure that the investment is well directed.

Finally, four critical success factors are key to a successful outcome of single product efforts. The relationships between these factors were described, and examples of failed projects illustrated the importance of each of these factors.

Desired Upper Management Behaviors:
Business Considerations for a Single Product

➤ Take personal interest in the new product investment process.

➤ Personally review each new product direction:

    Opportunity addressed aligns with strategic plans.

    Opportunity size is attractive.

    Product definition is on target and competitive.

➤ Track the four terms in the new product revenue gain equation for each product innovation effort. Ensure that they stay healthy.

➤ Understand the cost of time. Invest appropriately:

    Staff projects for minimum TTM.

    Remove obstacles that cause delay.

    Put needed resources in place when projects stall.

Chapter 4

Time Dynamics of the Innovation Engine

We each have a "learning horizon," a breadth of vision in time and space within which we assess our effectiveness. When our actions have consequences beyond our learning horizon, it becomes impossible to learn from direct experience. Herein lies the core learning dilemma that confronts organizations: We learn best from experience, but we never directly experience the consequences of many of our most important decisions.

Peter M. Senge
The Fifth Discipline

Business leaders are typically dynamic, action-oriented individuals used to taking control, implementing change, and seeing quick results. Their typical time horizon of interest varies from minutes to months—with occasional glimpses that extend out a year or two. This is fine for most business operations. Executives often can make decisions in a matter of minutes to hours. They can understand or correct problems with a manufacturing assembly process in days to weeks and can deal with personnel issues in weeks to months. Understandably, these same executives often get frustrated when dealing with product innovation matters, where the time between decision and results can easily extend to several years. Business leaders may feel as if they are climbing down from a race horse and trying to spur a glacier into motion.

To understand and effectively support product innovation efforts, executives must understand and adopt new mental models that accurately reflect how the innovation engine affects business results, both now and in the future.[1] These mental models must encapsulate how current business performance relates to earlier decisions and investments, and, how today's actions in product innovation may affect the company's future. As this chapter's quotation indicates, experience plays a vital role in the growth and learning of an organization. Learning from product innovation experience, however, requires that business leaders extend their learning horizon in new ways. Cause-and-effect relationships and response times typical of the innovation engine are sometimes unlike those of other business processes. Business decisions made without this understanding can produce seemingly excellent short-term results but in later years can lead to disastrous consequences.

Chapters 2 and 3 have provided important elements of the requisite mental models and the success criteria and interrelationships that they must reflect. Chapter 2 provided a broad-brush view of the collective enterprisewide innovation system and how it affects business performance and revenue growth. Chapter 3 described important aspects of a single product effort. This chapter fills out the definition of these mental models by describing important principles and interrelationships in product innovation with respect to the dimension of time. To achieve this end, a business case is developed here, based on a computer simulation, that realistically depicts performance issues and response times typical of an actual business.

The simulation begins by establishing a realistic revenue-versus-time response to a single project investment and then continues to develop a similar relationship for a full vintage year set of product investments. The revenue growth analysis introduced in Chapter 2 is then applied to determine quantitative relationships for our simulated business that connect investment rate, revenue gain, and revenue growth. Finally, the initial growth years of the business simulated, establish a backdrop for the business case.

---

[1] Senge, Peter M. *The Fifth Discipline: The Art and Practice of the Learning Organization* (p. 8). New York: Doubleday Currency, 1990.

■ BUILDING THE SIMULATED BUSINESS

➤ Time Dynamics of a Single Project

The perspective in this discussion is that new product effort *causes* the potential for revenue to exist. Once a company has introduced a new product, it is entitled to some level of revenues for a period of time as a return on its investment. How much revenue it can potentially receive and for what period of time depend on the market opportunity selected, the nature of the product and the business, and the excellence of the product. How much of the potential revenues are actually realized depends on how well the company sells and supports the product throughout its window in the marketplace. Nonetheless, completing a new product effort entitles the company to a return that extends from the moment of introduction to perhaps several years into the future.

The revenue entitlement created by a single project is depicted in Figure 4.1. In this simulation, the project time-to-market is set to 12 months and a revenue function versus time has been chosen that is typical for the particular business. The new product revenue gain was set to 13.0 for this example. The project investment is presumed constant at $300,000 per month over the life of the project. Revenues, of course, are delayed until the point of product introduction. Computation verifies that the total area under the monthly revenue curve is exactly thirteen times the total cost of

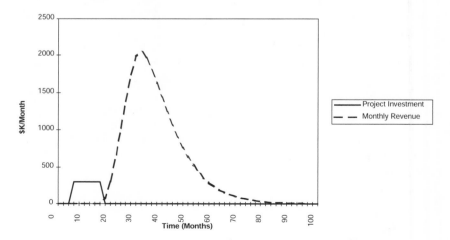

Figure 4.1   Revenue dynamic for a single project.

the project. If the company mounts an excellent sales and support effort for this product, it should realize all the potential revenue depicted in Figure 4.1.

➤ Revenue Entitlement of a Full Vintage Year

Companies typically distribute product introductions throughout each fiscal year. A reasonable approximation then is to assume that new products are introduced at the beginning of each quarter throughout a given vintage year. Figure 4.2 shows the total project investment required to complete one new product effort at the beginning of each quarter in the vintage year that starts at month 17 in the graph. Each project is again assumed to last 12 months and each project investment level is set at $300,000 per month. The project investment waveform in Figure 4.2 is the sum over time of all four projects, from beginning to end. That new product investment causes the vintage year revenue entitlement that follows.

The revenue entitlement for the vintage year begins as soon as the first product is introduced at month 17 and then builds as each subsequent new product is completed. Once again, the new product revenue gain for all projects is set at 13.0 so that the total revenue entitlement over the market window of this vintage year is 13 times the total new product investment in this vintage set. The same revenue-versus-time function that was used in Figure 4.1 is used again here for all four projects.

The vintage charts discussed in Chapter 2 depict the total annual revenues contributed over time by a given vintage year. Summing

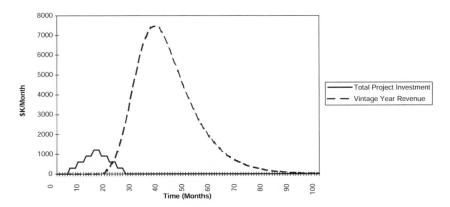

Figure 4.2 Revenue dynamic for an entire vintage year.

the monthly revenue depicted in Figure 4.2 into annual lumps produces the representation in Figure 4.3. This graph shows the annual revenue contributions that this vintage year will make in each year of its market window. The shape of this graph, while different from the monthly revenue curve in Figure 4.2, is still determined by the revenue versus time function chosen for this particular business simulation. Its shape will remain the same for all vintage years while its amplitude varies in proportion to total vintage year revenues.

➤ Growth Relationships for the Simulated Business

Examination of Figure 4.3 indicates that the vintage year revenue behavior of this business can be approximated by a five-year window with the following percentages of total revenues allocated to each year:

Year 1	8.5%
Year 2	42.0%
Year 3	32.5%
Year 4	12.1%
Year 5	4.9%

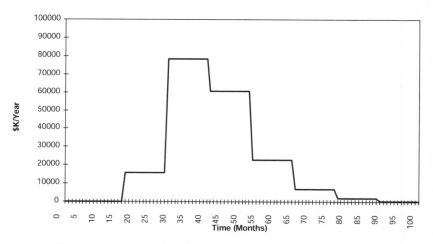

Figure 4.3   Annualized revenue for a single vintage year.

For simplicity, the small amount of revenue that actually occurs in year six and beyond has been lumped into year five. This normalized data can be used in the process described in the Appendix to establish the relationships between new product revenue gain, product innovation investment rate, and annual revenue growth. These relationships are given in Table 4.1.

■ A SIMULATED START-UP COMPANY

As with any start-up, our simulated business needs an initial investment in new product operations to start things off. An initial investment of $300,000 per month was assumed in the simulation, and this level of investment was kept in place until revenues created by the growing family of products could sustain at least this level of new product operations. In the subsequent growth phase of the business, new product operations are funded by a fraction of revenues that the business leadership team sets each year.

The vintage chart in Figure 4.4 depicts revenue growth in the early years of our start-up. During this period, annual revenue growth of about 10.4 percent is created by a new product investment rate of 0.09 and an average new product revenue gain of 13.0. The period of steady growth pictured here is fairly typical of a new company that has launched itself into a growing market with a good product contribution.

Table 4.1 Growth Relationships for the Simulated Business Case
(Growth = 1 + AGR)

IR	New Product Revenue Gain									
	10.0	10.5	11.0	11.5	12.0	12.5	13.0	13.5	14.0	14.5	15.0
0.060	0.750	0.769	0.788	0.807	0.827	0.846	0.864	0.883	0.902	0.92	0.939
0.065	0.782	0.803	0.824	0.844	0.864	0.885	0.905	0.925	0.945	0.965	0.985
0.070	0.814	0.837	0.858	0.880	0.902	0.923	0.945	0.966	0.988	1.010	1.031
0.075	0.846	0.869	0.892	0.915	0.939	0.962	0.985	1.008	1.031	1.054	1.077
0.080	0.877	0.902	0.926	0.951	0.975	1.000	1.025	1.049	1.074	1.098	1.123
0.085	0.908	0.934	0.960	0.987	1.013	1.038	1.064	1.090	1.117	1.143	1.169
0.090	0.939	0.966	0.994	1.022	1.049	1.077	1.104	1.132	1.160	1.187	1.215
0.095	0.969	0.999	1.028	1.057	1.086	1.115	1.144	1.173	1.203	1.232	1.262
0.100	1.000	1.031	1.061	1.092	1.123	1.153	1.184	1.215	1.246	1.277	1.308

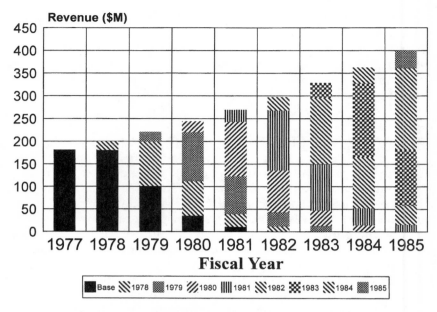

Figure 4.4 Vintage chart reflecting healthy growth
(Investment Rate = 0.09; Revenue Gain = 13.0).

➤ Psychology of the Initial Growth Phase

Launching a start-up company is somewhat like launching your-self off a cliff in an amateur-built airplane of your own design. A group of enthusiasts get together with some great ideas and con-spire to build an airplane. They cobble together a machine that has some of the right parts—an engine, wings, a tail, and control surfaces—and then they all climb in, roll down the hill together and off the edge of the cliff. If they have built the airplane well enough and if there is a good strong updraft at the launch point, the darn thing just might fly. Many don't, and you never hear about them again. The updraft wasn't there, the wings didn't cre-ate enough lift, the engine didn't develop enough power or some-thing. But some do fly. They soar to altitude very quickly and attract a lot of attention. Was it strength of the updraft or was it the fine qualities of the airplane?

Most start-up companies fly because they pick a spot where there is a good strong updraft—that is, a terrific market opportu-nity—and they can quickly put together a product line that will make a profit, despite high costs and flaws in product design. The business initially makes money and grows, not because it has efficient business processes and industry best practices, but because having the first product in a terrific new market generates an incredible amount of revenue. Depending on circumstances, this growth phase may create impressive wealth and last a long time. But for every updraft, there will eventually be a downdraft just as strong. Whether the company survives its first encounter with a serious market downturn will depend on several factors.

The crew of the home-built airplane and the leadership team of the start-up company face many similar choices during their initial experience. They can choose to regale in their success and enjoy the view from the wondrous heights they have achieved. They can soar this way and that as they savor the attention that they attract. They can congratulate each other on their outstanding cleverness and derring-do as they look down on other mere mortals. Or they can realize that the only reason that they are still alive is the serendipity of a strong updraft or an extraordinary market opportunity.

To survive in the long term, the wise air crew knows that they must tend to the deficiencies in their craft and in their own ability to pilot it. The wings must be properly trimmed, the engine must be made to deliver peak power. Those at the controls must learn the limits of their machine and how to get the most out of it. In the start-up company, ad hoc activity must be replaced with efficient business processes. The new product program must be brought to full effectiveness. Executive leaders must learn to manage their business for peak, long-term competitive performance. In both cases, those involved must transform themselves from lucky amateurs into seasoned professionals. And they must do so before a strong downdraft or market downturn creates catastrophe.

➤ The First Market Downturn

Often the first indication of a downturn that business leaders notice is a softening of revenue growth. It may be nothing dramatic, just revenue growth that is just a little lower than expected. These initial signs are easy to ignore. Next year, things will probably return to normal. In the business simulation developed so far, corporate leaders have had 10 years of successful experience, represented graphically by all of Figure 4.4 and years 1986 and 1987 in Figure 4.5. By now they are quite confident in their ability to

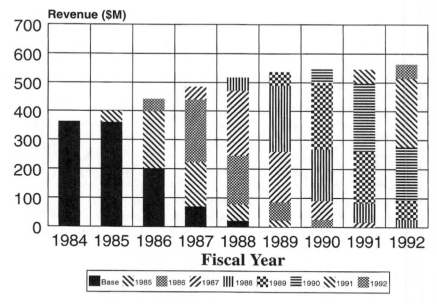

Figure 4.5 Vintage chart—Declining growth rate.

continue this success forever. They have just wrapped up 1988, however, and revenue growth was a little disappointing.

The reader should try to imagine the frame of mind that must exist among the executive staff at this point in the company's unfolding story. It is 1988 and you are looking back at 10 years of uninterrupted growth. And this year's revenue is considerably greater than last year, but the growth percentage is just slightly lower. What should you do? Should you be concerned? Should you do anything differently? What you have been doing has worked for 10 years, hasn't it? Sure the sales force has been grumbling about tough times, but that's nothing new. Maybe profit growth hasn't quite kept up with revenue growth in recent years, but doesn't 10 years of steady growth mean that you know how to run this business? Or has your success been due the strength of the "updraft effect" all this time? Is it finally coming to an end? Is there a downturn ahead and, if so, are you ready for it?

As Figure 4.5 shows, in 1988 the future did indeed hold a market downturn for this test-tube enterprise. As 1989 progressed, revenue growth became even weaker. New products introduced in 1988 and so far in 1989 were selling, but a little below expected levels. Efforts were launched to increase sales—increased quotas and incentives, alternative channels into the market. While this helped keep 1989 from being worse than it was, revenues for that year ended up even more disappointing than 1988, and as Figure 4.6 illustrates, profits were dramatically weaker. Soft customer demand and competitive pressure in the market pushed prices downward, while operating expenses and COGS continued to climb. As a result, operating profit, as a percentage of revenues, dropped sharply as did the price of the company stock. In early 1990, after the results of 1989 had been fully internalized, the business leadership team was willing to admit that they were in trouble. They were eager to attack problems and implement solutions, if they could only identify the root cause of their dilemma.

There are three places to look for the cause of a change in revenue growth rate:

1. A change in the new product investment rate.

2. A change in revenue versus time.

3. A change in the new product revenue gain.

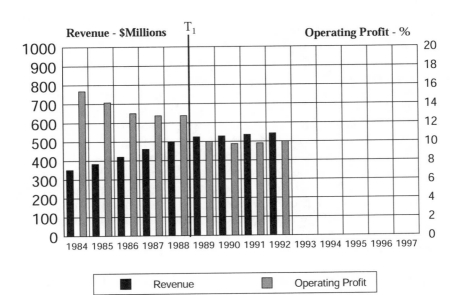

Figure 4.6 Market changes stall revenues and profit growth.

The root cause of the problems faced by this imaginary enterprise actually occurred in mid-1988 (T_1), almost two years earlier, when the new product revenue gain went from a value of 13.0 to about 11.3—a decrease of a little over 13 percent. As Table 4.1 shows, this small decline is enough to drop annual revenue growth from 10.4 percent to about 1 percent. As a close look at the vintage chart in Figure 4.5 reveals, it only takes a small decline in total vintage year revenues to nullify revenue growth. An instantaneous change in new product revenue gain is unrealistic, but it serves the purpose of this discussion.

A number of things can cause new product revenue gain to drop. A depressed economy, competing product alternatives in the market, and other changes in the customer world that reduce the demand for existing products are a few examples. Learning which of these factors is at fault, though, is often difficult for an executive team that has grown complacent. In this hypothetical situation, a combination of changing customer needs and new competition was the culprit. After 10 years, the original learning and assumptions about the customer base, on which the business was founded, had ceased to be as valid as they once were. Customer demand for the company's product offering was growing weaker. In addition, other companies were becoming familiar with the same customer base and developing new products that more specifically addressed its current needs. These competitors were doing very well since, over time, more and more of the customers' dollars were being diverted in their direction. But these subtleties were not yet clear to the leadership of our simulated enterprise in 1990.

Wanting to take some sort of action, the executive staff launched a number of improvement efforts. New training for the sales staff, total quality methods, and improvements in engineering practices and tools were implemented. While all of this helped in specific ways, none of these efforts got to the core problem confronting the enterprise and revenue growth continued near zero. These actions, however, took time to implement and to evaluate. Each improvement program started with high hopes and grand promises, but in the end, they did not add up to a solution to the fundamental business problems. By mid-1991, revenues were still flat, earnings were still down, and investors were protesting loudly about a stock price that had declined steadily for more than a year. Running out of patience, the board of directors quietly began a search for a new CEO who could take charge and turn the company around, restoring both earnings and the stock price to acceptable levels.

In the business scenario that has been developed so far, the executive staff clearly has not handled its first market downturn well. When they should have been tending to the fundamental ability of their firm to adapt and compete, they were perhaps too busy with other matters. The enterprise has remained largely ignorant of changes in the marketplace and new competitive pressures for too long. There must have been leading indicators of trouble long before revenues and profits began to fail, but management did not heed them. When the company finally woke up to its financial woes, the leadership team was not able to effectively apply business fundamentals and define corrective action. The CEO probably should be replaced along with, perhaps, some of the executive staff. But what kind of leadership should the board of directors seek?

The company has reached a defining moment, and the choices that the board of directors makes will determine its future. The following sections describe two alternative futures for this company that result from two different selections for CEO that the board of directors might make.

■ SCENARIO A—ATTACKING EXPENSES

The board of directors selected Al Adams as the new CEO. He had a well-established reputation as a tough, no-nonsense businessperson who focused on first principles and the bottom line. He had managed two other firms out of similar financial difficulties, and while he hadn't made many friends at either one, he had left them both with profits restored to their former levels. The rumor was that Al had made a bundle on his options when the stock price for each company rebounded. The board was well pleased with their choice, and Al started in his new job in early 1992.

Al was not happy with most of the executive staff that was in place when he arrived. Most were among the founders of the business. They were too impressed with their own importance, and they were soft—unwilling to make tough decisions and take the hard actions that would be necessary to turn this business around. One by one, they were moved out and replaced. In most cases, Al was able to find replacements from the ranks, individuals who knew the business and wanted a chance to show their stuff. In a few instances, Al brought executives in from outside who had the skills and fortitude that he wanted.

The year 1992 involved personnel changes, self-examination, and the defining of hard financial goals. Expenses had to be cut drastically. Inventory was too high, and manufacturing processes were sloppy. Administrative expenses were out of hand, and engineering was too fat and slow. By the end of 1992, Al had his staff and his plans in shape; 1993 would be the year of the turnaround.

Both the engineering and administrative budgets for 1993 were fully one-third lower than they had been in 1992. When the engineering vice-president went to Al to protest, he was told, "I'll tell you how to improve engineering productivity. Where you have ten engineers, lay off three and then put pressure on the other seven to get the job done. Make sure that they know that, if they fail, they too will go." Al was evenhanded, though, for all parts of the operation that he classified as "overhead" were cut by the same percentage.

Financial performance did turn around in 1993. As Figure 4.7 shows, revenues did not improve much, but profits came in sharply higher. Expense cuts at the beginning of fiscal year 1993,

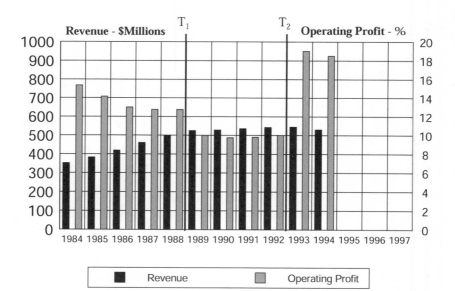

Figure 4.7 Cost-cutting restores profitability.

labeled T_2 in the graph, almost doubled the company's earnings in a single year. The board of directors was very pleased at the situation that emerged during the year. They had clearly made the right choice in leadership. Each quarterly earnings statement caused a sharp upward reaction in the company's stock price. By the end of the year, earnings per share were dramatically improved and investors were thrilled with the change. Al received a standing ovation at the shareholders' meeting, a first in the company's history.

As fiscal year 1994 progressed, things continued much the same: flat revenues but terrific earnings, at a percentage reminiscent of the early days. Al's success attracted a lot of media attention—articles in the financial papers, even a cover photo on a prominent weekly business journal. In late 1994, after about two and a half years with the company, he was hired away by another firm needing his clearly effective skills. Rumor has it that he, once again, made a bundle on his stock options as he left.

Figure 4.8 shows the legacy that Al left behind. While operating profits continued at a high percentage, in 1995 and beyond revenues declined sharply. By cutting new product investments by one-third, Al had moved the company's position in Table 4.1 from

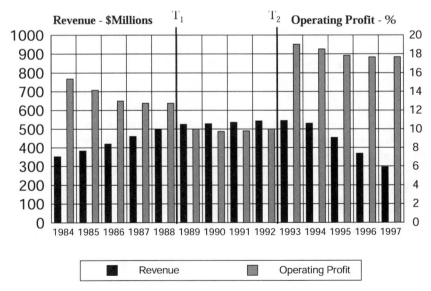

Figure 4.8 Cuts in new product investment cause delayed revenue decline.

an investment rate of .09 to .06 at a new product revenue gain of about 11.3. Since nothing fundamental was done to improve productivity, this changed the annual revenue growth rate from a positive 1.1 percent to roughly a negative 20 percent. Of course, revenue growth did not change immediately, because products already in the market or about to be introduced from the new product pipeline continued to generate revenue for several years. Even with investments levels cut by a third, new products continued to be introduced, but at a much slower rate. In this simulation, the company's revenue loop had enough inertia to run about two years before showing the impact of cuts in new product investments.

■ SCENARIO B—FINDING AND FIXING ROOT CAUSES

The board of directors selected Barbara Baker to be the new CEO. Although this was a risky step, for Barbara had never worked at this level of responsibility before, the board was convinced that she had the experience and the insight needed to pull off the needed performance improvements. While she possessed a firm grasp of the usual business fundamentals, she also had a unique understanding of new product processes and believed fervently that success was to be won by improving the company's capacity to deliver greater value to its customers.

Arriving for her new assignment in early 1992, Barbara's first impression of the executive staff that she had inherited was disappointing. She felt, however, that she could work with most of them. Some were surprisingly naive in business and management fundamentals, but several had a strong understanding of the company's products and customers. A couple of the executives were too impressed with their own success and importance to be salvaged, though, so they were replaced with outside people who brought new understanding of industry best practices in product innovation into the business.

Although she set high expectations for expense control, Barbara was careful to emphasize that only fat and waste should be cut, not fundamental capability. The focus was on productivity improvement, not expense cuts. Every department was expected to identify and prioritize the performance issues that impaired its ability to perform at competitive levels. Barbara asked each staff member to answer several key questions:

➤ What are the top three performance issues in your area?

➤ How do you know those are the top issues?

➤ What are you doing to improve performance in these areas?

➤ How are you measuring the progress of these improvements?

Drawing on her past experience in new product introduction at other companies, Barbara quickly recognized that new product processes throughout the company were particularly weak. The new product strategy was vague, and the company's sense of direction was unfocused. There were no set methods for identifying new product opportunities or focusing new product investments in the most lucrative areas. Product-innovation projects were not systematically tracked. At the occasional project review, people seemed to avoid asking the tough questions. Due diligence was simply not practiced routinely by the business leadership team. Handling of new product data was apparently sloppy too. A prevalent horror story heard in the hallways concerned a design file on the engineering information system that got erased by mistake. This had apparently delayed the introduction of a major new product by four months and cost about 10 engineering months of effort to replace.

The company had grown to its current level because it had found a high-growth niche market and had enjoyed almost uncontested dominance in this marketplace for years—but that was changing. Industry best practices in product innovation had not been adopted and activities in this crucial business process were as ad hoc now as they had been in the company's beginning. She vowed to take a personal interest in this important enterprisewide performance issue.

The company introduced intensive training in product-innovation practices and leadership roles—first at a high level for the executive staff and then later in more detail for the next layer of management. The entire management team needed to learn the same set of fundamental concepts and acquire a common vocabulary for new product operations. While the initial reaction from her staff was, "Why isn't this engineering's problem?" she quickly convinced her people that getting new products to market quickly was everyone's responsibility.

She and her staff met for several days off-site to explore the company's historical performance in product innovation. They identified the most critical issues that, when solved, would produce the biggest impact on business performance. A full-time project team was assembled to study industry best practices in product innovation and to explore in more detail the company's historical performance flaws in these targeted areas. By mid-1992, plans were ready for implementing specific performance improvements, and the needed resources were invested. Throughout this effort, Barbara and her staff closely monitored improvement activities and tracked results.

While implementation of product innovation improvements proceeded on schedule and was completed by the end of 1993, the duration of a full product development cycle had to pass before any effect could be measured in financial performance. Early in the improvement program, managers of product-innovation activities had acquired new skills in identifying market opportunities and defining competitive new products that better targeted customer needs. Project management skills were developed that vastly improved the productivity of new product teams. As a result, estimated new product revenue gain regained its former level of 13.0 by mid-1994 and seemed to be headed even higher. Throughout this period, the new product investment rate was held constant at 0.09 so, at long last, revenues again began to grow. As shown in Figure 4.9, annual revenue grew 2.2 percent in 1994 and the growth rate for 1995 was over 9.5 percent.

Although her course of action was exactly right for the long-term health of the company, it was not an easy career move for Barbara. In fact, she almost lost her job and her reputation because of it. Continued price pressure in the marketplace drove margins even lower in 1993. By the end of that year, revenues were still flat and operating profits that had once been consistently above 12 percent were now down to 9.4 percent. The company had apparently lost ground since she took control almost two years earlier. Shareholders were incensed and pressed the board of directors hard to fire Barbara Baker. The media was not kind to her either. Articles questioning the ability of Barbara Baker to handle a tough situation like this appeared in the business press. Despite this, Barbara convinced the board that the actions that she had underway would fundamentally change the competitive stature of the company so they stood by her and her program. By the end of 1996, the success of her leadership was apparent and she was well rewarded for her wisdom and tenacity, both financially and in terms of personal satisfaction.

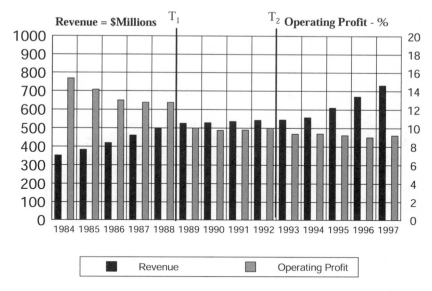

Figure 4.9 Effect of restoring new product revenue gain.

■ COMPARISON OF THESE TWO APPROACHES

The primary difference between the approaches to business success by Adams and Baker is that one addressed the most troublesome symptom while the other identified and resolved root causes of the problem. The fundamental problem here was a reduction over time in the ability of the company to create competitive value for its customers. Furthermore, the enterprise was unable to perceive early warning signals and adapt to changes in the marketplace. In addition, the original executive staff was ignorant of the business fundamentals of product innovation and, over several years, was unable to launch an effective response to the company's growing problems. In the language of the amateur-built aircraft metaphor, the crew had failed to make sure that their craft was airworthy when they had the chance and they had not taken the time to learn how to fly it well.

The symptoms of the company's problems were declining revenue growth and profit. In the aircraft metaphor, this is analogous to a reduction in the ability to climb to higher altitude. Attacking expenses is a straightforward and decisive response to one of these symptoms, declining profits. In the metaphor, cutting expenses is equivalent to throwing weight overboard to make the airplane lighter. This is a good idea only if the aircraft is carrying non-essential weight, and then it must be done with great care. Eliminating something important can cause the structure to fail or seriously hinder the performance of the aircraft. This kind of work should only be done by people who thoroughly understand how airplanes work. When Adams decided to cut new product investment expenses by one-third, he was effectively saying, "These engines are the heaviest things in the airplane. Cut them loose so we can climb better"—not very insightful. Such actions can make a dramatic improvement while you are still in the updraft but, in the long term, they cripple the aircraft.

In contrast, Baker's approach was equivalent to applying knowledge of how airplanes work to the performance problems of this particular craft. She determined and fixed root causes of the poor climb rate. In particular, a little nonessential weight was shed and the horsepower of the engines was improved over time until a good climb rate was reestablished. This approach required the application of a much higher level of expertise and required more time to implement. The result, however, was a permanent solution to performance problems.

In the language of shareholder value, Adams's solution had a dramatic and positive effect on the present value of cash flow from operations in the forecast period but at the cost of a terrific loss in residual value. As explained in Chapter 2, shareholder value usually is most heavily dependent on residual value, the present value of cash flow from operations beyond the forecast period. The actions taken by Adams may have caused the stock price to increase temporarily, as a reaction to short-term increases in earnings per share. But in the long term, his strategy had a devastating impact on shareholder value. The solutions implemented by Baker, on the other hand, did little to improve cash flow from operations in the forecast period. Instead, she focused on improving the long-term competitive performance of the company, which has a strong positive effect on residual value.

Figure 4.10 illustrates the difference in annual operating profit over time caused by these two different approaches to improving performance. The expense cuts implemented by Adams creates an obvious early advantage, but when revenues decline in 1995 and beyond, total operating profit declines as well. The advantage of a

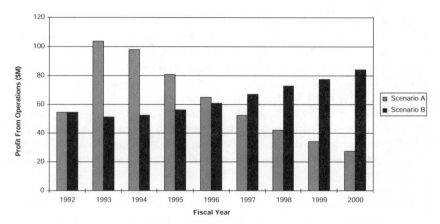

Figure 4.10 Differences in operating profit performance.

higher operating profit percentage is quickly lost as total revenues plummet. Baker's solution takes a while to get revenue growth going, but even with a lower percentage of operating profit, it is the clear winner in the long term.

■ CONCLUSION

Financial problems due to poor performance of the innovation engine can take a long time to develop, and they often take a long time to correct. New product programs can sometimes run for long periods without much executive attention and still generate growth for the company. They may only slowly drift away from a well-centered focus on market opportunity and customer needs. This was the nature of the simulated business case in this chapter. When top executives are simply tracking the bottom line and not paying attention to the actual performance of key business processes, the company can wander far off track before problems become apparent in visible, financial terms.

Due diligence and frequent review by the business leadership team keeps product-innovation operations competitive. In leading companies such as HP, executive leaders track new product efforts diligently, year in and year out, to make sure that they stay competitive and well focused on desired strategic directions. Frequent and effective review keeps situations like the one illustrated in this chapter from ever developing in the first place. When issues with the performance level of the innovation engine are discovered, leading executives invest quickly in corrective measures.

In terms of the aircraft metaphor, best practice indicates that the airworthiness of the aircraft should be inspected frequently and repairs should be made immediately when flaws are discovered. This highlights a key role of the executive staff—they are responsible for the ongoing competitiveness (airworthiness) of the key business processes in their enterprise. And the innovation engine is the business process that provides the power to make revenues grow.

Leading companies also provide ongoing development of executive skills in product-innovation practices so that they are able to provide effective leadership in this area. Industry best practices in the generation of new products change and evolve, sometimes rapidly. Staying abreast of these developments is essential if high-level managers are to provide effective decisions and leadership. This is equivalent to frequently upgrading the pilot's skills so he or she can most effectively operate the aircraft. Pilots keep themselves and their passengers alive by learning how others have dealt with new and unusual circumstances before they too are one day surprised by the same situation. As pilots of the enterprise, executives must not only set the direction for the company, they must deal with unforeseen circumstances in a way that preserves the health and well-being of the firm. To do this, they need a firm grasp of competitive business fundamentals, including those of the innovation engine.

Business executives should master operative mental models of the innovation engine to improve the effectiveness of their leadership in this area. This chapter began with a quotation from *The Fifth Discipline* about learning horizons in space and time. Learning from experience is difficult when the results of our decisions occur at some point beyond our learning horizon. The simulated business case presented in Chapter 4 has demonstrated the long lag time between cause and effect that can occur in new product efforts. Often the separation in time between action and results extends well beyond the learning horizon of those involved. Effective mental models that reflect the principles and relationships typical to new product activities offer an important supplement to experiential learning for executives. Chapters 2, 3, and 4 that make up Part I have outlined important elements of these models and the success factors and interrelationships that they must reflect. The remainder of the book continues this work.

Management practices at HP manifest many of the principles outlined in Part I. When the authors were leading product development projects at HP's San Diego Division in the mid-1970s, Bill Hewlett and Dave Packard used to visit the division at least once a year to review the business. A primary part of that annual review was a tour of new product development activities. Bill and Dave, along with other top HP executives, would listen to project managers describe their product contribution, technical issues, customers, and competition. They would ask insightful questions, probing for depth of understanding and soundness of judgment. Their interest in new product activities, as well as comments and questions, provided a role model for the company. Business division leaders and project managers alike knew the kinds of questions that would be asked. They also knew that you couldn't fool Bill and Dave. This leadership kept us honest and on track.

When revenue growth at HP would weaken, Bill and Dave would first examine new product programs because they knew that, ultimately, strong revenue growth depends on a steady stream of excellent new products. Were we working on the right new products? Were there any obstacles impeding early product introduction? Was there anything the company could do to help project teams get the most important products out sooner? Weak revenue performance always triggered expense cuts but Bill and Dave rarely cut R&D expenses. Instead, they would strengthen and focus new product efforts. Investment in new products was, and still is, viewed as the lifeblood of HP's future.

Desired Upper Management Behaviors:
Time Dynamics of the Innovation Engine

➤ Develop and maintain effective mental models that reflect the competitive operation of your innovation engine.

➤ Understand that growth is caused by an ongoing stream of excellent products. Focus management attention on the cause and let the effect happen.

➤ Track new product efforts with due diligence. Satisfy yourself that they are competitive:

  Investment levels support revenue growth goals.

  Projects are focused on the best opportunities.

  Productivity of new product processes and teams is competitive.

➤ Design executive incentives to emphasize long-term growth in shareholder value.

Part II

The Process of Product Innovation

Chapter 5

The Innovation Engine—
Fundamental Principles

in•no•vate, v.—l. to introduce something new; make changes in anything established ...

Random House Dictionary of the English Language

You, the reader, may now be thinking along these lines, "Okay, I'm convinced. My business needs to improve its new product operations to achieve better financial performance. But what does an effective new product operation look like? What should I change?" The answer to these vital questions is a resounding, "It depends."

Some sources insist that improved product innovation processes and tools will put business performance right every time. But too many start-up companies achieve outstanding business success with the most haphazard processes and tools for this single answer to be universally true. Others contend that all you need to do is provide an environment that empowers people and unlocks their creativity. Successful new products will inevitably follow. Empowerment and unleashing creativity in the workforce is important but creativity needs direction and focus to produce competitive business performance.

A competitive new product operation requires the right balance among three principal business assets:

1. Excellent product innovation processes.
2. Effective leadership from high-level management.
3. A supportive work environment.

The improvements needed in any particular enterprise will depend on which of these areas is inhibiting competitive performance. Part II of this book outlines important elements of the product innovation process. Part III outlines the critical roles and responsibilities of high-level management in a successful new product program. Part IV discusses the work environment and how it relates to successful new product activity. The material in Chapters 5 through 11 provides answers to many problems that executives must deal with in their own operations.

Part II begins with an overview of key elements of the innovation engine and describes fundamental process principles that determine their quality and productivity. Chapter 6 then describes in detail what goes on in the product innovation process and outlines some important opportunities for improving its performance. Chapter 7 discusses the project manager's role—a job that is often poorly supported and executed although it is critical to the success of new product activities.

■ THE INNOVATION ENGINE—A SYSTEM THAT SPANS THE ENTERPRISE

If the revenue loop in Figure 2.1 were on a computer screen and the reader were able to zoom and double-click on the innovation engine symbol, the detail in Figure 5.1 would appear depicting the key elements of the innovation engine. They form an enterprisewide system for developing and introducing a steady flow of new products.

The strategic planning and portfolio management process accumulates knowledge about trends in markets, customer needs, and technologies and develops the wisdom to excel in the business particular to the enterprise. Product strategies and family plans guide the flow and direction of new product efforts. This process determines the placement of new product investments and then applies due diligence to assure that those investments are well managed and yield expected results. This process is described more fully in Part III.

Below the broken line in Figure 5.1, the product innovation process provides the tactical muscle that addresses specific market opportunities with clearly defined project activity. This activity begins with the identification and development of new business opportunities. New customer needs and technologies that affect a

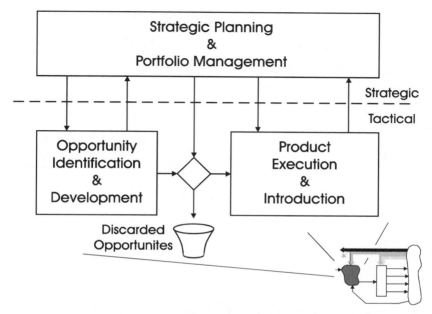

Figure 5.1 Inner workings of the innovation engine.

particular customer segment are investigated as possible opportunities and are developed into proposals for specific new products. After reviewing them, product portfolio management accepts and funds some of the projects. Others are discarded, either for lack of potential or lack of available resources.

Ideally, this system effectively engages and integrates the best efforts of people in almost every part of the business and at every level, from individual contributor through top-level managers. Operation of strategic planning will be covered in detail in Chapter 8. Tactical activities associated with specific products are described broadly here and in more detail in Chapter 6.

■ THE PRODUCT INNOVATION PROCESS

Zooming in on the tactical part of Figure 5.1 reveals a detailed view of the product innovation process, depicted in Figure 5.2. The product innovation process described here starts earlier than most

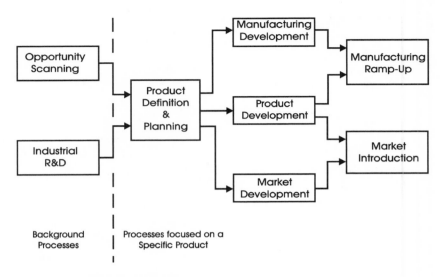

Figure 5.2 The product innovation process.

other representations and extends further into the future. It involves almost every functional department in the enterprise.

The purpose of the system shown in Figure 5.2 is to gather information and add value to it in a way that makes possible the manufacture, sales, and support of a specific new product. Each element in the diagram is also an information process that makes a specific contribution to the overall goals of the system. Information in one form or another flows between these elements. The major flow of information through this system is represented by the arrows in the diagram, but in reality, information is exchanged continuously in every direction between all elements of the system. The process begins at the left with general, approximate information about business opportunities or new technologies and ends at the right with highly accurate and specific information about a particular new product—how to manufacture it, sell it, and support it at mature levels. Once the enterprise has learned and archived this final information, the product innovation process has completed its work. The new information will have transformed the enterprise in a way that enables it to sell, ship, and support the new product at mature levels throughout the remainder of its market window.

Product innovation includes both background work and processes that are executed in conjunction with a specific new product. At the left-hand side of Figure 5.2, opportunity scanning and industrial research are shown as background processes. These on-going processes produce general information that may have value to a variety of new products. Opportunity scanning, which refers to the systematic search for new business opportunities that could provide value to the customer, is discussed in detail in Chapter 6. Industrial research involves finding and validating new technologies that might apply to customer needs. These two processes work together to identify new business opportunities.

When knowledge of a business opportunity is sufficient, it triggers investment in a project to develop that particular new product. The process elements to the right in the diagram are executed as part of each new product investment.

Each new activity begins with product definition and planning to investigate the business opportunity and its related technologies. Once an appropriate new product is defined, project and business plans are created to guide it to completion. The output of this system element should be, in effect, a business proposal much like that presented by a start-up company to a venture capitalist. The business opportunity is described along with the product offering. The financial return is estimated as well as the investment required to get the product to market. Developing the proposal generally involves technologists, marketing people, finance personnel, and manufacturing specialists.

Once the enterprise has accepted the investment proposal, development begins in earnest. The investment now grows significantly as product development engineers, manufacturing engineers, and product marketing people are added to the team. The three development processes shown in Figure 5.2 are executed more or less concurrently and each element needs a multifunctional team. Product development cannot be accomplished well without an understanding of both manufacturing methods and market requirements. Market development reflects information about product performance and features as well as manufacturing cost. Effective manufacturing methods and tools require information about the product design, product support requirements, and shipment forecasts. The three development processes in Figure 5.2 (1) create an information set that describes how to manufacture, sell, and support the new product, and (2) transfer this knowledge to the operational departments of the enterprise.

This key point deserves emphasis. *The purpose of the product innovation process is not to create new products; it is to create and archive information about new products.* This archived intellectual property represents the "crown jewels" of the enterprise. It enables the future sales and shipment of products worth perhaps tens or hundreds of millions of dollars to the company. It establishes both the present and the future competitive position of the firm. It forms the basis for future competitive actions. The growing pool of intellectual property created by the product innovation process represents a substantial part of the shareholder value of the enterprise.

Product innovation is not finished with the development of the product information set. The enterprise also must learn to sell, support, and manufacture the product at mature levels. Product introduction and manufacturing ramp-up elements provide this learning and finalize the information set to enable smooth sales and shipment of the new product into the future.

■ OWNERSHIP OF THE PRODUCT INNOVATION PROCESS

Ideally, the elements of the process in Figure 5.2 work together in a symbiotic way to develop and introduce successful new products. Each element must perform at competitive levels, and in addition, they must work together well for the overall system to be competitive. If the product innovation process is not performing satisfactorily, it must be diagnosed and repaired as a system. Those elements inhibiting competitive performance must be identified and corrected.

All too often, new products are presumed to be the responsibility of engineering, and executive leadership is likely to hold the engineering manager responsible for improvements. Product development then gets a lot of attention because it is the only element of the system over which this individual has control. This approach can result in improved business success only if the product development process is at fault. If the problems lie elsewhere (e.g., in market development or opportunity scanning), investing in the product development process will not solve the problem. It will simply divert attention from more important problems and waste both time and money.

Responsibility for competitive performance of the product innovation process rests, instead, with that individual who controls all its elements. Usually this is the CEO or business unit general manager. That person, along with his or her business leadership team, is responsible for elevating the performance of the product innovation process to competitive levels and keeping it there.

■ PRODUCT INNOVATION AS AN INFORMATION ASSEMBLY LINE

Many business enterprises are finding it harder to achieve financial growth and profitability. The new competitors invading their markets are changing the old familiar ground rules. These intruders are more clever at discerning customer needs and introduce new products at a dizzying pace. Because they provide more customer value with products that cost less to build, their profit margins are truly enviable. They are capturing market share and growing faster.

A similar destabilization of common business practice took place in the 1970s and 1980s, only the competitive playing field at that time was in manufacturing operations. Business leaders of the United States and Europe found themselves caught short in productivity, manufacturing cost, and product reliability. Hat in hand, they traveled to Japan to learn new ways of managing their manufacturing operations. The good news is that many of the lessons that management learned during that era can be applied intact to current performance issues in new product efforts. This section provides a method for reusing these hard-won lessons.

To begin, a discussion of process maturity provides necessary conceptual underpinnings that are common to both the manufacturing and product innovation domains. This is followed by a description of the information assembly line metaphor, an intellectual device for mining the wisdom that has been gathered by the manufacturing community over several decades.

➤ Process Maturity

As learning occurs, work processes evolve and mature. The corrective actions appropriate for a particular process will depend, in part, on its current state of maturity. A method of characterizing software development processes was crafted by the Software Engineering Institute (SEI) at Carnegie Mellon University.[1] This method involves a process maturity scale, described in Table 5.1, that can be adapted to work processes of any sort, not just software development. Understanding how work processes vary on this

---

[1] Paulk, M.C., Curtis, B., Chissis, M.B., et al. *Capability Maturity Model for Software* (CMU/SEI-91-TR-24, ADA240603). Pittsburgh, PA: Software Engineering Institute, Carnegie Mellon University, August 1991.

Table 5.1 Software Engineering Institute (SEI) Process Maturity Model

Level	Characteristics	Areas of Focus
5 **Optimizing**	Improvements fed back into process.	Automation
4 **Managed**	Quantitative. Measured process.	Changing technology. Problem analysis & prevention.
3 **Defined**	Qualitative. Process independent of individuals.	Process measurement. Process analysis. Quantitative quality plans.
2 **Repeatable**	Intuitive. Process dependent upon individuals.	Training. Technical practices. Process focus.
1 **Initial**	Ad hoc, chaotic.	Project management. Project planning. Configuration management

scale is important in describing issues and defining improvements associated with product innovation.

A work process at Level 1 on the SEI scale is ad hoc or even haphazard. Given an assignment, an engineer operating at Level 1 will invent the work process needed to achieve the assigned goals. Another engineer given the same assignment will likely invent a different process. Processes at this level are rarely reused and reflect highly variable productivity and quality of work.

At Level 2 on the scale, work processes are repeatable. Experience has taught the senior members of the group effective methods for accomplishing work. These methods are archived in the minds of these experienced individuals, who then pass them on to subordinates by word-of-mouth as needed. Work processes are thus repeatable, but only if the work group remains intact and these senior members are present.

At Level 3, work processes have been documented. These documents are sufficient to (1) convey overall methods for doing the work and (2) guide the efforts of individuals working in the process. If a work process has reached this level of maturity, it can be replicated in an isolated, uninitiated work group by simply transferring the appropriate documentation.

A process maturity of Level 4 implies that critical parameters of each work process can be measured quantitatively and tracked. These measurements can then be used to understand the state of the process and to make corrections if it wanders from desired performance levels.

Assembly operations in manufacturing are a good example of Level 4 process maturity. Quantitative measurements here might include units completed per day, reject rates, and amount of scrap accumulated per month. Measurements are usually expressed as variance from operational norms that have been established and, when performance wanders, these measurements can trigger corrective action.

The highest level on the SEI scale, Level 5, is assigned to work processes that not only can be measured, tracked, and corrected, but can also be improved over time. At this level, process understanding is so great that performance measurements can be used to imply process changes that will improve the speed and quality of results beyond current operational norms. To realize desired performance improvements, these changes can then be applied while the process is running.

➤ Product Innovation versus Manufacturing

If one were to apply the SEI process maturity scale to a collection of manufacturing processes and then to a collection of work processes in the product innovation arena, the levels of process maturity encountered would typically vary widely. A graphical representation of the results of this comparison might look like that depicted in Figure 5.3. Process maturity would vary over some range in each of these two domains. In general, though, the maturity of work processes in manufacturing would be about two levels higher than those found in new product operations. This contrast reflects the differing amounts of energy invested on process improvement activity over time in each domain.

This difference in process maturity highlights an opportunity. The higher level of process maturity in the manufacturing world represents a repository of knowledge that might be tapped to improve new product operations. An intellectual link is needed, though, to connect these domains and transform ideas in manufacturing into a form useful to product innovators. If this link can be found, the new product community might be able to reap the benefits of the immense learning that has occurred in manufacturing

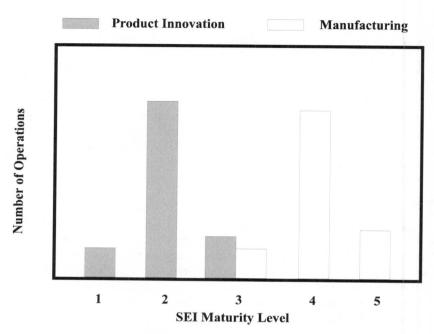

Figure 5.3 Process maturity—Manufacturing versus product innovation.

operations over the past two decades without having to duplicate the investment.

➤ The Metaphor

Most of us learned about metaphors as a form of communication while studying literature in school. They should actually be part of the engineering curriculum as well, for metaphors are *idea transforms*. They map ideas from one arena of thought into another—from a domain in which they have been conceived and proven valid into another domain in which they might also have value. An appropriate metaphor provides an alternative way of viewing a problem. Having the ability to view a problem from more than one perspective often leads to more creative and effective solutions.

Thinking of the product innovation process, represented in Figure 5.2, as an information assembly line provides the required

Purpose:
  **To add value to parts & materials as rapidly as possible
  until they become a quality, finished product ready to ship**

——————————— **Is Equivalent To** ———————————

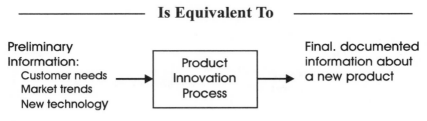

Purpose:
  **To add value to an information set as rapidly as
  possible until it describes how to manufacture,
  sell and support an exciting new product**

Figure 5.4 Product innovation as an information assembly line.

link between the manufacturing world and new product efforts.[2] In this metaphor, outlined in Figure 5.4, product innovation activity is viewed as an assembly line that applies value-adding effort not to parts and materials, but to new product-related information instead. Where the goal of a manufacturing assembly line is to create a finished product of high quality that can be shipped to the customer, the purpose of the information assembly line is to create an information set of high quality that completely describes how to manufacture, sell, and support an exciting new product.

Manufacturing concepts transform through this metaphor with the relationships depicted in Figure 5.5. Manufacturing processes perform operations that add value to parts and materials. They procure, fabricate, assemble, and ship parts and materials. Each of these words has an equivalent in the new product domain. The information assembly line gathers, creates, integrates, and

[2] Patterson, Marvin L. *Accelerating Innovation: Improving the Process of Product Development.* New York: Van Nostrand-Reinhold, 1993.

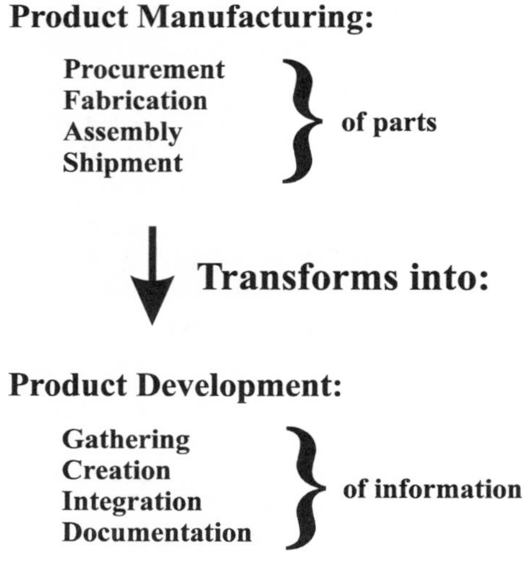

Product Manufacturing:

Procurement
Fabrication
Assembly
Shipment
} of parts

↓ **Transforms into:**

Product Development:

Gathering
Creation
Integration
Documentation
} of information

Figure 5.5 Transformation of concepts through the metaphor.

documents information. For example, any investment in the manufacturing arena that has improved the process for procuring parts and materials may point to an equivalent breakthrough in the gathering of information for new product efforts. Any concept related to the processing of parts and materials in manufacturing links to equivalent ideas in the new product arena that relate to the processing of information. In manufacturing, the payoff comes when you ship a finished product. In new product operations, the payoff occurs when you document the final information set for a new product.

■ LESSONS FROM MANUFACTURING EXPERIENCE

This section demonstrates the effectiveness of the information assembly line metaphor with real-life examples that point to opportunities in new product operations.

➤ Conveyors

In manufacturing, one area of improvement was in the handling of parts and materials. Implementing conveyors to move components and subassemblies from one workstation to the next reduced time and labor and prevented damage from mishandling. In the information assembly line of product innovation, the equivalent would be local area networks (LANs), and product data management (PDM) systems that move information related to the product from one workstation to the next. Engineers transfer data files instead of drawings. Information workers view three-dimensional models on a computer screen instead of two-dimensional representations on paper. The PDM system archives immensely valuable product information and maintains control over access to and modification of data files. In a manner similar to their counterparts in manufacturing, these information tools reduce the labor involved in transferring information and prevent damage from mishandling.

➤ The Improvement Paradigm

The best practices for systematically improving a work process that have evolved over time in manufacturing include the following five steps:

1. Stabilize and measure the process.
2. Improve process productivity and quality.
3. Improve the timeliness and quality of incoming parts and materials.
4. Redefine and eliminate waste.
5. Reduce the cycle time of the process.

The order for accomplishing in these steps is important. Attempting to reduce cycle time before stabilizing the process and getting productivity and quality under control, will only accelerate the creation of scrap.

The improvement paradigm transforms through the metaphor almost intact except that Step 3 shifts to a focus on information. The product innovation improvement paradigm becomes:

1. Stabilize and measure the process.
2. Improve process productivity and quality.
3. Improve the timeliness and quality of incoming information.

4. Redefine and eliminate waste.

5. Reduce the cycle time of the process.

Again, the order of execution is important for the same reasons.

A step-by-step comparison of the improvement paradigm, as it applies to each domain, highlights how concepts in manufacturing have equivalents in new product operations.

Stabilize and Measure

Before the manufacturing quality movement began, assembly line processes sometimes involved undocumented, handcrafted operations. Productivity and quality of output varied widely, and depended almost totally on the skill of individual workers. These processes were at Level 1 or 2 on the SEI maturity scale. At this level of maturity, each part created had to be inspected and measured individually to ensure it would work in later stages of the assembly operation. The first step in the improvement paradigm is aimed at fully defining and documenting such processes and then finding quantitative measures that reflect process productivity and quality.

Today, elements of the product innovation process in many businesses are still executed as undocumented, handcrafted operations. Each design has to be tested and reworked through several cycles to get it right. In these companies, members of the engineering team insist that you can't schedule invention and that product innovation cannot be managed as a process. Only a small fraction of the work involved in introducing a new product is, however, associated with invention. In reality, at least 85 percent of the effort involved in most product innovation efforts is similar to work that has been done on other projects. Performance of these tasks on all projects can be improved using the same methods that have worked in manufacturing. Stabilizing and measuring the process is thus a valid first step to improvement in product innovation, just as it was in the manufacturing domain.

Productivity and Quality

Once the process is defined and measured, the second step can be executed to improve productivity and quality. This involves understanding where effort is required to execute the process and how the process contributes to flawed results. The process is streamlined and tooling is altered to reduce required time and effort. The root causes of defects in the output are analyzed and systematically eliminated to improve quality. This step applies equally well to both manufacturing and new product operations. The difference is that, in manufacturing, the process output is in the form of parts or subassemblies, whereas in new product operations, the output is information about the product.

Control Incoming Materials or Information

The third step focuses on getting defect-free inputs to the process. In manufacturing, this means getting high-quality parts and materials to the assembly line just when they are needed. No time is wasted searching for parts to assemble because they are always delivered just in time to the line. Flawless materials passing through a perfect process involving error-free tools always creates a perfect output. Today much of the work accomplished in manufacturing operations is like this. The results are so nearly perfect that final tests to verify quality are not performed. The defect rate is so low that the cost of a final test is not warranted.

In product innovation, this step involves getting high-quality information to engineers working in various stages of the product innovation process just when they need it. Customer needs, manufacturing process constraints, and product safety regulations are examples of the information that must flow into the product innovation process. Having engineers search for this information is wasteful. Worse yet, they might proceed without the information that they need. This would be the same as leaving out some of the parts in a final product because they were not available when needed. In either manufacturing or new product operations, this practice is guaranteed to produce flawed results.

Redefine and Eliminate Waste

The next step is to creatively redefine waste and then eliminate it. The forms of waste that were initially measured in manufacturing operations included the amount of metal in the scrap bin or the cost of scrapped obsolete parts. Gradually, however, manufacturing operations began to view the length of an assembly line as an indicator of waste. Long lines implied that assemblies had to pass through many operations before completion. Each handoff from one assembly step to another involved wasted time and effort. Long lines were particularly vulnerable to bottlenecks. A snag at any stage on the line brought a lot of materials and labor to a standstill. A long line implied that each assembly spent a long time on the line, from start to finish. The cost of work-in-process inventory included the time value of money invested before the finished product was shipped to a customer. A longer line thus meant that more money was being lost to the time-value equation.

Once these forms of waste were recognized, improvement steps focused on reconfiguring the factory floor. Parallel feeder lines were created that concurrently delivered subassemblies to a short final assembly process. The total time that materials spent in assembly was reduced to lower the time value of WIP investments. Just-in-time (JIT) delivery of materials to the assembly line was implemented so that materials delivered to the receiving dock were taken immediately to the assembly line—no time sitting on the shelf in inventory and less handling costs.

Many of these forms of redefined waste have equivalents in the product innovation process. A long string of sequential process steps involves similar handoff problems and a longer time from start to finish. Product innovation activities have WIP inventory, just like that of manufacturing operations—except that, in many cases, the costs associated with this investment are substantially greater. Bottlenecks in a long, sequential new product process affect the overall flow of development in a manner much like the manufacturing example. The cost of time is a particularly important form of waste that has been traditionally overlooked in the new product arena. As was discussed in Chapter 3, a month of lost time in this cycle can cost millions of dollars in lost profit. This is true whether the month was lost from the beginning of the cycle or somewhere near the end.

The solutions in new product operations are similar as well. Concurrent development processes that deliver subsystem designs to a final integration and test phase are much like the parallel assembly line example. Manufacturing development and market development efforts are also conducted concurrently with product development activities. Supporting all project efforts with just-in-time information is a direct parallel to JIT manufacturing techniques and is discussed more fully later.

Reduce Cycle Time

When enough effort has been invested in the early steps of the improvement paradigm so that productivity, quality, and waste are sufficiently under control, the response time of the overall process can be reduced to improve business performance. Process changes to speed up manufacturing operations are implemented with careful attention to the fundamentals learned in earlier process improvement steps. Using these methods, some manufacturing operations have been accelerated to the point where they can build and ship products to order in the same day that orders are received. This results in very low WIP inventory, no finished goods inventory, and very happy customers. These levels of response time have been achieved only after bringing productivity, quality, and waste under control and keeping them there while reducing cycle times.

This final improvement step and its place in the sequence are just as valid in the new product domain. New product cycles can be dramatically accelerated as well but only after doing the preliminary work on process and quality. Sometimes businesses try to skip earlier steps and leap to accelerating the innovation cycle. This inevitably leads to mistakes, massive redesign, and a sharp drop in product quality. If products do get out sooner, it is because the project team makes a Herculean effort and puts in long hours. Business leaders may overlook these extra efforts and think instead that they have accomplished a bona fide process improvement. Business gains based on acts of heroism alone, though, are eventually lost as more and more energy must be diverted to correcting flaws in products that the business introduced prematurely. Further ground is lost as the workforce burns out and customer loyalty wanes.

➤ The Cost-of-Quality Principle

Another fundamental principle in manufacturing that transforms nicely concerns the cost incurred through creating a flaw in the process output. This principle holds that the cost of a flaw increases as the point in the process where it is created and the point where it is detected get farther apart. Examples will illustrate how this principle applies in both arenas.

Imagine an assembly line that builds an electronic device, a computer display. An early step in the process causes holes to be punched in a piece of sheet metal. For some reason, one of those holes is a half-centimeter off center, but this goes undetected. The metal sheet is bent to shape in the next process step, and at later stages, electronic components are installed in various locations on the sheet. Still the misplaced hole goes undetected. Eventually, the finished computer display is shipped to a customer who excitedly takes it out of the shipping carton, hooks it to his computer and turns it on. Now the flaw becomes apparent.

A large capacitor was installed in the misplaced hole and was thus located a half-centimeter closer to the blades of the cooling fan than planned. When power was applied, the spinning fan blades ground into the side of the capacitor with a horrible noise that terrified the customer. Before he could react, though, the electrical insulation on the capacitor failed, shorting out the high voltage inside. The capacitor then exploded in a cloud of foul-smelling smoke that filled the room. What was the cost of this process failure, and how does this cost compare with the cost would have been incurred had the flaw been detected early?

The cost of this flaw could have been a few dollars if it had been detected immediately after it was created. The bad sheet metal part simply would have ended up in the scrap bin. Instead, an entire new unit had to be shipped to the customer, free of charge, at a cost of perhaps $600. Worse than this, though, a dissatisfied customer was created. As it turns out, this customer was very vocal and an excellent storyteller. Several hundred potential customers eventually heard about the exploding computer display and associated it with the brand name on the product. The eventual revenue loss caused by this incident amounted to well over a hundred thousand dollars.

The cost-of-quality principle works exactly the same in the new product domain. Suppose an excellent new product opportunity for a desktop printer is identified in the opportunity scanning process on the left-hand side of Figure 5.2. An investigation is launched and the engineering team focuses on a thermal writing technology for the printer. A product is defined around this technology and the project is launched. In this particular company, however, new products are felt to be the responsibility of engineering. The executive staff is both too busy and disinclined to pay much attention to new product operations until market introduction is at hand. As a result, due diligence was not applied to this investment during its formative phases. The faulty information and logic that led to a flawed product definition were thus not detected.

Twenty engineers work on this project for about 18 months. The total investment required to get the product to market is over $8 million. The product is introduced, but sales do not ramp up as expected. In fact, the company sells less than three hundred units in the first six months. Feedback from customers indicates that they do not like the special paper required by the thermal writing technology. It is expensive, hard to get, and stays curled after coming off the feed roll. Furthermore, the list price of the new product is over $1,000 higher than competing products that provide similar value. As in the manufacturing example, the results of an early process failure were not detected until the product reached the hands of the customer.

Although the company discontinues the product after six months in the market, it must continue supporting the few units that have been shipped with paper supplies and repair service for the next five years. The total cost of this product failure eventually exceeds $12 million. Perhaps more important than this cost is that the company does not have a competitive product in this rapidly developing market during its early years. By the time they recover from their error, competitors have captured customer loyalty and market share. By being late, the company must attack a fortified hill.

If the executive staff, instead, had practiced due diligence early in the project, the cost of this information quality error could have been limited to a much lower value. An effective management review of the product definition phase results would have questioned the market viability of a writing technology that required special paper that was not readily available to the customer. The review would have questioned planned unit-manufacturing-cost (UMC) and would have found that the overall market viability of the product was lacking. At that point, the project could have either been canceled or redirected back into investigation to resolve these competitive issues. The total cost of the flaw could have been limited to $300,000 or less.

➤ Changeover Waste

As manufacturing operations reexamined sources of waste, the time required to set up a tool to produce a different type of part came into focus. In the automotive industry, for example, some of the tools for forming large sheet metal parts are as big as a small house and represent an investment of millions of dollars. The value provided by these tools in supplying parts for assembly operations can be tens of thousands of dollars per day of operation. In the 1970s, a 48-hour change-over cycle was typical. The cost in lost operating time could thus easily exceed $50,000 every time the tool had to be changed.

Over time, the design of these tools has been changed so that preparation for the changeover can be made as the tool continues to run. New forms are moved into place. Vehicles for carrying away the old forms are moved into position. When the changeover is initiated, cranes move the old forms out and the new forms into place so rapidly that operation of the tool resumes in less than 15 minutes. The reduction in downtime costs is like money in the bank.

Project teams in new product operations exhibit an equivalent form of changeover waste. As engineers finish their work on the current project, they often enter a time of less than full employment. Usually, nothing obvious marks the end of their work on the current project. As the product moves into production, its demands on their time simply diminish. In many operations, the nature of the next project is not yet clear and a few people are working to define what needs to be done. These people must finish this work before the engineering team can receive assignments and become fully employed on the new effort. So engineers enter a period of downtime that can last from weeks to months. An engineering team of 10 engineers will typically cost the company on the order of $100,000 per month during this changeover period. Most of this cost is a form of waste.

The solution to this form of waste in new product operations is similar to its counterpart in manufacturing. The changeover must be anticipated and preparations made for it while engineers are engaged with their current assignments. Opportunity scanning, technology investigation, and market investigation should be conducted concurrently with the final phases of the current project. The goal is to have the new product concept validated before the current project ends so that engineers can be reassigned to meaningful work immediately. Again, the changeover waste saved is like money in the bank. The extra bonus here, though, is that time saved in the changeover directly extends the new product market window. The company will thus reap an additional month of earnings at mature volume for the product for every month they save in project changeover delay.

➤ Just-in-Time Methods

The JIT factory is perhaps one of the most impressive improvements implemented in the manufacturing domain. As mentioned, the idea here is to reduce the amount of time that parts and materials spend in the factory, to dramatically reduce handling costs, and to speed up the assembly cycle time. This innovation requires in-depth knowledge and practice of the fundamental principles that support product quality.

To begin, vendors must be found that can deliver all the components required by assembly operations with flawless quality and with highly predictable delivery times. Incoming materials arrive at the receiving dock of the factory on the day they are required and are transported immediately to appropriate stations on the assembly lines. The flow of incoming materials is orchestrated with the movement of assemblies down the line so that, soon after they arrive, incoming materials are assembled into work moving by on the assembly line. Finished products flow off the line and are transported immediately to the shipping dock. Materials are thus assembled into finished products and shipped to the customer on the same day they arrive at the factory.

Information needs to flow like this through the information assembly line. In a JIT information assembly line, engineers would receive the information that they need (1) just when they need it, (2) in the format that they need, and (3) with flawless quality. The common set of information needed by all new product operations, depicted in Figure 5.6, would be understood and provided. Engineers would spend no time at all searching for needed information, and they would never proceed through their development tasks without that information. Information flow on the project would be as well understood and planned as the materials flow in a JIT factory. Information passed from one work team

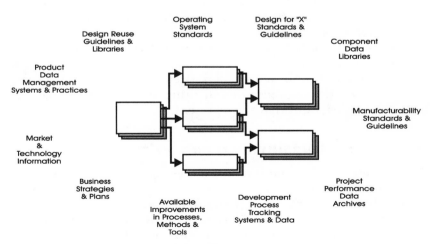

Figure 5.6 Managing the quality and timeliness of portfolio information needs.

to another would thus always be on-time, accurate, and in the appropriate format. Local and wide area networks would enable the effortless transfer of product information to other work teams and vendors located anywhere in the world.

To our knowledge, this JIT information factory concept has never been fully implemented in the domain of product innovation. It may, in fact, seem a bit outlandish to some. In the 1970s though, the idea of a JIT factory was just as outlandish. Twenty years of systematic improvements, however, can make a big difference. The current explosion in information technology is moving new product activities in this direction. With some effort and focus on process, the rate of progress should be considerably greater than that experienced in the manufacturing domain for we have their lessons and experience to draw on.

■ ADDING VALUE TO INFORMATION

The usefulness of the information assembly line metaphor depends on two conditions. First, those who use it must accept that they are in the business of adding value to information. Second, they should understand what determines the value of information.

A discussion of the factors that determine the value of information is provided in *Accelerating Innovation*.[3] The principles highlighted in that discussion are summarized here, but in the light of new learning from the field of situation theory.[4] Situation theory holds that the meaning of an utterance—their term for a packet of information—depends on both its content and its circumstances. In view of this, the factors that add value to information, outlined in Table 5.2, are organized into two parts: (1) those that control circumstances to add value, and (2) those that add value through actions that alter content.

➤ Increased Business Opportunity

The discussion of single product success factors in Chapter 3 described how the financial return from a new product effort depends directly on the size of the opportunity. When any given product innovation project finishes its work and archives a final information set, the value of that information to the enterprise is

---

[3] Ibid. Chapter 6.
[4] Devlin, Keith. *Logic and Information*. New York: Cambridge University Press, 1991.

Table 5.2 Factors That Add Value to Information

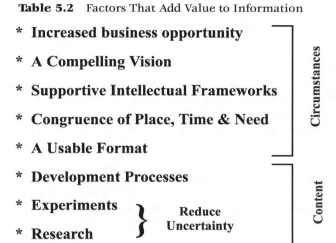

* **Increased business opportunity**

* **A Compelling Vision**

* **Supportive Intellectual Frameworks**

* **Congruence of Place, Time & Need**

* **A Usable Format**

* **Development Processes**

* **Experiments**

* **Research**

} **Reduce Uncertainty**

Circumstances

Content

in the financial return that it will enable throughout the market window. The value of the information set is thus directly related to the size of the business opportunity. This is true for the entire information set and for each element of information within it. The business opportunity establishes, in part, the circumstances in which the information exists. If the circumstances are more favorable, the information has more value.

➤ A Compelling Vision

An engineer who conducts a successful experiment, or a failure, learns something—he or she creates new information. The value of this new information depends, in part, on the existing vision of customer needs and product contribution. A project manager or a business executive with a strong product vision can sometimes find value in new information that the engineer cannot see. For example, the pervasive, yellow notepads with the semisticky adhesive that we post all over our offices are a product based on a failed adhesive experiment.[5] Someone with vision recognized the product possibilities and thus changed the circumstances around the information gained in this experiment. A compelling vision alters

---

[5] *3M Innovation, The Post-It Story*, 3M Web site: http://www.3m.com/intl/DE /english/about/ab_in_001.html.

the circumstances around new information and thus can dramatically increase its value.

➤ Supportive Intellectual Frameworks

The value of information depends on what else we understand at the time—the intellectual framework in which it exists. The detailed information set compiled to successfully manufacture a new 64-bit microprocessor might have had immense value in the year 1997. If we could transfer ourselves back in time with this same information, however, circumstances would change the value of our information set. Imagine trying to create financial success with this same information in the year 1940. Software technologies, memory systems, and computer applications are not yet even a gleam in someone's eye. The intellectual frameworks that are commonplace today do not yet exist. Without these supporting frameworks, circumstances in 1940 reduce the value of our hard-won information set to zero.

➤ Congruence of Place, Time, and Need

To have value, information needs to be needed. An application for the information must exist that has priority. In addition, information must be available at the place where it is needed at the time it is needed. An engineer, designing the outer case for a new electronic instrument, may need information on product safety regulations to create a suitable design. The information may exist at the time it is needed in an excellent technical paper on product safety that is located in the middle of a large stack of other papers in an office elsewhere in the same building. This information has no value. Later, the owner of this technical paper delivers it to the engineer, who—three weeks earlier—had committed his design to hard tooling. The information is now in the right place, but not at the right time. It still has no value.

➤ A Usable Format

The format in which information exists can have a major impact on its value. To have value, information must be delivered in a format that the user can understand and apply. A format that exactly matches that used in the current application increases the value of information dramatically. Imagine an engineer in Los Angeles receiving a design specification from an associate in Japan that is annotated with *kanji* characters. Unless the engineer is fluent in this form of writing, the information will have no value. On the other hand, if the information came instead in a computer file compatible with the engineer's system and was written in English, it would be much more valuable.

In our experience with one company, we discovered that each functional department had standardized on different systems for creating and communicating product-related information. Engineering used three-dimensional CAD systems and computer files. Manufacturing insisted on two-dimensional drawings. The stress analysis people used CAD systems but could not accept the formats available in engineering. This company estimated that it spent $5 million annually just changing the format of new product information from one form to another and then back again.

➤ Development Processes

A development process is a series of actions that systematically add value to information by transforming its content. An engineer who starts with a specification for a signal processor and then, through skill and labor, transforms this into the detailed design of a circuit board has increased the value of the information set significantly. A writer who takes technical information about the product and transforms it, through skill and labor, into a user manual that educates the nontechnical user on how to gain value from the product has added value to the information set. In both of these examples, information workers alter the content of the information set through systematic application of skill and effort. As these value-adding contributions accumulate, the information set advances toward the point where it will enable the enterprise to successfully sell, manufacture, ship, and support the product.

➤ Experiments

When new product activities involve steps that are uncertain in their outcome, experiments or prototypes may be required. Conducting experiments and testing of prototypes are other means for altering the content of the product information set in way's that add value.

A new and unfamiliar technology must be learned and tested to determine (1) whether it works at all, and (2) how much new functionality it can provide. Breadboard experiments can verify that the technology will work in the product application as needed. These experiments should also determine the critical design rules for the new technology that will enable engineers to apply it in the product with confidence. Prototype versions of the final product, either physically real or computer simulations, enable testing and verification of product performance. These prototypes are essential to remove many uncertainties:

➤ Do subassemblies perform according to specifications?

➤ Do parts fit together as planned?

➤ Will subassemblies work together as a system?

➤ Does the total product function over specified environmental variations?

➤ Does the total product satisfy regulations such as electromagnetic compatibility and safety requirements?

The value that these experiments and prototypes add to the information set depends on two factors. First, the value of the information gained depends on how essential it is to the total value of the product. In a printer product, experiments to verify that the mechanism will take paper successfully through the print path and deliver it to the output tray provide essential information in the evaluation of the product. Experiments to verify methods for labeling the shipping carton provide information that is less essential. Second, the value of the information gained depends on how much uncertainty is removed. In the preceding example, if the paper path design is fundamentally new and different, there will be a high degree of uncertainty in its performance. Testing of a prototype will thus provide much value. On the other hand, if the paper path mechanism is almost exactly like others that have been used in earlier products, very little uncertainty will be removed through these tests. They may not be worth the time and effort involved.

➤ Research

Another means of eliminating uncertainty is the investigation of prior art, learning from the work of others. This may alter the content of the product information set in a manner that increases its value. Research is often a precursor to product development activity. Occasionally, though, research can serve as an alternative to product-related experiments. Learning through research is usually less time consuming and expensive than building and testing breadboards and prototypes. As such, it should be exercised with due diligence first. Experiments that follow can then be better designed to eliminate only those uncertainties that remain.

Consider the first application of an unfamiliar fabrication technology such as a large, complicated plastic casting. One way to learn about this technology and verify that it will work in a particular product application is to build prototype parts and measure the results. Did the parts release from the mold as planned? How well did final dimensions match the design? How much touch-up work was needed to finalize the part? Another method for verification is to do library research on theory and applications, attend conferences where this technique is discussed, and visit other companies that have used it. Such research can often eliminate most of the uncertainties without the investigators having to learn through experiment.

■ STRATEGIES FOR IMPROVING INFORMATION PROCESSES

Strategies useful for improving information processes include:

- ➤ Select an excellent opportunity and align the project well.
- ➤ Provide customer-oriented, visionary leadership.
- ➤ Work on the most risky, most valuable tasks first.
- ➤ Creatively redefine and eliminate waste.
- ➤ Strive for effective design of experiments.
- ➤ Increase the rate of doing experiments.
- ➤ Squeeze experiments for information.
- ➤ Provide engineers with information resources.
- ➤ Design and manage project information flow.

➤ Select an Excellent Opportunity and Align the Project Well

As established earlier, the overall financial value of a new product effort is proportional to the size of the opportunity it addresses. The value of each action within a given project must then also be proportional to the opportunity of focus. The strategy for improving information processes that precedes all others is to focus efforts on substantial business opportunities. Once a good opportunity has been identified, the project must be aligned to that opportunity by a competitive product definition and effective project and product plans. Accomplishing these steps well ensures that every information process that follows will add the greatest possible value to the product information set.

➤ Provide Customer-Oriented, Visionary Leadership

When engineers get into the thick of the fray on a project, they sometimes fail to recognize the full impact of what they are learning. In effect, they can get lost in the forest as the trees obscure their view. A project leader who maintains a vision of how the new product relates to customer needs can often see value in project results that others miss. This perspective is essential in providing the direction and guidance that helps the engineering team ask the right questions, do the right experiments, and select a design approach that will lead to a successful product.

For a large format printer project, the initial investigation focused on verifying the technology for a full-color output capability with very high image resolution. After several months of excellent technical work, the project team finally had to admit that the color solution was simply not feasible. They were very disappointed with their result. In reviewing their results, however, the project leader discovered that high resolution black-and-white output was quite feasible. In fact, the technology that had been verified was sufficient to enable a very competitive product for a different customer set. The value in the information gained was there all along, but the broader perspective of the project leader brought it to light.

➤ Work on the Most Risky, Most Valuable Tasks First

Every project has risky elements, required outcomes that may prove unfeasible. Some of these outcomes are essential to a successful new product and others are less important. Proving that a questionable outcome can be achieved removes a measure of uncertainty and thus creates a quantity of valuable new information. Achieving an outcome that is essential to product success makes the information gained more valuable.

On the other hand, proving that an essential outcome cannot be achieved has immense value as well. Learning early that a new product is not feasible allows the project to be canceled with a minimum investment and the least wasted time. Gaining that same information at a later time has the same overall result—no new product. But the investment required to reach this conclusion will involve both lost time and added expense. Of the two, the lost time is usually far more valuable.

➤ Creatively Redefine and Eliminate Waste

This strategy comes right out of the manufacturing process improvement paradigm described earlier. The focus of project activity should be to gainfully employ every person in the work of increasing the value of the product information set. Anything that detracts from that work or slows it down is a form of waste. Someone proposed a conceptual metric that applies here, organizational velocity. Organizational velocity is defined as the ratio of time each person spends adding value for the customer to their total time spent at work. In an effective workplace, this ratio might be as high as 80 percent. In others, it can get as low as 5 percent. Information processes in the product innovation process should be streamlined to maximize organizational velocity.

➤ Strive for Effective Design of Experiments

Breadboard experiments and prototypes used in new product work should be designed to achieve maximum learning with minimum investment. Learning will occur only in areas where outcomes are uncertain, so effort and investment should be focused there. Creating finished-looking prototypes of outer covers and front panels early in the project is usually a waste of effort and time. These parts involve no uncertainty at all so early prototypes will not add value to the product information set. Experimental design methods, such as those of Teguchi, are useful in designing experiments that yield maximum insight for the number of measurements taken.[6] Experiments and prototypes represent a major portion of the project investment and add essential value to the product information set. They deserve careful

---

[6]Taguchi, G. *System of Experimental Design*. White Plains, NY: Kraus International Publications, 1987.

thought and planning and should be an area of leadership focus and due diligence.

On occasion, the behavior of business leaders creates a "Demo or Die" attitude among members of the new product community. Business leaders expect to see impressive demonstrations of prototypes from time to time, and their reactions and feedback during these reviews send clear signals about what they like to see. In some cases, teams can become more concerned with putting on flashy demonstrations than getting the new product out.

Undue attention to appearances is one symptom that too much priority is being given to demonstrations. Early breadboard experiments and prototypes should be ugly, with wires and bare metal everywhere. They should be strictly focused on learning. Early models to convey product design concepts are sometimes useful but should be limited to painted cardboard mock-ups or computer models. When the project team puts too much energy in making their early prototypes pretty, they probably have their priorities wrong.

➤ Increase the Rate of Doing Experiments

Another conceptual measure of product innovation effectiveness is the amount learned per unit time. Doing experiments rapidly is thus as important as doing them well. This means that, once new product-related experiments have been planned, resources must be in place to rapidly implement them. For hardware development, access to a model shop that can provide rapid turnaround on limited quantities of prototype parts is essential. Computer simulation tools may offer the ability to do "virtual experiments" very rapidly. Executive leadership can often play a key role here by eliminating obstacles that delay the implementation of experiments.

Creativity can also help speed up the experimentation process. On one project in the authors' experience, a large format drafting plotter concept was under investigation. A new technology was encountered in the research lab that was interesting, but it was implemented in a small notebook-size mechanism. People were skeptical of the ability of this technology to handle the large, heavy sheets of linen and film media typical in drafting applications. In response to this skepticism, the project leader of this research effort had the little mechanism literally cut in half on a band saw. Each of its parts was then extended in length to allow the mechanism to handle 24-inch-wide media. In less than a week, a prototype was working with the drafting media in question. Using normal practices of the day, fabrication of a new prototype of this sort would have taken perhaps four to eight weeks. This creative leap by the project leader thus accelerated the learning process by about a month.

➤ Squeeze Experiments for Information

Implementing a product-related experiment or a prototype is both time consuming and expensive. The payback is the information gained from the effort. To maximize this return, project teams should strive to learn everything they can from the apparatus that they have assembled. Once performance has been measured under nominal conditions, more information can be gained by varying environmental conditions to the specified extremes. When these tests are finished and recorded, even more information can be gained by stress-testing the apparatus—varying conditions beyond specified limits to determine design margins and failure modes. An effective set of experiments generally will reduce the prototype apparatus to dysfunctional scrap in the end.

➤ Provide Engineers with Information Resources

Some fraction of the new product budget should be invested in support services that facilitate engineering access to needed information. All new product projects in a particular business share common information needs such as design for manufacturability guidelines or preferred part specifications. Figure 5.6 gives further examples of shared data requirements. A central investment to cover these requirements in a manner that provides accurate, timely, and consistent information to all projects simply makes good common sense. It eliminates the need for engineers to chase down the information themselves, and it ensures that all projects will operate with the best available information.

➤ Design and Manage Project Information Flow

Project plans should consider who needs to know what by when. Activities to learn and communicate critical project information then need to be included in the plan. Each engineer on the project should understand who is depending on them for information and what these people require in both timeliness and format. A product data management system should be implemented that keeps track of scheduled information delivery. This system should also routinely back up and archive project information and maintain control over access to and modification of information files.

■ CONCLUSION

This chapter has described the product innovation process as an enterprisewide business process that systematically assembles the knowledge needed to produce, sell, and ship new products. This process adds value to information in much the same way that the factory assembly line adds value to parts and materials. This similarity is so strong that many techniques developed in the manufacturing arena to improve process productivity and quality can be applied successfully to the product innovation process. Examples were provided to illustrate how these manufacturing concepts map into new product operations.

The SEI maturity scale is a means of comparing the level of development of various processes. The implication is that a higher level of process maturity is better. While this is generally true in manufacturing, it is not always true in new product operations. A start-up company that is bringing a new technology into a new market probably needs to do product innovation at the handcrafted level while establishing their technology and position in the market. Such an operation would find highly mature development processes burdensome. When this company grows to the point where it is running several new product projects simultaneously, however, the highly flexible, handcrafted style can become an obstacle to further growth. A more defined process is then needed that provides scheduling of limited resources and structured interaction between project teams and management. Each business enterprise will thus have an ideal level of process maturity that depends on its circumstances.

Some principles that are fundamental to adding value to information were discussed and strategies for improving information processes were provided. The value of an information set is related to (1) its content, and (2) its circumstances. Experimentation and research are ways to add value to information by removing uncertainty. There are specific strategies for improving the information processes typical to new product operations, based on these principles.

Desired Upper Management Behaviors:
The Innovation Engine—Fundamental Principles

➤ Manage product innovation as a business process. Track process performance and make corrections.

➤ Pay attention to early phases of the process. Exercise due diligence on opportunity selection, product definition. Raise the maturity of these process elements to at least SEI Level 2.

➤ Periodically review new product efforts. Test their effectiveness in adding value to information.

➤ Invest in common information resources for new product teams. Make needed information easy to get.

Ch a p t e r

Operation of the Product Innovation Process

Every activity, every job is a part of a process. A flow diagram of any process will divide the work into stages. The stages as a whole form a process. The stages are not individual entities running at maximum profit.

W. Edwards Deming
Out of the Crisis

Chapter 5 introduced the workings of the innovation engine at a high level—the view from 15,000 feet—as an interconnected set of tactical and strategic elements. The tactical side of this system, the product innovation process, was then described as an interconnected set of subprocesses that add value to a product information set. This chapter continues to describe the tactical side of the innovation engine in more detail—the view from, say, 5,000 feet. At this level, the operation of each subprocess in the product innovation process is visible, and the work that goes into adding value product information is more discernible.

This process description is only one example of how the product innovation process might operate. At this level, differences related to the nature of individual businesses begin to appear. The candidate processes offered here are self-consistent, however, and highlight essential elements of a successful product innovation process. This discussion advances understanding to a point where business leaders can more effectively evaluate their own new product operations.

Figure 6.1, essentially a copy of Figure 5.2, provides a high-level road map for this chapter. The discourse here proceeds from

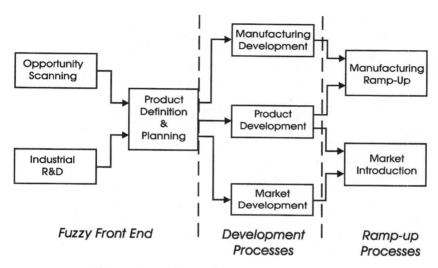

Figure 6.1 The product innovation process.

left to right through the diagram. If Figure 6.1 were reproduced on a computer screen, the reader might imagine moving the cursor to each element in the diagram and double-clicking the mouse button. In each case, the screen would fill with the next level of detail for that process element. These graphics, along with supporting discussion, are the substance for the remainder of this chapter.

■ THE "FUZZY" FRONT END

Smith and Reinertsen describe the initial, formative stages in product innovation as the "fuzzy front end."[1] In Figure 6.1, this formative work is included in the opportunity scanning, industrial research, and product definition process elements. These elements identify, describe, and verify new business opportunities and technologies that might lead to future new product activity, and then create a proposal for a specific new product effort. In the assembly line metaphor, this is equivalent to finding sources of raw material that may have value in future assembly operations, and then proposing a plan for their use.

---

[1] Smith, Preston G., and Reinertsen, Donald A. *Developing Products in Half the Time.* New York: Van Nostrand-Reinhold, 1992.

Work in this area of the product innovation process is indeed fuzzy, with a high level of uncertainty. The emphasis here is on searching for possibilities. Answers come later. This work is also fuzzy because it is often not recognized as real work. In many companies, these process elements are so low on the SEI maturity scale that they are subconscious.

Despite this pervasive lack of attention, these front-end processes are critically important. They set the direction for future new product activities and establish rich choices for the selection process. The quality of the information that flows out of these front-end process elements directly amplifies the value returned to the enterprise from future new product investments. The fuzzy front-end deserves close attention from the business leadership team. In many businesses, this part of the product innovation process offers an opportunity for dramatic improvement in long-term business performance.

➤ Opportunity Scanning

The purpose of the opportunity scanning process, depicted in Figure 6.2, is to identify and describe potential business opportunities that might be worthy of new product investment. The desired output from this process element is a prioritized queue of exciting product possibilities. This queue needs to be in place so that, when current new product projects finish, the team that becomes available can be quickly reassigned to the next most important investment. These opportunities will be exciting because they describe new ways in which the enterprise can move toward its desired future and provide value to its customers. The most exciting opportunities will align well with established strategic directions and core competencies of the firm. They will promise excellent growth in both revenue and profit.

This work begins with the scanning for new information in various communities of practice. Technologists in the firm, for example, read professional publications and attend conferences. They learn new technologies and practices from time to time that might have product importance. Marketing personnel attend trade shows and talk with customers. They learn about evolving customer needs and practices. They learn about new products offered by the competition. Technical professionals from manufacturing operations scan their world for new production tooling methods and fabrication practices. This scanning activity goes on all the

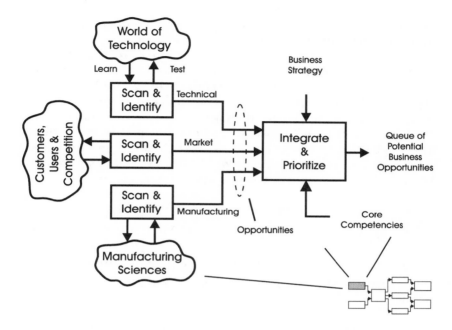

Figure 6.2   An opportunity-scanning process.

time in most business enterprises. Differences in performance arise, though, from how well management applies this incoming information to business operations.

Information from any one of these communities of practice can translate into an exciting business opportunity. In general, however, the most compelling possibilities are created by combining information from two or more of these operating arenas to identify a new product opportunity. Aligning understanding of a new technology with knowledge of evolving customer needs makes breakthrough product concepts more likely. A new manufacturing technology that can dramatically improve reliability or lower product cost is most exciting when it is combined with an understanding of market pressures.

An effective opportunity scanning activity will thus have some means of integrating the information learned by individuals throughout the enterprise. Scanning activities will be deliberate and planned. Information gained through these activities will be systematically reviewed in the context of the firm's strategic directions and core competencies. The most compelling business opportunities will emerge from this process.

While the diagram in Figure 6.2 and this process discussion may seem too formal to some readers, the implementation does not have to be very formal at all. In the authors' experience, the process represented schematically in the diagram was accomplished well when a product marketing manager and a product engineering manager teamed up to visit customers and attend trade shows. They talked with a sampling of customers in all important market segments. Rather than asking, "What kind of products would you like us to develop?" they learned to ask more insightful questions:

➤ What value are you delivering to your customer?

➤ How do our current products or our competitors products help you do that?

➤ What obstacles keep you from being more competitive?

➤ How would you like your operations to improve over the next five years?

The product marketing manager was able to discern customer needs and business opportunities, while the product engineering manager could identify possible technical solutions to these needs. They each gained different insights from their conversations with the customer. The integration process depicted in Figure 6.2 took place informally in restaurants all over the country as these two individuals discussed their experiences and compared notes at the end of each day. The integration and prioritization process continued as they reviewed their findings periodically with the business leadership team and others back at the plant. This ongoing activity allowed the company to develop a prioritized list of new product possibilities and kept it current and exciting.

A final and most critical outcome of the ongoing opportunity scanning process is that the individuals involved develop and maintain judgment in the business arena under investigation. This judgment eventually enables them to identify families of products that (1) address a broad range of customer needs, and (2) provide a stronger competitive position in the marketplace. This judgment is also essential in honing the definition of specific products and in making the decisions and compromises that will guide subsequent development projects to successful outcomes.

➤ Industrial Research

Industrial research provides a more intense exploration of available technology than that offered by the scanning activity. A few talented individuals can accomplish this process in a small company; large companies, such as HP or the Xerox Corporation, may maintain entire laboratories. As depicted in Figure 6.3, industrial research begins with a search for advances in product-related technologies. Candidate technologies are either found through research or created through creative application of fundamental principles. An understanding of desired strategic directions for the enterprise guides this work, and knowledge of market needs of specific business units provides focus. The result is a queue of possible technology opportunities.

The most promising opportunities are selected for further investigation. One to several people may take from weeks to months to provide information about the viability of a candidate technology and prove that it provides useful product-related functionality.

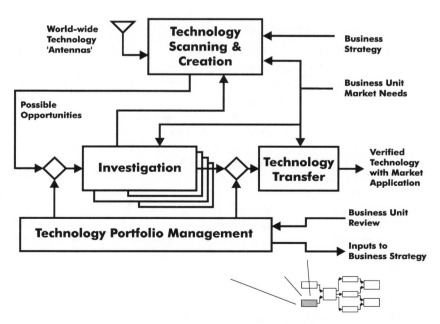

Figure 6.3 An industrial R&D process.

Key design rules for the technology are established that will help engineers adapt it to specific product applications. When an investigation produces promising results, individuals from product development operations in the appropriate business units are invited in to review the outcome.

The payoff from industrial research occurs when a verified new technology is transferred to a product development project and provides a proprietary edge over competitors in the marketplace. Often an industrial research champion for the technology joins the target development project for a time to ensure that the knowledge transfer is successful and to help work through initial difficulties in adapting the technology to product needs.

A second payoff is the wisdom and judgment in technology needed to establish effective long-term business strategies. This important business asset is developed over time through in-depth involvement in pertinent technical communities of practice. It is also developed in the ongoing struggle to advance product-related technologies from a state of laboratory curiosity to that of robust and dependable intellectual property.

➤ Product Definition

Figure 6.4 provides a graphical representation of the product definition process with some elements of current best practice. The process begins at the left with an infusion of information from the opportunity scanning and industrial research processes. It continues with steps to develop a focused understanding of customer needs that relate to the specific new product under investigation. This preliminary gathering of information launches concurrent investigations, to identify the market potential, to verify technical feasibility of the product, and to establish its competitive performance levels. These activities must remain tightly coupled, for the direction and success of each depends on the other.

The market investigation explores in detail customer needs for the product, sales potential, possible product positioning, and critical market success factors. Unit manufacturing cost constraints and pricing possibilities are also examined as is the competitive environment. Alignment of the new product with business strategies and sales and distribution channels is established. Throughout this effort, awareness of technical investigation results provides a current estimate of the probable product performance and feature set.

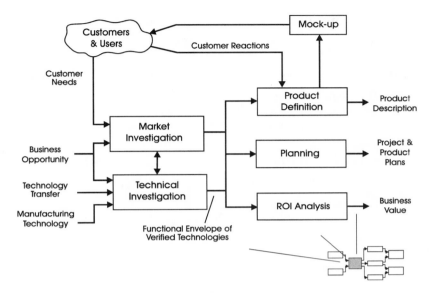

Figure 6.4 A product definition and planning process.

A process called *Concept Engineering*™ formalizes the market investigation and product concept creation processes.[2] An outline of this process, presented in Table 6.1, describes the flow of Concept Engineering activity but does not show the richness of thought and technique that it includes. Concept Engineering employs a cross-functional team and takes them through a market study, customer visits, and exercises to identify customer requirements and product concepts. These exercises combine logical and intuitive methods that work together to create an insightful product definition that will both delight the customer and fare well against competition in the marketplace. John Doyle, a retired executive vice-president at HP, used to lecture HP business leaders about the importance of developing "an imaginative understanding of user needs," which he tagged with the acronym, IU^2N. Concept Engineering is a well-thought-out process that focuses on developing IU^2N. More information on this process can be

[2] Hepner Brodie, Christina, and Van Winkle, Tag. "Developing Better Product Definitions Using Concept Engineering." Talk presented at the Product Development & Management Association's 1997 International Conference, Monterey, CA, October 22, 1997.

Table 6.1   The Concept Engineering Process

1. Develop understanding of customers' environment
    Research the market   Visit customers
    Develop a customer matrix   Reflect on their environment

2. Convert understanding into customer requirements
    Translate requirements   Use language processing
    Identify the vital few requirements   methods to gain insight

3. Operationally define requirements
    Identify valid measures   Survey customers
    Correlate measures and requirements

4. Generate concepts
    Decompose design into subsections   Generate concepts
    Generate ideas

5. Select concepts
    Screen concepts   Reflect on final concepts
    Select concepts   and process

obtained from the Center for Quality of Management™ in Cambridge, Massachusetts (617)873-8950.[3]

The technical investigation attempts to adapt product-related technology to specific customer needs in a way that will yield a sustained competitive advantage in the marketplace. Critical product features are implemented in breadboard form so that experimentation can verify technical feasibility and performance limits. A constant awareness of market investigation results keeps the technical investigation focused on activities and product features that will most likely contribute to successful business performance.

The magnitude of effort in these investigations depends on how much new information needs to be assembled. If the product is simply an extension of an existing product line, the order of magnitude may be simply one or two people working a few weeks to ensure that market and technical assumptions are still valid. If the product addresses a new market or employs an unfamiliar technology, then several people working a number of months is more realistic.

The information assembled by both the market and technical investigation enables a preliminary definition of the new product—

---

[3] *Concept Engineering* and *Center for Quality of Management* are trademarks of the Center for Quality of Management. All rights reserved.

including its feature set, user interface, performance specifications, desired unit manufacturing cost, and positioning in the marketplace. A mock-up of the product can then be fabricated to gather feedback on the product definition from key customers. The mock-up is also useful in garnering support for the product from the business leadership team in the enterprise.

The primary purpose of the mock-up is to convey the product concept in a way that engages the interest and imagination of both investing business leaders and customers. It should be realistic in appearance and include enough detail to show the primary functions and user interface features of the product. As always, speed is of the essence so the mock-up should be simple and easy to fabricate. Painted cardboard mock-ups with glued-on front panel buttons can be effective and can be fabricated in a couple of weeks. In the hands of a skillful designer, they can look very much like a finished product. Computer screen simulations of the product also are effective mock-ups. This technique can be used as well to simulate the intended operation of product displays and user interfaces.

Once the mock-up is in hand, a round of customer visits is conducted to determine whether the product is as exciting to real customers as it is to its creators. Several visits are made in each targeted market segment to sample attitudes of key customers. Knowledge and relationships established during opportunity scanning activities are useful in planning and arranging these meetings. At each visit, the company representative shows the mock-up and describes product contributions. Feedback from customers is carefully noted, especially their level of enthusiasm for how the proposed product will improve their operations. This information helps the company tune the product definition and better align it with real customer needs. The information is also useful in determining the value of the proposed product to the customer and will influence pricing decisions later. The customer feedback loop is repeated at least one more time, perhaps with different customers, to verify the adjusted product definition.

The effect of this loop is to test and improve the information in the product definition. As customer feedback is incorporated and the loop is repeated, the quality of the definition improves dramatically. After a very few cycles through this loop, customer enthusiasm for the new product will be so high that they will want it yesterday. This result reflects the high-quality information in the product definition.

As the definition takes form, project plans can be formulated and the financial analysis for this project investment can begin.

Table 6.2 Product Definition Success Criteria

➤ Understanding of customer and user needs.

➤ Alignment with business strategy.

➤ Understanding of competitors.

➤ Product positioning.

➤ Technical risk assessment.

➤ Clear decision trade-off criteria.

➤ Understanding of regulatory constraints.

➤ Assessment of distribution channel alternatives.

➤ Upper management support.

➤ Organizational support.

Project plans should include (1) a description of the work breakdown structure for the project including key objectives and milestones, (2) the development schedule, and (3) enterprisewide resources needed to complete the project. The financial analysis should include an estimate of the financial investment required, forecasts of unit sales and estimates of expected revenues and ROI. As discussed in Chapter 2, a forecast of expected revenues versus time and overall revenue gain would be useful as well. Together, the product definition, project plan, and financial analysis comprise an investment proposal that is presented to the business leadership team for consideration. The likelihood of acceptance should be related to the quality of this proposal, the confidence gained from customer feedback, and the confidence level created by the market and technical investigations. Table 6.2 lists other important criteria for a successful product definition.[4,5]

Questions that always come up when we reach this point in our executive seminars are, "Isn't it risky to share proprietary product information with customers like this? What if they leak your product plans to your competition?" There is some risk of this and the importance of that risk will vary from business to business. This risk must be traded off, however, against the value of

---

[4] Wilson, Edith. "Product Definition: Assorted Techniques and Their Marketplace Impact," Proceedings of the 1990 IEEE International Engineering Management Conference, pp. 64–69.

[5] Gaynor, Gerard H. *Handbook of Technology Management* (ch. 36). New York: McGraw-Hill, 1996.

the information gained during these customer interactions. Also, the perceived risk of possible information leaks to the competition is generally much larger than the real risk involved.

Imagine the tables reversed: your competition has shared proprietary product information with your customers and they have leaked it to one of your salespeople during a conversation. What is the probability that your company will use such information to foil the efforts of your competition? In most cases, information received in this way gets lost before it ever reaches someone in your company with the power to create a competitive response. In the worst case, imagine that the astute salesperson immediately picks up the phone and calls the right person in your firm with this information. What is the likelihood that the information communicated will cause this person to divert enough resources from current new product efforts to create a competitive response? Leaked information causes no harm unless it creates a significant shift in competitive behavior. The answers to the questions posed here will help you determine the real risk of these information leaks to your firm.

The risk of leaked information depends on the duration of your innovation cycle and that of your competition. By the time you visit customers with a product mock-up, you are well into the innovation cycle. You have perceived the opportunity, investigated it, and are about to launch a full-fledged project. In perhaps a year, you will introduce your new product. Assuming that your competition acts on the information that you leak through customer visits, what is the likely length of their innovation cycle from that point? If they have a similar product effort underway, it could be relatively short. If not, they have to work through opportunity perception and investigation themselves to reach a point comparable to your current competitive position. Any competitive response on their part will, in this case, be much later to market than your product offering presuming that your company can get products to market at least as quickly as they do. Having a fast innovation cycle is thus one of the best defenses against damage caused by information leaks.

■ TIME TO REFLECT

Taking time out at this point to reflect on the information processes described so far is useful in highlighting some of the principles described in Chapter 5. First, note how both opportunity scanning and industrial research gather vague, nonspecific information that may have some product value and transform it into valuable information with a specific product focus. The product definition process takes this information, adds to it, and creates an even more valuable output, the description of a competitive product response to the business opportunity along with detailed plans and financial analysis for the required investment. These process descriptions should make the discussion in Chapter 5 of adding value to information more tangible.

In each process described so far, the quality of the information produced is a function of the quality of incoming information and the quality of the applied process. The product definition process can be applied to an excellent business opportunity or one that is decidedly off track. While some self-correction may be provided by the customer feedback loop, the business value of the process output will vary directly with the quality of the information that flows into the process. Likewise, an excellent business opportunity can be operated on by an excellent product definition process or one that is haphazard. Again, the value of the information produced will vary, but this time as a function of the process quality. These relationships between inputs, process, and outputs are identical to those of an assembly line process that operates on incoming parts and materials.

The reader should view the process elements described here simply as examples of the functions that must be performed in the product innovation process. Internal details of actual business processes employed may vary from one enterprise to the next. The processes described here, however, embody some of the best practices encountered in the authors' experience and provide a good starting point for innovation process discussions in the reader's company.

Finally, the process diagrams provided so far highlight the value in creating even rather simple schematic representations for elements of the innovation engine. Designing a graphic representation of innovation process elements requires first a focus on key information required by each element and also on the important information delivered by the element. Where does required information come from and what are its principal ingredients? Where is this information used and what must it contain for smooth operation of the innovation engine?

The next set of questions that must be answered to create a process diagram concerns how work processes transform incoming information into the desired form needed to support effective product innovation. What key work patterns and relationships accomplish this transformation? How do these process elements relate to one another and to the outside world? Answering these questions begins to resolve the internal detail of the process diagram.

The real fun begins when an enterprise creates a conceptual model of how their product innovation process should work and then begins to compare it to how work really gets done in everyday operations. This comparison usually highlights flaws in current work processes with embarrassing clarity. Information necessary to a successful product may not be available to the project team when they need it and they routinely proceed without it. Or perhaps the goals and objectives of work processes in product innovation are unclear. Members of the development team are routinely unaware of others who depend on their work and fail to provide information when and where it is needed. Creating a conceptual model of how product innovation should proceed in the ideal case is a powerful step toward improving the business performance of the enterprise.

■ DEVELOPMENT PROCESSES

The objective of development processes in the product innovation process is to transform the product definition into an information set that describes how to manufacture, sell, use, and support the proposed new product. A further objective is to accomplish this outcome in accordance with the initial project and product plans. The information set produced collectively by the three development processes shown in Figure 6.1 will enable the enterprise to generate profitable revenue with the new product for months and perhaps years to come. This information set is an important addition to the pool of intellectual property that distinguishes an enterprise from its competitors. It should be treated with great respect—well recorded and carefully archived.

In general, three kinds of development are needed to create the required information set—product, manufacturing, and market. This does not imply a return to the old functional silo organization. It simply means that there are three interrelated work processes focusing on different aspects of the information set. The information from these processes should overlap and integrate into a seamless, well-documented package for use in day-to-day operations throughout the life of the product.

Each process should be accomplished by a multifunctional team with access to information from the other development activities. The product development team, for example, needs to include members from both marketing and manufacturing. Product development cannot be accomplished effectively without frequent infusion of information from both market and manufacturing development efforts. Detailed information about customer needs and related product features is required as well as an understanding of manufacturing tooling approaches and related design constraints. Manufacturing and market development efforts need similar information links and multifunctional involvement.

➤ Product Development

The product development processes begins with product definition information and the project plan and then systematically creates and documents knowledge concerning the detailed product design, how the product works, key assumptions made in its development, and constraints on product operation. The information assembled by this process must be sufficient to sustain product manufacturing and support operations throughout the market life of the new product. If changes occur in future operations—a vendor goes out of business, for example, and key components are no longer available—information assembled by the product development process must be sufficient to support recovery efforts.

As the product development process proceeds, it provides an ongoing stream of information to the manufacturing development process that describes in detail the unfolding design of the new product. Concurrently, the product development process receives and responds to information from manufacturing operations describing design constraints imposed by available tools and fabrication processes. The manufacturing and product development teams work together to achieve unit manufacturing cost goals.

Similar two-way information flow occurs between the product development process and market development efforts. Information about customer needs and applications provides increasing clarity on the product feature set and how it contributes to product value. As the design unfolds, information about the actual performance and cost affects market development efforts.

A caveat is needed here. As the market development team learns about customer needs and applications, they are often tempted to change the definition of the product, to make it better. Changes in the product definition at this point in the project will inevitably cause major portions of the engineering effort in product development to be scrapped. This is demoralizing, wasteful, and time-consuming. Unless the competition has introduced a major breakthrough that obsoletes current development efforts, changing the product definition in middevelopment is almost never a good business decision.

Best practice in product innovation is to first create the best possible product definition and then get that product out as quickly as possible. Product features that emerge from further learning about customer applications and needs during development are deferred to a future revision. If the development team decides during the middle of the development phase that the current product definition is not competitive, this means that either their work during the product definition and planning process was flawed, or they have taken too long to get the product out and the market has changed. Such an occasion should trigger a close scrutiny of new product processes and subsequent efforts to correct the fundamental defects that caused this outcome.

Figure 6.5 provides a schematic representation of a product development process. An initial system design activity considers

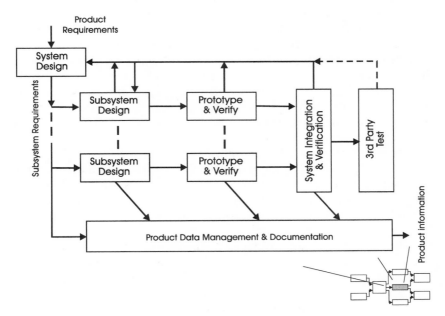

Figure 6.5 A new product development process.

product requirements and then crafts a corresponding product architecture. This architecture dictates how product functionality will be implemented. In a new electronic measurement product the system design establishes the performance that will be required of mechanical, electronic, or software subsystems. It also describes how subsystems will operate together and interface with one another. The product architecture embodies key decisions and trade-offs that profoundly affect product attributes such as manufacturing cost, development time, and performance. In fact, the basic feasibility of the product is often either established or undermined by the system design.

The system design for a product should align with the core competencies of the enterprise to establish the sustainable competitive advantage that the product must have to succeed financially. These competencies might include unique product technologies, strategic business directions, or product distribution and support capacity. A competitive manufacturing infrastructure is often one of the most important competencies in a world-class business. The system design approach should thus utilize as much as possible the manufacturing knowledge, processes, and supplier infrastructure that the enterprise has assembled over time.

There was a time when manufacturing operations were expected to assume the attitude, "You design it and we'll figure out how to build it." This gave product developers total freedom to pick technologies and design approaches. More recently, however, business leaders have realized that their manufacturing processes and infrastructure require major investments to achieve and maintain competitive stature. Investments must therefore be focused on the essential capabilities and strategic partnerships. Product developers must now align their efforts as much as possible to utilize this competitive manufacturing infrastructure lest they diffuse the competitive intensity of manufacturing operations.

The output of the system design activity is information about the basic product architecture and specifications that describe the requirements that each subsystem must satisfy. As shown in Figure 6.5, this system design information is archived as part of a growing product data set.

The system design information launches a set of concurrent subsystem design activities. Some will involve a single mechanical, electronic, or software engineer. Others will involve teams of several engineers working together to determine an efficient subsystem design that will satisfy requirements. The output of these efforts is a conceptual design for each subsystem. As an example, the information set created for an electronic subsystem might include schematic circuit diagrams, timing diagrams, state diagrams, performance specifications, parts lists, and circuit board designs.

Next, prototypes of each subsystem are fabricated and tested. These tests verify that each subsystem performs as designed and satisfies its requirements. Flaws in the conceptual design of a subsystem are often detected at this stage as the immutable laws of physics come into play:

> *The facts will eventually test all of our theories, and they form, after all, the only impartial jury to which we can appeal.*
>
> Jean Louis Rodolphe Agassiz
> 1807–1873

The final outputs of the prototype stage are (1) verification that each subsystem design works and (2) test information that describes performance limits. Preliminary outcomes, however, are likely to be that the subsystem design does not work well and subsystem requirements have not been met.

Essential learning occurs during both the subsystem design and prototype verification stages. As shown in the diagram, knowledge acquired by the engineers during these activities feeds back into the system design process. Perhaps system designers have specified something that cannot be realized with current design techniques. Occasionally subsystem designers come up with creative ideas that lead to a fundamentally better approach to the product architecture. In such cases, an iteration of the system design may result in a modified product architecture and new subsystem requirements.

Testing of subsystem prototypes often reveals that actual performance does not match what was expected of the subsystem design. Knowledge of performance limits and failure modes created by the testing of prototypes feeds back into either the system or subsystem design stages as appropriate and causes iteration of the design. Once the design is corrected, modifications are made to the prototype and performance verification tests are repeated. This loop is repeated until subsystem requirements, subsystems designs, and prototype verification test results converge to a workable solution.

These iterative loops are typical of product development activities. When flaws are detected at any stage of the development process, they must be corrected. The cost-of-quality principle tells us that the cost of a flaw is minimized when it is detected and corrected as early as possible. These iterative loops are, however, both time consuming and expensive. Performance improvement efforts often focus on minimizing both the number of iterations and the cost and time of each pass through the loop.

The lessons from manufacturing apply here as well. Perfect inputs operated on by perfect processes and tools will provide perfect results. As much as possible, then, development processes should be perfected along with the information and design tools available to development engineers. When such perfection is achieved, subsystem designs will always work the first time without fail. Until then, lessons from manufacturing teach that early inspection and correction can best achieve quality improvements. Design reviews by senior practitioners are a best practice that accomplishes this. The creator of each design presents it to a small gathering of senior engineers, who can apply their best experience and judgment to each design before it is implemented as a hardware prototype. Corrections at this point are quick and inexpensive. In addition, simulation tools may offer the opportunity to quickly verify design performance with a software implementation before making the expensive transition to hardware.

Once a workable set of subsystem prototypes has been assembled, they can be integrated into a system prototype and tests can be performed to verify performance of the entire product. If the system design and subsystem designs are sound, there will be no surprises and the product prototype will meet all expectations. Often, however, unexpected interactions between subsystems cause system failures. Electrical interference generated by one subsystem may impair the performance of other subsystems. The timing of actions generated by a subsystem may not match up with that required by other subsystems to which it interfaces. As Figure 6.5 shows, the knowledge of performance limits and failure modes gained through system verification tests feeds back to earlier stages to trigger changes in the system design or in the design of individual subsystems.

As shown in the diagram, a product management system captures and archives the information created at each stage of this iterative development process. Appropriate documentation facilitates communication and work flow throughout the enterprise. The product data management system should (1) contain current files on all pertinent design information and (2) control access to and modification of those files. All product data should be periodically archived and stored in a safe place. The information captured by the product data management system represents most of the value created by a new product investment. This information is an incredibly valuable business asset and should be well protected and managed.

Before the explosion of digital information tools, best practice was to maintain product information in the form of hard-copy drawings and other paper documents. Policies and procedures were in place to archive these documents and maintain revision control. As more and more product information began to exist in digital file formats, however, the old paper-based product data management systems began to break down. Horror stories exist in many enterprises that occurred during this transition from hard-copy to digital information management. In one instance, an engineer inadvertently purged a data file that contained the only copy of a complicated software subsystem program. Recreating this program required ten engineering months of effort. Worse than the cost of redesigning the software, the product introduction was delayed four months. In other cases, engineers have spent several weeks revising their design, only to discover that they were working with obsolete information about other parts with which their own design interfaced. In each case, the entire revision effort had to be repeated.

Since product innovation is essentially a process for adding value to a product information set, methods and tools used for storing and managing this information deserve special attention and should be reviewed for adequacy.

The product design created by the process depicted in Figure 6.5 passes through various stages of maturity. The initial pass creates an engineering prototype to prove that the product concept works and can meet all requirements. The engineering prototype may be rough and have wires hanging out all over. Many of the mechanical parts will have been hand-crafted in the model shop. Access covers and other housings may be simply pieces of unpainted sheet metal or missing altogether. Engineers will own this prototype, modify it frequently, and perform all tests personally. The intent is to prove the product concept as quickly and efficiently as possible so little effort should be expended on nonessential aesthetics.

The second level of product design maturity is the production prototype phase. Once testing of the engineering prototype is complete, the knowledge gained triggers a final, production-ready design of each part and subsystem. Once again, the process depicted in Figure 6.5 is followed. As much as possible, production prototype parts are fabricated with final tooling and assembly methods. Final access panels, paint, and front panels are in place. This prototype looks like a final product. Any flaws detected in engineering tests on this unit are corrected by further design iterations until the prototype performs like a finished product and the development engineering team is ready to declare their work finished.

At this point, ownership of the prototype usually transfers to manufacturing operations and several copies of the production prototype are created to be used in several ways. Some are used in design verification tests to prove that the product design is indeed ready for production and for use by the customer. Others may be installed in customer beta sites for field tests. Production prototypes may also be used for development of operating manuals or field support training.

The product development team remains involved with this activity primarily to (1) correct flaws that are found by others, (2) keep the product design information up to date, and (3) support the prototype units and keep them functioning properly. The team should also be finalizing the product information to adequately sustain manufacturing and support of the new product into the future.

➤ Manufacturing Development

The objective of the manufacturing development process is to transform information about product requirements and the project plan along with an understanding of the unfolding product design into the knowledge required to manufacture a cost-effective, reliable product. A further objective is to supply fabrication tools, assembly lines, and test fixtures needed to support initial manufacturing operations. This latter objective points to one of the few examples where an important output produced by the product innovation process is physical hardware rather than some form of information.

Figure 6.6 provides a graphical representation of a manufacturing development process. Information about the product concept, knowledge of product design directions, and initial sales forecasts provide a starting point for the development of a manufacturing approach that will satisfy unit manufacturing cost,

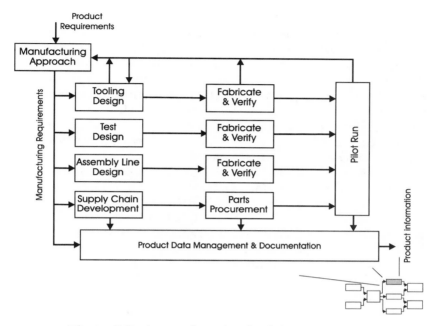

Figure 6.6 A manufacturing development process.

product reliability, manufacturing capacity, and budgetary constraints. This step is equivalent to the system design process described in the section on product development. Key decisions and trade-offs made during the formulation of the manufacturing approach will determine the viability and business success of future manufacturing operations. For example, should product assemblies be manually transported from one assembly station to the next or is an automated conveyor system required? Is a fully automated final test system with a custom fixture for the current product an appropriate approach or should a technician simply collect the right instruments on a workbench and test each unit by hand? The manufacturing approach largely determines the cost and productivity of tooling, assembly lines, and product test operations.

Appropriate manufacturing approaches vary dramatically, depending on the nature and shipment volume of the product. Each enterprise must learn the range of manufacturing practices that are appropriate to its industry and develop the skills to apply them competitively. An assembly line for an automobile plant employs tools and processes that are unlike those found at a facility dedicated to the packaging and shipment of toothpaste and mouthwash. An operation that turns out tens of thousands of personal computers each month is fundamentally different from one that turns out a few dozen expensive and sophisticated electronic instruments in the same time period. The investment in automation that typifies a PC factory makes no sense at all for an assembly line that ships only a dozen or so units per week. Each business must focus on manufacturing core competencies that are cost-effective and competitive for its particular product line.

Once the fundamental approach to manufacturing has been established for the new product, engineering efforts can be launched to develop tooling, assembly processes, and text fixtures. Development of outside sources for critical, long-lead-time components can also begin. The requirements established by the manufacturing approach should include information such as cost targets for each part, labor content targets, and expected parts volumes. The manufacturing plan should also specify schedule information, manufacturing resource allocation, and budgetary allowances for each effort. Once the manufacturing development activities shown in Figure 6.6 have been launched, their management and flow proceeds much the same as that described for the product development process.

The degree to which engineering concepts are implemented in prototype form in the manufacturing development process depends on the degree of uncertainty in their application. Implementing prototypes in manufacturing operations can be particularly expensive and time consuming. These costs must be weighed against the probability that the particular tool or assembly line simply will not work. In practice, engineering concepts involving the greatest uncertainty may be implemented first as prototypes, whereas proven manufacturing methods will proceed directly to final fabrication. As with the product development process, flaws detected during implementation and verification provide new learning that triggers redesign activity.

Once fabrication tools are in hand, assembly lines are in place, test fixtures exist, and parts have been procured, a pilot run of the newly developed product is manufactured to verify that all is ready for full production. The performance of fabrication tools is tested. Flow of materials and work on the assembly line are observed. Product test procedures and fixtures are verified. Units produced in the pilot run are exhaustively tested to ensure that they meet performance and reliability goals. This flurry of activity around the pilot run provides essential learning that will be critical to smooth operation of these manufacturing facilities when product shipments ramp up to full volume.

As with product development, knowledge gained throughout the activities in manufacturing should be captured by the product data management system. Documentation essential to future operations should be completed. All of this important intellectual property should be carefully archived to ensure its ongoing availability.

➤ Market Development

The market development process transforms information about product plans and the product definition into the knowledge and communications required to sell and support the new product at targeted mature volumes. This process also provides sales forecast information that is essential to preparations for volume production in manufacturing operations.

Figure 6.7 depicts a representative market development process. Beginning with the product definition and product plan created earlier, the marketing plan addresses issues related to the ability of the enterprise to sell and support the new product. A development activity assembles the information needed to establish new required capabilities. How the product will be distributed and sold, how it will be repaired when it breaks down, and how customers can use it to advantage in key applications are some of the business issues addressed in this phase. Some products require that customers have access to consumables such as paper, ink cartridges, staples, or other such materials. The supply, distribution, and sales of these materials must be included in marketing development efforts.

Customer feedback is needed to support this development activity. Beta testing of product prototypes by customers may be called for to ensure that the product works well in key applications in a real customer environment. Customer focus groups may be useful in gathering information to support decisions on marketing issues such as product positioning, pricing, and merchandising approaches. Information gathered from customer visits or focus group activities may highlight particular new applications for the product that should be targeted by applications engineering efforts.

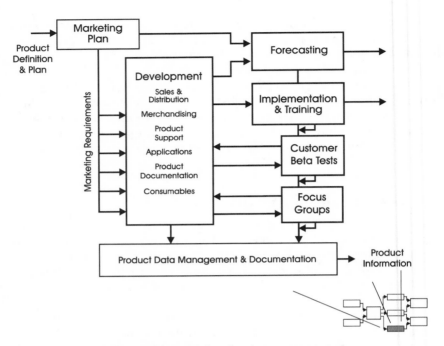

Figure 6.7 A market development process.

Each market development outcome will call for some form of implementation or training. Sales and distribution development, for example, will call for interaction with the sales force and distributors. They, at least, need to know this new product is coming and how it is positioned relative to the rest of the product line. They also need to know about the plans for advertising and merchandising the new product. Training of sales representatives and distributors may be required if the product is significantly different from others with which they are familiar.

The work involved in the market development process varies dramatically with the product and the enterprise. The marketing plan for a product line addition in an established business may simply call for a straightforward extension of capabilities that are already in place. Introduction of a new product platform into a new business arena, on the other hand, presents a significant marketing challenge. New distribution channels may be needed. An extensive investment may be required to create customer awareness of the new product and to educate them about its potential value. If unfamiliar technologies are involved, product support people may need extensive training and new tools in order to repair and maintain the new product.

As the market development process unfolds, information is gathered about the magnitude and intensity of customer demand for the new product. If a direct sales force is used, sales representatives must be introduced to the new product and annual sales quotas negotiated. On the other hand, if the product is to be distributed through dealer channels, the product must be shown to dealers and estimates of sales volume must be determined. This information must be translated into accurate forecasts of both mature sales levels and of initial product sales growth.

Forecast information acts as a throttle on ramp-up processes and is critical to enterprisewide preparations for the product introduction. The fundamental approach taken in manufacturing development will depend on mature shipment forecasts. The extent and nature of the distribution channel strategy will be affected by anticipated sales volume. Forecasts of initial sales will establish the size of early production runs and will drive the initial procurement of inventory for the new product. If these forecasts are too low, parts will not be on hand to support customer demand and delays will occur in initial deliveries. If these forecasts are too high, the enterprise will have to deal with excessive inventory levels, both in raw stock and finished goods.

The following real-life examples illustrate the potential impact that errors in sales forecasts can have on a business enterprise. In one instance, a new plotter product enjoyed customer demand that was about five times greater than the sales forecast. The flush of excitement from this rush of customer acceptance quickly dissolved into stress as the business team scrambled to deal with supply problems and customer frustrations. Assembly lines quickly used up all available inventory. Lead times on some critical parts were on the order of 8 weeks, so shortfalls in inventory could not be immediately corrected. Worse yet, this unexpected demand exceeded the capacity of the sole-source vendor of a critical stainless steel part. Other sources for this difficult part had to be developed as quickly as possible but this took time. Overtime premiums had to be paid to vendors so parts costs overran their targets. Delivery times quoted to customers started out at 4 weeks, then went to 8 weeks and finally stabilized at 20 weeks—5 months between the time a customer said, "Yes, I want one of these" until that buyer received the purchase. Frustrations ran high. Shipment volumes were well below what they could have been so revenues and profits came in far short of their potential. The first 6 months of this product's life were earmarked by excitement, frustration, turmoil, and chaos—all because a forecast was clearly out of line with reality.

In another case, the sales forecast for the product was several times higher than the real demand. Because this product was to be delivered through dealer channels, enough initial finished goods inventory was needed to fill the dealer pipeline at product introduction. Beyond that, production volume had to be running at a capacity that could meet forecasted demand. Inventories and vendor capacity had to be in place to support this level of production.

By the time the real customer demand for the product was perceived, the enterprise was already awash in finished goods. Flow of the product through the dealer pipeline proved to be only a small fraction of what was expected, so finished goods in shipping cartons quickly began to fill every square foot of empty floor space in the factory. Before the enterprise could rescale its operations to match the reality of customer demand, finished goods had overflowed into several semitrailers in the parking lot that were rented as temporary storage facilities. Assembly lines sat idle for months as the enterprise slowly used up this incredible stockpile of finished products. When production finally did start up again, the capacity of the production line was so much greater than demand that it was only operated for short periods and then shut down. The approach in the manufacturing process, which was based on early forecasts, had resulted in an expensive production facility that was clearly an overkill solution for the reality that unfolded.

If forecasting is so important, why don't we zoom and click on that box in Figure 6.7 and show the reader what goes on inside? Unfortunately, the details of the forecasting process depend too much on the nature of each particular business to allow a general discussion here. Instead, the reader simply gets a box labeled "Forecasting" and a discussion that highlights the importance of this process to new product operations. Each reader then has the challenge of developing an effective forecasting process for her or his business that can accurately predict the demand for new products.

■ RAMP-UP PROCESSES

The ramp-up processes in Figure 6.1 acknowledge that the innovation of a new product is not finished at the end of development.

The enterprise, in general, still has more to learn before the new product can be sold, shipped, and supported at mature volumes. Effective ramp-up processes will accomplish and institutionalize this learning quickly and efficiently.

➤ Market Introduction

The market introduction process creates awareness of the product in the marketplace and then builds order rates to targeted levels. The objective is further to ensure that early customers have the support that they need and can put the product to effective use. The strategy, messages, and materials for creating market awareness should have been created by market development efforts. In the market introduction process, these plans are launched. An effective introduction will quickly follow up the launch with steps to (1) evaluate the effectiveness of advertising and merchandising efforts, and (2) make adjustments as necessary to achieve awareness goals in targeted markets.

Initial customer response to a new product offers a critically important learning opportunity for the enterprise. Order rates will depend on how customers perceive the new product and relate its value to their needs. The new product offering and its associated advertising messages will be based, in part, on assumptions made earlier during market development. Those assumptions will be tested during market introduction and their validity or lack thereof will become clear. The market introduction process should thus include steps to measure this initial response, learn from it, and implement adjustments as needed.

Several questions need to be answered: Do customers perceive the product and its benefits accurately? Are assumption about their buying patterns and decision criteria proving valid? For those who buy the product, what features or benefits cause them to say "Yes"? What applications are they addressing with this product? How might the enterprise help them more effectively apply the product to their needs? Are there other related products or features that they might want in future products? What can be done to improve order rates? For those who reject the product, these questions need to be answered: Why did they say "No"? What competitive alternatives will they pursue instead of this product? What changes in the value proposition that was offered would turn their "No" into a "Yes"? An effective market introduction process will gather the answers to these questions effectively and then use that information

to make appropriate adjustments in advertising and sales operations. This information is also used to shape follow-on new product
activity.

Figure 6.8 provides a graphical outline of a market introduction process. This process is initiated by information of various
kinds that is assembled during market development efforts. This
incoming information might include sales and support training,
strategies for creating customer awareness, and plans for assessing
the effectiveness of initial sales and support efforts. Market introduction begins with training for sales representatives, dealers, and
customer support personnel to convey essential knowledge about
the new product and prepare them to effectively carry out their
assigned roles.

When sales and support channels are ready, the strategy for creating customer awareness is implemented. Advertising through various media communicates major messages about product features
and benefits to the targeted customers. Merchandising materials

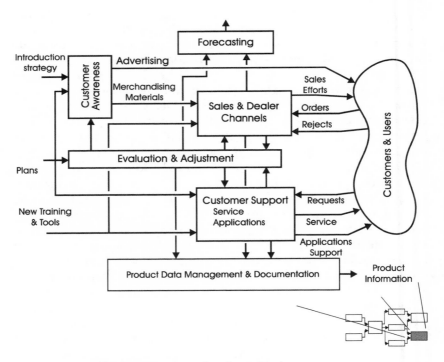

Figure 6.8 A market introduction process.

might include point-of-sale posters, brochures, and product demonstration materials. Sales efforts are launched to begin bringing in the orders. Customer reaction to these initial sales efforts will provide information critical to the accuracy of updated sales forecasts. This information may also indicate the need for urgent adjustments in advertising and merchandising efforts or, perhaps, in product pricing structures. Perhaps initial sales are adversely affected by flaws in the dealer channels, or by inadequate preparation of sales representatives. Evaluation and adjustment activities need to closely track these initial sales efforts and then quickly implement performance corrections as needed.

As initial customers receive the product and begin to use it, they may have questions about their application, or perhaps they will need service or repairs. The response of the enterprise to these early requests for support must also be tracked closely. Is the customer support group able to satisfy customers? Are requests handled smoothly and professionally? Are the responses to incoming requests timely? Do early service requests indicate flaws in the product design or, perhaps, in the manufacturing process? Initial customer support issues may be the harbinger of major product reliability or support problems just around the corner. Early detection and correction of flaws in either the customer support process or in the product can lead to huge savings later, in both support costs and customer loyalty.

Learning that occurs during market introduction activities should be added to the accumulated product information set as appropriate to support future operations associated with this product. Knowledge of what customers really value in the product can help future sales efforts and shape follow-on product development activity. An understanding of how customers are applying the product to their needs will help applications engineering provide better support in the future. Knowing how the product performs in real customer environments and how it typically fails will help service and repair people respond more effectively to customer needs.

Effective product introduction strategies vary widely as a function of the product and the buying patterns of the target customer. For example, consumer products must be in place on dealer shelves at the time introduction occurs. The product introduction strategy will probably include an advertising blitz to create awareness of the product and motivate the customer to try it. Introduction of a new toothpaste might include mailing small samples of the product to every household. Once you get your customers' attention, you want them to be able to walk into the store and buy your product. If you pique their interest and your product isn't readily available, they may very well go out and buy your competitor's product instead. The introduction strategy for a product such as this will thus include early production runs and filling the product pipeline before product launch.

Introduction of products that are intended to be used by other companies in the design of their own products—integrated circuits or fasteners, for example—is quite different. In this case market introduction involves creating awareness among designers of the customer's product and then supporting them with samples and information throughout their own design cycle. When their product comes out, large-scale orders for these components will eventually occur. Ramp-up of new component sales is determined by the customer's design cycle and can be slow. The market window for these products, on the other hand, is determined by the collective market window of customer products and can be quite long.

At the high end of the scale, introduction of so-called big ticket items, (e.g., a new luxury car) will occur well before initial production because these purchase decisions take time to develop. Advertising is designed not only to create customer awareness but to stimulate contemplation of how the product fits into the customer's lifestyle and value system better than competing alternatives. Assembly lines are designed to build products customized to individual orders and the customer expects this to take a little time. Order-to-delivery cycles of several weeks are usually acceptable. As the advertising for a luxury car continues to work on potential customers, they begin to see the product on the road, driven by others who appear to represent the image that they aspire to project. This works in synergy with advertising efforts to increase order rates to mature levels.

Product introduction practices thus vary widely among enterprises. In every case, however, this phase of the product innovation cycle is "where the rubber meets the road." Assumptions and estimates are replaced with reality. Advertising either influences the customer or it is ignored. The customer either likes the product or not. The product works reliably in the customer environment or it fails. The real world offers essential learning here, and an effective market introduction process should be designed to capture this knowledge quickly and use it to an advantage.

➤ Manufacturing Ramp-Up

The manufacturing ramp-up process eliminates any final uncertainties or lack of confidence that vendors, production tooling, assembly lines, and assembly personnel are all ready to support full-scale production. As with market introduction, this is a process of learning from real-world experience and then rapidly applying the lessons to improve manufacturing operations. In a real sense, if development processes were executed perfectly, no manufacturing ramp-up would be required at all, since all uncertainty would have been removed in development. Manufacturing operations could simply be launched on schedule at full volume. Scrap rates, unit manufacturing cost, labor content, and product reliability would all immediately assume targeted values. The need for a ramp-up to full volume production simply reflects the degree of uncertainty that remains in the results of development efforts. The amount of learning that takes place in manufacturing ramp-up is a measure of the work left undone in development.

Figure 6.9 depicts a manufacturing ramp-up process. Introduction plans and initial forecasts trigger the scheduling of early procurement activity and launch the first production runs. Evaluation of experience in these initial operations provides the learning to make needed adjustments. Conversations with early customers determine their satisfaction with the shipments that they have received. Did the product arrive on time and in good shape? Was initial setup and operation satisfactory? Are they happy with their purchase? Likewise, evaluation of early shipments from vendors will identify any corrections that are needed in the procurement process. Did the right parts arrive on time? Was the quality as expected? Did initial parts and materials work well in the assembly process? Vendors receive any necessary feedback to make adjustments in their operations. Lessons learned that have value to long-term operations are, once again, captured in the product information set.

■ THE INDIVIDUAL LEARNING PROCESS

The fundamental purpose of all of the elements of the product innovation process described in this chapter is to facilitate learning in the heads of individuals. If everyone involved with a new product

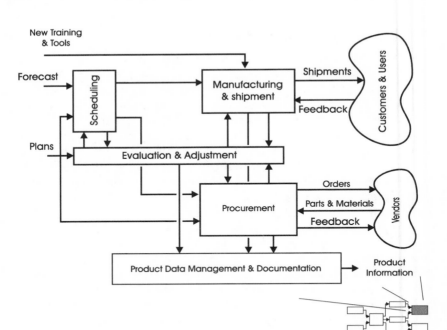

Figure 6.9 A manufacturing ramp-up process.

effort was, in the very beginning of the project, smart enough to write down all of the truth and wisdom needed in the final product information set, there would be no need for most of the processes described earlier. Final tooling could be ordered immediately and parts could be ordered right away from vendors for full-volume production. While waiting for tools and parts to arrive, the project team could then teach those in operations what they need to know to sell, ship, and support the new product.

This situation is highly unlikely. Instead, each individual on the project has to engage in some sort of learning process before he or she can record with certainty any particular contribution to the product information set. If the processes outlined here are not effective at expediting this learning, they need to be altered until they become effective. If processes that were once effective at supporting needed learning cease to be as effective because conditions have changed, then they need to be altered as well. The goal must always be to establish and maintain a business process with an effective work pattern and flow to support the learning of individuals engaged in the new product.

A common problem in many enterprises is that, once successful business processes have been found, people try to institutionalize them—cast them in concrete for all time. Occasionally, "process police" are created in these companies to make sure that no one strays from the righteous path. This approach works until the competition invents a new way of working that is more responsive to changing customer needs and market conditions. Then the company stuck in old work patterns begins to realize that its business processes have become a weight to be dragged along instead of a competitive business asset.

■ FINAL REFLECTIONS

Every business enterprise that depends on the shipment of products for its livelihood already has in place every element of the product innovation process described here. The only difference between the best and the worst examples among these companies is the level of process maturity and information quality that they have implemented in each element of their innovation engine. Every company identifies new business opportunities—somehow. Is opportunity scanning a defined, well-managed process or is it an unconscious, knee-jerk reaction to the last customer input? In some companies product definition and planning is a well-thought-out process with clearly outlined success criteria that routinely define the most competitive new product offering for a given business opportunity. In other firms, this process is ad hoc. Development projects seem to come into existence on their own. No one can describe how they have reached their current direction and focus. Whether these elements are conscious or not, whether they are managed or not, and whether they are competitive or not—every aspect of product innovation described here already exists in each company that introduces new products. The question readers should be asking themselves is "In what state is my product innovation process? Which elements operate at competitive levels, and which ones need to be overhauled?"

The goal of the discussion in this chapter, and in Chapter 5 as well, has been to create a vision of an effective product innovation process, that operates with a relatively high level of process maturity. This mental image depicts how product innovation can operate like a well-oiled, smoothly running, information machine that businesses can manage and improve. The intent is to arouse the reader's curiosity, to create a tension between the reality of what may exist in his or her own company and this new understanding of a better way.

■ CONCLUSION

This chapter has described how the tactical elements of the product innovation process work—individually and together. The discussion has demonstrated in tangible terms how value is added to information throughout the enterprise to prepare the firm to introduce and manufacture a new product. The information assembly line metaphor, introduced in Chapter 5, becomes less abstract and the applicability of manufacturing quality principles are more clear. This material provides a convincing example of how

---

Desired Upper Management Behaviors:
Operation of the Product Innovation Process

➤ Ask the responsible parties to explain their part of the product innovation process:

How it works.

Key interrelationships and deliverables.

How they know it is competitive.

➤ Ask insightful, process-related questions at project reviews. Expect good answers.

➤ Assign someone to manage new product processes. This assignment includes:

Developing and maintaining process documentation.

Providing process training.

Providing consulting services to project teams.

Tracking and improving process quality.

➤ Pay attention to lessons learned from experience. Track their integration into the product innovation process.

➤ Be alert for situations where enforcement of the process causes people to do something dumb. Fix these quickly.

product innovation can operate and be managed as a process—as an information assembly line, in fact.

The goal of this enterprisewide information process, though, must always be to facilitate the quick processing and flow of information to satisfy customer needs. Once an enterprise has an effective innovation process, it must thus be applied consistently and effectively in each new product effort. This key role of the project manager is covered in Chapter 7. As customer needs change and market conditions shift, though, the product innovation process must be adapted quickly to remain competitive. This requires due diligence by an individual or team charged with the responsibility of owning the product innovation process and keeping it up to date and competitive.

Chapter 7

Project Management Considerations

[Push decisions] as far down in the organization as we think we possibly can, on the very sound principle that the farther down you get, the closer you're getting to where there's true knowledge about the issues.

Don Peterson, Former CEO
Ford Motor Company
Forbes Magazine, 1988

A key factor in establishing the level of product-innovation performance is how new product efforts are organized and managed. The business process described in Chapter 6 is complex. It includes many concurrent tasks and objectives. It involves almost every department in the enterprise. It often takes a long time. Its success depends on the coordinated efforts of many people. The management of an undertaking such as this requires the dedicated efforts of a project manager with unique leadership skills combined with effective support from upper-level management.

As the chapter quotation suggests, best business performance happens when day-to-day decisions about product innovation activities are made at a level in the organization where true knowledge about the real issues exists. An effective project manager provides leadership in the trenches, so to speak, and has the experience and firsthand knowledge needed to make good decisions about day-to-day project issues. For best business results, though, this person requires occasional guidance and support from higher level managers who have a broader business perspective and control of additional resources that may be required from time to time by the project. In addition, periodic review of the project by upper-level managers instills in the project manager a sense of accountability that helps ensure a successful project outcome.

In Chapter 6, the importance of an effective, multifunction product innovation team was described. This is a "horizontal" project team that draws on resources across the enterprise. In addition to this team, however, a "vertical" team is required. The vertical team consists of the project manager working in cooperation with those upper-level managers who set business strategies, define product family plans, and assign project resources. The project manager acts as an agent of this upper-level management team in leading detailed activities related to the development of a specific new product. The upper-level management team, in turn, provides the project manager with the guidance and support to keep the project on track.

This chapter highlights the critical role of the project manager and outlines leadership principles that will enable upper-level managers to establish and support a competitive project management capability within their own organization. Following this introduction, the preferred project structure is described. Next, roles and responsibilities of the project manager are outlined and some principles for managing project risk are examined. The chapter closes with a discussion of key steps that are required to develop the project management capacity of the enterprise to competitive levels.

■ THE PREFERRED PROJECT STRUCTURE

Both the organizational and physical project structure affect the level of performance that is achieved. This section offers observations of best practice in these areas.

➤ Organizational Structure

Companies manage their product innovation projects in many ways. Some use a matrix management structure in which a program manager requests support and receives the services of individuals who are assigned to the project from various functional departments. Sometimes the project management responsibility is assigned to a "core team"—a group of managers from selected functional departments that manage the project as a committee.

In small, start-up operations, the engineering vice-president may manage projects directly, along with his or her other duties.

The most effective structure for product innovation projects is a clearly defined project team that is accountable to one dedicated individual—the project manager. This team will almost always include engineers and other professionals from functional departments such as marketing and manufacturing. Project team members are assigned to the project by their home department and remain with the project, in general, until it is finished.

Each person assigned to the project should understand that he or she is on the project full time, or for the greatest fraction of full time that makes sense for the assignment. To the greatest degree possible, each member should be physically located with the rest of the project team. A full-time job assignment helps remove ambiguity from each person's work objectives and accountability. It also eliminates, to a large degree, those distractions and interruptions that erode productivity. Having collocated project team members enormously improves the level of communication and coordination on the project. Product innovation has been described as an information assembly line that depends on the right information being available when it's needed, where it's needed. The informal, free flow of information that occurs when members of a multifunction team are physically located next to each other in the project work space improves the performance of the team immeasurably.

➤ Physical Structure

The physical layout of the project area is important as well. People who must work together should be physically close. In HP, the product manager from the marketing function would move his or her desk into the engineering project manager's cubicle. These two people would, in effect, become roommates for the duration of the project. They most often worked on different aspects of the project, but they inevitably shared a common information base because of their physical proximity and frequent interactions.

The project floor plan should be arranged with a large space in the center for work on product breadboards and prototypes. This serves two important functions. First, a dedicated prototype area in a protected space allows experiments to be set up and left intact for long periods without disruption. Second, having office space for the project team arranged around the prototype area stimulates awareness and information flow. People tend to get involved with the prototype activity spontaneously as they are needed.

On large projects that involve a great deal of complexity, a "war room" arrangement is often useful. This is a dedicated meeting area in the project floor plan with lots of wall space to display and track project information. The wall space is allocated to working groups in the project for the display of their working plans and documents. Meetings held in the war room have instant visibility into all the complex aspects of the project issue set.

A final aspect of the physical layout of the project area is the need for balance between the high degree of interaction required between members of the project team and the need for creative knowledge workers to have a quiet workspace where they can concentrate without interruption. Tom DeMarco, an industry software consultant, claims that every interruption, even a one-minute phone call, costs a software designer at least 20 minutes of lost productivity.[1] Three phone calls an hour can completely disrupt useful work. One HP software development team grew so desperate for a quiet place to work that they rented an apartment near the plant as a software design retreat. Each enterprise must address these conflicting needs as they assign physical space to product innovation activities.

■ ROLES AND RESPONSIBILITIES OF THE PROJECT MANAGER

The project manager should be picked from the function in which the greatest project risk is likely to occur. Often the greatest risk will be associated with the technology in the new product, so the best choice for project manager will be a person from the engineering department. A project that brings existing technology to an unfamiliar new market situation, though, may be best managed by a person from the product marketing group. Regardless of their home department or the nature of the project, the project manager should fulfill the roles and responsibilities outlined in Table 7.1.

---

[1] DeMarco, Tom, and Lister, Tom. Notes from "Controlling Software Projects" from a seminar by the same name. Palo Alto, CA, 1986.

Table 7.1   Project Manager's Roles and Responsibilities

➤   Verifying the opportunity.
➤   Defining the right product.
➤   Creating project plans.
➤   Assembling and directing the project team.
➤   Acting as product champion.
➤   Managing the innovation process.
➤   Interfacing with internal/external partners.
➤   Steering the project to committed results:
    Managing tradeoffs.
    Mentoring project team members.
    Managing risk.
    Launching contingency actions.
➤   Elevating problems to the right level.

➤ Verifying the Opportunity

Earlier we described the value of a new product opportunity in terms of its revenue and profit potential, its feasibility, and the ability of the resulting new product to achieve a sustainable competitive advantage. The first responsibility of the project manager is either to develop this information or to gather it together from where it has been developed and verify its validity. One way or the other, the project manager must become completely convinced that the project addresses a substantial new opportunity. This person will be viewed throughout the entire enterprise as the one who owns this opportunity and who is responsible for delivering a competitive new product to address it.

The project manager must understand the business case, all feasibility issues (technical, market, and manufacturing), and the competitive environment into which the new product will be launched. From the very start, the project manager must become and remain convinced that all important aspects of the opportunity are in place. If issues concerning the validity of the opportunity arise at any point, project resources must be applied to resolve them. If, for any reason, the opportunity ceases to remain valid—a required product feature proves to be technically infeasible, or perhaps a competitor introduces a much better product—the project manager must call this fact to the attention of upper management. Under these extreme circumstances, the project manager may even have to instigate the graceful termination of the project.

➤ Defining the Right Product

Project managers are responsible for defining a new product that will provide the most competitive response to their assigned business opportunity. In doing this, they should be intimately involved with the market and technology investigations described in Chapter 6 and should personally participate in interactions with selected customers. In formulating the detailed product definition, an effective project manager is able to tap the full wisdom and judgment of the enterprise and bring it to bear on this critical step. As the final product definition emerges, the project manager should provide compelling information substantiating the feature set that has been selected and explaining the decisions and trade-offs that were involved.

The project manager should document the product definition and associated specifications well and then defend them and keep them from changing as the project unfolds. One of the most prevalent causes of project schedule delay is an unstable product definition. As new requirements are added and "feature creep" occurs, project engineers find themselves designing toward a moving target. Immense amounts of engineering time are wasted as existing designs are scrapped and new designs have to be created. The excuse usually given is, "The market changed." But this is rarely true. In most cases, the market and business opportunity were just not well enough understood at project launch so the initial product definition was flawed. One of the most important contributions that the project manager makes is to create the best possible product definition at the beginning of the project and then keep it stable through project completion.

➤ Creating Project Plans

Once product requirements have been established, the project manager can plan the project. An effective project plan includes (1) a breakdown of the work involved in achieving project objectives, (2) an outline of the people and other resources required to do this work, and (3) a detailed schedule of project activities. Ideally, these plans will reflect a good understanding of both the performance achieved on other similar projects that have been recently completed and any lessons learned from those experiences. Project plans should also show consideration of key areas of risk and include development of alternative solutions that can be used in case a preferred but uncertain approach is not feasible.

➤ Assembling and Directing the Project Team

Next, the project manager assembles the project staff and creates work assignments for each member of the team. The project plan is communicated to upper management along with requests for specific people and other resources. As people are assigned to the project, the project manager determines how each person can best contribute and works with them to establish the work objectives that will focus and guide their efforts. As the project unfolds, the project manager closely monitors each individual's work and provides guidance, coaching, and coordination. When bottlenecks or other obstacles are encountered, the project manager either redirects project resources to work them out, or brings them to the attention of upper management when they cannot be resolved within the project.

➤ Acting as Product Champion

At various times, new product efforts have to be explained, justified, defended, or sold. The project manager is an essential resource on these occasions. This person will always have the most up-to-date information and will generally have the greatest insight and judgment concerning the new product, its contribution, and its competition. Just as a good defense lawyer vigorously protects the best interests of her client, a good project manager can always be depended on to look out for the well-being of the project.

➤ Managing the Innovation Process

Success of the innovation process depends on the smooth flow and development of information—knowing who needs to know what by when, adding value to incoming information, and then delivering the required result in the form needed. In addition, it depends on systematically removing uncertainties by designing and executing experiments, or perhaps negotiating with a distributor to nail down volumes and discount rates. Each phase of the project should have specified deliverables that must be accomplished by a particular date. There will be gate reviews to prepare for and attend. The project manager must be familiar with all these aspects of the product innovation process and proactively see that they are accomplished effectively and on time.

➤ Interfacing with Internal/External Partners

To succeed, a development project often depends on work done by others. The enterprise may depend on a technology partner, either internal to the enterprise or external, to deliver and support a new technology for the product. Critical parts for the product may be designed and manufactured by outside suppliers. Distribution and sales may be provided by other firms. Either the project manager or another designated project representative must work with each partner to (1) establish the direction and objectives for their involvement in the project, (2) evaluate any risks associated with their involvement, (3) monitor their progress, and (4) resolve issues when their work does not proceed according to plan.

➤ Steering the Project to Committed Results

As a project unfolds, numerous influences tend to drive it off track. Issues arise, almost on a daily basis, that jeopardize achievement of project objectives. A subsystem turns out to be too expensive or perhaps an engineer's design cannot achieve a critical performance specification. Feedback from the sales force calls for a feature that wasn't in the original definition. Maybe an engineering approach to the product design proves unworkable and has to be reconsidered. The project manager must "ride herd" on all this activity and make daily decisions on how to keep the project moving down the right path.

The decisions that a project manager must make in response to these influences involve the trade-offs between key project objectives depicted in Figure 7.1.[2] For example, if the project gets a little over budget and behind schedule, deciding to not implement expensive manufacturing tools for the product may save both development cost and time. But this decision will impact unit manufacturing cost unfavorably. A higher manufacturing cost generally means reduced profitability. Deciding to leave out a product feature is another approach that may save both time and development cost, but at the expense of product performance. Reducing product performance may also have a negative impact on sales

---

[2] Smith, Preston G., and Reinertsen, Donald G. *Developing Products in Half the Time: New Rules and New Tools.* New York: John Wiley & Sons, 1998.

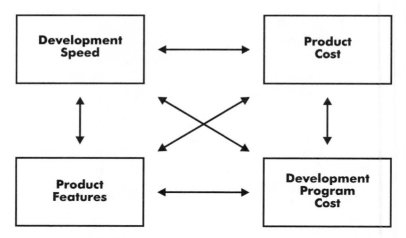

Figure 7.1 Trade-offs between product development objectives.

and profits. Deciding to hold the line on product features, even though this has proven more difficult than originally thought, may protect product performance and mature sales volume. This decision, however, might cause the introduction date to slip and reduce the market window. The ultimate impact of these decisions on overall business success is not inherently clear and calls for further analysis and understanding. The project manager must internalize these trade-offs and develop a consistent model for making decisions that leads to the best possible business outcome.

Keeping the project on track also means mentoring members of the project team. A good project manager spends time each day wandering around the project, checking in with each team member. The purpose of these informal visits is to see that each person is gainfully employed and making progress toward his or her assigned objectives. These visits also provide early warning of possible feasibility issues or other obstacles that may lie ahead. Project managers must always know which members of the team are in the "critical path." These are the individuals that are responsible for that subset of project tasks that determines the product's ultimate delivery date. If their work is delayed, product introduction will be late. An effective project manager will pay special attention to the needs of these people and provide whatever resources they need to keep their work on schedule.

The path between project launch and product introduction is often fraught with risks and uncertainties. To navigate it, a project manager must first understand where the real risks lie and then define and manage a set of activities that systematically addresses these risks and resolves the uncertainties. This is an important aspect of the project manager's job that deserves special attention. This topic will be covered in more detail in the next section.

Despite a project manager's best efforts, a project rarely unfolds in precise accordance with the original plan. Anticipating and planning for all the work involved in a complex project is nearly impossible. Furthermore, unanticipated issues and obstacles always arise. Careful planning of the project up front will minimize these surprises, but not eliminate them altogether. An important part of keeping the project on track toward committed results, then, is the definition and execution of contingency actions that address the unexpected.

➤ Elevating Problems to the Right Level

Skillful project managers can resolve most of the issues that arise in their project through effective application of the resources that they have at their disposal. Nonetheless, occasionally an obstacle is beyond the span of control of the project manager. When this occurs, the project manager must bring the problem to the attention of upper management and ask for help. Realizing that the project needs outside assistance and taking quick action in this regard can be critical to a successful outcome. These situations will tax the project manager's communication skills and exercise the credibility and working relationships that she or he has managed to establish throughout the enterprise. Sometimes, though, a successful project outcomes depends on the project manager's ability to lobby for and obtain needed outside assistance.

■ MANAGING RISK

The risk associated with a new product effort is defined as:

The likelihood that unexpected situations or outcomes will occur that reduce the business success of the project below expected levels.

Most people tend to think of new product risk in technical terms—projects fail because the technology was not ready or invention failed to occur on schedule. However, more projects fail to create expected business success because of management or work process flaws. Even technical problems that occur late in the development cycle are usually due to process and management issues. Lack of rigor in early technical experiments and an inadequate level of due diligence by upper-level managers often allows projects to proceed before the technology is ready. The discussion here includes all forms of risk that might cause a project to deliver disappointing business results.

Engineers and engineering managers often describe their work as risky. They disparage the idea of a product innovation process, claiming that their primary responsibility is inventing new products and that processes cannot be applied to invention. In reality, most work on most new product projects is routine and does not involve the creation of new technology at all. Instead, conventional engineering techniques are applied to design requirements using standard tools. These methodologies and the work processes around them, either defined or undefined, are very much the same from one project to the next. A successful design outcome almost always occurs. If this is true, then where is the risk? Why do project schedules slip? Why do new products produce disappointing business results? What can be done to manage and minimize project risk?

➤ Risk versus Uncertainty

A prevalent attitude among product developers is that their work involves a great deal of risk—project outcomes are precarious. This was certainly true at HP when the authors were involved in product development activities there. In reviewing literally hundreds of HP projects, however, we discovered that perhaps 19 out of 20 were completed and produced some level of business success. Statistically speaking, the probability of outright project failure was thus on the order of 5 percent, and yet the perception of technology risk was much higher.

These HP project teams were uncertain at the beginning of each project about how to achieve their project objectives and they tended to misinterpret this initial uncertainty as risk. There is a fundamental difference between risk and uncertainty. A parable borrowed from *Accelerating Innovation* illustrates this difference.[3]

---

[3] Patterson, Marvin L. *Accelerating Innovation: Improving the Process of Product Development* (p. 87). New York: Van Nostrand-Reinhold, 1993.

The King's Challenge

In olden times, a king sought a suitable mate for his son, so he offered to any young woman in his kingdom, who could solve a particular puzzle, his son's hand in marriage and half the kingdom to boot. The king's challenge was to determine which of ten gold coins, identical in appearance, was false using only three trials with a balance scale, as illustrated in Figure 7.2. The only clue offered was that the false coin differs from the genuine coins by weight, although it may be heavier or lighter than the other coins.

Is there uncertainty here? Is there risk? Certainly uncertainty is present. There is uncertainty which of the ten coins is false. There may be uncertainty in whether three experiments with the balance scale can be designed that will determine without fail which coin is false.

Is there risk? What if a young woman tries the puzzle and fails? What is her loss? If she simply goes back home and resumes a normal life; there doesn't seem to be much at risk. She has only lost the effort that she has invested in attempting the king's puzzle. Risk requires that the failure to achieve a successful outcome results in a substantial loss or penalty.

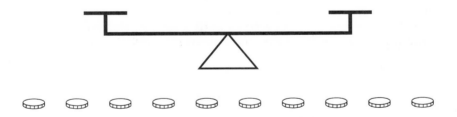

a. Find the false coin in three experiments or lose your head.

$$I = Log_2 (1/p)$$

b. The underlying intellectual framework that changes risk to uncertainty.

Figure 7.2 Uncertainty and risk are not the same.

What if the king changes the rules of the challenge so that any young woman who tries the puzzle and fails will lose her head at the hands of the royal executioner? Apparently the king has decided to eliminate losers from the gene pool. Now is there risk? The answer is, "It depends."

Whether a young woman is at risk in this situation depends on whether she can design three experiments that will identify the false coin with certainty. This, in turn, depends on whether she possesses an intellectual framework suitable for designing those experiments. If she does, she can take on the king's challenge with no risk at all. To be sure, in the beginning of her work there is uncertainty. The false coin has not yet been identified, the experiments have not yet been designed. These things are, as yet, uncertain. But as she goes about her work in solving the puzzle, applying her intellect to the design of experiments and then doing those experiments, uncertainty is systematically removed. In the end, the design of the experiments is in hand, the false coin has been identified and only certainty remains. And the young woman will one day be queen of the kingdom.

If our challenger does not possess the needed intellectual framework in the beginning, then she must invent an algorithm for designing experiments as she goes. In this case, she is very much at risk for there is a reasonable probability that she will lose her head, in a very physical sense.

The intellectual framework required to solve this puzzle comes from the field of information theory and includes only the following information:

$$I = \text{Log}_2(1/p)$$

where I is the amount of information gained by each experiment, measured in bits, and p is the probability of the particular outcome of an experiment. In addition, the challenger needs to know that there are three possible outcomes for each experiment—tilt clockwise, tilt counterclockwise, or balance—and that the most information is gained when experiments are designed so that the probabilities of these three outcomes are as nearly equal as possible. If she possesses this information at the beginning, the young woman can first calculate whether the puzzle can be solved in three trials and then, if so, she can systematically solve the king's puzzle with no risk at all.

The amount of information needed to solve this puzzle is calculated by letting p equal 0.1, the probability that any given coin is false, in the equation. This calculation determines that 3.32 bits of information are needed to identify the false coin with certainty. If ideal experiments could be designed, the probability of each outcome would be $1/3$. Using the equation again with this value for p shows that each experiment can thus yield as much as 1.58 bits of information. In three such experiments, about 4.74 bits of information can be accumulated, more than enough to solve the king's challenge without any risk at all. In the actual solution, however, experiments have outcome probabilities that are slightly different than $1/3$ so that, in three well-designed trials, only 4.32 bits of information are gained. This is, however, 1.0 bits of information more than is required to identify the false coin. This extra bit of information determines whether the false coin is heavier or lighter than the other coins and is nonessential to a successful outcome.

The complete solution to this puzzle is published as an appendix in *Accelerating Innovation*.

Relating the King's Challenge to Project Risk

At HP, a high project success rate occurred because relevant intellectual frameworks had evolved over time in each business arena. These intellectual frameworks enabled development teams to design experiments that could systematically reduce uncertainty about any given new product. In product innovation, these experiments take the form of performance tests on breadboard and prototype designs. In other cases, they may involve market studies or customer surveys. The results of these experiments reduce uncertainty and provide information about how to best move the new product effort toward a successful conclusion. As with the king's challenge, each subsequent experiment is designed to best capitalize on the information gained in earlier trials. After enough prototypes have been tested, enough design iterations have been completed, and enough customer surveys have been done, all uncertainty will be removed and the information that describes a workable new product will exist.

Projects that involve work in an area where these intellectual frameworks do not yet exist will, however, experience a much greater likelihood of failure. In a product effort that employs an untested new technology, for example, the intellectual framework that describes how to design with confidence using the new technology must be created before engineers can apply it. In other instances, the company addresses new and unfamiliar markets with a new product offering. The pertinent intellectual frameworks that must be developed here will include knowledge of the benefits that are required by these new customers and an understanding of the buy-decision criteria that they will employ. These frameworks must be created to effectively address uncertainties about the required new product. In creating these frameworks, information flaws often occur that can lead a project astray and prevent it from achieving its goals.

The degree of risk that exists for a product innovation project depends directly on how much new intellectual framework must be created to succeed. In the king's challenge, the young woman who has to invent information theory to succeed in winning the prince's hand in marriage assumes a very high risk of losing her head. Likewise, a project team that must invent substantial extensions to available intellectual frameworks takes on a serious risk of failure.

➤ Factors That Cause Project Delay

One of the greatest forms of project risk, given the definition offered at the beginning of this section, is project delay. As noted in Chapter 3, the cost of a project slip can have an immense negative impact on business success, through lost market window, lost market share, and added development expense. Many factors that contribute to project delay, summarized in Table 7.2, are managed by the project manager, but can be either resolved or aggravated through actions taken by upper-level managers.

The most common reason projects take longer than necessary to complete is that they are understaffed. New product organizations typically take on more projects than they should. Sometimes

Table 7.2 Common Issues That Delay Projects

➤ Too many projects, too thinly staffed.

➤ Unclear processes and deliverables.

➤ Drifting product requirements.

➤ Organizational silos.

➤ Bottlenecks:

Inadequate support resources.

Specialists versus generalists.

An engineer's progress stalls.

upper-level managers simply have new product desires that exceed their means, and they lack the discipline to select and staff only the most critical few. In other cases, there is a lack of agreement between project managers and upper-level managers about the right level of staffing. Since the Golden Rule of Management applies—"He who has the gold, makes the rules"—projects end up understaffed and with overly aggressive schedules. In other instances, the process for launching projects is out of control. Projects get started without determining whether the necessary resources are available. Since available resources are always constrained, too many projects means that most will inevitably proceed with fewer people than they need to achieve the shortest possible time-to-market. These project staffing concerns are covered more completely in Chapter 8.

Another common cause of project delay is an unclear development process and poorly defined deliverables for each phase. Projects proceed without a clear focus on what needs to be done by when. Clear exit criteria for each development phase are not defined so the project moves ahead without necessary work being finished. As these flaws are discovered, expensive and time-consuming rework results. As the cost-of-quality principle dictates, flaws that are discovered later in the project create the greatest amount of rework, delay, and anguish.

In the late 1980s, HP became increasingly concerned about lengthy product development cycles, as time-to-market had become an important competitive issue. A study of companywide new product efforts revealed that the most important root cause of project delay was drifting, unstable new product requirements. This, in turn, was the result of ineffective processes for opportunity discovery and new product definition. As the authors have gained experience with other companies since 1993, this issue has proven pervasive and is often a primary cause of project delays. Due diligence by upper-level managers can avert this problem by testing the quality of the opportunity and the product definition before launch. This high-level scrutiny, however, is often missing as well.

As described in Chapter 6, an effective product innovation system involves close cooperation and an effortless flow of information between the functional departments of the enterprise. Even today, however, these functional departments still operate in many companies as fiefdoms or silos—deep vertical structures with impenetrable walls. When this condition exists, the cooperation and information flow needed for effective product innovation break down and new products take much longer to reach the marketplace.

Product innovation delays often occur as bottlenecks, where work on one part of the project stalls and holds up progress in other areas. Bottlenecks are sometimes caused by inadequate support resources. Development of support functions such as the engineering model shop or, perhaps, the marketing communications department has not kept pace with the number of new product activities underway at any given time. Inevitably, a time occurs when two or more projects need support at the same time and these demands exceed available capacity. The solution is to maintain a proper balance between the workforce invested in project teams and the groups that support product innovation activities.

Occasionally, bottlenecks are caused by overspecialization. In a heavy equipment firm, mechanical engineers were permanently assigned to specialty areas. A single individual designed fuel tanks for all new vehicles. Much of the time this person was underutilized, but when two or more projects needed fuel tanks designed at the same time, he became a bottleneck. A better practice is to encourage people to maintain a broader skill set so that they can be assigned more freely to the tasks at hand. This allows individual employees to stay fully employed and provides the flexibility needed to avoid these problems.

Bottlenecks sometimes occur when the progress of a single person grinds to a halt. An engineer may have trouble creating an effective subsystem design. The root cause may be inexperience or, perhaps, unanticipated technical difficulty. Regardless of the reason, progress has stalled and something must be done. Often the project manager can deal with this situation by focusing other project resources on the problem and resolving the issue. Sometimes, though, this is not possible and outside help is needed.

Another lesson from the manufacturing domain applies here. Operations managers know that the likelihood of bottlenecks on the manufacturing floor, and their severity, both increase exponentially as the scheduled utilization of resources approaches 100 percent of capacity. Maintaining some margin of underutilized resources allows the flexibility to quickly resolve bottlenecks.

The same phenomenon occurs in product innovation. As the number of projects increases and the aggressiveness of schedules pushes resources to 100 percent of their capacity, the likelihood and severity of bottlenecks increases dramatically. When a bottleneck does occur, no one is available who can help. Everyone is already fully employed, in over their heads with more time pressure and high-priority work than they can handle. Furthermore, if spending levels are at 100 percent of budget, with no funds available for contingency actions, the firm cannot seek outside help either.

A practice that was common in HP new product laboratories helped a great deal to reduce the severity of bottlenecks. About 10 percent of the workforce at any given time was assigned to investigation activities. These investigations were in the product concept phase of the development process, prior to the project launch milestone. If a bottleneck occurred on another project that was closer to introduction, people working on investigations could be temporarily reassigned to help resolve the problem. The business impact of a slight delay in a product concept investigation was much less severe than a lengthy bottleneck in a fully staffed project. Furthermore, keeping about 10 percent of the product innovation workforce employed on new product concepts ensured a continuous supply of exciting new product investment opportunities.

➤ Strategies for Reducing Project Risk

Thus far, the discussion has laid the groundwork for understanding how managers can actively work to reduce project risk. Referring back to the definition of project risk at the beginning of this section, any action that increases the likelihood that a project will fulfill its business expectations, by definition, reduces risk. Some of these actions will be initiated by the project manager, whereas others must be undertaken by upper-level managers. To succeed, however, both parties must work together, in the spirit of vertical teamwork mentioned earlier, to implement each of the strategies outlined here.

Table 7.3 provides a summary of the six risk reduction strategies discussed in this section. These items have been selected for their relevance and potential impact on the business results achieved by product innovation projects.

Define, Manage Front-End Processes

The work that precedes the project launch decision provides the technology and market foundations for a new product effort and sets the direction for the entire project. This work includes opportunity discovery, technology and market investigations, product definition, project and product planning, and the business case

Table 7.3 Strategies for Reducing Risk

➤ Define, manage front-end processes.

➤ Improve development processes.

➤ Develop competitive management practices.

➤ Manage the portfolio information environment.

➤ Improve the design and execution of experiments.

➤ Recognize and manage extensions to intellectual frameworks:
  Technology.
  Market.
  Manufacturing.

analysis for the project. If the information assembled by these early process steps is sound, the project has a good chance of creating business success. If not, the project has no chance at all of meeting expectations. Despite the critical importance of these early innovation process elements, in many enterprises they remain largely undefined and poorly managed.

The symptoms created by information flaws generated in these early stages are common and easy to spot. Most common is a product definition that changes throughout the development cycle. As the project unfolds, information leaks into it from the marketplace that is inconsistent with both the project and product plans. Eventually these discrepancies become too great and the product definition and product plans have to be adjusted to take the new information into account. These changes cause some of the work completed up to that time to be scrapped and reworked, at the cost of added engineering labor, schedule slips, and frustration among project team members.

Technical problems that arise late in the development cycle are another symptom. Inadequate early investigations fail to discover all performance issues with a new technology and do not fully identify and validate critical design parameters. Consequently, engineers attempt to apply the technology in ways that ultimately fail to perform as needed. In the worst case, the entire approach to the product design can be rendered invalid as the laws of physics prove yet one more time that they will not be broken, or even bent a little. More often, though, the project is simply delayed as engineers scramble to invent a solution to a technical problem caused by avoidable ignorance. In addition to a slip in the introduction date, these late inventions usually cause unplanned increases in unit manufacturing cost and a corresponding decline in overall revenue and profit margin.

The symptoms created by poorly executed project and product plans include schedule slips and budget overruns. These results are due to major tasks that were simply overlooked until late in the project or that took far longer to complete than planned. As these tasks are completed late, their delayed outcome often causes rework in other parts of the project.

A poorly executed or missing product plan can lead to cancellation of the project late in the development phase as the management team discovers that this product effort has too few real customers and too little potential profit. All to often, though, the lack of market response after product introduction is the first signal that makes the enterprise aware of these flaws in their product.

The strategy for eliminating these risks is to first become conscious of these important front-end process elements and to evaluate how they are working in the current product innovation process. Next, a concerted effort should be initiated to (1) define generic subprocesses that describe how this early work should generally be accomplished on each project, and (2) outline the deliverables and success criteria for each of these critically important process elements. Chapter 6 provides a starting point for this work. Following this, roles and responsibilities must be defined that describe who is responsible for managing and executing the work required by these process steps. Upper-level managers must decide how they will make work assignments in these areas of the innovation process and how they will track and evaluate the results. Finally, the management team needs to (1) put these plans into effect, (2) be prepared to learn from early experience, and (3) adjust processes and policies accordingly.

Improve Development Processes

The second strategy for reducing risk is to improve development processes. Many new products fail to meet schedule, cost, and profitability goals because of flaws created during development. These flaws can result in (1) excessive rework cycles that delay product introduction, (2) product performance shortfalls, (3) product reliability problems, and (4) failure to meet unit manufacturing cost targets. While needed improvements vary from business to business, they fall into broad categories that are fairly universal:

➤ Improving the initial system design.

➤ Bringing the best available wisdom to bear on initial plans and designs.

➤ Clarifying information needs and deliverables.

The initial system design can be improved in a manner similar to that described for front-end processes. First, raise to a conscious level the fact that there is a step called "system design" and then make this step explicit. Define a general process for creating system designs and then see that it is effectively applied on each project before subsystem design begins. Of particular importance is getting the best system talent in the organization involved in this step. To ensure effective system design, upper-level managers can require a milestone review at the completion of this phase and then applying due diligence by asking the right questions and pressing for solid answers during this review.

We used to say, "If HP only knew what HP knows, we would really be great." A shortcoming in many companies is that they have difficulty integrating and applying the wisdom gained by individuals from their experiences over time. In product development, senior engineers have accumulated a far greater understanding of design techniques and potential pitfalls than that of more junior engineers. And yet, in most organizations, junior engineers are left alone to repeat the same mistakes that a more experienced engineer could easily avoid.

A simple technique for bringing accumulated wisdom to bear on product innovation issues is the design review. Each person who is responsible for a subsystem design, or perhaps a significant product marketing task, is required to hold a design review after formulating initial plans or a design approach. Several senior practitioners are then provided with reading material that describes the individual's initial work. At the review meeting, the preliminary plan or design approach is discussed and the senior people express their ideas and concerns. The individual under review then integrates the information gained into a more robust approach and moves forward with the work.

Surprisingly, this straightforward and effective technique is often not applied. A possible reason is that the culture on many product innovation teams emphasizes individual expertise and effort. People are reluctant to "open their kimono," so to speak, and expose their work to criticism by others. In other cases, individuals are simply unwilling to put forth the effort required to prepare for and hold a design review. They apparently feel that the potential return is not worth the effort invested. Getting design reviews to happen under these circumstances requires a degree of project management discipline that is often missing.

Individuals often create flawed results during development because they are either unaware of information that is important to their work or not clear on who is depending on them to deliver specific information at some point in the future. The solution requires first that project managers understand the product innovation process for a particular enterprise. Each project manager must then assign objectives to the team members that make their information deliverables clear. Each team member should be able to describe the information for which he or she is responsible, the format in which it must be delivered, and who needs it by when. The project manager also needs to coach each member of the team to make sure that everyone has the information inputs needed to do the work.

Develop Competitive Management Practices

The discussion up to this point has described ways in which both project managers and upper-level managers can significantly influence the risk associated with each new product effort. One of the most important strategies that an enterprise can implement is to (1) train both project managers and high-level managers in their roles and responsibilities with respect to product innovation, and (2) redefine the recognition and reward system in ways that emphasize effective product innovation behavior at these two levels of management.

In its efforts to improve time-to-market in the late 1980s, for example, HP discovered that its system for training new project managers was in disrepair. A period of about six years had elapsed during which little effort had been invested in developing project management skills. In that time frame, several hundred people had been promoted to the role of project manager with very little training. Moving from a role as individual contributor to that of project manager is a fundamental career change. The typical engineering school education did little to prepare a person to plan a project and to lead a team of technical professionals toward a successful outcome. Consequently, these new project managers were ill prepared to lead projects and this deficiency was an important contributor to HP's lagging time-to-market performance.

HP responded by making world-class project management skills an objective on its annual Hoshin plan. This action focused companywide attention on this important issue and set the stage for needed investments. A project management initiative was launched that included an insightful project management curriculum and a significant investment in developing skills that continues to this day. The HP project management initiative is one of the best efforts in the world of this kind. Over perhaps three or four years, it helped HP transform this serious performance issue into a competitive advantage.

HP's project management initiative also recognizes the important roles of upper-level managers and includes courses on managing project managers. In addition, however, upper-level managers must create and maintain the strategic context within which each project exists. They, in fact, own other very important roles in product innovation that are discussed in depth in Chapter 8. Training and coaching provided for upper-level managers thus not only should include a focus on how to manage project managers, but should also develop their ability to define and manage a successful product strategy and corresponding new product portfolio.

Manage the Portfolio Information Environment

All new product efforts in a given business enterprise require information unique to the particular product opportunity as well as information that is common across all projects. As was depicted in Figure 5.6, a wide range of common information is needed to support product innovation activities. This information set might include items such as commonly applied environmental design standards or, perhaps, safety regulations that apply to all products. Knowledge of preferred components to be used in the product design is another example of information that is the same for all projects. Project teams also need an understanding of common guidelines and constraints that are imposed by the existing manufacturing processes and infrastructure. While these common information requirements will vary from one company to another, they represent an opportunity to substantially reduce project risk.

If projects are not routinely supplied with this common knowledge, each engineer or project manager must be responsible for researching and developing this information independently. Often they either overlook important information or simply do not have the time needed to find it, so the project proceeds in a state of ignorance. When this happens, the risk of a disappointing business outcome increases substantially.

One project team, for example, failed to fully understand international safety regulations that applied to their product and took their product design to completion without having this required information. Their product was a small graphic plotter to be used as a computer peripheral device in an office environment. The design team decided to try a new approach to the power supply design, moving it out of the main chassis and installing it instead as a lump in the power cord at the wall receptacle. As the product neared completion, it failed in its attempts to pass safety inspection in Germany. The design of the external power supply clearly violated German safety standards. The product was introduced and sold in the rest of the world, but a six-month redesign effort had to be completed before it could be sold in the German market. This caused a serious shortfall in initial sales and profits.

A business enterprise can greatly reduce this form of project risk by investing in a systematic support effort that first identifies common information needs and then makes this information readily available to each member of every new product team. This investment both improves productivity and reduces time-to-market by eliminating the need for redundant discovery efforts on each project. It reduces risk by ensuring that people on each project proceed in their new product efforts well-armed with the best information available.

Improve the Design and Execution of Experiments

Competitive performance in product innovation requires that experiments—the breadboards and prototypes—associated with each project be well conceived and executed. Broadly speaking, the objective of each experiment is to add value to the information set as quickly as possible by removing uncertainty. The information theory presented in the discussion of the King's Challenge lends some insight into how best to do this. It states that the amount of information gained by the outcome of an experiment is related to the degree of uncertainty in the particular outcome. Consequently, the focus of each prototype implementation should be on those aspects of the design that are most uncertain and most critical to business success. Conversely, anything about the prototype that will certainly succeed—the probability of the outcome is 1.0—yields no information at all. From a management perspective, the key measures should be how well prototype efforts are focused on the important questions and how quickly the project team is removing uncertainty.

Creation of prototypes and breadboard designs is both time-consuming and expensive, and their only purpose is to provide learning for the project team. Their use should thus be rigorously managed toward that end. Some prototypes and breadboards are used to verify design performance. Others are used to gain initial customer feedback or ensure proper operation in the customer's application. Technical publications writers need access to product prototypes so that they can exercise the product and document its normal use and operation. Only a few prototypes are created, so there are often conflicting demands on those that are available. Since prototypes are always costly and the product development team usually has to support them and keep them working, there is good cause to keep the number of prototypes as small as possible. Consequently, frivolous uses of prototypes that do not contribute to the learning process should be vigorously discouraged.

Recognize and Manage Extensions to Intellectual Frameworks

Product innovation must inevitably push the limits of understanding—that is, extend existing intellectual frameworks—at some point. As illustrated by the King's Challenge, the need to extend intellectual frameworks substantially increases the level of risk. A key strategy for minimizing this added risk is to recognize when new intellectual framework needs to be created and to manage the process appropriately. For example, the extension of intellectual frameworks should be confined, as much as possible, to investigation activities that take place before product dèfinition and project launch. Here the costs of slipping schedule or outright failure are much less than they would be later in the innovation cycle when the product extinction time has already been frozen and the entire enterprise is poised to introduce a new product.

Inventing an extension to existing technology, for example, should be completed as a well-managed technical investigation effort. The team should be kept to a small number of the smartest people. They should be given clear objectives and a limited time in which to demonstrate progress. Their work should be reviewed periodically by high-level management. They are finished with their work only when they have (1) demonstrated that their technology provides new capabilities that have business value, and

(2) reduced the uncertainty associated with their new technology to a level that allows development engineers to confidently include it in their design approach.

The level of project risk is increased greatly when the intellectual framework must be extended in more than one dimension to achieve business success. The project that, for example, takes on an untested new technology and applies it in an unfamiliar market arena assumes a tremendous level of risk. A better alternative would be to first apply the new technology in existing and well-understood markets. Once the technology is proven, it can then be applied to new market segments with a much greater chance of success. An equivalent tactic is to first approach new market arenas with products that utilize existing technology. Once a niche has been established and the new market is more completely understood, products that include new technologies can be implemented with a greater likelihood of a positive business outcome.

The history of the electronic game market illustrates the latter approach. When electronic games first appeared, the successful competitors universally employed existing microprocessor, memory, software, and display technologies. Once the market had been established, however, the key players began to introduce leading edge user interface, display, and microprocessor technologies to stay competitive.

The project launch milestone review provides an important opportunity to limit intellectual framework risk associated with both new markets and new technology. Before this checkpoint is passed, the project team should have demonstrated that new technologies can deliver all functionality required by the proposed new product. Furthermore, they should have identified all design parameters that are critical to the performance of the new technology and measured the design margins available in each. With regard to market-related intellectual framework extensions, the project team should be able to describe the customer benefits that the proposed new product will provide and state the value proposition that will compel targeted customers to buy the new product. The size of the market opportunity should be characterized in terms of the number of customers available and the profit margin that they will support. The means by which the product will achieve a sustainable competitive advantage should also be explained. The approach to product distribution and sales should be outlined. All this information should be substantiated with specific and compelling data gathered from the proposed new market arena.

High-level managers can limit the risk associated with intellectual framework extensions by holding the project team accountable for developing and delivering the information described in the previous paragraph. They enforce this accountability in both investigation reviews and, most importantly, the project launch milestone review. Due diligence applied at the project launch review should ensure that no project gets beyond this point without a convincing presentation of this required information. In HP, the project launch review was called the "I to L" review (Investigation to Lab prototype). Some of these turned into "I to I" reviews when project teams failed to demonstrate an acceptable understanding of either their technology or their marketplace. The project was either canceled at this point or the project team was sent back to complete their investigation.

■ BUILDING PROJECT MANAGEMENT CAPACITY

Capable project managers are essential to competitive performance in product innovation. Every enterprise needs people who can carry out the roles and responsibilities outlined in Table 7.1. In fact, the quality of the project management workforce can make the difference between healthy business growth and outright failure of the enterprise. The best strategic plans and project funding in the world will come to naught if the enterprise cannot effectively execute its plans and investments. But where do these people come from? Can you hire them or must they come from the existing workforce? How does a company develop and institutionalize competitive project management practices?

This section provides some answers to these questions. It begins with a discussion of required project management skills and how they might be developed. Following this, key elements of the necessary management framework for product innovation work are described. The intent of this section is to provide the reader with an understanding of steps that they might take in establishing an effective project management capability in their own enterprise.

➤ Developing Project Management Skills

Effective project management requires a great deal of judgment, the kind that is born of both training and on-the-job experience.

The best project managers will thus have experience with both the product line and the technologies of the business enterprise. Furthermore they will be familiar with its internal infrastructure and product innovation process. Consequently, project managers are much more likely to be developed from the internal talent pool than hired from outside the enterprise. If they are hired from outside, they should have gained extensive experience in the same industry so that they are familiar with both the technologies and the customers.

The best candidates for project management are engineering or product management professionals who, in addition to excellent vocational skills, have better-than-average interpersonal skills and a demonstrated aptitude for leadership. As mentioned, moving from the role of individual contributor to that of project manager is a fundamental career change. The vocational skills that have made people successful up to this point in their career can provide a sound basis for the judgment required of a project manager. These skills, however, usually are not sufficient to enable these individuals to effectively plan a project and lead a team of technical professionals to a successful business outcome. To succeed in this career change, candidates for the role of project manager must receive further training and development specific to their new responsibilities.

The business enterprise that desires to improve its project management capacity must develop an effective curriculum for this training and see that suitable candidates participate in the development program. Accountability for this effort might be assigned to the head of human resources or possibly the head of engineering. The program developed in HP was initiated and coordinated by the corporate engineering department, but course work was acquired from outside the company through a carefully screened group of firms who specialized in project management training.

The Project Management Curriculum

Table 7.4 illustrates a structure that has proven effective in building the required project management curriculum and offers a few topics that are representative of the kind of material that should be included. Training should be provided as close as possible to the point in their career where each individual first needs the information. Experienced project managers are receptive to different

Table 7.4 A Representative Project Management Curriculum

	Fundamentals	Business	People	Marketing
Potential Project Managers	Problem solving Quality methods Project management as a career change		Managing interpersonal relationships	Quality Function Deployment
New Project Managers	PM fundamentals	Finance for project managers Basic legal principles	Technical leadership skills	Product definition
Experienced Project Managers	Advanced PM techniques Managing Partnerships	Negotiating skills Intellectual property management		Building market-focused organizations
Upper-level Managers	Managing Project Managers			

topics than those who have just become project managers. Consequently, courses are categorized according to the recipient's level of experience. Furthermore, to be most effective, project managers need exposure to a wide range of information, not just management techniques. Financial and legal fundamentals, personal skills, and marketing techniques all add valuable depth to a project manager's judgment and skill set.

As the table indicates, development of potential project managers should begin well before they are promoted into that role. General skill development at this level might include basic problem-solving techniques, interpersonal relationship skills, and perhaps training in general principles of quality management. These courses will improve the effectiveness of individual contributors whether or not they decide to move into management. Of particular value is a course that addresses the topic of project management as a career change. The purpose of this training is to introduce potential candidates to the role of project manager and prepare them to make a good decision on whether to pursue this career path. All too often, excellent technical contributors accept a promotion to project management only to find that their aptitudes are not well-suited for the job. Not only does this job change largely eliminate their technical contribution, both they and the people who work for them are likely to perform poorly until this situation is somehow corrected. The intent of this course is to (1) deter those individuals who are not right for the job, and (2) better prepare those who are.

Individuals who have been assigned to the role of project manager must be trained in project management fundamentals such as establishing project objectives, creating the project work-breakdown structure, setting realistic schedules, and managing the project team. Exposure to financial and legal principles helps them deal more effectively with business matters with which they may have been, up to this point in their career, completely unfamiliar. Training in technical leadership skills will prepare them to more effectively manage the efforts of technical professionals. Finally, the marketing techniques associated with creating a competitive product definition will better prepare them to execute this critical step.

Once an individual has managed one to several projects, they can use further training. Table 7.4 lists several topics in the Experienced Project Manager category that are typical of those that might be useful in this regard (the "graduate school" of project management).

Finally, to create an effective project management work force, even upper-level managers need training. They need to understand the methods and tools that project managers are being encouraged to use so that they can provide needed support and hold project managers accountable for employing these techniques effectively. Consequently, the curriculum suggested in Table 7.4 includes a course for upper-level managers that addresses the topic of managing project managers. This course provides a high-level overview of project management methods and introduces business leaders to the critically important roles that they must play in leading and supporting project managers.

Training Methods

As an initial step in overhauling its project management capability, HP studied the effectiveness of its past training efforts in influencing the business-related behavior of participants. Up to that time, training had been executed in traditional classroom style. Participants would travel to the course location, listen to presentations for several days, and then travel back home with a new binder for their bookshelf. The business intent of these investments, though, is to alter the work behavior of trainees so that they contribute more effectively to successful business outcomes. The evidence indicated that new methods and tools covered in the classroom were not being adopted in the workplace.

A survey of former participants and their supervisors revealed the factors that reduced the business impact of these training investments to almost nil. In some cases, trainees could not employ the new methods they learned because others on their project were using a different approach and consistency was needed. In other cases, participants tried to employ the new techniques only to encounter difficulties that had not been covered in the classroom. Unable to overcome these obstacles on their own, they reverted to old, familiar methods to keep their project moving. New methodologies learned in the classroom occasionally required expensive computer tools for effective application. Some trainees found, when they returned home, that there was no money in the budget for such tools. In other instances, upper-level managers, who were unfamiliar and uncomfortable with the new techniques, actually prevented the implementation of more competitive new practices that their employees had learned. For these and other reasons, HP had not been getting a very favorable return on its training investments.

In setting up its project management development program, HP adopted new training methodologies that overcame these difficulties and more effectively achieved needed changes in work behavior. For example, participants are more likely to use new methods if they learn them just when they need them. Furthermore, their behavior is more likely to undergo permanent change if they successfully apply a new concept immediately after they have been exposed to it. The probability of success is also greater if everyone on the project learns and employs the same methodologies.

Consequently, project-centered training was implemented in the HP program that involves an entire project team in the training experience. New methods are introduced just before they are needed in the project cycle. A combination of classroom training and on-the-job application is used. As participants attempt to apply a new technique, consultants or other expert practitioners are made readily available to help them over the hard spots. HP makes every effort to ensure that each training exercise is followed immediately by a successful experience with the new methods learned.

These new training techniques were instrumental in improving the level of project management skill practiced throughout HP. As this development program was rolled out, it developed a track record of success, and even the most skeptical of HP's business units were transformed into enthusiastic customers. Acceptance of HP's project management initiative has been so strong that, for a number of years, it has completely supported itself and even grown in size with funds received from enthusiastic internal customers.

➤ Establishing an Effective Project Framework

In addition to skilled project managers, successful new product activities depend on a well-established, enterprisewide project management framework. This framework establishes the direction of each project and keeps it on track toward that goal. It defines the roles and responsibilities of people associated with the project and establishes the flow of both work and information. It establishes accountability for success. Key elements of the project framework are listed in Table 7.5. If this framework is not already in place, one of the first priorities for upper-level managers must be to define and institutionalize it in their firm.

An Institutionalized Phase-Gate Process

The flow of a new product activity and the key points at which it is reviewed by upper management should be well defined and common to all projects. An effective means for accomplishing this is

Table 7.5   Elements of a Project Framework

➤   An institutionalized phase-gate process.
➤   The product specification.
➤   The project plan:
Work-breakdown structure.
Schedules—Major milestones, individual.
Resource requirements.
➤   The product plan.
➤   A contractual relationship.

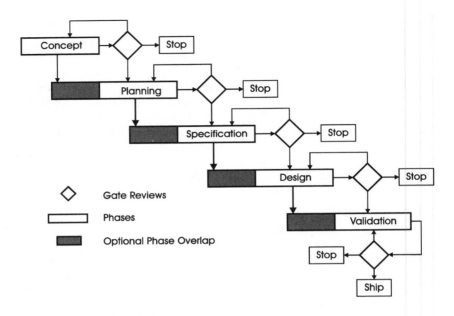

Figure 7.3 Phase-gate project flow.

the *phase-gate process*.[4] Figure 7.3 provides a graphical example. Work within each phase is focused on well-defined objectives that are essential to successful completion of the phase and moving the project forward. In this example, activity in the product concept phase is primarily focused on verifying the market opportunity and defining the right product. Each phase is followed by a gate—a high-level review of the project.

In gate reviews, upper-level managers examine the results of work accomplished in the current phase. There are three possible outcomes of a gate review. The reviewing managers may confirm that the objectives of the current phase have been met, and approve advancement to the next phase. Alternatively, they may decide that the phase has not been successfully completed and direct the project team to continue work on the current phase. On occasion, the information presented at one of these reviews may call the viability of the project into question and result in its being canceled.

---

[4]McGrath, Michael E. *Setting the PACE in Product Development.* Stoneham, MA: Butterworth-Heinemann, 1996.

As the diagram shows, the phases may overlap in some cases, where selected tasks in the next phase begin before all work in the current phase is finished. This overlap can substantially reduce time-to-market, much like collapsing a telescope reduces its length. Schedule overlap has its price, though, and can increase the risk of creating scrap and rework. The decision to overlap phases should thus be discussed during gate reviews and only done with prior planning and approval.

In general, each enterprise needs to define a phase-gate structure that works best for its own operations. There are many different ways to get from a product concept to the point where the product has been introduced into the marketplace and is being manufactured at full volume. Figure 7.4 provides a glimpse of some of the alternatives, albeit from an engineering-centric point of view. The first phase is generally some form of product concept definition. Next, a translation of the product concept into a system design is almost always necessary. During this phase, the scope and nature of the project becomes better defined and project and

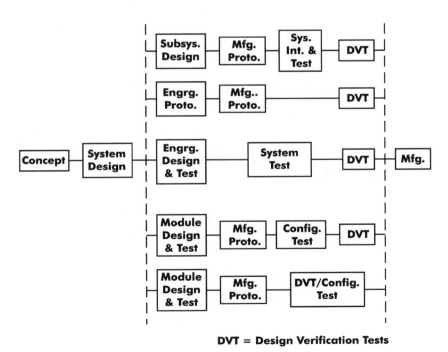

DVT = Design Verification Tests

Figure 7.4 Phase-gate process alternatives.

product plans can be finalized. Beyond this point, however, the sequence of activities may vary widely between enterprises.

A company that develops electromechanical products may utilize the second option from the top in Figure 7.4. The engineering prototype phase answers the general question, "Does this design work?" Once the engineering design has been proven, the manufacturing prototype phase addresses the question, "Can we manufacture this mechanism at target volumes and within cost and reliability constraints?"

An enterprise that produces electronic modules that plug into larger systems may opt for the alternative in Figure 7.4 that is second from the bottom. Here the first phase after system design involves developing a module design and verifying its performance. Once the module design has been verified with engineering prototypes, a large number of manufacturing prototypes are fabricated. The manufacturing prototype phase accomplishes two purposes. First, the manufacturability of the design is verified. Second, many prototype modules are made available for field tests in a wide variety of customer systems. This phase-gate approach works best for those situations in which product designs cannot be fully verified in the engineering laboratory, but instead, must be exercised in existing field situations.

Each phase-gate approach needs to include some form of design verification testing (DVT). The group that performs DVT acts as a customer advocate, verifying that both the product that engineering has created and its associated documentation are ready for delivery to the marketplace. Engineering owns the design and all testing up until the DVT phase. The gate review that precedes DVT examines the work that engineering has done and determines whether all engineering objectives have been met. The purpose of the DVT phase is to provide an independent, third-party affirmation that the product is indeed ready for introduction.

A first step in building project management capacity in an enterprise is to evaluate the definition and operation of any existing phase-gate processes. Is the purpose of each phase well defined and does the phase structure serve the needs of the company well? Are the entry and exit criteria for each phase spelled out? Are roles and responsibilities clearly described? Is the involvement of upper-level managers in gate reviews clearly outlined? Is the process actually used or does it exist only in a binder that gathers dust on someone's bookshelf? If this evaluation reveals that the phase-gate process is in a state of disrepair, the business leadership team should launch an initiative with the objective of identifying a process that will be more widely accepted and hence more useful.

The Product Specification

A second element in the project framework is a clear and stable product description. This description should outline the product, its feature set, and the value that it provides for customers. Technical specifications for the performance of each product function should be provided. If the product has to interface with other products or systems, the technical details of these interfaces should be described. Product specifications are usually created in either the product concept, feasibility, or system design phases. Whatever the phase structure, a product specification must exist and be approved at the gate review where upper-level managers decide to fully staff the project effort.

This product specification should be the result of extensive technical and market research so that it accurately represents a competitive product offering that addresses a well-understood market opportunity. If this condition is satisfied, the product specification will likely remain stable throughout ensuing project activities and will thus serve as a solid part of the framework that guides the project toward successful completion. If this condition is not satisfied, the product specification will most likely change, shifting and moving as the project team gradually learns about market and technical realities. This inevitably leads to scrapped engineering efforts, rework, and schedule delays.

The Project Plan

The project plan provides another key element in the project framework. A good project plan includes (1) a work breakdown structure, (2) a top-level schedule that includes primary project tasks and the major milestones and gate reviews, and (3) a resource map that outlines the people and other resources the project needs. The work breakdown structure describes how project objectives translate into specific tasks and work assignments. Once work has been assigned to specific individuals, a second level of schedules should be created that reconcile individual efforts with the top-level schedule.

The quality of the project plan is a direct function of the quality of the information and judgment that were applied during its creation. The best project plans are well researched. Effective project managers, in creating their project plans, will discuss the work involved with individual engineers and people from other departments that will be involved. They will review historical records from similar projects that have been recently completed. Having gathered all this information, they will apply good judgment, born of earlier career experience both as a project manager and as an individual contributor. Their plans will thus include an insightful work breakdown and the best possible schedule and resource estimates. As steps are skipped, the quality of the project plan will degrade accordingly.

Like the phase-gate process, project plans are a valuable part of the project framework only if they affect the way people work. A project plan that only exists in an unopened notebook somewhere is not worth much. In an interview with one engineer at a client company, the engineer was asked if he had a second-level plan that described his work on the project. He answered, "Yes," and then began rummaging through piles of paper. After considerable effort, he found his work plan buried deep on a side table. It was a well-constructed document, but a quick review revealed that this engineer was months behind schedule and was not even working on the tasks called for in the plan. Project plans must be kept relevant and current, and project personnel must feel accountable for doing their part.

The Product Plan

The product plan describes (1) the product, (2) the business case, (3) the value proposition that the product provides to target customers, (4) how the product will be positioned in the marketplace, and (5) how it will be introduced. While the project plan addresses the development, verification, and manufacturing of the product, the product plan will address issues such as distribution channels, merchandising requirements, sales support, and customer support. The business case will address the size of the market opportunity, product pricing and manufacturing cost issues, revenue and profit estimates, and the expected overall financial return. Like the project plan, the product plan should also include a work breakdown structure, schedule, and resource requirements. The work breakdown structure, in this case, describes how product marketing objectives translate into individual assignments.

The quality of the product plan, just like the project plan, is directly related to the information and judgment that are applied as it is assembled. The best plans are created by experienced product managers who do their homework, researching market factors and prior new product efforts extensively before they formulate the product plan. To serve as an effective element in the project framework, a product plan must also remain stable as the project unfolds. It will be more likely to do this if it is based on solid information and judgment from the beginning.

A Contractual Relationship

The final element in an effective project framework is a contractual relationship between the project manager and upper management. Both parties should mutually agree on the product that will be developed, the time it will take, and the investment that will be required. They should also agree on the expected financial return. In effect, the project manager is acting much like a general contractor that the reader might hire to build a house. After an initial investigation, the project manager assembles a description of the product proposed for development, outlines the value proposition that will be offered to the high-level management team, and prepares an estimate of the schedule and resources required for the project. Upper management, who is being asked to approve the product description and invest the necessary resources, is in effect, the customer. This is the same pattern followed by a general contractor preparing plans for a house, estimating the schedule for construction, and setting the price for the job. The project moves forward only after there is agreement on the terms of the contract and it has been signed. Likewise, the project manager and upper management should reach agreement on the terms of the project before it moves forward. As with a contract, both parties should feel bound by their agreement and accountable for satisfying its terms.

There is an important difference, though. The housing contractor is self-employed and moves, over time, from customer to customer. The project manager is a long-term employee of upper management. They control, to a very large degree, the project manager's career advancement and financial well-being. This can inject political overtones into the project launch process that distorts the quality of the project plan and destroys any contractual relationship. In some enterprises, upper-level managers dictate project schedules that are based on their desires rather than on realistic estimates. The project manager offers a product description with an estimated schedule only to receive a response like, "That's too long.

We need this more elaborate product out six months earlier." At that point, the project manager can either argue, which might have career-limiting effects, or succumb.

If project schedules are decreed by upper-level managers, their relationship with the project manager is no longer a contract. It is, instead, like the relationship between a dictator and his subjects. As the demands of upper-level managers exceed the project manager's estimates, the project team may feel pressure to increase performance—but only up to a point. When upper-management demands become too unrealistic, pressure felt by the project team stops increasing and actually subsides. They begin to regard the project plan and, in particular, the project schedule as some sort of joke that has no real bearing on their work. Their only pressure at this point is to avoid getting hurt when the schedule inevitably slips.

If product innovation in the enterprise is in good shape, the project manager—like the housing contractor—will be closest to the real issues and will have the best expertise. This person will therefore be in the best position to estimate the schedule and resource requirements. If upper management treats these estimates with respect and negotiates the terms of the project in good faith, the project manager will come away from the project launch review feeling committed to the agreement that has been reached. This desired state of affairs is an important earmark of a successful project.

■ CONCLUSION

This chapter has focused on the importance of a strong project manager in achieving successful business outcomes from product innovation efforts. The strength of the project manager is a function of personal skills, of the organization within which the project is executed, and of the support that the project manager receives from upper-level managers. The project manager is the leader of a horizontal team that spans all departments involved with a specific product innovation effort. This person, though, also works as a member of a vertical team and acts an agent for upper management. In this role, the project manager leads a single new product effort that is but one of several in the company's new product portfolio.

This discussion has described important roles for upper-level managers that are critical in establishing a strong project management capability:

➤ Establishing an organization that supports product innovation projects managed by a single person.

➤ Investing in the development of project management skills.

➤ Seeing that an effective phase-gate process is established and followed by each project.

➤ Treating each project as a contractual relationship with the project manager.

➤ Tracking projects and holding project managers accountable.

➤ Supporting project managers when they need help.

A final way in which upper-level managers can ensure the competitive performance of each new product team is to remain interested in their work. Attention from upper-level managers, in which they show genuine interest in the project and ask intelligent questions, helps keep project personnel motivated. Business leaders who communicate an accurate understanding of new product efforts and frequently endorse the importance of this work can have a big impact on its competitiveness. Part III continues this discussion of how upper-level managers can most effectively interact with and influence the performance of product innovation efforts.

Desired Upper Management Behaviors:
Project Management Considerations

➤ Revise the organization of product innovation efforts as necessary to place control of each project in the hands of a single project manager.

➤ Assess the competitive strength of your project managers. Set objectives to bring their skills to world-class levels.

➤ Establish and maintain an effective, ongoing development program for project managers.

➤ Review and strengthen key elements of the project framework.

➤ Become appropriately involved with product innovation projects.

Part III

Leading Product Innovation—Upper Management Roles

Chapter 8

Leading, Managing, and Building the Innovation Engine

Wisdom for those who would be general:
Know the enemy, know yourself; your victory will never be endangered.
Know the ground, know the weather; your victory will then be total.

Sun Tzu
The Art of War

Thus far we have provided a high-level description of the innovation engine and how it drives business growth. The operation of a single product innovation project has been described in some detail and we have outlined the crucial role of the project manager. As success factors to business growth, however, these topics fall in line somewhere behind excellent high-level leadership in overall importance.

An enterprise with an effective upper management team that provides needed leadership to product innovation efforts can, over time, create a successful, growing business. This is true almost without regard to other factors such as existing work processes and project management skills. Effective business leaders will inevitably address these factors as they confront the obstacles to their success. The converse, however, is not true. That is, excellent project managers and product innovation processes will usually not generate long-term business success if the high-level management team does not provide the necessary direction, focus, and support. The best of all worlds is to have excellent performance in every area. But if the authors were forced to choose only one, they would pick effective high-level leadership every time.

Part III focuses on these crucial leadership roles and responsibilities in some depth and breadth.

■ THE PRODUCT PORTFOLIO LEADERSHIP TEAM

Chapter 5 provided a glimpse of the inner workings of the innovation engine as well as the operation of a single project. Figure 8.1 begins with that same view of the internal structure of the innovation engine, but this discussion zooms in on the upper part of the diagram: (1) setting effective product strategy, (2) establishing and managing a portfolio of projects, and (3) building and maintaining a competitive capacity to create new products.

The business team that owns the roles and responsibilities covered in Part III begins with the individual who has span of control

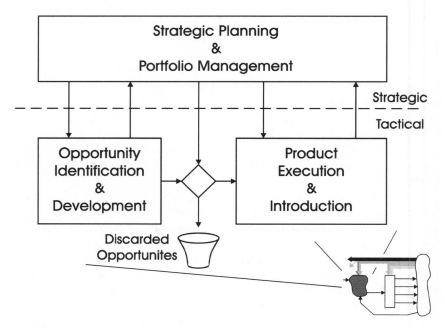

Figure 8.1 Inner workings of the innovation engine.

over all the resources required to create and introduce new products. In a small to medium-size company, this is most likely the president or CEO of the firm. In a large, multinational firm, this person will have a title such as Business Unit President or General Manager. This person's staff will, in general, include the engineering and marketing leaders for the business, and often a manufacturing or operations leader as well. These people form the product portfolio leadership team for the enterprise and they are the primary owners of the roles and responsibilities covered in this part. In addition, however, they may delegate specific assignments to other individuals who report to them.

Figure 8.2 graphically illustrates the business management team and these key product innovation roles. The product portfolio leadership team sets strategic directions, makes final decisions on new product investments, and tracks each product innovation project. They might, however, assign specific tasks to people who report to them. For example, a product manager from marketing and an

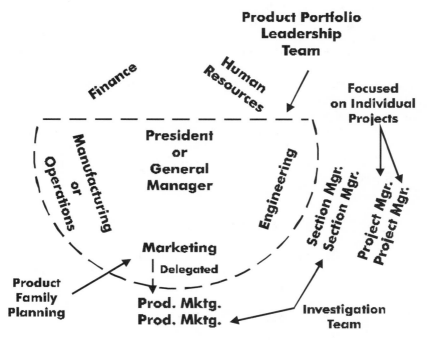

Figure 8.2   New product portfolio management roles.

engineering section manager might be assigned as an investigation team to explore new opportunities in a particular business arena. Another product manager might be assigned the logistics involved in creating the new product family plan. The results from these assignments are always reviewed and approved, however, by the product portfolio leadership team. Managers of individual product innovation projects are generally one or more management levels below this group and are devoted entirely to getting their own particular product to market. In general, they should not be distracted by other assignments.

Other members of the top-level business staff may include a finance manager and, perhaps, a human resources manager. These individuals do not usually play primary roles in setting product strategy or managing the new product portfolio.

The people included in the product portfolio leadership team are among the busiest people in the enterprise. They very often are completely consumed by other work—sales calls, vendor problems, customer relations, operational problems. As a result, they spend little time on new product issues. The good news is that a major improvement in business results usually is possible by simply shifting the focus of these people to the essential roles and responsibilities described here. The bad news is that, to do this, they need to shift their focus away from seemingly high-priority distractions, and that is hard to do. Experience shows, however, that when strategic plans are solid and product innovation projects are well tracked, especially in the early phases, new product introductions proceed much more smoothly. A steady flow of successful new products ensures both satisfied customers and excellent business performance. And when all this is in place, demands on high-level management time eventually drop to a much reduced level.

■ THE NATURE OF LEADERSHIP

The word *leadership* is used a great deal throughout Part III, and some clarification of what this term means will be useful. John W. Gardner contrasts leaders with managers in the following way:[1]

> *Leaders and leader/managers distinguish themselves from the general run of managers in at least six respects:*

---

[1] Gardner, John W. *On Leadership*. New York: Free Press, 1993, (p. 4).

1. *They think longer term—beyond the day's crises, beyond the quarterly report, beyond the horizon.*

2. *In thinking about the unit they are heading, they grasp its relationship to larger realities—the larger organization of which they are a part, conditions external to the organization, global trends.*

3. *They reach and influence constituents beyond their jurisdictions, beyond boundaries . . .*

4. *They put heavy emphasis on the intangibles of vision, values, and motivation and understand intuitively the nonrational and unconscious elements in leader-constituent interaction.*

5. *They have the political skill to cope with the conflicting requirements of multiple constituencies.*

6. *They think in terms of renewal. The routine manager tends to accept organizational structure and process as it exists. The leader or leader/manager seeks the revisions of process and structure required by ever-changing reality.*

Part III encourages behaviors among the members of the product portfolio leadership team that are in line with these distinctions drawn by Gardner.

■ OVERVIEW

The roles and responsibilities discussed here involve (1) setting fruitful directions for new product activities, (2) managing the portfolio of projects underway, and (3) systematically building and maintaining the capacity to compete effectively. Figure 8.3 provides a graphical overview of these leadership roles and serves as an outline for the remainder of this chapter.

The elements of Figure 8.3 form an ongoing loop of activities, all focused on product innovation issues for the enterprise and all interconnected with each other to form a closed-loop system. A good starting point in this loop is the business leader's knowledge base. To set competitive new product strategies and keep product innovation efforts on track, business leaders must accumulate knowledge about their business and the context within which it exists. As the chapter quotation suggests, those who would presume to lead must strive to be knowledgeable about their undertakings. The most knowledgeable leaders are most likely to emerge as winners.

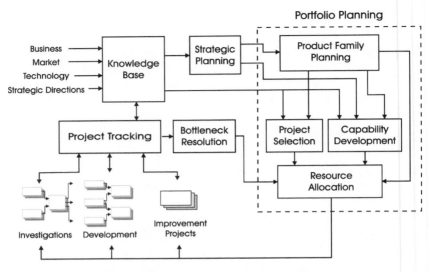

Figure 8.3 The product portfolio leadership process.

One application of this knowledge base is to establish an effective strategic direction and focus for the new product program. This new product strategy and the knowledge base then enable development of specific plans for the new product portfolio. These will include a product family plan that outlines the flow of current and future products. The product family plan and the knowledge base provide information for selecting the next project. In addition, they provide the background needed to guide development of those capabilities that will keep the enterprise competitive in both its current and future new product efforts. Both of these processes place demands on inevitably limited resources, so choices and trade-offs have to be made in the process labeled "Resource Allocation."

Resources can be allocated to product development projects, technology, and business opportunity investigations or capability improvement efforts. In general, a balanced investment in all of these types of activity is desirable. Once launched, project activity in each category represents an ongoing investment that the product portfolio leadership team must track with due diligence. Just like stocks in a portfolio, these project investments should be expected to achieve their objectives and should be periodically reviewed to ensure that they continue to make business sense. Once again, the knowledge base enables business leaders to apply this due diligence with wisdom and insight. Review of project activity is, however, also a learning experience for business leaders and adds to their knowledge base.

Bottlenecks in project activities occasionally can jeopardize successful business results. These emergencies must be factored into the resource allocation process. The bottleneck resolution process provides a proactive means for assessing these situations and minimizing the damage caused by unplanned snags and obstacles.

To echo a point made in Chapter 6, every business enterprise already has each element of Figure 8.3 in place, whether they know it or not. The pertinent questions for the reader are, "What level of maturity has been achieved in each of these process elements in my enterprise and how well do these elements work together as a closed-loop system?" For example, a product plan unfolds in each enterprise. Is it a forecast three years into the future that results from a well-crafted strategy, or is it simply a knee-jerk reaction to the last customer visit? Resources get allocated to project activities in every business. Does this process facilitate judicious investment of these resources in the best possible business opportunities or does "the squeakiest wheel get oiled"? Differences in business performance between enterprises are due, at least in part, to how each company views and implements the leadership roles and processes outlined in Figure 8.3.

■ THE KNOWLEDGE BASE

In an earlier era, the prevalent attitude about the role of high-level management was, "Those in top management positions think, and those at lower levels do." The pendulum seems to have swung far from this extreme. These days it seems as if top-level managers in many firms are too busy to think. They put in 90 hours or more a week on all sorts of important, but mostly nonstrategic, activities. Very few, however, can point to even two hours per week in which they have had time simply to think about what they know and how to apply this knowledge to their business situation.

The business leadership team with the best knowledge, wisdom, judgment, and imagination is most likely to succeed. Each member of the leadership team must strive to develop and maintain current and in-depth knowledge that addresses (1) the firm's particular business arena—their customers, their technologies, the structure of their marketplace, (2) the strengths and weaknesses of their own enterprise, and (3) the larger context within which their business exists—economic, political, and social. To stay ahead, business leaders must be mentally prepared to both out-think their competitors in their current lines of business and imagine how to reinvent their industry. Gary Hamel and C. K. Prahalad state it this way:[2]

> . . . in many companies, process reengineering and advantage-building efforts are more about catching up than getting out in front. . . . A company surrenders today's business when it gets smaller faster than it gets better. A company surrenders tomorrow's businesses when it gets better without getting different.

➤ Required Business Knowledge

Beyond the usual education in management theory and practice, the knowledge required to lead a business enterprise includes an understanding of market factors specific to the business such as customer and user needs, the criteria that they use when deciding to buy, the nature of the competition, and distribution channel issues. A working knowledge of relevant product technologies and operational concerns is also required. This knowledge base should include a perspective on the historical underpinnings that have led to the current state of the business as well as an awareness of trends that will shape its future. Each member of the business leadership team should bring both personal experience and their understanding of these matters into the group. As the business team works together, the different perspectives of individual members should combine to provide both a broader and more complete understanding of pertinent business issues, and a richer imagination about possible futures for the business than any single member of the team can muster.

Perhaps the most important element of this required knowledge base is an imaginative understanding of customer and user needs. Each member of the business leadership team should be able to draw on recent and personal experience with the people

---

[2] Hamel, Gary and Prahalad, C.K. *Competing for the Future: Breakthrough Strategies for Seizing Control of Your Industry and Creating the Markets of Tomorrow.* Boston: Harvard Business School Press, 1994.

that receive value from their business. These experiences should not be limited simply to sales calls. Interactions also should be focused on learning more fully about the customer's world. Fruitful avenues of inquiry might include what customers strive to accomplish in their own business, the aspects of current products and services that they value most, the frustrations and obstacles that they face, and their visions, aspirations, and directions for the future. Learning about the realities of the customer's experience in doing business with your firm is also crucial. How well did the process of shopping for and purchasing your products work? Did products provide the expected value? Were interactions with customer support services satisfying? Interacting with customers who have said, "No" to your products and services often offers a particularly rich learning experience. How was the competitor's value proposition more attractive than yours? What might you have done to turn their "No" into a "Yes"? As busy as high-level managers are, they must make time for ongoing customer involvement so that their knowledge and judgment always remain personal and current.

Other ways that high-level managers acquire the knowledge to support their leadership efforts include attending trade shows and symposia relevant to their business. Trade shows offer an opportunity both to view the efforts of competitors firsthand, and to scout for new customers and areas of opportunity. Attending conferences where leaders in the industry speak increases awareness of leading-edge issues and future directions.

Busy managers may be thinking, "I don't have time in my schedule for all this!" That may be true, but there doesn't seem to be any better way to gain the judgment and insight needed to effectively lead and manage product innovation in a business. A thoughtful evaluation of those things that managers currently spend time on, compared with the ongoing development of needed business judgment and insight, may assign a higher priority to the activities described here.

➤ Required Self-Knowledge

Effective leadership of enterprisewide product innovation efforts also requires an ongoing and realistic understanding of one's own company—its strategic directions, the strength of its product line and distribution channels, the effectiveness of its people, its tools and facilities, and those business processes that are critical to its success. A business is a symbiotic collection of interdependent systems and all have to perform at competitive levels for the overall business to remain viable. Each part of the business is a living, dynamic element that requires ongoing attention and investment.

The product portfolio leadership team must always strive to be cognizant of the true strengths and weaknesses of the business for these will change with time as business conditions vary. As technologies pertinent to the business evolve, the skill set of the engineering workforce may erode from a source of competitive strength to a handicap that must be addressed. Progress in the microprocessor industry, for example, has shifted the way many products are implemented, from a focus on electronic or mechanical ingenuity to one that involves primarily software design. This change has left many companies with too many electronic or mechanical engineers and a scarcity of software design talent. For these firms to remain competitive, they must somehow realign this balance of skills with the needs imposed by current technologies.

Product innovation processes that have been competitive for many years can be rendered obsolete and noncompetitive by outside forces. A number of U.S. industries, for example, lost market share in the 1970s to Japanese competitors who were better at discerning customer desires for reliability and economy. To combat this trend, new methods for understanding customer needs had to be developed and these needs had to be translated into high-quality new products. As U.S. firms caught up in this arena, the Japanese developed dramatically faster product innovation cycles. This meant that a Japanese company could study market trends and customer needs longer, launch its new product development activity, and then have a better product in the market ahead of U.S. firms who were addressing the same opportunity.

Business leaders must be in touch with the relative performance of these critical business processes so that they can make timely corrections. Better yet, business leaders should be imagining how they can implement strategic improvements to capture customer loyalty and put other firms at a disadvantage.

Changing business conditions can also obsolete a company's approach to sales and distribution. When HP moved its focus from electronic instruments to computers and peripherals, sales and distribution methods had to move from direct sales at the customer site to selling through dealer channels. More recently, as the personal computer business has evolved, leading competitors are moving away from dealer channels and back to direct sales, only now through interaction with the customer by telephone and over the

Internet. These new distribution methods are radically affecting market shares, cost structures, and profit margins in the industry. Any firm that wants to stay competitive must thus evaluate these trends and react quickly to realign its internal skills and business processes.

Business leaders must make sure that every major process and facility that their firm supports becomes and remains a core competence.[3] Leading firms focus their investments in strategically vital areas where their performance can be elevated to and kept at world-class levels. Twenty years ago, companies tended to develop and maintain almost every capability that was needed to deliver their product or service. An appliance manufacturer, for example, would install and maintain a complete range of facilities; for fabrication of sheet metal parts and printed circuits, for painting, and for product assembly. Some even designed and fabricated their own electric motors and solenoids. Almost none of these facilities, however, operated with costs and productivity equal to that of worldwide leaders. Over time, these manufacturers have learned to outsource many operations, choosing strategic partners for this work who can provide needed services at competitive performance levels. High-level managers must develop a level of understanding that enables good decisions on these matters, for they are essential to long-term competitive performance.

A final area of self-knowledge critical to the enterprise is an in-depth understanding of the workforce; who is making a positive difference, who is impeding progress, and the overall mental and spiritual health of the people who do the work. Are people enthusiastic in general, or burned out? Are working relationships healthy or do bickering and internal politics impede the effective flow of work and information? Do people communicate openly and with candor or is intellectual honesty a rare thing? In Chapter 5, we described product innovation as an information assembly line. Trying to develop new products in an organization that operates more on fiction than truth is like trying to run a physical assembly line with parts that are made out of paper rather than metal. Ultimately, what matters is the people who do the work and the quality of the information at their disposal. An enterprise needs a capable, well-informed workforce to be competitive. These things should be a primary focus for upper management attention and understanding.

---

[3] Prahalad, C.K., and Hamel, Gary. "The Core Competence of the Corporation," *Harvard Business Review* 68, No. 3 (1990), 79–91.

➤ Required Knowledge about the World Context

Each business operates not only as an economic force in its marketplace, but also as a citizen of the world within which it resides. Business leaders must become and remain aware of social and political issues as well as the economic environment in which their enterprise exists. Worldwide economic trends and cycles are obviously important to the business, both in the near and long term. Social and political concerns, though, can also be highly relevant.

Concerns for the environment can greatly influence the choices made by potential customers. Every business that manufactures and ships products has been affected by a growing body of regulations to protect the environment. Companies who deliver products to customers in Germany must be willing to accept the return of their packaging material for disposal. The cost and environmental impact of disposing of these materials now, by law, belongs to the manufacturer. Customers, angry at the sheer volume of packaging material received, have been known to dispatch huge shipments of used packaging directly back to the CEO of the company from which it came. On the other hand, companies that demonstrate concern for the environment and develop more efficient and recyclable packaging methods can win greater market share in an ever-more concerned customer base.

Sustainability is an even broader issue that is emerging to influence global marketplaces.[4] Can a corporation deliver its products and services in ways that avoid damaging either the environment, or replaceable or nonreplaceable natural resources? In other words, can a corporation do its business in ways that enable our planet to remain healthy and able to support humankind?

Generally, such matters first emerge as social concerns and then become political issues. Governments eventually respond by enacting new laws and regulations that attempt to control those factors affecting the environment and, hence, the well-being of its citizens. These laws and regulations alter the business landscape, creating both obstacles and opportunities. Some firms choose to fight these trends, undermining any alleged benefits associated with new legal requirements and highlighting the added costs that

---

[4] Hart, Stuart L. "Beyond Greening: Strategies for a Sustainable World," *Harvard Business Review,* January/February 1997.

will be imposed on society. The reaction of automobile manufacturers to air bag regulations is an example of this response. Other firms find opportunity in this new business landscape. Government tax incentives for environmentally friendly practices have created entirely new markets in California. A market for toilets that use less water has been created within the past few years, in response to both tax incentives and public concern for the water supply. Solar water heating systems are popular for essentially the same reasons: tax incentives and public concern for pollution associated with energy usage.

As issues such as these emerge and grow in importance, business leaders must remain aware and ready to alter their firm's strategy as necessary. Ultimately, customers vote for the business enterprises of their choice with each dollar that they spend. They will place these votes with the companies that provide them with the best overall value. As time goes on, and economic and environmental pressures grow and change, the value proposition that customers consider is broadening to include more than just the products or services that they receive for their money. Business leaders must always strive to maneuver their enterprise to keep it aligned with shifting customer needs, preferences, and concerns.

As societies evolve and learn, new issues of importance emerge. People generally learn over time to envision a better future; for themselves, for their families, and for the world. Governments can create laws that act as a catalyst for action. But it is the incredible power of business, responding to customer needs and choices, that actually moves the world toward its future. The muscle that moves the world and makes it different is embodied in the energy and creativity of product innovators everywhere. And the intelligence that guides this incredible force for change resides in the business leaders who establish the strategy and direction for each enterprise.

➤ Contemplation

Having time to gather knowledge, such as that described in the preceding sections, is only part of the requirement. Business leaders also should set aside time to contemplate—to consider what they have learned and to imagine creatively about the future of their business. Most high-level managers have little or no time at all available for effective contemplation. Their time is completely consumed by other urgent demands that seemingly have a higher priority.

Successful leadership requires both insight and creativity: insight to see the real meaning behind events and trends; creativity to devise strategies that will outmaneuver competitors and guide the enterprise to more fruitful, uncontested markets. These essential attributes do not come automatically with the gathering of new knowledge. Such knowledge may provide the soil, but a watering of time alone to think and the warmth of thoughtful discussion with others are required as well, before insight and creativity will grow and flourish. The business value of insight and creativity among business leaders is immeasurable. But these properties are so nebulous and intangible that high-level managers ignore their development, and invest their time instead in more concrete and urgent matters. In the words of Hamel and Prahalad:[5]

> *It takes substantial and sustained intellectual energy to develop high-quality, robust answers to questions such as what new core competencies will we need to build, what new product concepts should we pioneer, what new alliances do we need to form . . . These questions go unanswered because to address them senior managers must first admit, to themselves and to their employees, that they are less than fully in control of their company's future. . . . So the urgent drives out the important; the future goes largely unexplored; and the capacity to act, rather than the capacity to think and imagine, becomes the sole measure of leadership.*

■ STRATEGIC PLANNING

Establishing a strategic direction for the enterprise and outlining the major steps that it must take to achieve long-term goals is a critically important application of the management knowledge base. These plans will establish in broad terms which markets the business will pursue, which technology investments it will make, and how broadly or narrowly it will focus its new product efforts. A good strategic plan will reflect an in-depth understanding of the shifting business terrain and where the competition is both strong and vulnerable. It will point the way to the richest business opportunities that are available to the enterprise. The strategic plan

---

[5] Hamel, Gary, and Prahalad, C. K. *Competing for the Future*, (pp. 202–211). Boston: Harvard Business School Press, 1994.

should establish the "theater of operations" for the product family plans that follow. Finally, it should reflect an understanding of the strengths and weaknesses of the enterprise and outline both new capabilities that are needed and corrective actions that must be taken. The strategic plan should identify capabilities that (1) are to be developed as core competencies, (2) will be acquired through strategic partnerships with other companies, and perhaps (3) will be eliminated over time. It should also identify new skills, methods, and tools that are needed and highlight business processes that must be developed or overhauled.

The most successful businesses provide a kind of leadership to their customers, and this leadership is largely articulated through a firm's strategic plans. The late W. Edwards Deming defined leadership as "Removing obstacles that keep people from taking pride in their work." The products and services provided by some business enterprises do this for their customers. But leadership also means pointing the way to new possibilities, identifying the direction toward a more effective future. Leading companies identify new possibilities for their customers and then bring these possibilities to life in the form of exciting new products and services. Often customers cannot envision these products for themselves, but they quickly perceive their value and learn to apply them. Leading companies very often provide new products that, in important ways, redefine the future for their customers.

The product portfolio leadership team should focus on the strategic plan at least once each year. Figure 8.4 illustrates how

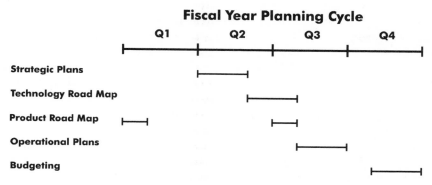

Figure 8.4 Recommended annual planning cycle.

this activity might fit into an overall annual planning cycle. The strategic planning effort may involve anything from a simple review and endorsement of the existing plan to a total strategic redirection of the enterprise. Regardless, the leadership team should ensure that the published plan reflects their best insight and judgment relative to current business conditions and future directions.

Creating the right strategic plan for a business enterprise is somewhat like mining for gold. Gold miners search for the mother lode, the long vein of gold that stretches deep into the earth providing a rich source of wealth into the unforeseeable future. Once they find this lode, the miner's tactical plan is simple: Stay in contact with the mother lode, and follow it wherever it leads. Businesses use this same approach with current markets. Inevitably, though, every mother lode eventually peters out. Either another vein must be found or the mine closes down. Leaders in the gold-mining business must periodically assess their situation and choose where to invest their resources. Should they put everyone to work on the mother lode and thus maximize production, or should they also explore for new veins to exploit when the mother lode becomes exhausted? When they explore for a new mother lode, they must apply every ounce of intuition and judgement that they can muster in picking fruitful directions for their search. As their search reveals new veins, they must decide whether they should mine them in earnest or pass them over for better opportunities in the future.

Just like these miners, business leaders must periodically choose whether to invest their resources exploiting current markets or launch a search for rich, new opportunities. Like the mother lode, every existing market will eventually peter out. When this happens, revenue growth becomes problematic, profits decline, and the time is at hand for exploration. Establishing new strategic directions for the enterprise calls for all the judgment, intuition, and creativity that the business leadership can muster. The path to fruitful new markets will depend on technology trends, market trends, and worldwide economic conditions, as well as on social and political climates throughout the world. As the search unfolds, the product portfolio team must decide which new markets to pursue and which to pass over. The future of the enterprise will depend on the knowledge held by the product portfolio leadership team and the level of insight, intuition, and creativity that they bring to bear on this search for new markets.

➤ Strategic Planning Process

Table 8.1 shows a sample of contents for a business unit strategic plan. The process for creating a plan like the one outlined here, however, does not start with Item 1. The planning discussion usually starts with Item 3, moves to 4, then perhaps to 1, and then to 5. This loop is repeated until the thoughts in each of these areas have converged into a well aligned and logically sound set based on the best wisdom, business judgment, and insight available. With this information as a backdrop then, Item 6 can be discussed effectively. Only after Item 6 has been outlined should an attempt be made to address Item 2. Once Item 2 has been solidified, Items 7 through 9 become a rather straightforward process for planning the execution of these objectives.

Once it has been finalized, the business leadership team must communicate the strategic plan throughout the enterprise, endorse it, and see that it influences business investments and activities appropriately. On a selective basis, elements of the strategic plan may also be shared with important customers to help them understand what to expect from the firm. While this may involve some risk of tipping off the competition, sharing strategic directions with key customers can help both establish and maintain

Table 8.1   Contents for a Business Unit Strategic Plan

1. Purpose statement for the business unit
2. Long-range objectives
3. Analysis of markets and customers
4. Analysis of competition
5. Required products and services
6. Required capability development and adjustment
7. Financial analysis
       Long-range financial projections
       Outline of major expenditures
       Long-range budgets for functional areas
8. Assumptions and recommendations
       Interdependencies
       Potential problems
9. Plans for the coming year

their loyalty as well as gain important feedback on the firm's strategic direction.

■ PORTFOLIO PLANNING

The high-level management team is also responsible for identifying, launching, and managing an ongoing portfolio of new-product-related activities. The purpose of this effort is to translate the strategic plan into specific product innovation projects and capability development activities. The new product revenue gain performance, as discussed in Chapter 2, and hence the revenue growth rate for the enterprise will largely be determined by how well the business team executes these responsibilities. As illustrated in Figure 8.3, the portfolio planning effort includes processes for product family planning, project selection, capability development, and resource allocation.

➤ Product Family Planning

A business enterprise reshapes itself and propels itself toward the future through its ongoing stream of new products and services. The specific products that are introduced, the way they are positioned relative to each other and to the market, and the order in which they emerge are determined by the product family plan. In a well-managed firm, this product family plan translates the broad strategic directions established earlier into specific new products that will best achieve the strategic goals of the business. As with the strategic planning process, the product family plan should reflect the best wisdom and judgement that the enterprise can muster.

The objectives of the product family plan should be to:

➤ Identify specific products that will achieve targeted revenue growth and profit performance.

➤ Move the enterprise aggressively toward its strategic goals.

➤ Emphasize application of the firm's core competencies.

The balance in the product portfolio—between short-term, incremental product-line improvements and long-term investment in major new platforms, for example, or perhaps between the use of current technologies versus aggressive technology advancement—should result from efforts to make concurrent progress on these three objectives.

A graphical new product road map is a concise representation of the product family plan. Figure 8.5 provides a hypothetical example of this method of communicating the new product vision for the enterprise. Product lines are plotted on the vertical axis with time extending from the present out to the future limits of the product vision on the horizontal axis. Icons representing each new product are plotted at the approximate introduction dates. Every enterprise should maintain an ongoing new product road map that evolves somewhat like a moving belt. Concepts for new products are added at the extreme future limits of the graph as the business vision dictates. As time unfolds, they move toward the present and evolve as the vision gets clearer.

When a new product concept gets within range, a small team is assigned to perform market and technology investigations specific to that particular product. As these efforts progress, the vision for that product stabilizes, creating a detailed product definition and product plan. Eventually, the project expands to include a full multifunction development staff. Product icons continue to move

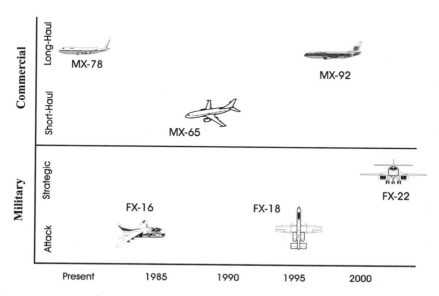

Figure 8.5 Ajax Aircraft—Product road map.

to the left over time until they reach the present end of the graph and are introduced into the market. At any given point in time, the road map will provide both a snapshot of current new product activity and the long-term new product strategy for the company. As Figure 8.4 indicates, the new product road map should be updated perhaps twice a year.

Product family planning is critical to the future of the enterprise and should involve the best minds and the best information available. One member of the product portfolio leadership team, generally the marketing manager, should have this as an ongoing assignment. This individual should, however, involve others in product planning efforts including, in particular, the best strategic thinkers in the product marketing, engineering and technology research functions. As interesting opportunities arise, the product portfolio leadership team should launch investigations with the objective of developing an in-depth understanding of each area of opportunity. These investigations typically involve a product marketing manager who works with a product engineering manager as a "scouting party" that maps out the business terrain ahead. These individuals might spend as much as one week each month

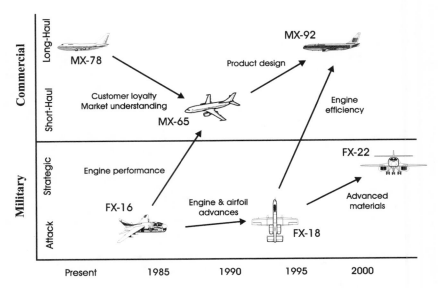

Figure 8.6 Ajax Aircraft—Product plan rationale.

traveling together, visiting potential customers, going to trade shows, and attending conferences. The information gathered in these investigations is vital to the creation of insightful new product plans.

Product family plans should include more than just an outline of future new products. There should be a rationale to the plan and a synergy between new product offerings. The development of core competencies and strategic partnerships should be evident in the unfolding of the product family plan. As Figure 8.6 shows, the new product road map can serve as a backdrop for highlighting these aspects of the plan.

Another element of a thorough new product plan is the technology roadmap.[6] As illustrated in Figure 8.7, this device connects emerging new technologies to the product family plan and identifies critical timing and dependency relationships. This information helps management focus and motivate new technology efforts, and enlist involvement and support for these activities at all levels in the firm. It also helps provide a balanced perspective

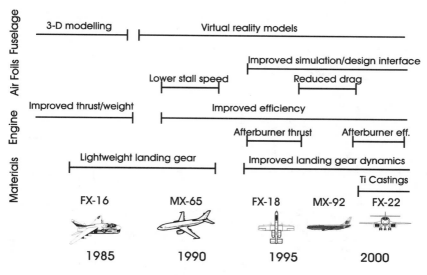

Figure 8.7   Ajax Aircraft—Technology road map.

---

[6] Wilyard, Charles II, and McClees, Cheryl W. "Motorola Technology Roadmap Process," *Research-Technology Management,* September–October 1987, pp. 13–19.

on investments in new technology development that establishes their priority relative to other possible uses for the same resources.

➤ Project Selection Process

The objective of this process is to make certain that the resources of the enterprise are well invested in the best possible new product opportunities, both short and long term. The product family plan and the management knowledge base provide information to guide this process and support high-quality investment decisions. As Figure 8.8 illustrates, if this selection process is sound and is provided with excellent investment alternatives from the product family planning process, it will establish an ongoing portfolio of new product efforts with the highest possible value to the business.

Table 8.2 offers a checklist for the attributes of an effective project selection process. First and foremost is a "venture capitalist" mind-set. In selecting a proposed new product for investment, high-level managers should consider its merits from the viewpoint of a private investor. They should ask themselves, "Is this investment opportunity so good that I would risk my own money on its success?" Adopting this perspective will lead the product portfolio

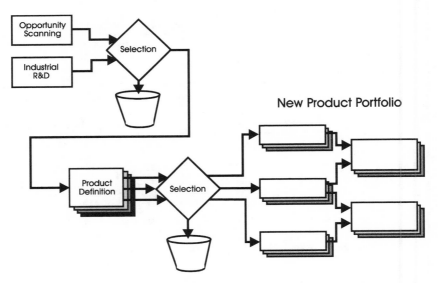

Figure 8.8 Opportunity selection establishes the value of the new product portfolio.

Table 8.2 Earmarks of a Successful Selection Process

➤ A "venture capitalist" mind-set exists.

➤ Process is explicit rather than clandestine.

➤ Decisions are made by a "benevolent dictatorship."

➤ Decisions utilize the best available information.

➤ Investments are reviewed periodically:

All projects are considered, existing and proposed.

Portfolio is adjusted for best business value.

➤ Project results are systematically reviewed. Lessons learned are used to improve the selection process.

leadership team to ask the right questions when evaluating a new product proposal. What is the promised payoff? Does this project offer the best return among the available investment alternatives? Does this investment offer significant strategic value? What are the risks to the success of this project? Does the project team speak with a single voice in this proposal? Are they enthusiastic? Are they believable? Are they likely to deliver a competitive project effort?

An effective project selection process is explicit and follows well-known guidelines in considering proposals. The criteria to select projects for investment are understood not only by the portfolio leadership team, but by those who propose projects for investment as well. An explicit selection process means that no project gets launched without a successful review.

Each business should establish a list of project selection criteria for acceptable proposals reflecting the experience and best judgment of the enterprise. The specific detail of this list may be somewhat different for each business but will include some common elements as well. Table 8.3 offers a template for consideration.

In an effective selection process, project proposals are reviewed and approved by a "benevolent dictatorship"—a person or a small group of people who can listen well, gather required information, and then make a clear, quick decision based on best judgment. This person or group is a dictatorship because it has the power to make its decision stick. If more than a single person, this group should be able to work well together, easily combining the perspective and judgment of each member into a collective view held by all. Once a proposal has been accepted, the power of this

Table 8.3 Characteristics of a Successful Project Proposal

➤ The project promises to create high returns in both revenue gain and profit. Explicit performance standards should be met.

➤ The project aligns well with established strategic directions.

➤ The proposal reflects an insightful understanding of customers and customer needs.

➤ The proposal reflects an insightful understanding of competitors and competing products.

➤ The proposed product promises to create a sustainable competitive advantage.

➤ Project risks have been well assessed and contingency plans exist.

➤ The proposal reflects an understanding of applicable regulatory constraints.

➤ Product marketing and distribution channel issues have been considered. A viable approach is included in the proposal.

➤ The proposal is supported by upper management.

➤ The proposal has the support of key functions in the organization.

"benevolent dictatorship" ensures that the project will have the resources and support that it needs through to completion.

In some organizations, a committee reviews project proposals. These decisions are more likely to reflect the consensus of the group, rather than a wholehearted commitment by each member. Such decisions take longer to make and are susceptible to the "pocket veto" phenomenon—members who succumb to group pressure in committee may later refuse to provide necessary support for the project.

An effective project selection process should make a deliberate attempt to acquire and utilize the highest quality information available. Certainly the business case and product definition must initially be based on approximations and guesses. Nonetheless, every effort should be made to validate the information used for project investment decisions. Each guess and approximation should be backed by a sound rationale. Initial product descriptions should reflect information gained through thorough market investigation and recent feedback from specific customers. The selection process should include an explicit discussion of information quality and the assumptions that will affect the project outcome.

In subsequent phases, the information and assumptions that supported the initial investment decision should be reexamined in the light of new learning to ensure that the intellectual underpinnings of the project remain valid.

One purpose of the project selection process is to ensure that the business value of the ongoing portfolio of project investments is as high as possible. As new proposals are considered, they should be compared both with other alternatives in the queue and with other projects that are underway. Investment resources are inevitably limited, so the people needed to staff a new project are rarely just "waiting in the wings" for their next assignment. Staffing a new project usually means either waiting for another project to finish or canceling a present effort to free up the needed resources. In considering each new proposal, the portfolio leadership team must weigh the business value of this new effort against the value of other projects that are currently underway. Occasionally, canceling an existing project to launch a more lucrative effort might make good business sense, particularly if the existing project has fallen far behind schedule, or is proving to hold less business promise than originally thought. The possibility that a project might be canceled to free up resources for a better opportunity can create a healthy tension in the enterprise that intensifies both the business focus and the sense of urgency felt by existing project teams.

Another purpose of the project selection process is to create a desired balance between current projects.[7] Each enterprise must decide for itself which dimensions are important in balancing the portfolio. Some will strive for a balance between incremental improvements to existing product lines and fundamental new product platforms that gain strategic ground and open new markets. Others may emphasize a balance in investments across all pertinent market segments. Still other firms might decide to distribute investments based on the risk and reward associated with each project in the portfolio. Whatever dimensions are selected for the portfolio balance, a graphic like that shown in Figure 8.9 can be a useful tool in establishing and communicating the current state of balance in the product portfolio.

---

[7] Cooper, Robert G., Edgett, Scott J., and Kleinschmidt, Elko J. *Portfolio Management for New Products,* (chap. 3). Reading, MA: Addison-Wesley, 1998.

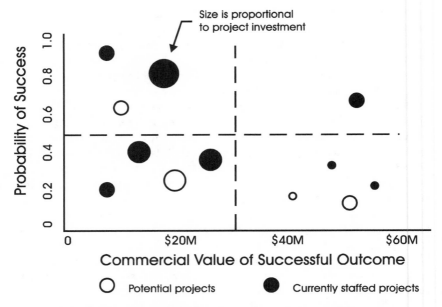

Figure 8.9 Balancing the new product portfolio.

➤ Capability Development

Information from the knowledge base, strategic directions and plans, and the product family plan provide an information backdrop that allows the product portfolio leadership team to manage the competitive stature of their current and future new product capabilities. These capabilities include (1) work processes, (2) information tools that support new product activities, (3) broad areas of competency that support the creation of new value for customers, (4) the size and nature of the product innovation workforce, (5) the knowledge and skill sets embodied in this group, and (6) the motivation and morale of these people. The portfolio leadership team is responsible for building and maintaining a competitive capacity to introduce new products, for this establishes a significant part of the shareholder value for the firm. The exact nature of the work involved in building needed capabilities will depend on the current state of the people and processes involved, the future products that must be developed, and the desired future state of the business outlined in the strategic plan.

The desired output of the capability development process is (1) a comprehensive strategic direction for capability improvements, and (2) plans for specific improvement projects that will move new-product-related capabilities of the firm toward desired goals. Typically, an enterprise can only manage perhaps two or three capability improvement projects at a time. Consequently, these efforts must be well managed, well staffed, and focused on the most important competitive issues at hand. In executing its capability development responsibilities, the product portfolio leadership team should address the following questions:

➤ How must our product innovation capability evolve to become/remain competitive throughout the range of our strategic plan?

➤ What three product innovation performance issues have the biggest impact on our ability to compete, both near- and long-term?

➤ What makes these the most important performance issues?

➤ What specific steps and investments are required to completely resolve these performance issues?

➤ What progress measures will indicate that these performance issues are being effectively resolved?

Work Processes

The portfolio leadership team is responsible for tracking the effectiveness of the firm's processes for identifying the best new product investments and then smoothly moving products through development and into production. Frequent reviews of process performance, both for work associated with single projects and for efforts related to the new product portfolio, should be conducted. Particular attention should be paid to process learning that can be derived from recently completed project experiences. The leadership team must compare the performance of these processes in their enterprise with equivalent performance that can be discerned from the actions and product introductions of their competitors, and then identify specific improvements to remain competitive. As the firm grows and its market and competitive circumstances evolve, these processes need frequent attention and insightful investment to remain viable. As with many of its other responsibilities, the leadership team should delegate the primary responsibility for improving these work processes to specific individuals—one person should own product innovation processes for the single project while another individual assumes responsibility for the new product portfolio process.

Information Tools

Once an enterprise has installed effective work processes for its new product efforts, attention should be turned to the information tools—computers, networks, and applications—that will best facilitate the work flowing through these processes. A common mistake in many firms is that information tools are identified and purchased by individuals or departments with little regard to the integrated needs of the total product innovation process. The result can be a hodgepodge of hardware and software that fails to support competitive levels of performance, consumes inordinate quantities of scarce resources, and unnecessarily constrains the firm's ability to establish effective work processes. In one company, the engineering group uses one set of tools, the stress analysis department uses a different brand, and manufacturing uses yet another. One high-level manager estimated that the firm spends over $5 million and enormous amounts of time each year just converting the information format of new product data between departments. The role of information tools in product innovation is to support work processes, not the other way around.

The opportunity for installing effective tools exists at three levels. First, individual engineers need effective tools to create a successful design quickly. These information products should facilitate the engineer's access to information needed for their design, assist in the creation of a high-quality design, and provide realistic simulation that allows rapid, first-pass design evaluation. At a higher level, project managers need information tools that facilitate the tracking and management of project expenditures, schedule and track completion of project tasks, and manage product-related information throughout the project. The latter of these, the product data management (PDM) system, should both provide routine archiving of product-related data, and control of data file access and modification. Finally, product portfolio managers need tools for managing and tracking the new product portfolio. These tools should provide standard project performance measures that highlight the status of all projects in the portfolio. They should facilitate the management of project-related resources and help identify potential bottlenecks. In effect, new product portfolio managers need the equivalent of an aircraft instrument panel—a standardized display of information for all projects that they can readily access, and that allows them to quickly focus on trouble spots and initiate needed corrective action.

Core Competencies and Strategic Partnerships

Often a business enterprise finds that, to remain competitive, it must acquire more new capabilities—new technologies or, perhaps, new distribution or support capacities—than it can develop on its own. Sometimes available resources limit the firm's ability to develop new capabilities and, at other times, there is simply too little time. The leadership team must decide which capabilities are to be developed in-house, as core competencies of the firm, and which will be acquired through strategic partnerships. Important elements of the output of the capability development process are thus (1) identification of the core competencies that the firm will develop and support, (2) plans to build capacity in existing and new core competencies, and (3) a plan for developing those strategic partnerships that are essential to the long-term goals of the enterprise. Along with this, another critical capability that must be developed and maintained is the ability to establish and manage successful long-term strategic partnerships. Training and development in this important skill set should be readily available to product innovation managers at all levels.

Product Innovation Workforce

In examining its competitive capabilities, the product portfolio leadership team should dispassionately assess the quality of its existing product innovation workforce and of its processes for acquiring new talent. In many ways, building a competitive new product capability is like building a winning athletic team. Managers need to start with the best possible talent, and then provide these people with the best methods, the best training, the best coaching, and the best tools available. The training and coaching provided must be responsive to the competitive situation. Just as an athletic team strives over time to gather together the best players, a new product organization needs also to assemble the best available talent for the jobs that must be done.

Building a winning athletic team, though, is not simply a matter of finding the best players. These individual contributors must work together effectively as a team as well. The same is true in product innovation. Individuals on a product innovation project team must be able to rely on each other and work well together. New product efforts are most effective when a feeling of mutual respect and trust exists throughout the project. Either highly talented, but self-centered, individuals or poor performers can have a disproportionate, negative impact on project performance. Prima donnas on a project team generally strive to draw an undue amount of credit for their own accomplishments. Often such individuals will also minimize the value of work done by others. Poor performers can cause delays or create errors that thwart the efforts of the team to meet its objectives. These individuals inevitably increase the workload of others around them. When managers fail to deal effectively with poor performers, others on the team can become demoralized. "Why should I work so hard and care so much, when that person over there does half as much and creates flawed results without reprimand?"

To build the most competitive product innovation capability, managers must work to resolve both of these issues as they occur. The easiest approach is to avoid these problems by improving recruiting methods so that potential problem employees are filtered out before they are hired. The interview process should include effective screening for not only vocational skills, but values and work ethic as well. Having three or four potential peers interview each candidate for employment on different aspects of the work involved will usually provide a good measure of that person's vocational skills. Interviewers should also be coached, however, to watch for potential interpersonal problems as they conduct their interviews. Along with answering questions about a candidate's professional ability, interviewers should be prepared to answer the question, "Would you like to work with this person on your project?" In one case, the hiring manager detected a personal dislike for a candidate from a prestigious engineering school in hallway conversations with each of the engineers who interviewed this person. The candidate's professional skills, however, were outstanding. At the meeting to review the interview results, only the preceding question was asked. A unanimous negative response sealed this candidate's fate at that company. He was sent off to start his career somewhere else.

Performance problems with existing employees are more difficult to solve. Nonetheless, they must be dealt with quickly and effectively to build and maintain the most competitive new product capability. Initial efforts to resolve these issues should be focused on altering the adverse behaviors at the core of the problem. The goal is not only to improve the performance of the problem individual, but also to communicate to others that there are clear, enforceable standards of performance and behavior within the organization. Excellent employees find peace of mind in this fact and focus their energy on the work at hand. When these signals are clear, marginal employees will take heed and be motivated to keep their own work within acceptable limits. Effective efforts to deal with problem employees create a healthy sense of fairness and accountability among all members of the product innovation workforce.

When reasonable efforts to modify adverse behavior have failed, the only recourse is to "de-cruit" the problem individual. This is, perhaps, the hardest job that a manager ever has to do, but is often essential in building a competitive new product capability. As with the athletic team, a product innovation group cannot afford to carry a weak or disruptive member. There are only a given number of seats on the bench or a limited number of employees devoted to product innovation. For the athletic team or the project to be competitive, each individual must contribute fully to the achievement of the goals at hand and support the efforts of other members of the team. Poor performers who cannot be salvaged, in the end, require too much investment and distract management attention from more important matters. Furthermore, they degrade the working environment for other members of the team. They must be removed and replaced with other individuals who can contribute at a higher level of performance.

➤ Resource Allocation

The resources devoted to product innovation represent an important investment for a business enterprise and must be diligently managed to achieve the best business results. A process is necessary for allocating these limited resources between competing demands. Demands are generated by recently approved product innovation projects, market and technology investigations, capability development efforts, and bottlenecks on existing projects. The product portfolio leadership team is responsible for tracking the employment of all product innovation resources and assigning them to these demands as they become available. Often, though, the resources to address an urgent demand are not readily at hand and trade-offs have to be made. Which project effort should we put on the shelf to free up the people needed to deal with this new obstacle? These crucial business decisions are an important part of the ongoing work performed by the portfolio leadership team and have a significant impact on the overall business success of product innovation efforts.

Staffing Product Innovation Projects

An important earmark of an effective resources allocation process is that all projects are staffed close to the level that minimizes time to completion. A common mistake of many businesses is investing in too many projects at one time so that each project is delayed by inadequate resources. In Chapter 3, an example was described that outlined the effect of altering the staffing approach on total revenue generated by two development projects. Serial projects that are fully staffed were shown to provide significant business advantages over concurrent understaffed projects.

Figure 8.10, illustrates the tradeoffs between staffing level, time to market, and project return. The numbers in this graph were derived from the authors' product development experience and reflect the relationships typical of a particular business situation that occurred years ago.[8] While every enterprise has relationships similar to those illustrated, the reader should not try to apply Figure 8.10 literally to a specific business case. This graph simply provides a visual model that higlights important relationships.

Introducing a particular new product generally involves a fixed amount of work. A few people can do that work in a long time, or more people can get it done in a shorter time. Over a fairly wide range of staffing levels, the total cost of doing this fixed amount of work remains fairly constant. Given these conditions, the project illustrated in Figure 8.10 takes a little over three years to complete with a staff of 8 and about two years with a staff of 12. With a larger staff the work gets done quicker, so the product is introduced sooner. As described in Chapter 3, the extinction time for

---

[8] Figure 8.10 is a plot of numbers generated by a spreadsheet model that approximates the nondiscounted cash flow depicted in Figure 3.1 between Definition Freeze and Extinction. The model was adjusted to match the performance of several projects from the authors' experience that addressed a particular business segment. The extinction time of the market window remains constant, while the introduction time varies with time-to-market (TTM). TTM, in turn, varies with staffing level. Monthly revenues and profits at maturity are assumed to be unaffected by introduction time. The model further assumes that the total work and cost to introduce a product is constant over the midrange of staffing level. The model is adjusted mathematically to reflect additional work required to introduce a product with both low and high staffing levels.

Return-On-Investment (ROI)

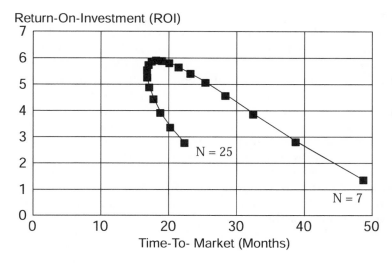

Figure 8.10   Effect of project staffing on time-to-market.

the product is unaffected by an earlier introduction so the market window gets wider as the time-to-market shrinks, and the total financial return from the product effort increases. A larger financial return divided by a fixed total cost implies that the total return-on-investment (ROI) grows as the time-to-market declines. ROI in Figure 8.10 thus grows from a value of about 3.0 at a staffing level of 8, to about 6.0 at a staffing level of 14 people.

Adding people to speed up a project, however, only works up to a point. Every project has an optimum staffing level, where the ROI is as high as possible. Below this staffing level, people may work efficiently but the project takes longer to complete. Above this level, time-to-market continues to decline a little, but people are underutilized and tend to get in each other's way. Productivity drops off and total project cost increases, so ROI declines. As even more people are added, the amount of communication required goes up dramatically and more time is spent in meetings. Time-to-market stops declining and productivity drops even further. A point is eventually reached where adding people to the project actually increases time-to-market and, coupled with even further reductions in productivity, causes ROI to plummet. The ROI curve for every project thus tends to reach a peak as staffing level is increased, fall off, and then tuck back under itself like the case illustrated in Figure 8.10.

The challenge for each product portfolio leadership team is to understand how these relationships work in their own business. Their business goal should be to maximize the ROI generated by each project, so they should strive to staff each project at its optimum level, which will generally be a just a little bit short of its minimum time-to-market point. Knowing the optimum staffing level for a given project with precision, though, is not usually possible. Instead, the leadership team must develop judgment and intuition about such things. Their leadership skills must include (1) knowing intuitively when to say "No" to a project manager who clamors for too many people, and (2) when to add people to a project effort that is understaffed. Since ROI is strongly affected by staffing level, the leadership team can greatly influence the business success of their new product efforts through the project staffing policies that they implement.

Staffing Capability Development Projects

Each product portfolio leadership team should assess its need to build and maintain a competitive product innovation capacity and then allocate an appropriate percentage of total product innovation investments to this purpose. The portion of the product innovation budget devoted these improvement efforts should vary with competitive circumstances. If the firm is behind the competition in key markets and fighting for survival, perhaps 15 percent of the budget or more should be invested in well planned and managed improvement initiatives. If a company is well ahead of the competition and simply desires to maintain that position, an investment of about 5 percent of the budget may be adequate until the situation changes.

Establishing and protecting this investment in building competitive capacity takes strong leadership. Each dollar spent here is a dollar that is not being spent getting new products out. The revenue impact of a new product is usually well understood throughout the enterprise, and it starts when the product is introduced. But the revenue impact of an improvement project is more obscure. An effort to improve the way that product innovators identify new business opportunities and define corresponding new products may require four people and a year to complete. When finished, this improved process may increase the revenue gain as much as 50 percent for each affected project. The revenue impact will eventually be tremendous, but before it can start, the improvement project must be completed and then the first projects to use the more effective process must complete their entire innovation cycle. The revenue impact of the improved process may not be felt until two or three years after the decision is made to invest in this effort. Launching and managing these projects requires clear vision and steady nerves on the part of the product portfolio leadership team.

To not make these investment, though, is a decision to leave things the way they are. There is an old saying:

If you keep on doing what you're doing,
you'll keep on getting what you're getting.

In business it is even worse than this. With no investments in competitive improvements, an enterprise will only continue with business as usual until the competition decides to change the ground rules. In marketplaces that are becoming ever more global, many enterprises have experienced a startling invasion of their markets by an unexpected competitor who refuses to play by the old rules. These competitors can change both the competitive terrain and the market fundamentals. They destabilize customer expectations and profit margins. They steal market share at an alarming rate. On the other hand, when leaders in an existing market invest in systematic improvements in their ability to introduce more competitive products faster, they actively discourage invasion by new competitors. Shareholder value depends to a large degree on the competitive position of a firm at the end of its forecast period. The fraction of the budget spent building product innovation capacity can thus directly impact shareholder value if these improvement efforts are well conceived and managed.

Improvement efforts, like product innovation projects, should be staffed for minimum time to completion. Just as with a new product effort, the payoff starts when the project is finished—the sooner the better. These efforts should also be managed and tracked as rigorously as product innovation projects, even more so. Because their financial return to the business can be far in the future, improvement projects need to have excellent plans and clear progress measures. These will relieve the anxieties of business leaders by assuring them that the effort is unfolding as it should. As long as improvement projects proceed as planned, business leaders will continue to invest and remain confident that these investments will eventually deliver their promised payback.

Staffing Investigations

Often the initial phase of a new product effort is to verify the product concept, both the market viability of the proposed product and its technical feasibility. The purpose of these efforts is to assemble enough information to enable the definition of a competitive new product and the project plans that will move it smoothly through development and into the market. Staffing at this point in the project will depend on the key questions that need to be answered. It may vary anywhere from a product manager and an engineering project manager working together part time, to perhaps two people working on the market investigation and three or four engineers investigating the technology. The people assigned to these tasks should have an affinity for this kind of work—not all individuals do. In making these assignments, product portfolio leaders should either work from a strong understanding of the inclinations of their own people, or rely on the recommendations of subordinates. Investigations can be a source of joy for some employees and a source of agony for others. This early work has a tremendous impact on the business outcome of the project so only the best people for these jobs should be assigned.

New product investigations should be an ongoing effort in a business enterprise, with a fairly constant percentage of the workforce assigned to these activities. At HP, for example, about 10 percent of the engineering staff was engaged in technology investigations at any given time. This level of activity produced good product ideas—and revealed some that didn't work—at a rate slightly higher than the capacity of the enterprise to introduce new products. As a result, there were always a few pretty good product concepts that were never developed. This is the desired balance for new product investigation activity. Of course, the right level of investment in investigations will vary from business to business. Each product portfolio leadership team must decide on the right level for that particular enterprise.

Staffing Bottleneck Recovery Efforts

Almost every project encounters obstacles and bottlenecks along the way. Support resources, such as technical publications or the engineering model shop, have limited capacity and sometimes cannot get the work out fast enough to keep all projects on schedule, so bottlenecks develop. Perhaps an engineer encounters unexpected technical problems with a design, and progress stalls. Often project managers can work these problems out among themselves, shifting work and schedules a little, or moving people around on the project. Occasionally, though, the solution of more serious problems lies beyond the control of the project manager. At this point, they become the responsibility of the product portfolio leadership team.

Bottlenecks and other obstacles to progress are always unplanned, so they call for unplanned redeployment of resources. As discussed in Chapter 3, the business cost of time lost to bottlenecks can be immense, so they need to be resolved quickly. The right people and resources need to be identified and brought to bear on the problem as soon as possible. An effective approach is for members of the product portfolio leadership team to meet with the project managers involved and discuss the best way to solve the issue. These discussions should be unconstrained—any person on any project in any department can be accessed, so long as their current task is of less priority than solving the current roadblock. Often the people who are best able to help are those who are assigned to new product investigations. Delaying an investigation to help a stalled project that is close to introduction is almost always a good business decision.

People and equipment outside the company should be considered as well. Specialists who can bring additional expertise to the problem are expensive, but can often save time that is worth many times their fee. Sometimes a special instrument or other kind of equipment can speed up the solution. An unexpected and very infrequent failure of an electromechanical product prototype required the use of a high-speed video device that could record the failure whenever it occurred and enable engineers to study the failure mechanism during replay. This specialized recording device was discovered at a local equipment rental firm, and was essential to the eventual solution of the problem. When project bottlenecks occur, the product portfolio leadership team must be ready to provide guidance and every resource needed to get the project moving again.

■ PROJECT TRACKING

Once project investments have been launched, they should be tracked and managed to ensure that they make acceptable progress toward their objectives and continue to make good business sense. Each of these investments, in its own way, is critical to the long-term success of the enterprise. They represent a significant fraction of the firm's investment portfolio and thus deserve ongoing attention and due diligence from the product portfolio leadership team.

Project tracking serves three very important functions. First, it creates a sense of accountability among the members of each project team. To get their project funded and staffed, they will have created plans, provided a business case for their project, and made commitments to deliver results. Knowing that they will be required to periodically demonstrate their progress to an interested product portfolio leadership team creates a healthy sense of urgency and accountability.

The second function of project tracking is that it provides information and learning for the product portfolio leadership team. It expands their knowledge base. As they review projects and respond to issues, the members of the leadership team learn what works on these projects, and what does not work. They see and experience the pitfalls that derail project efforts and cause delays. They develop judgment about all aspects of the project—staffing levels, schedules, and business impact. As project teams investigate, learn, and report, the leadership team gains valuable information about the realities of the new products and capability improvements that are in progress.

A key element in this learning process is the postmortem or retrospective analysis. Each project, whether successfully completed or cancelled, should end with a retrospective analysis. A common format for this analysis is a facilitated workshop that involves key members of the project team in an informal setting. The objective of this event should be to identify and record lessons from the project experience. These lessons can relate to the formal phase-gate process, the business plan, assumptions that were made, things that went right, things that went wrong, or anything else about the project. The goal is to learn from the experience and to apply this new knowledge for the improved execution of subsequent projects. The portfolio leadership team is responsible for receiving this knowledge and seeing that it is applied effectively to improve future product innovation activities.

Finally, project tracking provides essential feedback and guidance for project teams. As the product portfolio leadership team interacts with each project, they bring their broader perspective and judgment to bear on project issues. As projects move from the planning phase into harsh reality, decisions and trade-offs have to be made. Initial designs fail and new approaches have to be crafted. Product features are altered and manufacturing cost is impacted. While most of these decisions are made by the project manager, they are reviewed by the product portfolio leadership team and judged against strategic and financial requirements. As a project deviates from plan, the leadership team should carefully assess and monitor risk areas. Occasionally, a project manager will be asked to change direction or focus on a different goal. The portfolio team may decide that manufacturing cost for a given product has moved beyond acceptable limits. In this case, they would direct the project manager to redouble efforts to reduce product cost even, perhaps, at the expense of reducing product performance or slipping the introduction date. The product portfolio leadership team is ultimately responsible for the business return from each project investment. They should keep track of their portfolio and make the best possible decisions with regard to each investment—whether to continue on course, change direction, or pull out and cut their losses.

➤ Product Innovation Projects

The phase-gate process, discussed in Chapter 7, is the primary tool for tracking product innovation projects. Each phase in the process should have clearly defined deliverables. The periodic and gate reviews designed into this process give portfolio managers frequent opportunities both to review progress on these deliverables and to assess the performance of the project relative to its plan. Both project and portfolio managers should be familiar with the deliverables that will be discussed at each review and the questions that must be asked. A project manager should not call for a gate review until the project team is ready to answer these questions.

The behavior of portfolio managers at these reviews greatly influences the performance of each product innovation project team. This is much like a situation in which a teacher has assigned homework to students. The teacher's behavior determines the response of the students to the assignment. If the teacher fails to collect assigned work and grade it, students quickly learn to ignore these assignments. Likewise, the behavior of portfolio managers in periodic and gate reviews has a major influence on the performance of the project team. The goal should be to instill each project team with a sense of both urgency and accountability so that the members come to each review well prepared. Effective execution of project review responsibilities is discussed later in this chapter.

In addition to periodic and gate reviews, informal project tracking methods are also important. Effective product portfolio leaders frequently wander around and interact with members of project teams, particularly with those who are within their own department. These informal conversations facilitate a high level of intellectual honesty and allow the portfolio manager to gain clear, accurate, and timely insight into project issues. A friendly smile and a cup of coffee in the hand will help ensure that this happens. Bottlenecks and other important project issues can be discovered and dealt with much more quickly this way.

➤ Capability Development Projects

Projects aimed at improving product innovation capacity are generally relatively few in number and unique in nature. In view of this, having an standardized phase-gate process for these projects makes little sense. Instead, each capability development effort generally settles first on a process for achieving its objectives and then creates a plan that reflects that process. The plan should outline the major task milestones as well as describe their key objectives, deliverables, and overall schedule for completion. It should also describe the resources required and indicate the times of periodic and milestone reviews. Finally, the plan should identify project progress measures that the portfolio leadership team can monitor. As mentioned, the payoff from capability development work can sometimes take a long time. The resources invested in these efforts subtract directly from those available for new product efforts that can create a known level of revenue growth and financial return. Unless they have a clear plan to follow and can see that progress on capability development efforts is happening according plan, high-level managers can get impatient with continued investment in these efforts.

➤ Investigations

The goal of investigation efforts is to learn and explore—to scout the market and technology terrain ahead. The product portfolio leadership team should make sure that each investigation team has clear questions to answer, and clear time constraints on their effort from the start. Tracking these projects becomes a simple matter of periodically reviewing what has been learned, assessing the rate and direction of progress, and providing feedback and guidance to the investigation team. The perspective and judgment of the product portfolio leadership team are essential in establishing the business impact of the knowledge gained. Their understanding and guidance is required to keep each investigation project focused on the most important areas of uncertainty.

The deliverables from investigation projects are answers to key questions about a specific area of business opportunity. A market investigation will answer questions such as:

➤ How much new revenue does this new opportunity promise?

➤ Who are the customers and what criteria do they use in their decisions to buy?

➤ What profit margins will this market support?

➤ Who are the competitors in this market arena and how do we compare?

➤ What is our value proposition for customers in this market?

➤ What new products will best address this area of opportunity?

➤ What sales and distribution issues are related to this opportunity?

Technology investigations will answer these questions:

➤ What technologies are required to address the given market opportunity?

➤ What level of product functionality can be achieved?

➤ What are the critical design parameters and design rules for each new technology?

➤ Do these technologies imply new product support issues?

➤ What are the relevant intellectual property issues?

A new product effort can be launched whenever the answers to these questions become sufficiently clear and favorable. The role of the product portfolio leadership team is to keep each investigation effort on track toward this goal.

➤ The Gatekeeper Role

The reviews in the phase-gate process described in Chapter 7 are called "gate reviews" because they are like gates that each project must pass through to move from one phase to the next. An important responsibility of the product portfolio leadership team is thus to provide "gatekeepers" for these reviews—appropriate members of the leadership team who can ensure that each project has satisfied prescribed criteria before it leaves its current phase. As gatekeepers, members of the portfolio leadership team apply due diligence to their new product investments and create a sense of accountability among the members of each project team reviewed. Ideally, candidates for the role of gatekeeper should be specified in documentation that describes the firm's product innovation process. When a new product effort is launched, specific members of the portfolio leadership team should be assigned to act as gatekeepers for that project. Members of each project team should thus understand from the start who will be reviewing their work.

The Gatekeeping Process

Figure 8.11 shows how the gatekeeping process works to keep projects on track. An important criterion for a successful project is a clear set of objectives, depicted at the left-hand side of the diagram. These objectives launch the project in a direction that, at least at the time the project is begun, aligns with both business needs and the priorities of the product portfolio leadership team. Unless a means for tracking projects is in place, however, the work done by a project team can eventually diverge widely from the expectations of high-level managers.

The project team and the portfolio management team live in different worlds, and both are influenced by different forces over time. Even with the best intentions, the actual results achieved by a project team can wander off track under the influence of project realities—ambiguities and inconsistencies in the original product specification, the laws of physics, and unexpected results from vendors, to name a few. While the portfolio management team understands the initial objectives given to the project team, they will interpret these objectives differently as time passes and their perspective changes. The expectations formed by these business leaders depend on their view of the business world in which they operate. Over time, they learn new things about this world. Other

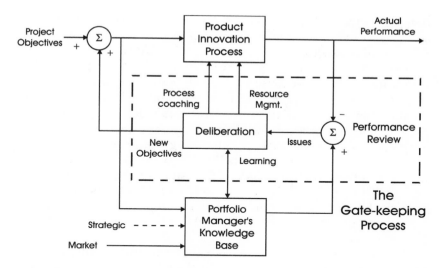

Figure 8.11   The gatekeeping process aligns project results
and management expectations.

companies, for example, are becoming more competitive by improving their work processes and speeding up time-to-market. Or perhaps customers are pushing on product cost. Maybe a new competitor is invading the company's "home turf." As their views change, so do their expectations of the new products under development in their portfolio. Without a gatekeeping process to periodically involve high-level managers with each project in the portfolio, actual project results and management expectations can become disconnected.

The gatekeeping process is included inside the dashed outline in Figure 8.11, and includes both a review of project performance and deliberations on the information gathered. The performance review includes an examination of the current versions of the project plan and the business case. Actual project results are scrutinized as well. As portfolio managers compare the actual state of the project and its plans with their presumptions, they can either recalibrate their expectations or identify performance issues that need to be resolved. For example, the manufacturing cost of a new product may have grown a little higher than promised. In some situations, this may be acceptable and portfolio managers simply reset their expectations. In other cases, however, market conditions may have changed to a degree that makes the new manufacturing cost unacceptable. Under these circumstances, a product-cost issue must be addressed.

Once the performance review is complete, gatekeepers deliberate on issues that have arisen. Their objective is to determine how to best manage their ongoing investment for business success. The actions that they can take include altering the resources for the project, coaching the project team on more effective application of work processes, or, perhaps, changing the project direction or objectives. Before the gate review is closed, action items related to the issues being worked are identified and assigned to individuals, along with completion dates and follow-up plans. The issues may be such that they must be resolved before the project can move on to the next phase. In this case, the plan for achieving phase completion is established.

The results of an effective gatekeeping process include both learning and guidance. Both the portfolio managers involved and the project team learn from an effective gate review. Portfolio managers learn about the project's specific results to date, and about issues and obstacles that have occurred. They gain experience from examining the current situation on each project. The project team receives feedback from portfolio managers that reflects a more current view of business realities and, perhaps, a higher level of business perspective and judgment. They may also receive guidance and coaching as a midcourse correction to keep the project well aligned with desired business goals.

Occasionally, the business case for a project is no longer viable. Perhaps a competitor has introduced an unexpected new product that obsoletes the product under development. Or a technical issue may have arisen that threatens the feasibility of the product or compromises product performance to an unacceptable degree. When these circumstances arise, portfolio managers have no choice but to cancel the project and cut their losses. This outcome from a gate review is rare and uncomfortable, but represents a tough and extremely valuable business decision.

The Power of Effective Gatekeeping

Portfolio managers who carry out their gatekeeping responsibilities effectively can have an incredibly powerful and beneficial influence on the firm's product innovation capacity. If they understand best practices in product innovation and use this understanding as a standard of comparison during gate reviews, they can, over time, install these practices in their own new product efforts.

Imagine a new product organization that, in the beginning, uses only the most haphazard processes for product innovation, but that has an enlightened group of people on the product portfolio leadership team. A new product effort is launched with clear objectives and the project team proceeds with its work in the usual ad hoc and disjointed manner. Because portfolio leaders have a solid understanding of how an effective new product effort should proceed, their expectations are both high and realistic. At the first gate review, the results achieved so far by the project team are disappointing, and many serious issues are identified. The project team is informed of the shortcomings in project results and provided with coaching on objectives, work processes, and methods that will help them in achieving a more acceptable output. They are then sent back to work on the issues identified at the gate review. Through their resolve and unmistakable expectations, the gatekeepers have instilled a strong sense of accountability in the project team. Work on the issue set proceeds until the project team feels that it is ready to pass the gate review, and another review is scheduled. At this point, their work will either be acceptable to reviewing gatekeepers or the rework cycle is repeated until results reach an acceptable level.

When portfolio leaders are finally satisfied with the results achieved in the first phase, they allow the project to proceed, but provide the project team with a clear message about how to do the work in the second phase. They describe both the process to follow and the desired results at the next gate review. Once again, the project team leaves the review meeting with a clear understanding of both the expectations and the resolve of the gatekeepers.

As work proceeds, portfolio leaders take note of who on the project team is responding appropriately, and who is resisting the efforts of gatekeepers. Recalcitrant members of the team receive special attention, and the most resistant offenders may even be removed. Only two responses to pressure from gatekeepers should be allowed. Project team members can either respond appropriately or offer a rationale about work processes or project results that is good enough to reset the expectations of gatekeepers. One way or another, the expectations of gatekeepers and the work of the project team must move into alignment. If the gatekeeping process is performed in this manner, the behavior and performance of even the most disorganized project team will inevitably improve and mold itself to the expectations of the product portfolio leadership team. As word gets around that the gatekeepers are a force to be reckoned with, other project teams will fall in line more easily and new product efforts will begin to flow more smoothly.

But this is a double-edged sword. If gatekeepers fail to have high and appropriate expectations or fail to enforce a sense of accountability among project team members, gate reviews will, over time, become simply rubber-stamp affairs, with little or no authority over project efforts. When this happens, the discipline and best practices exercised by project teams tend to fall into disrepair as people learn that they can cut corners without reprisal. The gate review becomes like a homework assignment issued by a professor who never collects or grades the papers.

Earmarks of a Successful Gate Review

Regardless of the details of the product innovation process, effective gate reviews share some common attributes. First of all, those who are present in the role of gatekeeper behave as if the project is spending their own, personal money—they have the mind-set of a venture capitalist. High-level managers who come into gate reviews with this attitude test everything they learn and every decision to ensure that it supports the best possible business outcome from the project. Their objective for participating in gate reviews is to exercise due diligence on their investments in every way they can.

A second attribute of successful gate reviews is that information appears in a common format across all new product efforts in the enterprise. Both gatekeepers and project managers know the important issues that must be discussed at any particular review and a common and efficient format has evolved for presenting this information. Each project keeps and presents a current project data sheet that has the same look and feel as those from other projects. Project plans and schedules are presented in a familiar format. Project expenditures and budget information are always presented in a familiar way. Common presentation formats minimize the time that project managers have to invest in preparing for a review and they minimize the effort that gatekeepers have to invest in understanding what they see at gate reviews. Finally, common formats serve as a checklist to ensure that all important issues are on the agenda.

The formal definition of each project phase should include a statement of objectives for the phase and a list of deliverables to be generated by the project team. The high-level managers responsible for reviewing this work should be armed with a standard checklist for each gate review based on this definition. This checklist provides gatekeepers with an outline of what to cover at the review and prompts them to ask key questions. In an effective phase review, the project manager will use the gatekeepers' checklist in preparing for the review to ensure that all important issues are covered. Everyone on both sides knows what needs to be discussed and how it should be presented—there are no secrets and no surprises.

A successful gate review will simply focus on progress according to plan. Members of the project team who are present will have the look and feel of a team—they will agree with and support each other and generally speak with one voice on all important issues. Estimates of schedule, budget, product cost, and product performance will remain consistent with previous disclosures, with only small adjustments that are well justified. Irreconcilable differences between key members of the project team—particularly marketing and engineering—should serve as a red flag to gatekeepers. Also chronic instability in project schedules or other estimates is a sign of trouble on a project. Finally, gatekeepers should watch for lack of progress on key issues that have been reported earlier. Any of these signals indicates that a project may need more help staying on track. More frequent and less formal monitoring of the effort by high-level managers is probably a good idea.

Common Mistakes by Gatekeepers

As important as the gatekeeper role may be, in many companies it is not executed effectively. The causes for this breakdown in the product innovation process can be lumped into five categories:

1. Poor attendance.
2. Lack of preparation.
3. Poor meeting participation.
4. Ineffective follow-through.
5. Inappropriate recognition or punishment.

The members of the portfolio leadership team who are assigned to gatekeeper roles are usually very busy people. They have many conflicting demands on their time. Having to attend gate reviews is often viewed as just another item on a plate that is already overflowing with other important obligations. Their reactions to this situation often undermines the gatekeepers' effectiveness. Sometimes they respond to what they believe are higher priority interruptions, and simply fail to show up at gate reviews. The review proceeds without them and their absence casts a shadow of doubt over the importance of the event and any decisions that are made. In less severe cases, they show up late and cause a delay in the start of the meeting. Some high-level managers let other work bump gate reviews from their schedule so that these events are subject to chronic rescheduling. When they finally do occur, they are long overdue. Often the project has had to proceed without review to stay on schedule. In each case, the signal to the project team is the same, "This gate review is not important enough to deserve appropriate attention from high-level managers." This signal from gatekeepers is likely to cause project team members to also view gate reviews as unimportant, and shape their behavior.

Sometimes gatekeepers show up for review meetings with a thousand other things on their mind. They have not read prestudy material that was distributed prior to the meeting. Sometimes their comments and questions reflect a disturbing ignorance: either of project details that they should know or of the product innovation process itself. These symptoms are readily apparent to project team members at the meeting and undermine the sense of accountability that should be instilled by the gate review process. How can project team members feel accountable to someone who doesn't understand what is going on? Instead, they tend to discount that person's opinions and authority.

In other cases, the behavior of gatekeepers at review meetings may reflect a lack of commitment to the success of the project, or perhaps, a lack of high expectations for project team performance. For instance, gatekeepers may simply listen impassively as the meeting progresses, and never indicate approval, disapproval, or even curiosity. Gatekeepers need to show interest and ask tough questions that reflect their sense of importance for the project outcome as well as their ability to understand and evaluate project results. Their behavior during gate review meetings is of primary importance in establishing an appropriate sense of accountability throughout the project team.

Project teams often must look to gatekeepers for decisions and support that affect the continued success of the project. The people assigned to gatekeeper roles should have full authority to represent the entire product portfolio leadership team at each gate review. They should come to review meetings ready to make necessary decisions and then back these decisions up with appropriate follow-through. If they are uncomfortable making a decision on the spot, they must commit to any further action required to get the project what it needs. On occasion, decisions made at gate review meetings fail to stick for various reasons, or promised follow-on actions fail to occur. Perhaps someone higher on the portfolio leadership team overrules a gatekeeper's decision. Or perhaps gatekeepers simply fail to implement what they promised. Whatever the reason, the failure of gatekeeper promises undermines the trust that project team members place in their high-level managers.

Gate reviews provide an excellent opportunity for gatekeepers to recognize and promote role-model behavior on project teams. Recognizing this behavior appropriately is a sure way to encourage more of the same. Appropriate recognition, however, should exhibit three criteria. First, it should highlight behavior that is important to project success. Second, it should acknowledge appropriately all individuals who have contributed to a particular accomplishment. Third, it should demonstrate the intelligence and credibility of the manager who is handing out recognition. Sometimes managers give the wrong person credit for an achievement, or in handing out accolades, they reflect an ignorance of what has really happened or what really matters. Recognition such as this rarely accomplishes its intended purpose and, instead, undermines the authority of these managers among members of the team.

The cultural situation can affect which forms of recognition are appropriate. In Western cultures, public recognition of individuals who have demonstrated exemplary performance can be very constructive. In some Oriental cultures, on the other hand, such recognition can be completely humiliating to the individual who has been put in the spotlight. A good test is to pay attention to what forms of recognition invoke happiness or envy among peers. If a particular form of recognition makes people happy for the person who is receiving it, or if it creates a mild sense of envy among that person's peers, it is probably appropriate. If an act of recognition is to encourage more of a given behavior, everyone who witnesses it should want to receive some of the same.

On rare occasions, the authors have seen punishment handed out to individuals at gate review meetings. The old rule of four Ps always applies, "Praise in Public, Punish in Private." Sometimes tough feedback is needed at gate review meetings. If a project team has failed to meet expectations, they need to be told this—impersonally, clearly, and simply. They should, however, hear this as a message to the team. If particular individuals have failed and are in need of corrective feedback, these personal messages should be saved for a later, private discussion. When a manager delivers punishment to an individual in public, it has a terrible effect both on the individual, and on everyone who witnesses the act or even hears about it later. "If this can happen to that person, it can happen to me." On one particular project team, the fear of punishment was so strong and so pervasive that individuals backed completely away from taking any initiative at all. They simply waited to be told what to do. If things didn't work out, the responsibility then fell on the manager who had assigned the task. The impact on project productivity was devastating.

■ BOTTLENECK MANAGEMENT

Early detection is critical to successful management of bottlenecks that occur in new product efforts, but this is sometimes difficult. Those whose work is in trouble are often reluctant to publicize that fact. The best method for overcoming this reluctance is the technique of management by wandering around (MBWA) that is commonly associated with HP. Project managers and higher-level managers alike take time to wander through the project area and have frequent and informal chats with various members of the project team. "Hi, how's it going? How's the family? What are you working on? What's your approach to solving that problem? How's it working out? Do you have everything you need?" Symptoms to look for during these encounters are signs of stress, skepticism toward the project plan or schedule, a lack of viability in the approach to a solution, frequent changes in approach, or little progress since the previous chat. This gentle probing for information should, above all, be nonthreatening to members of the project team.

In the authors' early product development experience at HP, the engineering manager and our boss, Tom, was rarely in his office when we needed him. To find him, though, all we had to do was stand quietly for a moment and listen. Sure enough, before long we would hear his distinctive laugh from somewhere out in the R&D lab. Homing in on this sound, we would always find him in some engineer's cubicle, with his cowboy boots up on the desk swapping stories with the engineer and laughing. Later we might learn that engineer's design was in trouble. Tom would, with little fanfare, temporarily assign another person with just the right skills to help out. Tom's style was always friendly and the engineers generally enjoyed his visits. His MBWA was instrumental in keeping all projects in the development lab moving smoothly.

In this new age of telecommuting, geographically dispersed project teams, and virtual corporations, the kind of physical wandering around that Tom did can be difficult, even impossible. Other methods of informal information gathering are needed that will undoubtedly involve emerging telecommunications and Internet technologies. E-mail, videoconferencing, and chat rooms all help, but they are not yet like eye-to-eye contact, arm waving, and huddling over a tablet together, sketching diagrams. Managers will continue to struggle with this until a suitable solution evolves.

Once contingency action has been taken for a bottleneck, progress should be tracked by a member of the product portfolio team, usually the relevant functional manager, very closely. Are the steps that were taken working? Are there visible signs of progress? Can we try other resources or solutions? Is the effort back on track? Is the solution that has resulted sufficiently robust? This close management should continue until the bottleneck has been completely resolved. Once this has occurred, other people or resources that have been applied should be released back to their original assignments.

■ CLOSING THE LEARNING LOOP

Each project experience provides an opportunity for the product portfolio leadership team to learn about the capacity of their enterprise to innovate new products and services, and can highlight opportunities for making new product efforts more competitive. The aspects of each project that went well, and those that went poorly, both provide information about how well product innovation processes and tools are working. In particular, understanding the root causes of bottlenecks on a given project can point to improvements that will make subsequent projects proceed faster and more smoothly. Capitalizing on this learning, though, takes conscious and ongoing effort.

A final step in the formal product innovation process employed by each project team should be a project retrospective analysis that reviews the events of the project and systematically identifies ways it could have proceeded more smoothly and effectively. In this process, project team members are led through a workshop experience that systematically captures both their recollections about the project just completed and their ideas for improvement in both work processes and tools. A report on this analysis should be both archived and presented to the product portfolio leadership team. In response, the portfolio team can then identify actions to implement desired improvements. Ideally, these steps will be integrated into (1) plans for capability improvements, (2) current gatekeeping methods and practices, and (3) documented product innovation processes. An enterprise that learns well from experience will grow in its ability to serve its customers. In the words of de Geus:[9]

> *The ability to learn faster than your competitors may be the only sustainable competitive advantage.*
>
> Arie P. de Geus
> Royal Dutch/Shell

■ CONCLUSION

This chapter has outlined critically important leadership roles that, to a significant degree, establish the success of the innovation engine in a business enterprise. These roles have been linked to a closed-loop process that highlights the key elements of product portfolio planning and management. The long-term growth in both revenues and shareholder value that a company enjoys are strongly influenced by how well the roles defined here are executed. This chapter has stressed an understanding of the importance of each of these leadership roles and how they work together to establish a competitive new product program.

---

[9] de Geus, Arie P., "Planning as Learning," *Harvard Business Review,* March/April, 1988, p. 70–74.

In Chapter 2, critical success factors were described that drive growth in both revenues and shareholder value. Successful execution of the leadership roles described in this chapter has a direct impact on the performance levels for these growth drivers. Excellent strategic planning and an insightful product road map dramatically increase the levels of revenue gain performance. They also influence profit margins and thereby increase the product innovation investment rate that can be supported.

The discussion in Chapter 2 highlighted the competitive position of a firm at the end of its forecast period as a primary determinant of shareholder value. The growth in market value for firms such as Microsoft, Intel, and CISCO Systems serves as a compelling example of this relationship. Successful execution of the high-level management roles described here has a direct and decisive effect on the competitive level of future performance for a business enterprise. Strategic planning and efforts to build its knowledge base both improve a firm's ability to compete in the future. Investments in both performance improvements and capability development also directly impact the competitive level of future performance. If these efforts are well conceived, and if they are more effective than similar investments made by competitors, they will ensure future growth in shareholder value.

Above all, this chapter makes clear that ownership of the new product program lies not with the engineering manager, as some may believe, but with the entire product portfolio leadership team that is led by the person in the business unit who has profit-and-loss responsibility. To be sure, the engineering manager is a member of this group and thus shares in these responsibilities, but this individual is only one among several members of the team. The entire team is responsible for guiding the new product program with wisdom, insight, and judgment. The leadership team working together must establish its direction and its priorities. The team is responsible for investing resources in only the best new product opportunities. Once these investments have been made, the team is responsible for tracking progress with due diligence. The leadership team is collectively responsible for preparing the enterprise to meet the new product challenges of the future. And, if the new product program is not performing at a competitive level, the entire leadership team is responsible for improving its performance. They are the stewards of the innovation engine and jointly determine whether it competes successfully.

Desired Upper Management Behaviors:
Leading, Managing, and Building the Innovation Engine

➤ Strive to become smarter than the executives at firms with whom you compete.

➤ Invest yourself in setting an exciting, long-term direction for your new product efforts.

➤ Manage new product investments as if you are spending your own money.

➤ Make project teams feel both empowered and accountable.

➤ Commit to resolving your three most critical issues that impair competitive performance in product innovation.

➤ Wander around and talk to people in a way that encourages intellectual honesty.

Chapter 9

Managing Improvements to the Innovation Process

> [Leaders] think in terms of renewal. The routine manager tends to accept organizational structure and process as it exists. The leader ... seeks the revisions of process and structure required by ever-changing reality.
>
> John W. Gardner
> *On Leadership*

An important responsibility of high-level managers, as described in Chapter 8, is developing the capability of the enterprise to compete more effectively in the future. Achievement of this goal has a direct impact on growing shareholder value. Developing new capabilities, however, and overhauling old ones that no longer perform at competitive levels, requires change—in work processes and tools, in management methods, and in the way individuals behave at work on a day-to-day basis. Along with their other important duties, business leaders are also responsible for initiating and managing this change. To do this, they must identify key performance issues, initiate corrective actions, and then monitor these initiatives to make sure that they produce the desired improvements in business performance.

Once performance issues have been identified—in business processes such as product innovation, order fulfillment, or customer service—benchmarking similar processes at other companies has been a popular method for learning more competitive methods. Alternatively, companies turn to university executive programs, consulting firms, and even plain old inventiveness and

251

common sense. Even when better methods are discovered, though, business leaders sometimes have great difficulty implementing new work patterns and methods. It often seems as if their firm has developed an enterprisewide "immune system" that rejects these new ways of working with almost 100 percent efficiency.

The purpose of this chapter is to outline methods for defining, planning, and managing performance improvement efforts that can suppress the corporate immune system and enable substantial advances in business results. These techniques have evolved through experiences—both good and bad—with dozens of business process improvement efforts. They have proven effective in a wide range of industries and business situations, and can transform the improvement of capability into a systematic, straightforward process.

This discussion begins with an outline of the improvement cycle that must be undertaken by the high-level management team. Following this, some general principles are offered to explain the immune response and highlight opportunities for improving the effectiveness of changes. Building on these principles, a general framework for performance initiatives delineates the essential elements of an effective project. Common barriers that frustrate improvement efforts are outlined next; this chapter then closes with a discussion of the time dynamics typical to performance improvement activities.

■ THE BUSINESS IMPROVEMENT CYCLE

Improving the competitiveness of a business without disrupting ongoing operations is tricky. Doing this is, in many ways, like a practice that was common to automobile racing in the early 1900s. Engines were so unreliable in those days that each car would carry both a driver and a mechanic. As the race progressed, a car's engine would inevitably begin to lose power. Perhaps oil seeping past poorly fitted rings would foul a spark plug. A skilled driver could feel even slight changes in performance and alert the mechanic to the symptoms. The mechanic would then climb out on the fender and work on the engine, diagnosing and then repairing the problem while speeding down the track. A winning effort included not only the ability to drive the car fast, but also to quickly sense changes in performance, and then execute repairs while hurtling down the course. A winning effort in business requires these same abilities (1) to manage normal operations, (2) to quickly sense a loss in competitive performance, and (3) to diagnose and repair performance issues without disrupting normal business operations.

Figure 9.1 outlines the elements of a business improvement process that works to identify performance issues and restore competitive performance. Just like the driver of the race car, business leaders need to develop a feel for the operation of their business and its performance relative to competitors. They must be able to sense when the business is falling behind and initiate corrective action. This is accomplished by the "summing junction" at the left side of the diagram, the circle with the Σ in it. This symbolic device designates a comparison or difference operation. The information carried by arrows coming into this junction designated with a minus sign are subtracted from or compared with the information brought in by those arrows designated by a plus sign. The outgoing arrow conveys the difference or comparison.

Business issues are identified in Figure 9.1 by comparing the knowledge accumulated by business leaders, and their visions and goals for competitive performance with knowledge about the level of performance of current business operations. As current performance falls behind what it was in the past, or behind that of competitors, the summing junction produces relevant issues. Likewise, as the vision and goals of business leaders for more competitive performance exceed the performance available from

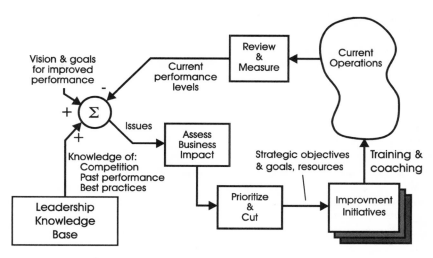

Figure 9.1   The business improvement cycle.

current operations, issues are identified that point the way toward new capabilities that are needed. As the diagram indicates, the accumulated knowledge of business leaders, as discussed in Chapter 8, and their goals for more competitive performance are important inputs that motivate and set the direction for future improvements.

For example, imagine that current operations in a company are producing revenue, but at a declining annual growth rate, much like the scenario described in Chapter 4. High-level managers are aware that this is due, at least in part, to loss of market share to competitors that have recently invaded the company's home turf. The current rate of revenue growth compares unfavorably with historical performance, the growth in revenues enjoyed by competitors, and the vision of success held by high-level management. In this case, the line coming out of the summing junction in Figure 9.1 will convey an issue regarding unfavorable revenue growth rates.

Business leaders should periodically meet as a group to consider the state of their business, identify competitive issues, and create a strategic plan for possible corrective actions. A facilitated workshop is an effective format for this activity. Typically, though, a long "laundry list" of issues will be identified that must be analyzed and prioritized. Only a few improvement efforts should be supported at any one time. Generally, resources for such investments are limited and launching too many concurrent activities simply diffuses the attention and support that each effort gets. As Figure 9.1 shows, the issues set should, instead, be assessed on the basis of business impact. The issues that, if corrected, would yield the greatest impact on business results should go to the top of the list. A business with three or four well-staffed improvement efforts underway is usually doing about all that it can to become and stay competitive.

Once the strategy for performance improvement has been set and the short list of issues to be addressed is in hand, projects should be planned and launched to correct each issue in the shortest possible time. The output of each project will, in general, be training and coaching to alter various business processes and shift the on-the-job behavior of targeted work groups. The rule is: No change in behavior means no improvement in business performance. If you keep on doing what you are doing, you will keep on getting what you have been getting. So each project needs to focus on changing behavior in ways that improve business performance.

As each initiative has its beneficial effect on current operations, the measured level of performance will improve. The information fed back to the summing junction will then, over time, reflect the desired increase in competitive capability. As this happens, the comparisons will become more favorable and the specific issue being addressed will become less of a concern. The corrective loop described in Figure 9.1, if effectively implemented, thus acts over time to reduce the severity of performance issues and transform them into areas of competitive advantage.

The authors first experienced this loop at work in HP during the late 1980s. Top executives, in comparing HP's performance with that of the competition, became increasingly concerned with the time that typical HP product innovation efforts took to bring new products to market. This issue became one element in an overall performance improvement strategy and was assigned to the corporate engineering group. As discussed later, the corporate engineering group implemented several corrective actions that, over several years, helped improve HP's time-to-market performance and changed this area of concern into a source of competitive advantage.

■ ECONOMIC FUNDAMENTALS THAT GOVERN INDIVIDUAL BEHAVIOR

Changing the behavior of individuals in the workplace is often difficult. Individual workers, especially professional employees, are often autonomous in planning and executing their daily efforts. Once people have learned a pattern of activity, they may be loath to adopt new work methods. Thus efforts aimed at improving a work group's results often meet with stiff resistance. One label for this resistance is the "Not Invented Here (NIH)" syndrome, a phenomenon particularly prevalent among engineers and other professionals who are convinced that they already know the best methods for doing their work. The NIH syndrome is, in effect, a mental immune system that repels new ideas about work methods such as how to accomplish an engineering solution or how to implement a new product.[1]

But why would people reject ideas or work methods that can make their efforts more effective? Why are they more comfortable continuing with old, familiar work patterns? What governs the choices that they make and attitudes that they form relative to

---

[1] Patterson, Marvin L. *Accelerating Innovation: Improving the Process of Product Development.* New York: Van Nostrand-Reinhold, 1993.

proposed improvements? The answers to these questions are essential in designing and implementing an effective improvement initiative.

The way people behave and the choices that they make on a day-to-day basis seems to result from an inherent ability that they have to work a kind of mental economic equation. The idea is simple: Most people are skilled at optimizing their personal resources and protecting their sense of well-being. The choices they make and their behavior in both their work and personal lives reflect their efforts to do this. The difficult part is understanding what currencies they are considering in their mental economic equation at any given time. Each of us values many different forms of personal currency, and the present value of our mental balance sheet establishes our sense of well-being. The value of each form of currency rises and falls, depending on the specifics of our immediate situation. Money is the form of currency that everyone assumes is most highly valued, but even its worth rises and falls with circumstances. Discerning the personal currencies that an individual is concerned about at any given moment will make that person's behavior much more comprehensible. A few of the kinds of currency that individuals may value are:

➤ Self-esteem.

➤ Sense of accomplishment.

➤ Appropriate recognition.

➤ Freedom from fear.

➤ Financial reward.

➤ Comfort level.

➤ Fun.

➤ Personal values, such as honesty, trust, integrity, and respect.

As people work their mental economic equations, they make cost-benefit trade-offs, and different people in similar situations may exhibit radically different behaviors. Everyone knows people in their organization who work hard and others who hardly work. Why are there such different responses to the work situation? Those who work hard may value a sense of accomplishment, or they might hold integrity and honesty as strong personal values. They may thus feel compelled to produce an honest day's work for a day's pay. Or those who work hard may just be looking for a raise in pay. Those who hardly work may place more value on fun or, perhaps, on their own comfort level than they do on their sense of accomplishment. If hardly working carries a low risk of penalties, in terms of personal currencies that they value, these individuals can optimize the enjoyment they experience at work or their comfort level with little or no apparent cost.

As to why people might respond to well-intended improvement efforts with the NIH attitude, well-established professionals are used to being rewarded for solving problems and accomplishing objectives. They typically develop a sense of pride in their personal capabilities. Depending on their level of experience, they have seen and tried many new ideas and have selected a reliable set of operating principles over time. In fact, those principles have been instrumental to their current success. They have seen many new approaches that initially seemed valuable, but proved unworkable in the end. They understand the cost in time and energy involved with trying a new idea, and are justifiably cautious when asked to adopt new approaches to old problems. They feel that, in the end, they will be rewarded if they get the job done, and if not, they will be held responsible for any delays or failure. New approaches or methodologies that are pushed on them from outside their own group are, in their mind, likely to cause problems for which they will be held accountable. Even if new methods are effective, they are someone else's brainchild and not a source of pride or reward to the local professional. So the NIH response is the result of people having to assume new risks without any apparent promise of reward. NIH is therefore simply a good solution to each person's personal economic equation.

Overcoming this resistance requires modifying the personal economics for each involved individual in a way that is favorable to their acceptance of needed change. The next section describes an effective approach for doing this.

■ FACTORS THAT ENCOURAGE CHANGE

Figure 9.2 describes four essential elements of an improvement program. These elements, when effectively applied in balance with each other, have proven effective in overcoming the natural resistance to change, enlisting people's best efforts in improvement initiatives, and managing and guiding these projects. In

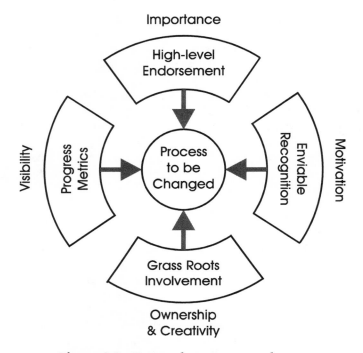

Figure 9.2 Factors that encourage change.

mathematical terms, this set of four factors that encourage change seems to be both necessary and sufficient to get the job done.

➤ High-Level Endorsement

The first role that high-level managers play in effectively launching an improvement initiative is to endorse the need to resolve a particular business performance issue. This endorsement instills a sense of importance for the business issue throughout the group of involved employees. Effective endorsement is sincere, ongoing, and consistent. It focuses on the problem at hand and the need for a solution. Every opportunity to communicate about the issue should be seized. The business issue should be described in simple terms that everyone can understand. Under no circumstances, though, should this communication dictate specific remedies for the problem. The objective instead is to make this competitive business issue a common goal that all must work on to resolve.

If this endorsement is effective, it will alter the value of personal currencies in each individual's economic equation in a motivational direction. Those with strong personal values for accomplishment or responsibility will perceive an increased value in these currencies. For others who are more interested in recognition, power, or financial rewards, the sense of importance from effective endorsement may offer an opportunity to gain attention and advance in terms of either salary or position.

➤ Grassroots Involvement

Once a sense of importance for resolving a particular issue has been established, expert practitioners and other thought leaders in the organization should be engaged in assessing the situation, and defining and planing appropriate steps toward a solution. A facilitated workshop is an effective way to bring these people together in an off-site setting. This event demonstrates the importance that top management places on the issue and underscores that high-level managers are seeking the help of those closest to the problem.

The objective of the workshop is to empower those people who know the most about the work processes involved, and will be the most affected by any solution. The workshop facilitators must, however, keep this group focused on the need for a solution that results in a competitive new capability. Doing business in the same old ways will not suffice. The group needs to understand that this initiative will most likely require an investigation of industry best practices, and an infusion of new information, work processes, and tools into the company. If these individuals employ their creativity in crafting the eventual solution, though, and feel a sense of ownership for the success of the improvement initiative, they will be much less likely to resist changes in their work patterns. When they become thus invested, the success of the program optimizes their personal currencies. Because they are respected among their peers, their influence will also help quell resistance to the change by others.

➤ Progress Metrics

Improvement initiatives often take a considerable length of time to complete and their conclusion does not usually result in an immediate impact on measurable business results. The impact of the initiative is to correct the performance of an important business process such as product innovation. The business impact is generated by more effective performance of that process, and thus will be delayed by the process cycle time. Management of improvement initiatives thus requires (1) a credible plan of action, (2) steady nerves on the part of high-level managers, and (3) suitable progress measures that will accurately reflect the successful execution of planned improvement activities. These progress measures make the unfolding of planned improvements visible to the organization. Without effective progress measures, high-level managers can only judge an improvement initiative by watching the financial bottom line. When immediate financial results are not evident, business leaders often get nervous and are likely to pull the plug on improvement efforts before they have the desired effect on targeted business processes.

Progress measures that are defined without grass roots involvement, though, can trigger many different reactions. If these metrics are defined and imposed by high-level managers, they can trigger a "malicious compliance" reaction. Individual personal economics, once again, can explain this behavior.

Malicious compliance occurs when the individuals who are being measured by a particular performance metric find alternative ways to achieve desired measurement levels that undermine the intent of the measurement. One somewhat outdated example occurred in a typing pool where secretaries worked at typewriters together in a large room. In their efforts to increase efficiency, management decided that the way to determine productivity in the typing pool was to measure keystrokes per hour. One day a technician visited the typing pool and installed little counters on each typewriter. Each time a keystroke occurred, the count displayed in the little window incremented by one. About a week later, a man with a clipboard wandered through the typing pool and wrote down each secretary's name along with the number displayed on his or her typewriter. He returned each day after that to repeat this process. The numbers recorded each day began to increase, eventually reaching a significantly larger value than the original baseline value. The managers were quite pleased with their "increase in productivity" until one day the man with the clipboard arrived during lunch break. He found an empty room filled with clattering typewriters. Each secretary had placed a book on the spacebar and the unattended machines were busy running up the count.

When performance becomes both visible and important, personal economics will generally change in a way that causes measurements to improve, one way or another. The little counters had made one aspect of secretarial performance visible. The fact that management was recording each person's numbers made them important. When a number became associated with each secretary's performance, they became vulnerable in a new way. Someone could now see the result of each individual's effort and compare them with their peers. Fear of reprisal thus emerged as an important personal currency. In some, the desire to excel might have also become important. To rebalance their personal economics, the secretaries might have worked harder and typed faster. But a book on the spacebar produces a greater return-on-investment.

Malicious compliance is less likely if those people being measured are asked to define their own performance metrics. This is another way of enlisting the creativity and ownership of people working at the grassroots level. If they have been involved in defining improvements to resolve a particular business performance issue, they are often in the best position to suggest insightful ways to measure successful implementation. When they have had a hand in defining the progress measures used, their personal economics are more likely to be optimized by having those measures improve as a result of genuine achievements toward program goals.

Once effective progress measures are in place, high-level managers must track those measures and set performance expectations. In effect, these measures are the performance meters on the improvement initiative. When high-level managers periodically show interest in an initiative and demonstrate their understanding by reading these meters with intelligence, they underscore the program's ongoing importance. Furthermore, their expectations instill a healthy sense of accountability in those who are responsible for implementing improvements according to plan.

This sense of accountability has a direct and motivating impact on personal economic currencies. Currencies such as responsibility, sense of achievement, or fear of failure will all be optimized when progress measures fall within a successful range.

➤ Enviable Recognition

Even with high-level endorsement, grassroots involvement, and effective progress metrics in place, some people will still resist adopting more effective ways of working. A further influence is needed to tip their valuation of personal economic currencies toward embracing the new practices. Enviable recognition of role-model behavior by high-level managers provides this final motivation.

The strategy of high-level managers in launching an improvement initiative should be to (1) endorse its importance, (2) invite grassroots involvement, and then (3) support those who show interest in addressing the targeted issue and improving performance. Others who may be resisting the change should be ignored initially. When early adopters of improvements begin to show performance gains, however, they should be recognized and rewarded by upper management in ways that their more recalcitrant peers will envy.

Enviable recognition directly affects the valuation of personal currencies by the peers of those being commended in a way that motivates them to emulate the behaviors and choices being praised. The early assessment by those resistant to a change initiative most likely places a high cost on the risk that a new practice poses. Furthermore, their assessment probably attaches a high value to current practices that seem to offer a reliable means for continued success. Once early adopters of improved methods have achieved some level of success and are receiving recognition, however, this early assessment must be revised. Those being recognized have demonstrated that the new methods lead to success, not failure. High-level managers, in recognizing this success, are sending clear signals that success and rewards in the future will depend on a willingness to embrace these new methods. Those who are resisting change must reevaluate their personal economics, and they inevitably move the value on their personal currencies in a direction that is more supportive of change.

Enviable recognition should continue until new practices are fairly well proven and have demonstrated a clear advantage over earlier methods. The new methods should then be moved into the category of "business as usual." Once this transition occurs, anyone still clinging to old methods and practices should be provided with career counseling focused on the person's poor judgment. In effect, enviable recognition disappears over time and is replaced by reasonable management expectations for high levels of performance.

➤ A Real-Life Example

In January 1981, early in John Young's term as president and CEO of the Hewlett-Packard Company, he set an objective for the company that addressed concerns about the reliability of HP products. His objective was that the failure rate of all HP products should improve by a factor of 10 over the next decade. A normalized measure of failure rate was defined that would be used to assess progress toward this goal—the average annual failure rate for each product divided by its list price in thousands of dollars. For example, an oscilloscope that, in 1981, cost $10,000 and had an annual failure rate of 50 percent would set a standard for comparison of 5 percent per thousand dollars. To achieve John's objective, that same product line would have to achieve 0.5 percent per thousand dollars by 1991. If the price of a similar instrument were to fall to $5,000 over this span of time, then the annual failure rate of this particular product would have to be 2.5 percent—a 20-fold decrease—to meet the objective.

Reactions to John's objective around the company mostly ranged from skepticism to indifference. John was untested in his new role, and grand, corporatewide objectives were uncommon in HP. Most assumed a "wait and see" attitude toward this program.

In the fall of 1981, John asked HP's quality manager to provide an assessment of how this program was progressing. The answer came back, "Not very well. In fact, on average, product reliability is in worse shape than it was in January." There were, though, a few bright spots. In particular, the Loveland Instruments division had taken John's objective very seriously and was making great strides.

With HP's annual general managers meeting coming up in January 1982, John devised a plan to put his program on more solid ground. He asked the quality manager to prepare one slide for his speech to the general managers, and then he scheduled a trip to Loveland, Colorado. He spent several days reviewing the product reliability project at the Loveland Instruments division. He learned about their approach, he met and talked with those responsible for their progress. And he took notes.

John's speech to the general managers in January took place in a darkened auditorium with John at a podium on the stage. John's one slide was projected on a large screen during his entire 30-minute speech for all to see. On it were the names of HP's divisions, the name of the general manager of each division, and a number representing the degree of improvement each division had made in product reliability over the past year. The list was arranged in descending order so that the Loveland Instruments division was at the very top of the list. The list clearly showed that only a few divisions had made progress and, in fact, most had lost ground during the year.

John never mentioned the slide at all. Instead he talked about his visit to Loveland, the people he had met, and the creative solutions that they had implemented to improve product reliability. He talked about the importance of product reliability to HP's customers and relayed some customer satisfaction stories that he had heard in Loveland. His speech clearly demonstrated his endorsement of product reliability as an important element of business success, his ability to read and understand product reliability progress measures, and his recognition of the outstanding efforts by the people in Loveland. His speech closed with a comment about how the folks he had met in Loveland were role models for those who would lead HP in the future.

Throughout 1982, people in other HP business divisions beat a path to Loveland to learn more about their program. In fact, the rush of visitors nearly brought the Loveland Instruments division to its knees. But John's product reliability program took off and began to make serious progress. John continued to endorse these efforts, track results, and recognize exemplary achievements. By 1991, the company had achieved his goal.

The four factors that encourage change described in this section provide high-level managers with powerful tools to both initiate and guide improvement efforts. These factors can transform the often frustrating task of change management into a straightforward process that routinely delivers successful results.

■ A FRAMEWORK FOR CHANGE INITIATIVES

Once strategic objectives for improvement have been set by high-level managers, they need to be addressed by well-staffed project efforts led by capable and credible individuals. By this time, the business leadership team will most likely have communicated the need for improvement broadly throughout the organization. People will be watching to see signs of commitment behind these words. How important is this new program? Will business leaders "put their money where their mouth is"? The best signal that the leadership team can send at this point is to assign ownership of each improvement objective to one of their most respected managers and then provide this person with the resources to get the job done.

The first task for the newly assigned leader of an improvement effort is the definition and planning of the project. Figure 9.3 depicts key elements of an improvement initiative that should be included in the project plan. Assigned strategic objectives and goals determined in the business improvement cycle of Figure 9.1 provide direction for the project and set targeted performance standards. In addition, early research related to each strategic objective will help define the work that must be done. What issues have limited our past performance in this area? How do other companies implement this business process and what levels of performance do they achieve? What can we learn about the apparent performance of our competitors? Are methods or tools available that we can adapt to help improve our performance? Are there pitfalls that we need to avoid? Answers to these questions help shape a successful improvement initiative.

As with Figure 9.1, the summing junction in Figure 9.3 signifies a comparing operation. The performance of current operations is compared with both the strategic goals for the improvement program and the best-in-class role models identified through research. The discrepancies identify specific performance issues that characterize the path that the business must take in achieving more competitive performance. Typically, this comparison yields another "laundry list" of issues that must be analyzed and prioritized into the most critical few. This short list then is used to launch specific

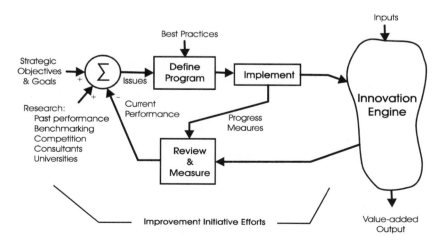

Figure 9.3 Framework for improvement initiatives.

improvement efforts. The following example makes this part of the process more tangible.

Earlier, slow time-to-market was discussed as an example of a performance issue that was identified by business leaders in HP. After some discussion, the specific strategic objective that was assigned to the corporate engineering group was to cut the average breakeven time (BET) for new products in half. This is the length of time, measured from the start of a new product effort, that it takes for a new product to pay back the investment that was required to get it to market. More is said about this performance measure in Chapter 12. Nonetheless, the corporate engineering program was launched with a clear objective in mind.

Improvement efforts began with a survey of past project experience that involved expert practitioners throughout HP's product development community. This survey identified three issues that were the most prevalent causes for delays in new product efforts:

1. Unstable product definition.

2. Weak project management skills.

3. Ineffective software development practices.

There were more concerns on the list, but these three were the most important. The potential for performance improvement in these three areas was estimated to be enough to meet the goals of the improvement program.

Further research was launched to learn about state-of-the-art methods in each of these areas. Comparing the results with current HP product innovation practices provided clear definition of the specific issues that had to be resolved by subsequent improvement efforts. As a result of this initial work, three separate projects were launched to improve performance in the areas listed.

As shown in Figure 9.3, an improvement program is defined that will address the issues identified and bring business performance in these areas to competitive levels. The program definition should include both a description of new practices that will be implemented and a discussion of how the change management principles described earlier in this chapter will be employed. New practices may be acquired from sources outside the company, or they might be defined locally. A well-managed effort to bring the collective ingenuity and common sense of expert practitioners from around the company to bear on the issues at hand often produces very workable solutions. The goal of any so-lution, though, should be to alter specific behaviors of those work-ing in product innovation in ways that will yield the desired business results: *The design of an improvement program should focus on changing behavior. You must improve the way people work on a day-to-day basis to improve business results.*

Another HP story underscores the degree of passion that the authors have for this point. In our efforts to solve the product defi-nition problem identified in the survey, the corporate engineering team identified some excellent best practices that could make a tremendous difference in the performance of new product ef-forts.[2,3] The improvement program that was defined and imple-mented, though, included only the design and delivery of a self-study course on product definition best practices. This course was published as a three-ring binder that was shrink-wrapped and sent, without explanation and at considerable cost to the com-pany, to every project manager in HP. The project managers who received this surprise package were hard-working, busy people; the likelihood that they would take it on themselves to open this binder, study the contents, and alter their own behavior in product definition was very low. For years after those binders were shipped, one could wander around HP and see them sitting in bookcases, still in their shrink-wrap. Even good ideas do not flow through shrink-wrap. In its initial implementation, this program had al-most no effect on individual behavior, and hence almost no busi-ness impact.

Later, HP implemented an on-site training program for project teams using the principles described in the discussion on training methods in Chapter 7. This program included on-the-job coaching and consulting in product definition best practices. This service became very popular and eventually began to have the desired im-pact on HP performance.

Another key element in the definition and implementation of an effective improvement program is the description of effective progress measures. These measures should initially make visible a project's progress in working its plan. Later, as the project begins

---

[2] Wilson, Edith. "Product Definition: Assorted Techniques and Their Market Im-pact," Proceedings of the IEEE International Engineering Management Confer-ence, 1990.
[3] Gaynor, Gerard H. *Handbook of Technology Management* (chap. 36, by Edith Wil-son). New York: McGraw-Hill, 1996.

to affect the performance of product innovation teams, these measures should also demonstrate the desired impact on behavior. As discussed earlier, improvement efforts sometimes take a long time to produce a payoff in measurable financial terms. High-level managers can get nervous about continuing to invest in such an effort unless progress measures show that the program is on track.

As in Figure 9.1, the elements in Figure 9.3 act as a performance correcting loop. Initial performance issues trigger the acquisition or invention of better methods. An improvement program is then defined to install these practices in ongoing product innovation efforts. As implementation begins to affect the behavior of new product teams, performance measures reflect the improvement. The performance comparisons at the summing junction thus move over time in a favorable direction. The loop continues to work in this manner until the performance issues addressed are transformed from problems into sources of competitive advantage, and the initial strategic objectives and goals have been achieved.

■ BARRIERS TO CHANGE

Influences that act to derail effective improvement efforts exist in almost every company and are pervasive in the culture and the psychology of the workplace. They include:

➤ Misalignment of recognition and rewards.

➤ Functional parochialism.

➤ The learning curve barrier.

High-level managers should (1) be alert to the symptoms of these common obstacles, and (2) be prepared to take appropriate action to nullify their effects on improvement efforts. The following discussion describes each of these factors and outlines ways to neutralize their influence.

➤ Misalignment of Recognition and Rewards

Often a company may espouse the need for performance improvement while supporting a system of recognition and rewards that actually penalizes executives for investing in such efforts. The salary increases, bonuses, and stock options that high-level managers receive are frequently based on current operational parameters such as revenue growth, profitability, return on assets, or economic value added. Rewards of this kind create an intense interest and enthusiasm for short-term financial results. This form of reward structure, however, discourages improvement efforts. A business leadership team that invests in improving its innovation engine will be spending money that could instead be reported as profits. They may be diverting their best people away from activities that can have a material effect on short-term rewards, and assigning them instead to projects that may not create a financial return for two years or more. While high-level managers may understand the importance of these long-term investments to the continued viability of the business, the impact that these investments will have on immediate rewards puts them in a conflict of interest.

To remedy this situation, when it exists, the formula that determines executive compensation should be altered to include consideration of effective investment in the long-term success of the business. Bonuses should be linked, at least in part, to the viability of improvement efforts. Does the business leadership team understand the three performance issues that are most critical to their long-term competitive position? Are their investments in correcting these issues well placed and appropriate in size? Have they assigned the responsibility for resolving these issues to good people? Have they identified progress measures for these efforts? Are they tracking the performance of these initiatives? The financial rewards that high-level managers receive should be influenced by the answers to these questions as well.

Another form of misalignment in recognition and rewards that tends to shift the priority away from improvement efforts is more subtle. The inherent behavior of high-level managers often includes recognizing and rewarding firefighters—those highly visible people who, in a crisis situation, leap into the fray, take charge, and lead the way to a solution. After they have stepped in and saved the day, high-level managers are inclined to reward their contribution and acknowledge them publicly as both hero and role model. Right now the reader may be thinking, "What could be wrong with this? Aren't these the kind of people that we want to encourage and promote in our organization?" The answer to these questions is a definite "Maybe." But there are broader implications for this kind of recognition.

High-level managers should reward the behaviors they want to encourage. Enviable recognition of role model behavior sends powerful signals throughout the workforce that will cause others to emulate that behavior. If solving business crises leads to recognition and reward, then somehow there will most likely be more fires to fight. The real heroes in an organization, though, are those people who work to eliminate those flaws in each business process that lead to crisis late in a program. This involves foresight, planning, and discipline, but usually is not nearly as visible or as dramatic as fire fighting. These are the people, though, who will transform a business from a noisy, inefficient, herky-jerky affair into a smoothly running, competitive, profit-making machine. This is the behavior that needs to be emphasized. These people should thus be recognized and rewarded at least as often and as well as firefighters.

There is another issue with recognizing firefighters. Whether a firefighter is a hero depends on who caused the fire. A person who steps in and resolves a crisis he or she had no part in causing is indeed heroic. But, on closer examination, a business crisis is usually found to be the result of either flaws in a fundamental process or errors in its execution. As discussed in Chapter 5, a major crisis that occurs toward the end of a program is usually due to mistakes committed early in the process. And often the person who gets credit for resolving a crisis is someone who could have, at an earlier time, taken steps to prevent it. In fact, chronic firefighters often disdain established business processes, and instead tend to take matters into their own hands and invent their own process as they go.

Before high-level managers hand out recognition and rewards, they should strive to fully understand what has really happened, and they should consider carefully the kind of behavior they want to replicate. When they reward fire-fighting behavior, they shift the values and the culture of the workplace in a direction that makes the systemic improvement of business processes more difficult.

➤ Functional Parochialism

In some businesses, functional departments become isolated centers of power—the so-called functional silo, a tall structure surrounded by an impenetrable wall. The flow of ideas and information between these isolated departments tends to be slow and restricted, causing frequent errors and rework in cross-functional activities such as product innovation. This kind of environment creates serious obstacles for the improvement project that is focused on streamlining product innovation as a cross-functional activity.

Chapter 5 described the cross-functional product innovation process, and pointed out that, to improve business results, you have to fix what is broken, regardless of what functional areas own the flaws in the process. Projects to improve product innovation performance thus usually need the wholehearted involvement of team members from several functional areas to succeed. Each team member brings unique expertise and experience from their functional area into the improvement effort that fosters the kind of multifunctional solutions that are necessary. Furthermore, implementing cross-functional solutions requires access to the established work processes in each functional department. These processes must be first understood and then later modified to create a smooth-running process that operates as a seamless, enterprisewide system. The narrow focus and protective attitudes characteristic of functional departments is some enterprises can render improvement efforts such as this unfeasible.

The antidote to functional parochialism is the commitment and management skill of the top-level executive who has span of control over all the functional departments. This individual first must see that clear objectives are established for the cross-functional improvement effort. Next, this person should become an outspoken advocate for the importance of these improvements. Everyone, including the functional department managers, should be clear on what the boss wants and expects to happen. Third, this top-level leader must closely monitor progress measures for the improvement effort and set challenging expectations for everyone involved. These expectations should be communicated clearly and often to each functional department manager. Finally, each functional department manager should be informed that his or her bonus and next salary increase depend on the enthusiastic support of this improvement effort by everyone in that person's department. If effectively employed, these steps will usually overcome this barrier and clear the path for cross-functional improvement efforts.

➤ The Learning Curve Barrier

Most performance improvement efforts include an intrinsic learning curve that acts as a barrier to change. Understanding and applying new processes, methods, or tools requires significant effort, and will often initially degrade productivity and slow a new product effort down. First attempts to apply new methods frequently result in errors and rework. The improvement project team must be prepared to take each new product team fully and successfully through this learning process, or they will backslide and revert to old, familiar work patterns. If any team is ever allowed to fail in the middle of the learning process, they will likely adopt the attitude, "We tried that and it didn't work." Once this rumor gets started, it can spread quickly and discourage other new product teams from ever trying the new methods and tools offered by the improvement team.

Figure 9.4 shows this learning curve barrier. The upper curve represents the energy required over time to employ current methods in doing a given job, such as introducing a new product. Often, as the world gets more complicated, the amount of work required to introduce a new product will grow so there will be an upward slope to this curve. New safety standards, more stringent electromagnetic compatibility regulations, and the like add work to the process and increase the total energy required to get a new product out. So, as time goes by, the effort required of a new product team moves up this curve to the right.

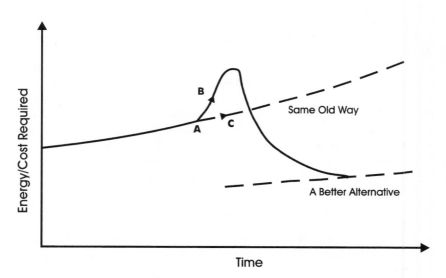

Figure 9.4 The learning curve barrier.

At point A, however, someone intervenes and makes the new product team an offer: "If you will adopt these new practices and learn these new tools, we will introduce you to a whole new world in which it takes much less energy to get a new product to market. Your efforts will be much more competitive in the future. All you have to do is let us lead you up this learning curve." All the new product team has to rely on at this point are these promises, their own insight and intuition, and the credibility of the improvement team.

Based on the personal economics of the situation—the promise of increased productivity and speed versus the energy required to learn and the possible risk of outright failure—the new product team leader decides to buy into the promises, and commits the project team to embrace these new methods and tools. And the project moves up the learning curve to point B.

By the time it reaches point B, the extra effort invested in learning has put the project behind where it would have otherwise been, and errors and rework have been introduced into the new product effort by the attempt to employ unfamiliar methods and tools. The personal economics of the project leader have changed. Schedule pressure is building, and no payoff from these new methods and tools is in sight. The learning curve stretches seemingly ever-upward into the future, with only more work and more delays visible from point B. The temptation to give up, return to familiar ways of working, represented in the diagram as a jump from B to C, is great. If this happens, though, the "We tried that and it didn't work" syndrome is born. The experience of this new product team, and their comments and attitudes will provide powerful negative signals to others that may prevent further consideration of these new methods and tools. Such a failure on the first try at improving product innovation performance often rings the death knell on an improvement program, and on the new work methods that it has tried to implement.

To succeed, a performance improvement team must be prepared to take each project team up the learning curve and over the top, without fail. On-the-job training, personal coaching, and expert consultants can guarantee that each project team that adopts the new methods will have a successful experience. These services can reduce the total learning effort required of the new product team, and minimize the investment in errors and rework. Once a new product team has experienced promised increases in speed, productivity, or market impact, they frequently become outspoken advocates for the new approach. These positive signals can make other new product teams eager to take on the improvements.

■ THE TIME DYNAMICS OF PROCESS IMPROVEMENT

The lengthy delays that can sometimes occur between the investment in product innovation improvement efforts and the financial payoff has already been mentioned several times. This section provides a more thorough look at the time relationships involved in product innovation improvement efforts.

Figure 9.5 illustrates the steps that occur between the decisions to invest in business process improvements and the resulting financial return. Most importantly, this graph illustrates the time relationships between these steps. To begin, the lowest curve in the graph represents investment decisions and the top curve indicates the firm's relative market position in terms of revenues, or perhaps market share. Imagine that, at time zero, top management becomes troubled by the company's steadily declining market position. This decline is correctly linked to an inadequate capacity to

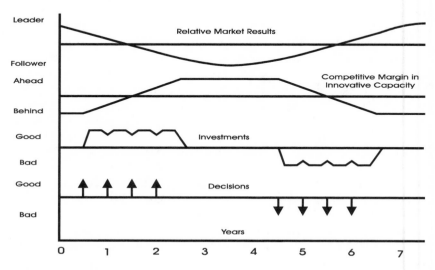

Figure 9.5 The dynamics of product innovation improvement efforts.

innovate new products, shown by the second curve from the top. Even though they are still ahead of the competition, they assign the objective of improving new product performance levels to a capable improvement program manager. After assessing the situation for six months, this person makes a decision to invest in effective improvement efforts, indicated by the first upward arrow on the lowest curve. Improvement investments are shown as the second curve from the bottom in Figure 9.5. In six months, the program manager reviews the progress created by these investments and sees that they have indeed begun to improve the firm's ability to innovate new products. Another good decision is made and the investment continues. This cycle repeats every six months.

The competitive capacity to innovate new products continues to grow as long as this positive level of investment is in place. At one and one-half years into this illustration, the firm has moved from being well behind in the performance of this critical business process to being even with competitors. More importantly, the capacity to compete is rapidly improving. A review of market results, though, shows that the firm's relative position has fallen steadily so that they are now slugging it out toe-to-toe with competitors that they used to dominate. At this point, their capacity to generate new products has just drawn even, so the products currently being introduced were largely created without the benefit of recent improvements. The relative market performance of the company will continue to fall until more competitive products can be created with the improved innovation process. Top management is not happy with this explanation, however, and they issue a stern warning to their improvement program manager. They want to see results.

A year later, at two and one-half years into this illustration, the competitive capacity of the product innovation process has improved to the point where it is the highest in the industry. New products moving through the process these days are very exciting and promise to restore the firm to its earlier position of market dominance. The firm has a two-year product development cycle, though, so these new market winners will not be introduced for awhile. By now, though, top management has lost patience with the improvement program. The bottom line has continued to drop so the program has been a failure in their eyes. Completely disgusted, they fire their improvement program manager and cancel any further investment in this person's program.

Another year goes by, and the firm's market position has now reached an all-time low. Revenue and profits are both in terrible shape. In desperation, the business leaders begin a search for out-side talent, someone who can take action and "stem the flow of blood." After a six-month search, a new improvement program manager is hired who promises to take a no-nonsense approach to the problem.

After a six-month assessment period, four and one-half years into this illustration, the new program manager decides to "in-crease productivity" and cuts expenses across the board. The prod-uct innovation activity takes its fair share of these cuts and begins to decline in competitive capacity. In the meantime, the exciting new products generated by the product innovation process at its competitive peak are beginning to take hold in the marketplace. Revenues have turned around and are on the increase. The recent expense cuts have had an immediate impact on the bottom line so profits are higher than they have been in years. Business is look-ing good.

At six and one-half years into this illustration, the market po-sition of the firm again dominant, expenses are down, and profits are at an all time high. The no-nonsense improvement program manager is promoted to vice-president as a reward for his excellent results and moves on to other work. The competitive capacity of the product innovation process, though, is back to a level that se-verely trails the competition, so more trouble looms just over the horizon.

This scenario is a fictionalized account of events that happen all too often in real business situations—the innocent are pun-ished while the guilty get promoted. Many readers will recognize the pattern described here in the history of their own careers. The authors have observed this cycle many times in various com-panies. The problem that this scenario illustrates is that market position indicators, such as market share and revenues, are all se-verely lagging indicators of improvement program performance. Managers who focus narrowly on these indicators can sometimes make terrible decisions.

A more effective approach to the management of improve-ment efforts includes (1) evaluating decision quality, (2) tracking the size and quality of investments, and then (3) tracking progress measures to make sure that the desired impact of these efforts is happening. In this scenario, the business leaders should have re-viewed the decisions made by the improvement program manager to ensure that they made sense and then assessed the size of the in-vestment made and the quality of the project plan. These steps are, in effect, attempts to measure the bottom two curves in Figure 9.5.

As time progressed, they then should have reviewed progress measures to assess the impact of these investments on the product innovation program. This is equivalent to measuring the second curve from the top in the graph. If these three states—decision quality, investment quality, and progress measures—are in good shape, the bottom line will, in time, take care of itself.

■ THE EARMARKS OF A SUCCESSFUL IMPROVEMENT INITIATIVE

The following list summarizes the critical success factors for a performance improvement project that reflect the points made in this chapter:

- ➤ Clear ownership is established.
- ➤ Issues to be resolved are compelling.
- ➤ Initiatives have high-level sponsorship.
- ➤ Investments are visible, measurable, and appropriate.
- ➤ Change-management principles are effectively employed.
- ➤ Progress measures are identified and tracked.
- ➤ Desired behavior changes are happening.
- ➤ Impact on business results is likely.

➤ Clear Ownership Is Established

First of all, someone should be clearly responsible for the improvement project and be accountable for its success. This person should feel as if the success of his or her career (including the next salary increase) is linked to the outcome of this initiative. This person will be empowered to manage the project as needed to achieve its success and will act as the champion for this effort.

➤ Issues to Be Resolved Are Compelling

Next, the performance issues that are addressed by an improvement program must be compelling—they need to be broadly considered as both important and repairable. There should be a sense of urgency, among high-level managers and others, for the success of the improvement initiative. Ideally, the promised results from the project will be considered valuable by people at all levels in the organization.

➤ Initiatives Have High-Level Sponsorship

The business leadership team should be deeply committed to each improvement effort, and this commitment should be reflected often in both their words and deeds. Their endorsements should effectively convey a sense of importance for the improvement effort to all departments and all levels that will be affected.

➤ Investments Are Visible, Measurable, and Appropriate

The importance of an improvement effort is, at least in part, communicated by the investment that high-level managers are willing to place in it. The size of this investment should be big enough to create a successful outcome in a timely manner. The people assigned to an improvement initiative should be both capable and credible. As much as possible, these individuals should work full-time on the improvement project so that they can give it their undivided attention. There should be no ambiguity about either their responsibility for this project or their loyalty to it.

➤ Change-Management Principles Are Effectively Employed

The plan for an improvement initiative should explicitly reflect consideration of the four factors that encourage change. It should enlist high-level managers in a well-thought-out program for providing ongoing endorsement. The methods to enlist grassroots involvement should be described. Progress measures should be spelled out and the means for reporting and reviewing these measures should be described. Finally, methods for identifying those worthy of enviable recognition should be discussed, and the roles of high-level managers in providing this recognition should be outlined.

➤ Progress Measures Are Identified and Tracked

In a successful improvement initiative, progress measures are clearly defined and routinely tracked by high-level managers in a way that creates a sense of urgency and accountability among members of the improvement project team. In their review of these metrics, high-level managers demonstrate both their ongoing commitment to the program and their ability to understand the important elements in the effort. This attention by business leaders should also reflect their eagerness to see a successful return from their investment.

➤ Desired Behavior Changes Are Happening

Once a successful improvement initiative begins to implement its plan and work with product innovation teams, the expected changes in behavior happen as planned and are reflected in the progress measures gathered. Evidence of resistance against new methods and tools among new product team members is within expected bounds.

➤ Impact on Business Results Is Likely

Finally, those business leaders who keep an eye on successful product innovation improvement efforts have steady nerves. These high-level managers understand the intended impact of the initiative on new product team behavior and work patterns. They are convinced that this impact is closely linked to future improvement in financial results. As a result, they are satisfied to track improvement project progress measures and wait with considerable patience for the financial results that will follow.

■ CONCLUSION

One of the most important responsibilities that high-level managers own is building the capacity of their business to compete in the future. Successful execution of this duty includes establishing effective strategic directions for investment in new or improved capability, and launching and guiding project efforts that succeed in increasing the level of business performance in designated areas. This chapter has offered some tools and guidelines for carrying out this responsibility.

It is easy to tell if a company is on track toward a more competitive future. Each member of the business leadership team will be conversant with the most important competitive issues of concern. Each of these issues will be addressed by project efforts that are well planned as well as effectively led and staffed. In fact, a significant portion of the product innovation budget, between 5 and 15 percent, will be devoted to these activities, depending on the degree and urgency of competitive issues that the company faces. The high-level management team will demonstrate strong interest in these projects and track their investments with due diligence.

On the other hand, symptoms in firms that have work to do in this area include:

➤ High-level managers who are too busy to worry about something as nebulous as "ability to compete in the future."

➤ A tendency among business leaders to delegate these issues to lower levels.

➤ A belief that committees can solve these problems.

➤ An absence of improvement projects with full-time people assigned.

This chapter has attempted to provide a vision of how well planned and managed improvement programs operate. This vision may affirm the steps that are already underway in the reader's own company. If not, then perhaps this chapter will have generated a sense of urgency for work that needs to be done.

Desired Upper Management Behaviors:
Managing Improvements to the Innovation Process

➤ Communicate with a sense of urgency about competitive performance issues and efforts to resolve them.

➤ Read the meter on improvement projects with intelligence and set high performance expectations.

➤ Recognize and reward those behaviors that most effectively build the capacity to compete.

➤ Manage and track capability improvement investments in the same way as other important components of the new product portfolio.

Part IV

Creating the Environment

Chapter

10

Organizational Vision— The Guiding Force Field

A leader is a person who has an unusual degree of power to create the conditions in which other people must live and move and have their being . . .

> Parker J. Palmer
> *Leading from Within*

We have covered the role of product innovation in driving business growth and described how work processes and the leadership of high-level managers contribute to the success of new product efforts. Building a competitive product innovation capacity, though, takes one more critical element. The most successful companies simply get more from the people who do product innovation— more work, more creativity, more initiative, more enthusiasm, more honesty, more integrity—than do their competitors. Part IV outlines steps that business leaders can take to create an enterprisewide setting that supports the highest levels of performance from each individual on each new product team. Chapter 10 addresses the nature and impact of enterprisewide direction and goals, while Chapter 11 focuses on the working environment—the ambience in which, in Palmer's words, "people must live and move and have their being."

Some readers may be about ready to bail out at this point. To paraphrase a line from a favorite movie, they may be thinking something like, "Ambience! Ambience! We don't need no stinking ambience!"

Where's the business value in ambience? *The Random House Dictionary* defines ambience as "the mood, special quality, or atmosphere of a place or situation." Consider the three pillars that support the business purpose of product innovation (see Figure 1.1)—work processes, leadership roles, and working environment. Which of these are truly essential to business success? The authors have worked with a number of companies that have developed a substantial revenue base without competitive work processes. These companies reach a point, however, where their usual ad hoc methods begin to break down and further growth depends on their ability to install effective business processes. So work processes are nonessential to small, start-up operations, but become more essential with growth. A start-up operation can also succeed and grow initially without much consideration of the leadership roles outlined in Part III. They may only have one or two products, so portfolio management leadership roles may not seem important. Once again, these roles become critical if the firm is ever to become a competitive large company. Every truly competitive operation, even the smallest start-up company, needs hard work and creativity from its product innovation workforce. And this, in turn, depends on the ambience within which these people "must live and move and have their being." The working environment can either support the highest levels of performance from each individual, or it can drag them down and practically nullify their productivity. The ambience in which product innovation occurs has terrific business value.

If the working environment is so important, then what can we as business leaders do about it? How do we get people aligned and working together on the business needs of the enterprise? How do we enlist their hard work, their creativity, and their enthusiasm? What mental models will help us do this part of the job? The answers to these questions begin with consideration of the individual personal economics described in Chapter 9. People will align their efforts and work hard only if it makes sense, in terms of their own personal economics, to do so. And they will unleash their personal creativity only if their own personal economics support such behavior.

Different models exist for how to influence and use these personal economics. The military model assumes that the personal economics are in place that will encourage soldiers to follow orders. Loyalty to one's own unit, fear of punishment, a sense of duty, loyalty to the flag, respect for officers, and confidence in one's training and abilities are all personal economic factors that align the efforts of an army. The fact that a soldier is committed to the military establishment for a set enlistment period has a great influence as well on each person's personal economics. A soldier simply is not allowed to resign from his or her position if the situation gets dangerous or unpleasant. The indoctrination and training applied in boot camp ensure that these personal economics are installed in a way that will support the objectives of the military. If boot camp and the training that a soldier receives are effective, then a military leader need only issue the appropriate orders to achieve alignment of action and enthusiastic participation.

But what about a business enterprise, what models and methods apply there? The conditions that affect personal economics are certainly different from those in the military example. People can decide to quit and go to work at another firm anytime they want. What will alter their personal economics in a way that makes them stay and help achieve success, even when the going gets rough?

An effective organizational vision, as outlined in the remainder of this chapter, will do this. Included in this organizational vision are:

➤ Understanding of and care for the customers to be served.

➤ Strongly held organizational values and beliefs.

➤ A common sense of purpose.

➤ A shared understanding of the current situation.

➤ An aggressive organizational goal for midterm achievement.

➤ An understanding of core capabilities that are essential to success.

➤ A rational organizational structure that effectively supports achievement.

Before discussing these important elements of the organizational vision, it is helpful to consider an interesting model of natural systems that has emerged and how it might relate to activities in a business enterprise. This discussion develops a metaphor that puts the role of organizational vision and its influence on individual behavior in perspective.

■ CHAOS VERSUS CONTROL

Throughout the eighteenth and nineteenth centuries, Newton's laws of motion were considered the ultimate truth that governed the motion of massive bodies in response to the forces that influenced them. At the core of all science during those times, these immutable laws held the promise that the universe was deterministic. That is, if humankind could just learn enough about the current state of matter, they would be able to determine, through the diligent application of scientific principles, the future of the universe for all time. Science in those days offered the promise of total knowledge, power, and control over the physical world.

As the industrial revolution unfolded and large business enterprises were founded, these ideas of scientific laws and control had significant influence over the new institutions.[1] The way they organized work and their methods for measuring and accounting for the flow of both materials and wealth were reminiscent of the methods of science. Business leaders felt that they had every right to understand their operations perfectly and to have perfect control over their dominion. Undoubtedly, military thinking had some influence as well, for businesses evolved in pyramidal form, with thinking and decisions accomplished by a very few people at the top, with ever broader ranks of middle managers and workers below to carry out the directives of top management.

The personal economics of the rank and file were probably simpler in those times as well. Poverty was prevalent, jobs were scarce, and people would do whatever was required to keep the boss happy. The cost of losing one's job to another more willing worker was high enough to overshadow most other personal currencies.

In the twentieth century, science has become significantly more complicated. Newton's laws are now understood to be mere approximations of how matter behaves in a rather limited domain of size and velocity. This new science can no long offer the promise of determinism, for in the last half of this century the emergence of chaos theory has revealed that even simple physical systems, while obeying straightforward natural laws, can exhibit highly unpredictable behavior.[2]

---

[1] Wheatley, Margaret J. *Leadership and the New Science*. San Francisco: Berrett-Koehler, 1992.

[2] Gleick, James. *Chaos: Making of a New Science*. New York: Viking Press, 1987.

The Earth's atmosphere and the weather, for example, respond to well-understood physical laws that govern the flow of fluids and the behavior of gases. For years, scientists have labored under the deterministic illusion that, if they just had big enough computers, and enough information about current weather conditions throughout the globe, they could use mathematical models to predict the weather well into the future. The energies of meteorologists and their investment of resources were focused in this direction for years. Recently, however, they have come to realize that weather as a system exhibits chaotic behavior. It will never be predictable more than a few days into the future, for even the tiniest shift in initial conditions can cause wild fluctuations in the state of the system beyond a time horizon of only a few days. While our mathematical models may be valid and the computing resources may be available, we will never be able to measure the current state of the atmosphere with enough precision to allow long-range prediction.

Although unpredictable, a chaotic system is not random. It obeys well-understood principles, and the state of a chaotic system always quickly converges on a narrow range of possibilities that has been labeled the "strange attractor." In a mechanical chaos system that has moving parts that influence each other through the pull of springs or magnets, the strange attractor will be a particular set of positions and velocities that are natural to that particular system. If one were to plot the actual velocities in the system versus position, the strange attractor would become visible over time as a discernible shape in this plot that is created as the system moves. With some, the shape is like a figure eight; others resemble a clover leaf. The shape of a strange attractor is sometimes complex and beautiful. Their general form and detailed shape, though, depend on the nature of the system and its specific parameters. If you launch a chaotic mechanical system at a position and velocity that are well away from its strange attractor, the system will very quickly move toward its attractor and converge with it. Regardless of how precisely you measure the current velocity and position of the system, though, you can never predict what the position and velocity of the system will be more than a short time into the future. All you know is that the physical behavior of the system will be somewhere near the strange attractor.

Businesses today seem to operate more like a chaotic system than the rigid, deterministic institutions envisioned in the nineteenth century. High-level managers these days really do not have as much control over the day-to-day actions of each employee. The personal economics of employees are certainly different than they were. Personal currencies such as career growth, sense of accomplishment, and self-esteem will generally rank much higher now, relative to the fear of losing one's job. The detailed activities of individuals, particularly product innovation professionals, in a modern company are usually quite unpredictable, but they are not random. There is a pattern to this activity and, in a well-run business, it adds up to a great deal of meaningful and competitive results. The efforts of individuals and of entire departments in a successful company seem to respond to a kind of strange attractor in a way that aligns and focuses this energy on the goals of the business. The attribute of a business enterprise that contributes to this essential influence is described here as the organizational vision.

The attention of high-level managers should thus not be on command and control over individual efforts, but instead on how to establish and maintain an effective organization vision for their business. Once this is in place, their role shifts to tracking its effect on collective efforts to ensure that the business is making good progress in the right direction, and to adjust their "strange attractor" as needed from time to time.

An effective organizational vision will affect the behavior of individual workers in several important ways. First, it will urge the efforts of the entire organization toward strategically important business objectives. Second, it will influence each employee to work hard in achieving business-related goals. Next, it will align the efforts of groups of employees in ways that enable them to cooperate in accomplishing common goals that are important to the business. It will influence each employee to remain employed by the firm, regardless of occasional difficulties and hard times. Finally, it will attract new employees to the enterprise and quickly align their efforts with the others.

The degree of alignment and effectiveness of individual effort in a firm is directly related to the clarity, intensity, and appropriateness of the extant organizational vision. To reflect a point made in Chapter 5 and again, in Chapter 8, every firm has the elements of an organizational vision already in place, in one form or another. Their differences in performance arise, at least in part, from the clarity and quality achieved in each element, and in the way the elements work together to influence results. These elements of an effective organizational vision are outlined in the following sections.

■ THE FRAMEWORK FOR AN ORGANIZATIONAL VISION

The organizational vision for a business enterprise begins with a focus on customers and ends with the detailed organizational structure that delivers value to those customers. Depending on circumstances, parts of the organizational vision must change from time to time. But other parts remain constant for decades and form, in effect, the bedrock on which the firm is founded. All parts of an organizational vision are essential, though, and work synergistically to create the influences described earlier.

Figure 10.1 outlines the framework for an organizational vision. This framework begins at the top with the identification, in broad terms, of the customer focus for the firm. Who are our customers and, generally speaking, what needs do they have that are of interest to our business? The next element in the vision is an understanding of the purpose of the enterprise. The purpose is a general, timeless statement that describes a company's "reason for being." What value does this company bring to the world? What would the world lose if we ceased to exist? The purpose of a

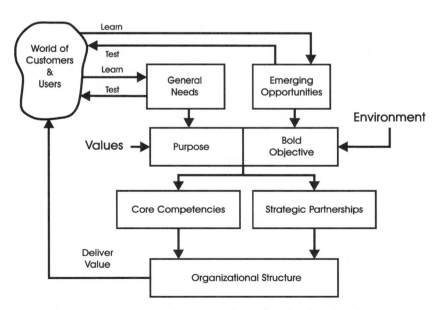

Figure 10.1 Key elements of an organizational vision.

business enterprise will reflect both its customers and key values and beliefs that are intrinsic to the people in the firm, and that are deeply held by them. The purpose serves as a "guiding star" for the enterprise and keeps it aligned and moving in the right direction over the long term.[3]

The next element in the vision is a specific and exciting strategic goal for the firm, labeled here the "Bold Objective." Collins and Porras, in their landmark book, *Built to Last,* call this the Big Hairy Audacious Goal (BHAG). This stretch goal for the firm, achievable in perhaps two to three years, will ideally reflect an exciting opportunity in the customer world as well as the current business environment and circumstances of the enterprise. It should also, of course, be well aligned with the purpose and values of the firm.

Of course, a company will pursue other aims and goals besides the single bold objective. These other pursuits, though, should all also fit well within the core ideology of the firm. Those that do not should be closely scrutinized and either altered or eliminated. Above all, none of these other activities should be at cross-purposes with the bold objective.

The purpose and bold objective provide a necessary backdrop for understanding the core capabilities that the firm must develop and maintain. These include both the core competencies that will be developed and supported in-house, and those capabilities that are to be acquired through strategic partners.[4] The core capabilities should be a necessary and sufficient set that will ensure the competitive performance of the firm as it pursues its purpose and objectives. Over time, as the enterprise achieves one bold objective and moves on to the next, as new technologies emerge, or as business conditions change, the required set of core capabilities may change. As this happens, though, the shift should be a logical response to the changing business environment and objectives of the company.

Finally, the purpose, bold objective, and core capabilities provide the underpinnings for the organizational structure of the business. The purpose of organizational structure is to effectively support the work that needs to be done. It should therefore be responsive to both long-term directions and midterm objectives. The specific detail of core competencies will impose demands

---

[3] Collins, James C., and Porras, Jerry I. *Built to Last: Successful Habits of Visionary Companies.* New York: Harper Business, 1994.

[4] Hamel, Gary, and Prahalad, C. K. *Competing for the Future* (pp. 202–211). Boston: Harvard Business School Press, 1994.

and constraints on the organizational structure, as will the requirement to manage and work with strategic partners. If, for whatever reason, the organizational structure gets in the way of competitive performance, it should be changed and improved.

Together, these elements of the organizational vision can provide focus and motivation for each employee in a company, at all levels. To do so, however, they should be broadly communicated. To have their effect, they need to make sense to each individual. If the company purpose reflects an employee's own deeply held values and beliefs, it will matter to him or her. Employees should understand the bold objective and how it reflects current competitive challenges and opportunities. Achievement of the bold objective should be an exciting possibility, and its alignment with both the company purpose and important customer needs should be inherently obvious. The rationale that relates core capabilities to the purpose and bold objective of the company should be clear and understood by all. The reasons behind the focus on a specific set of core competencies should be both widely understood and compelling. Finally, employees should understand how the organizational structure is designed to support the work of the enterprise. For the organizational vision to be effective, its elements must make sense to all employees and seem important to them. They must be able to see how their own work fits into this vision and how their personal efforts are important to its success.

■ THE CORE IDEOLOGY

In *Built to Last,* Collins and Porras describe the defining attributes of excellent companies—firms that had thrived for over 50 years and which, on average, had created shareholder value at a rate of about 16 times the market average. The authors studied and compared 18 excellent companies with 18 comparable companies that had not done as well over the same span of time. The lessons learned from this research are instrumental in identifying and defining some of the key elements in the framework for organizational vision outlined here.

➤ Organizational Values and Purpose

A characteristic that was common to each of the 18 excellent companies studied in *Built to Last* was that, despite their remarkable financial performance, their primary focus was not on profit, or on a particular product line or technology either. Instead, each company was focused on building an enterprise that mattered to its community, its customers, and the world—an enterprise based on principles. In the words of Collins and Porras:

> *Like the fundamental ideals of a great nation, church, school, or any other enduring institution, core ideology in a visionary company is a set of basic precepts that plant a stake in the ground: "This is who we are; this is what we stand for; this is what we are all about."*

In the framework offered here, these principles are embodied in the deeply held values and beliefs that are common to the group of people who work together in a business enterprise, and in their common sense of purpose.

In one of the 18 companies, the Hewlett-Packard Company, a set of commonly held values emerged through the influence of the founders, Bill Hewlett and David Packard, that reflected their inherent quality of character. This value set has been labeled "the HP way." Over the years, considerable effort has been invested to understand, articulate, and institutionalize these values, which include:

➤ Trust and respect for individuals.

➤ A high level of achievement and contribution.

➤ Uncompromising integrity in all business matters.

➤ Achieving common objectives through teamwork.

➤ Flexibility and innovation.

These values are broadly held throughout the company. Applicants for employment who exhibit them tend to be the ones who get hired. Employees who embrace them and demonstrate them in their day-to-day actions tend to be the ones who remain with the company for a long time and progress into upper management ranks. Once there, they tend to select their successors for these same qualities.

In its first 50 years, HP's purpose was articulated in various ways by various leaders. But it always came out as something about making a technical contribution in the products that HP develops. Or providing affordable quality for HP's customers. In an internal newsletter in 1961, David Packard stated it this way, "Our main task is to design, develop, and manufacture the finest electronic equipment for the advancement of science and the welfare of humanity."[5] This statement indeed reflects the values listed previously.

In the early 1990s, a select group of high-level managers, led by CEO John Young, created a "statement of strategic intent" for the Hewlett-Packard Company—a purpose statement. By this time, HP's primary business had evolved from electronic instruments to computers and computer peripherals. Electronic instruments were still important though, and the company's instrument products addressed needs in diverse areas, such as medical applications, the automotive industry, scientific research, and military applications. The challenge was to articulate the common purpose that drove these disparate activities. After a significant investment of time and effort, the group articulated HP's purpose as:

To create information products that accelerate the advancement of knowledge, and fundamentally improve the performance of both individuals and organizations.[6]

This statement still deals with making a technical contribution, but the language is broader and spans not only electronic instruments, but computers and peripheral equipment as well. People from HP's electronic instruments group who helped craft this statement balked briefly at the phrase *information products,* but quickly realized that HP has been building information products from the very beginning. The language in this statement has helped people throughout HP better understand the unity that ties their efforts together.

Merck & Company, another of the visionary companies studied by Collins and Porras, provides another excellent example. The values and beliefs held by individuals in that company include honesty and integrity, as well as social responsibility, and science-based innovation. As quoted in *Built to Last,* their purpose is stated this way:

We are in the business of preserving and improving human life. All of our actions must be measured by our success in achieving this goal.[7]

---

[5] Packard, David. "From Our President's Desk," *Watt's Current,* Internal employee newsletter, November 1961, courtesy Hewlett-Packard Company archives.
[6] Presented with permission from the Hewlett-Packard Company archives.
[7] Collins and Porras, p. 69.

This statement reflects deeply held values and beliefs and, as Collins and Porras put it, "drives a stake in the ground." The value that Merck brings to the world is implicit in this simple statement. Employees at this company are most likely eager to invest their best talents and their best efforts in a firm that stands for such a noble purpose.

➤ Walking the Talk

Of primary importance is the authenticity of the core ideology. The values that are cited must be heartfelt and reflected in the everyday actions of people at all levels in the firm; they cannot be borrowed or adapted from those of another company. Values are thus not an appropriate focus for benchmarking. Each firm must discover and articulate its own value set.

Likewise, the purpose of a company is personal to that enterprise. It cannot be borrowed or paraphrased from that of another firm. Instead it needs to be an aspiration that business leaders sincerely embrace and that evokes a sense of pride and commitment from employees. Statements of purpose that outline intentions to make money, typical of some enterprises today, simply do not measure up in this regard.

Many firms create high-minded and articulate credos and value statements that are not authentic and thus do not qualify as elements in an organizational vision. They are mere words and are worse than nothing at all. These creations are often embodied as posters on conference room walls. Employees get so used to seeing them that they blend into the background and, in effect, disappear. They are made meaningless by their lack of connection to the informal words and behaviors of high-level managers. After awhile, employees become hardened and cynical, and learn to ignore these empty messages.

In contrast, business leaders at Merck "walk their talk." A dramatic example of this occurred when scientist at Merck came up with a cure for "river blindness," a disease that affected over a million people in Third World countries.[8] In attempting to market this cure, the company discovered that those who needed it couldn't afford to pay for it. So Merck decided to give it away. In fact, they invested significant amounts of their own money in distributing this remedy to those who needed it, just to ensure that it

---

[8] Collins and Porras, p. 47.

got into the right hands and was properly applied. In terms of their own statement of purpose, this program was a big success, even though it lost money for the company. In deciding to go forward with the product at a loss, Merck leaders were concerned that to do otherwise would demoralize Merck scientists. In the words of chief executive P. Roy Vagelos, "The long-term consequences of such actions are not always clear, but somehow I think they always pay off."

➤ Implementation

In the 18 companies in *Built to Last,* the core ideology seems to have been in place forever, installed first by the original founders and then supported and protected by subsequent leaders. So what actions can a company take that does not have a clear core ideology? How can high-level managers put something in place that makes sense?

In articulating the values and purpose of an enterprise, sincerity and authenticity are of paramount importance. Business leaders need to first get in touch with their own feelings and attitudes on these matters, and then attempt to communicate them honestly and in simple language. Over time, a consistent message that aligns well with other signals from both formal actions and informal behavior will transform these words into a serviceable core ideology.

Depending on circumstances in the firm, an assessment of values and purpose may involve simply the founder, president, or CEO, or it might involve the entire top management group. A review of the HP way at the Hewlett-Packard Company in the early 1990s involved the members of their management council, the top 35 or so managers in the firm. Each member was interviewed as part of a well-designed assessment program and the results of these interviews were integrated into a restatement of the HP way values and practices. The important outcome is that, when the values and purpose for an enterprise have been established, all the business leaders who influence attitudes at lower levels communicate with one voice on these matters.

Occasionally, discussions of these issues may reveal deep, fundamental, and irreconcilable differences between key leaders. These individuals may embrace incompatible values, or they may have fundamentally different views on the purpose of the business enterprise. Discovering these differences is a positive step forward for, until they are resolved one way or another, the firm will operate, either overtly or covertly, at cross-purposes. Bringing these issues to the surface and dealing with them, once and for all is a major step in the development of the company.

A key point to keep in mind when exploring matters of values and purpose is that there are no "right" answers. Any set of values and beliefs is just fine, as long as key managers sincerely embrace it. Managers at the Nike corporation, for example, may espouse values related to athletic competition, whereas leaders at the Disney corporation might embrace commonly held family values. The purpose statement for Nike may be something like "To compete and win," whereas Disney's might be "To make people happy." Each value set and purpose statement can be quite different from the other, but each one may be just right for the particular company that embraces it.

■ THE ENVIRONMENT AND THE BOLD OBJECTIVE

A bold objective is the second key element in the organizational vision that amplifies its influence as the strange attractor for employee behavior. As mentioned, this objective is labeled a BHAG (Big, Hairy, Audacious Goal) by Collins and Porras and should reflect the current competitive circumstances of the firm and spell out a goal that gets employees excited and involved.[9] A firm will undoubtedly have many other goals and objectives, but each company needs a central bold objective that establishes a tangible vision for concrete and aggressive achievement that is line with the purpose and values of the firm. An effective bold objective lays down the direction for competitive transformation, and challenges each and every employee to "throw their shoulder to the wheel" and help move the firm toward the goal.

➤ Setting the Objective

The ideal bold objective is (1) clearly important in light of current circumstances, (2) time-limited in extent, (3) inherently measurable, and (4) aggressive enough to, at first, seem impossible. In ad-

---

[9] Collins and Porras, chap. 5.

dition, a successful bold objective must have the passionate and unwavering commitment of high-level leaders. A stellar example of a bold objective is John F. Kennedy's proclamation on May 25, 1961, "that this Nation should commit itself to achieving the goal, before this decade is out, of landing a man on the moon and returning him safely to earth."[10] At the time he laid down this challenge, the United States was reeling from a string of spectacular failures in our attempts to launch rockets into space. The Russians seemed far ahead of the United States and were pulling away in a race to dominate this exciting new field of endeavor. This was the perfect bold objective for the time—clearly important, time-limited, inherently measurable, and seemingly impossible. It was supported by Congress and by JFK's successors. It had a remarkable effect on NASA, on the U.S. economy, and on the attitudes of citizens throughout the country. It was instrumental in transforming the United States into the world leader in space technology.

Development of an effective bold objective for a business enterprise requires the highest degree of situational awareness. High-level managers should work together as a team on this and pool their knowledge, their intuition, and their imagination. This work should take into account emerging market opportunities, technology trends, and current circumstances, both internal and external to the firm. It should consider both the strengths of the firm and its current weaknesses. In fact, establishing an effective bold objective will most likely utilize every scrap of information in the management knowledge base discussed in Chapter 8.

To start, long-range trends in the marketplace need to be understood and an effort must be made to discern major, emerging opportunities. What will the market terrain look like in three years? What will the customer learn to want by then? Which of these opportunities do we want to own? What new capabilities will it take to dominate the market in this target area? Next, attention needs to be directed toward internal and external circumstances. Who might be our competitors for these target opportunities? What can we discern about their growth, development, and directions for the future? How do we compare with our competitors? What new capabilities do we need to compete? What capabilities do we currently maintain that may not be needed in the future? What is the outlook for the world economy, and for foreign

---

[10] Boorstin, Daniel J. *The Americans: The Democratic Experience.* New York: Vintage Books, 1974 (p. 596).

markets and competitors? What new constraints are visible within our time horizon that might impact our business (e.g., environmental concerns, increases in energy cost, political obstacles)? How can we turn these constraints to our advantage?

With some answers to these questions in mind, the next step for business leaders is to envision the future that they want to create. JFK certainly had a tangible grasp on the future that he wanted to see unfold. Perhaps that is why he is remembered as a great leader. Occasionally when high-level managers are asked to envision the future of their company, they fall back on numbers: "My vision for the future is that, in three years, our revenues will be over twice what they are now!" This kind of vision will not excite the imagination of the rank and file. The future that is to be created must instead be described in terms of what the firm will do differently—bold, aggressive, imaginative extensions or additions to current capabilities—to create unusual financial success.

To be influenced, employees need to see how the company will be transformed in its capability to provide value. They need to envision a role for themselves in this transformation that will be rewarding in terms of their own personal currencies, whatever they may be. They want to be part of the effort to put a man on the moon, or to provide customers with an unimaginably wonderful new line of products. They want to be part of an effort that stuns the competition, and leaves them bewildered and hopelessly behind. They want stories that they can tell their grandchildren.

➤ Some Examples of Bold Objectives

Built to Last provides several excellent examples of bold objectives— BHAGs—that visionary companies pursue. Boeing Company developing the 747 aircraft, Ford Motor Company democratizing the automobile, and Sony reversing the image of poor quality that plagued Japanese products in the 1950s are all examples highlighted by Collins and Porras.

In the late 1970s the Hewlett-Packard Company set a bold objective to become a major computer company. At the time, HP was primarily an electronic instrument maker. Only a small fraction of their new product effort was devoted to computer products, which included handheld calculators, desktop computers, and measurement system controllers. IBM and Digital Equipment Corporation (DEC) were the major players in the computer industry at the time and they were slugging it out in a struggle between mainframe-based, enterprisewide systems and minicomputers. Apple and Microsoft, partnered with IBM personal computer (PC) clonemakers, were going head-to-head for the fledgling PC market. For HP to aspire to compete in this arena was indeed audacious, and seemingly impossible. Growth in the electronic instruments industry was declining rapidly, though, making the rapid expansion in computers highly enviable.

➤ Sustaining the Bold Objective

Once a bold objective has been declared, it must have the steadfast support of business leaders through to completion. They communicate this commitment to the rank and file in both conscious and unconscious ways. Their words, their actions, their policies, where they invest available funds, who they promote, and their body language are all important signals that individuals at all levels in the organization detect and accurately interpret. Commitment can't be faked. People quickly see through hollow, insincere messages and inconsistencies between words and deeds.

A story about the chairman of the Boeing Company, William Allen, was told in *Built to Last*. When Mr. Allen heard a member of the board suggest that, if the 747 aircraft didn't pan out, Boeing could always back out of the project, he stiffened and said, "Back out? If the Boeing Company says we will build this airplane, we will build it even if it takes the resources of the entire company!" Real commitment is conveyed by body language, tone of voice, *and* the right words and actions.

In HP's 10-year product reliability initiative (see Chapter 8), John Young's objective didn't exactly stir the hearts of HP employees when he first announced it. While it might have been necessary, working on product reliability was not their highest priority. Once the program got rolling, though, and people started seeing some success, this objective began to generate some excitement. The sustained commitment of John and HP's other high-level managers, and their due diligence over this period, were essential to the success of this program.

Another example of the importance of high-level management commitment is HP's transition to computer products. In transforming itself into a computer company, HP was forced to reorganize (many times during the 1980s), to learn new technologies, and to invent new ways of selling, distributing, and supporting products. This bold objective required HP employees to learn new skills. A surplus of electrical and mechanical engineering talent was resolved, at least in part, by reeducating these individuals in software engineering techniques. None of this could have happened without strong and sustained commitment by HP's high-level management team. That, and diligent application of the four factors that encourage change (discussed in Chapter 9), caused steady progress toward this bold objective. Growth in the price of HP's stock, though, was not so steady. In the late 1980s, HP's share price fell to about half of its peak value. HP's business leadership team endured significant pressure and criticism at such times. They persevered, though, and remained committed to completing this important transition. By 1992, when John Young retired as CEO, HP had become the number two computer company in the world, second only to IBM. And HP's growth at that time—in revenues, profits, and shareholder value—was the strongest in the industry.

■ BUILDING CORE CAPABILITIES

The first part of the organizational vision is about establishing direction and figuring out what the company should do. The second part, building core capabilities, is about how the company intends to create the capacity to accomplish those goals competitively. This capacity to compete is achieved through either (1) developing and maintaining internal core competencies, or (2) acquiring needed capabilities through strategic partnerships with other firms. The reason these issues are included as part of the organizational vision is that employees need to know how business leaders intend to compete and why they have selected a particular approach before they can help make these plans work. The "How" is as much a part of the organizational vision as the "What." If both are made clear to employees, then they have the information they need to align their own efforts with the program. And, if the goals are compelling and the rationale for the approach to building needed capabilities makes sense, they will be motivated to work hard on the right things.

The intent of this section is not to provide a tutorial on how to build core capabilities. This information exists elsewhere. The reader may, for example, turn to *Competing for the Future,* by Hamel and Prahalad. Instead, this section will focus on issues that are important to ensuring that efforts to build core capabilities contribute to a strong organizational vision.

➤ The Balance between Internal and External Capability

The choice between developing internal facilities for providing a core capability and depending on someone outside the firm for this know-how presents business leaders with a dilemma. For example, a semiconductor manufacturer wanting to implement a new device with state-of-the-art chip density either must invest in an extremely expensive upgrade of its own fabrication facilities or depend on another company to fabricate the chips. Should the company invest, suffer the impact on the bottom line, and try to stay competitive as a silicon foundry? Or should it find a strategic partner for fabrication needs and focus its own investments elsewhere? Shifting to a strategic partner may mean laying off a significant number of valued employees, and it may cripple the firm's ability to compete in the future.

Figure 10.2 provides an equation for return-on-investment (ROI) that serves as a useful framework for the discussion on

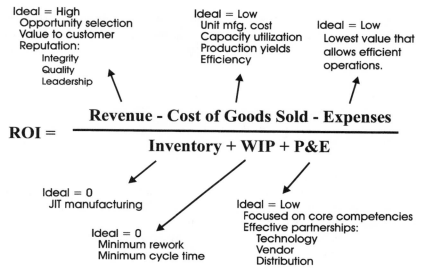

Figure 10.2 Optimizing return-on-investment.

balancing internal and external capabilities.[11] The numerator of this equation is the before-tax profit from a manufacturing operation, and the denominator contains terms for the forms of investment that are made. The comments attached to each term highlight the goals and focus for improvement efforts.

In general, the capabilities that a firm uses to deliver value to customers are included in the plant and equipment term (P&E) in the denominator. Lowering this term reduces the investment level and, as long the return stays high, causes ROI to increase. This desirable result motivates business leaders to look to strategic partners rather than make large investments in internal capacity. On the other hand, if one pushes that strategy far enough, a company can rid itself of all capacity to create value for its customers. It becomes, instead, a mere broker for the services of other companies who provide value. In the short term this can make ROI look terrific, but in the long term it can cripple a firm's ability to create revenue growth. The idea behind core competencies is that a firm needs to focus its P&E investments on those few areas where it intends to develop and maintain world-class competitive stature. It then needs to find strategic partners that can provide other required capabilities at competitive levels of cost and quality. The ideal value for P&E investments is thus low but not zero.

A better strategy for managing P&E investments is thus to focus them on core competencies. A business should select its areas of core competency carefully and then commit fully to whatever investment is required to be better at each of these capabilities than their worldwide competitors. Any capability that is currently supported, and is not in this set of selected core competencies, should be phased out over time and replaced with the services of a suitable strategic partner. This strategy decreases the size of the P&E term and focuses it on those investments that will best enable the firm to provide value for its customers, and differentiate itself from its competitors.

While this strategy may result in some layoffs and divestiture of facilities, it has a strong business rationale. It offers the promise of even bigger investments in truly competitive capabilities. It further promises to strengthen the ability of a firm to provide value for its customers in the future. Presuming that the strategy

---

[11] Based on comments presented by C. K. Prahalad at the University of Michigan Executive Program, May 1992.

results from sound business judgment and high-quality decisions, and that it is communicated to employees in a sincere and credible fashion, it will become a key component in a firm's organizational vision.

➤ Including Product Innovation Capabilities in the Organizational Vision

General accounting practice can distort the way business leaders manage new product activities. Most new product-related expenditures are included in the expense term in the numerator in Figure 10.2. As such, current new product expenses are subtracted from current revenues to determine current profits. They are managed in the same category as telephones and janitorial services. Expense controls aimed at keeping profits up during hard times thus usually impact the product innovation investment rate along with all other items in the expense category. As described in Chapter 2, this has an inevitably negative impact on long-term revenue growth.

In terms of its impact on the business, though, money spent on new product activities is much more like that invested in both the P&E and work-in-process (WIP) terms in Figure 10.2. The management approach to new product-related expenditures should thus be similar to that applied to these investment categories. Investments in R&D related to a new technology have a business impact that is equivalent to the construction of a new semiconductor facility. The new facility will enable shipment of specific new products currently under development and those yet undreamed of. The facility adds to the asset base of the firm and increases its book value. Likewise, a successful new technology provides an intellectual framework that enables new products currently under development, and also those yet unimagined. A new, proprietary technology adds to the intellectual property base of the firm and also increases its value. Both investments increase the capacity of a firm to generate revenue. Yet the semiconductor facility is accounted for as P&E, whereas the R&D investment is treated as an expense.

The business impact of money spent on the development of a specific new product is equivalent to that of money spent fabricating a product on the assembly line. A company spends money today to build a product that will be sold to generate revenue in the near future. These investments are accounted as WIP and placed in the denominator in Figure 10.2. Likewise, a firm spends money developing a specific new product now, and expects to make revenue from it in the future. The time delay between the new product investment and its return is longer, but the eventual business result is the same. This expenditure, though, is handled as an expense in the numerator. Lumping new product development expenditures in with expenses makes as much sense as accounting for all fabrication expenses on the assembly line as scrap. Business leaders should think about and manage the development of new products as if they are investments in WIP.

Regardless of how accountants handle the money then, business leaders should manage their capacities for industrial R&D and new product development as they do other core capabilities. What new technologies do we need to master to remain competitive? What kind of engineering tools and test equipment do we need? What skill sets will our engineering workforce need in the future? What current capabilities are becoming noncompetitive or obsolete? Which new product-related capabilities should be obtained through strategic partners? Once core competency and strategic partnering decisions are made with regard to product innovation, they should be managed with the same philosophy and the same degree of long-term commitment as are those in other areas of the business. This suggested shift in thinking will help ensure that new product-related core capabilities are an important element in the organizational vision.

■ ON ORGANIZATIONAL STRUCTURE

➤ Creating an Effective Organizational Structure

The reason that organizational structure is at the bottom of Figure 10.1 is that it should be the last part of the vision created. Organizational structure should be somewhat like the floor plan for a new building. Before an architect designs the floor plan, she must first understand the purpose of the structure, and the kinds of activity that it will support. She must take into account how people who are outside will access the functions that go on inside the building. The design should be responsive to these constraints. Likewise, organizational structure should be responsive to the other elements in the vision, so these other elements need to be established first. Then the structure of the organization can be designed to facilitate achievement of the bold objective, support execution of core competencies, and provide for effective interaction with strategic partners.

Occasionally an old residence will be converted into a restaurant. The effect is sometimes quaint, but the floor plan never works very well. The tables are always too close together, so waiters have to squeeze by patrons and carefully pass the food over their heads. The kitchen is usually cramped and in the wrong place. Food often needs to be carried long distances, even up stairs, to reach the customer. A business that tries to adapt a traditional organizational structure to a new bold objective, and its supporting core competencies and strategic partnerships, can create serious and unnecessary obstacles for its workforce. Like the walls of an old house, old organizational boundaries and constraints are strong. But sometimes they need to be torn down and rebuilt to facilitate the flow of work. And occasionally this cycle needs to be repeated several times before the organizational structure is finally right. Business leaders must sign up for this difficult work when they take on the implementation of an effective organizational vision.

When John Young established the bold objective to turn HP into a computer company in the late 1970s, he was managing a company that was structured to develop, manufacture, and sell electronic instruments. The core competencies included strong electronic engineering talents, and the capabilities required to manufacture electronic instruments—sheet metal fabrication, printed circuit assembly, and so on. The sales force was optimized to interface with electronic instrument customers, such as engineers and scientists working in laboratories. The company was organized into autonomous business divisions, each addressing its own segment of HP's marketplace such as oscilloscopes, voltmeters, gas chromatographs. HP's initial attempts to develop computer systems were very much like trying to run a restaurant in an old house.

Computer systems were more complicated than electronic instruments, and they involved new core competencies. Software technologies and engineering expertise, were required, but were not available in sufficient depth in HP, at least initially. Computer systems included multiple assemblies: a mainframe, tape drives, a system console, remote access terminals, and disc memories. Initially, HP assigned the development of each of these system components to separate business divisions, just as if they were independent electronic instruments. But that didn't work very well because these components had to come together and work as a system. The business divisions had to work together in new ways, and the old organizational structures did not support these new work patterns. Decisions and trade-offs had to be made, but each division had only a piece of the system under its control and all divisions had equal power. A simple decision about the number of interface slots on the back of the computer mainframe became complicated. The mainframe division needed only a small number for its purposes, but divisions that developed the peripheral products wanted more. The engineering teams could only argue over the right number. So they elevated such problems to higher management, and business division managers would then argue over these issues.

To resolve these conflicts, a high-level management group was established called the Computer Business Executive Council (CBEC). This group met once a month for a full day. The CBEC had the final word on all computer-system-related issues, and they had the span of control to make their decisions stick. The problem that quickly surfaced with this plan was that so many low-level technical issues got elevated to the CBEC that their agenda filled up to overflowing almost from the start. And this group of executives was poorly equipped to make low-level technical decisions. So the CBEC became a severe bottleneck to timely decisions and began to delay projects. Furthermore, the quality of their technical decisions was sometimes suspect, and this damaged their credibility at lower levels. In reality, the CBEC was a stopgap measure to help make an outdated organizational structure work.

Instead, the organizational structure needed a complete redesign, and some walls needed to come down. This difficult work took place through the early 1980s and involved not just one organizational restructuring, but many. It took several attempts to learn how to build a competitive computer company. In fact, there is no one, stable answer to this problem. The truth of the matter is that you have to be willing to change and adapt your organization often—its internal boundaries, roles and responsibilities, and operating ground rules—to stay competitive in a dynamic business.

► Making Organizational Structure Part of the Strange Attractor

The structure of an organization should make the people who work in it more effective. Their impact on progress toward the objectives of the enterprise should thus be amplified. This is best accomplished by aligning organizational departments and policies reasonably well with the work that must be done, and then encouraging people to "step out of the box" occasionally in getting the right things to happen. No organization can ever be designed and specified so completely that it addresses all the issues that may arise. Instead, broad charters ought to be assigned that get people generally focused in the right direction and then each individual should be encouraged to do what makes sense in moving work results toward desired objectives.

This works best when high-level managers have communicated the intent of the organizational structure along with their best guess about how it should look. Their communication should also include an invitation for each individual to raise issues about organization-related obstacles. When employees understand the importance of high-level objectives, and how business leaders are trying to implement steps to achieve them, they are better equipped to see waste and detect flaws in day-to-day activities. This, along with freedom from the fear of reprisal, will give each individual the license to help shape organizational processes in ways that will lead to more competitive performance. This can enlist the enthusiastic involvement of everyone and make their behavior on the job seem to be very much under the influence of a strange attractor.

■ THE STEWARDSHIP PHASE

Once the high-level management team has implemented the key elements of an organizational vision, their role shifts to tracking the performance, progress, and needs of their people. They become stewards of the organizational vision, communicating it, endorsing its importance, adjusting it, and improving its effectiveness as needed. Perhaps a snag may occur in developing a core competency. One of the business leaders should assist and coach those working on the problem. A problem in the organizational structure may surface. High-level management attention should be applied to help resolve the issue.

Above all, as employees come forward with questions and requests for help and guidance, they should be encouraged as much as possible to use their own judgment and do what makes sense. Business leaders should resist the temptation to tell people what to do, for this will preempt the influence of the strange attractor.

Instead they should attempt to amplify people's understanding of the organizational vision and then expect them to make progress in the right direction. Those closest to the work that must be done should be encouraged to make needed decisions whenever possible. They generally have the best information and the best judgment in the matters at hand. The magic in an organizational vision is that, when it is well implemented, it elicits that best from each individual at each level in the enterprise—hard work, creativity, good judgment, and quick, independent action.

During this phase, though, business leaders need to remain sensitive to changes in the business environment that may affect the viability of either the bold objective or established core capabilities. Changes in the marketplace, in technology, or in the mix of capabilities required to be competitive may require decisive adjustments to the elements of the vision.

■ CONCLUSION

The leaders of the most competitive business enterprises of our time have learned to get more out of their people, particularly those individuals who create and introduce new products. Product innovators at these firms work harder and compete more effectively than their counterparts in other companies. To keep up, business leaders in other firms must learn to evoke the same level of spirited competitive intensity from their workforce. But they are unlikely to do this by issuing stern orders and demanding results. These actions are unlikely to alter the personal economics of people in a way that produces the desired shift in behavior.

This chapter has offered an alternative management approach, based on the excellent work of Collins and Porras, and that of Hamel and Prahalad. This approach seems better aligned with the natural flow and patterns of work in a business enterprise than the old ideas of command and control. Product innovation professionals are often free to work on those tasks that are the most appealing. The trick is to make the work that leads to business success most appealing. A well-crafted organizational vision does this, and by influencing the personal economics of each individual, it promises to unleash more of the latent power that resides in the workforce of a business enterprise.

Furthermore, once it has been effectively installed, an organizational vision will largely unburden high-level managers. People who have embraced a vision and are passionately pursuing it require very little supervision, only occasional monitoring, and some coaching once in awhile. And those pursuing a well-conceived vision are less likely to create catastrophe but, instead, are likely to present their leaders with an occasional nice surprise—results that are well beyond those expected.

Desired Upper Management Behaviors:
Organizational Vision—The Guiding Force Field

➤ Apply the "parking lot" metric. Does the parking lot for the cars of your product innovation people fill up early each day and empty out late? Do you see people going home early? Or do they sometimes have to be chased out with a stick to get them to go home at all?

➤ Apply the "Monday morning" metric. When a new product engineer comes in early on Monday morning, before the supervisor gets there, what does the engineer do? Does this person know what work needs to be done, and does he or she want to do it?

➤ Apply the "Grandparents" metric. Can each employee explain, with pride and in simple terms that someone disconnected from the work situation (i.e., their grandparents) can understand, what the company does, and why their own job is important?

➤ Consider the results of the preceding measures. Decide whether or not your organizational vision needs work. Keep it vital.

➤ Communicate your deeply held values and beliefs and your sense of purpose whenever possible. Be authentic.

Chapter 11

Leadership and the Creative Environment

One of the tasks of a leader is to help the group achieve the sense of security and freedom from fear that enables it to risk renewal.

John W. Gardner
On Leadership

Product innovation can be risky. As discussed in Chapter 7, project risk is associated with flaws in work process, flaws in management process, and extension of intellectual frameworks. But that is not the kind of risk we are addressing here. Product innovation can be risky to the people who are involved. They can be personally damaged through their association with a product innovation project. A new product effort attracts a lot of attention. It has a schedule that others depend on. As mentioned in Chapter 3, project delays can cost a great deal of money. Project results can dramatically affect near-term revenue and profit growth. Other people's bonuses often depend on the successful outcome of product innovation projects. These other people are sometimes very powerful. Anyone who gets in the way of a successful outcome—who gets on the so-called critical path of the project—can be subjected to immense pressure, unwanted attention, and even career-altering censure.

In one real-life example, the unit manufacturing cost (UMC) of a new product was higher than expected. Initial cost targets had been unclear, but late in the project people in the marketing department grew nervous about the list price of the product implied by recent UMC estimates. In a meeting to review this issue, the

CEO asked the project manager to remove over 20 percent from the product cost. The project manager respectfully responded that this would require a complete redesign of the product, which would delay the introduction by almost a year. A delay of this magnitude, of course, was unacceptable. The CEO ordered the project manager to take the cost out and meet the current schedule. Since this was simply impossible, the project manager chose to lower costs where he could, but to continue with the current design and introduce the product on time—all good business decisions. The high UMC resulted in a list price that was higher than the marketing people wanted, but customers loved the product. It sold well above fore-casted unit volumes and made a terrific profit. The CEO, however, was not satisfied with the project manager's performance. The project manager was reprimanded and demoted back to the level of development engineer. He was personally damaged by the experience and his confidence and self-esteem were never the same. The job of project manager became known throughout that organization as the "gladiator" position. As long as you always win, you are a hero. But one slip and you get killed, careerwise.

Why then would any sane person ever want to get anywhere near a product innovation project? The answer is that the work environment—the ambiance in which product innovators live and move and have their being—is not always this hazardous. This example, though, illustrates the powerful impact that business leaders can have on the creative environment and hence on the work-related behavior of new product innovators. As implied by the quotation that opens this chapter, business leaders have the important task of helping product innovators achieve security and freedom from fear. Successful accomplishment of this task is essential to attain a competitive level of performance in new product efforts.

An effective work environment must achieve two important business objectives:

1. It must encourage and support the most competitive behavior from each individual and each team.
2. It should help attract and retain the best available talent.

To achieve these objectives, the working environment must affect the personal economics of each product innovator in ways that enlist his or her creativity, hard work, and willingness to take risks on behalf of the business needs of the company. Second, there must be a consistency to the ambiance over time so that people can adapt to it, become comfortable in it, and count on it. Finally, the work environment must be trustworthy. Product innovators must know that conditions and operating principles at work are solid, and that these conditions and principles apply equally to all.

Many styles of working environment can satisfy these conditions. As with the core ideology discussed in Chapter 10, there are no single right answers for the working environment issue. Working environments that satisfy these constraints, though, all share common attributes. This chapter outlines the essential characteristics of an effective product innovation environment. In addition, it describes the strong influence that leaders have on the working environment and discusses some common leadership pitfalls.

■ THE DISPROPORTIONATE EFFECT OF LEADERSHIP

Business leaders have an incredibly powerful influence on the ambiance in their company. Everything they say is analyzed and tested by subordinates for hidden meaning and consistency with what has been said before. Memos, policy statements, formal speeches, and informal conversation are all scrutinized closely. What they praise and what they punish also provide important messages about high-level managers, who they are, and how they might influence the careers and lives of subordinates. Keeping mentally centered under all of this scrutiny takes considerable strength of character, but these circumstances just seem to come with the territory.

The actions of high-level managers also provide important signals to subordinates. Whom they hire, whom they promote, what they expect, and where they spend their time all help set the working environment and establish de facto priorities. Their lack of action is important, too. Their willingness to overlook dishonesty can have far-reaching implications on the way people act at work, both toward each other and toward customers. Their lack of response to poor performance can lower performance standards across the organization and demoralize high achievers. Their tolerance of criticism and hostility between subordinates can lead to an environment that erodes mutual trust and cooperation. In fact, the actions of leaders sometimes speak so loudly that people have trouble hearing their words.

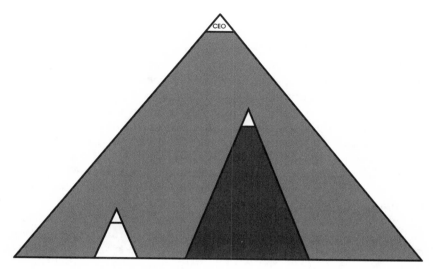

Figure 11.1 Leaders extend a cone of influence.

Through words and actions, then, leaders send clear signals, both consciously and unconsciously, that influence the working environment. In the words of Parker Palmer:[1]

> A leader is a person who has an unusual degree of power to create the conditions under which other people must live and move and have their being—conditions that can either be as illuminating as heaven or as shadowy as hell.

➤ Cones of Influence

The influence that a high-level manager has on the working environment spreads throughout the ranks of the organization within his or her span of control like a cone. As depicted in Figure 11.1, the cone begins with the individual leader at the top and spreads out to encompass all those who report to this person, either directly or through others. Depending on the values and integrity of

---

[1] Palmer, Parker J. *Leading from Within: Reflections on Spirituality and Leadership.* Transcription of a speech published as a pamphlet by The Servant Leadership School, Washington, DC, 1990.

the high-level manager, and on the effectiveness of his or her words and actions, this cone can either be "light" or "dark"—meaning that, respectively, it can either have a positive influence on the work behavior of individuals and thus improve business performance, or it can have a negative effect on performance.

Inevitably, the quality of life experienced by people who "live and move and have their being" within one of these cones corresponds to the lightness or darkness of the ambiance created by their particular business leader. Good people are generally happier on the job when they are engaged effectively in meaningful work. Their frustrations run high, though, and their sense of self-worth suffers if their energy is diverted into nonproductive activities mandated by an unhealthy work environment.

When Bill Hewlett and Dave Packard founded the Hewlett-Packard Company, their collective character and integrity permeated the organization with the HP way value system. They were more interested in creating an environment for accomplishing excellent engineering than in tracking the particular projects that were underway at any given time. In effect, they created a cone of light that encompassed the entire company. As the company grew and individual business divisions were established, Bill and Dave assigned people to the role of division general manager who shared the HP way values, and who understood the importance of a healthy working environment. So as the company grew, new cones of influence were created, but they were usually simple extensions of the already prevalent conditions.

Bill and Dave were diligent, though, and frequently traveled around the company to sample the working environment in each division. During their visits, they always created occasions to talk with individuals at all levels, from general manager through individual contributor. This "management by wandering around" (MBWA) allowed them to detect the occasional cone of darkness that might be evolving in their company, and to make appropriate corrections. Their persistent MBWA and their willingness to cull the HP management ranks to keep working environments healthy were instrumental in building HP into one of the world's most admired companies.

► Cones of Influence Outlast Their Creators

The cone of light or shadow projected by a particular high-level leader seems to grow a skeleton over time and thus becomes a semipermanent structure. The leader at the top of a cone will promote people into management positions that form part of the organizational framework. These people will inevitably have qualities that the leader appreciates. Their style and their values will thus tend to reflect those of the leader. And they, in turn, will promote people and extend the skeleton below their own level. The value system and style that have become prevalent affect hiring decisions. New people coming into the organization thus pass through a filter that reflects the dominant value system and attitudes that have been established. All these factors, in effect, solidify a cone of influence and give it permanence. A well-established cone of influence may thus continue to exist, even long after the high-level manager who created it has left.

➤ Shadows That Leaders Can Cast

Since the behavior of business leaders has such strong leverage on the working environment, their character can directly affect the business performance of their organization. Some character attributes—a strong self-image, strength of purpose, honesty, and integrity—can have a positive impact. Others—such as personal insecurity, dishonesty, or indecisiveness—can have a equally strong negative influence. In this regard, Palmer has identified five fundamental types of shadow that leaders can project onto those who are employed by them that are worthy of consideration.[2] These categories are outlined in Table 11.1.

Table 11.1 Categories of Shadow That Leaders Can Project

1. Deep insecurity about their own identity, their own worth.
2. The perception that the universe is essentially hostile to human interests and that life is fundamentally a battleground.
3. Functional atheism—the belief that the ultimate responsibility for everything rests with me.
4. Fear—in particular, fear of the natural chaos of life.
5. The denial of death, such as the end of old ways, the obsolescence of an organization or a process.

---

[2] Ibid. p. 13.

Insecurity Over One's Own Identity

Leaders who are not fully in touch with themselves as people, at the deepest levels, and who lack self-confidence and a sense of self-worth can cast a characteristic shadow over the work environment that they control. They tend to derive their own sense of identity from their position and functional power. They often have little regard for or understanding of the good work people accomplish in their organization. In fact, these leaders tend to be stingy with praise, and instead are more likely to itemize the mistakes and weaknesses of an individual in the presence of his or her peers. They create an environment to build their own esteem while depriving others of identity and importance.

A person who casts this type of shadow might be the business leader who personally presides over daily or weekly project reviews. This individual finds much to criticize in each person's presentation, and is fond of pointing out lapses in the application of institutionalized tools such as quality methods or other formalized approaches to problem solving. The content of the discussion seems of less interest to this leader than apparent flaws in the work process. These meetings generally involve more people than are necessary, but missing one of these meetings can set an individual up for sharp criticism. Even though this leader's demeanor may be aggressive, extroverted, or even authoritarian, this outward appearance may simply be a defense against insecurity.

Another good example of this type of leader is a medical doctor who places himself on a pedestal of respectability while diminishing his subordinates and patients. This person likes to be addressed as "Dr. Peterson," while his assistant is always referred to as "Judy." Regardless of the reason for their visit, his patients usually must shed their clothes and wear a standard hospital gown that does not fully close in the back. This and other details of the office visit create an environment that unsettles visitors and keeps them off balance. The fully dressed doctor, in contrast, can appear calm and in control.

In contrast, leaders who know themselves all the way to their core tend to create environments that give others identity, and empower them to take risks and deliver their full measure of creativity and productivity. Such leaders tend to give credit to others rather than taking it for themselves. These leaders understand that who a person is does not depend on what he or she does. And they apply this principle to themselves as well as to others. They tend to accept people, regardless of their position, and honor each one for that person's special contribution.

The Universe Is a Hostile Place

Leaders who project this shadow tend to view everyone else in the world as having a hidden agenda. Furthermore, this agenda is always somehow aimed at them and, unless they are ever wary, it will take something away from them. In a business environment, this attitude is usually directed not only at competitors, but at employees, customers, vendors, and everyone else. To these leaders, business, and every other aspect of life for that matter, is a zero sum game—if someone wins, then someone else loses. The solutions and visions that a person such as this imagines will usually be focused on winning, but at someone else's expense. The idea of a win-win solution does not usually occur to this person, and when one is offered, it is likely to be rejected.

People who work in the shadow projected by a leader such as this learn to stay close to accepted methods and solutions. Since the leader is basically a fearful person, the ambiance in his or her organization usually makes those who work in it fearful as well. This environment thus tends to stifle creativity and, instead, encourages small steps in familiar directions and a methodical approach. This leader is unlikely to want anyone too close, and will thus tend to keep everyone, subordinates in particular, at arm's length. People who are promoted in this environment will therefore most likely be those who are inclined to remain aloof as well. Relationships between boss and subordinate are thus likely to remain on a formal plane.

Leaders who have grown beyond these fears, in contrast, recognize that the biggest opportunities occur not in beating a competitor, but in discovering new opportunities that no one has thought of before, neither competitors nor customers. Instead of going head-to-head with competitors, they move the business in directions that are relatively free from competition. These individuals are more likely to focus their people on how to create new value for the customer than on how to beat the competition. They create an environment that is free from fear and that invites bold, creative leaps.

Functional Atheism

Leaders who project this shadow feel that to make anything worthwhile happen, they themselves must take full responsibility and cause it to come about. Such leaders are afraid to give away responsibility, for they do not trust others to assume it. Perhaps they fear failure if they are not personally in charge of every detail. Or it might be related to identity insecurity. In this case, identity may attached to responsibility rather than power and position, and delegating responsibility in effect is losing one's identity. Another possible cause is that the leader is afraid a subordinate might demonstrate superior knowledge and skill, thus damaging his or her own self-image. By picking the approach to every problem and controlling subordinates' work, the leader is able to keep others from demonstrating their ability. The individual who projects this shadow tends to assign tasks to subordinates rather than broad objectives. In this organization, there will thus really only be one mind at work—the leader's. Everyone else will simply be engaged in doing what they were told to do. Productivity in organizations that labor under this shadow is inevitably low. People spend an inordinate amount of time either waiting to have their work reviewed, or waiting for their next assignment.

The leader who has outgrown this fear is more interested in the long-term objectives for their organization than the day-to-day tasks that must be done. They assign major objectives to subordinates, and then give these people total responsibility for their assignment. They make themselves dispensable by creating an organization that can operate without them. This leader is not only unafraid of being bested by the superior knowledge and skills of subordinates, he or she actually relishes the nice surprises that employees create when they make a breakthrough, or advance the project farther and faster than expected. This leader routinely recognizes the good work that occurs throughout the organization and diligently searches out and removes obstacles that impede work progress. The leader who has grown beyond functional atheism realizes that the horsepower required to make the organization successful is distributed throughout the rank and file. He or she understands that the leader's job is not to do the work, but to unleash the power in others and then to focus this energy on the right objectives.

Fear of the Natural Chaos in Life

Leaders who project this shadow onto their organization are afraid to let circumstances out of their control. Reacting perhaps to the chaos of circumstances outside their company or their department, they may overcompensate by trying to control everything that moves within their own organizational boundaries. These individuals plan their work and then work their plan—and they expect everyone else to work this way too. To this leader, the method by which work gets done is more important than the result. The shadow projected into the organization is characterized by a requirement for overly rigorous plans as well as severe rigidity in rules and procedures. This shadow creates a culture that is imprisoning rather than empowering. Productivity tends to be low, since a lot of energy is lost to meetings and overly meticulous plans and processes. Creativity tends to be nonexistent.

In Chapter 10, we contrasted the traditional "command and control" style of management with the idea that organizations really operate unpredictably, and move instead in response to a strange attractor that can keep energy generally focused on the right activities. Leaders who fear the natural chaos in life will have nothing to do with strange attractors. They want absolute command and control over everything. And even though this is impossible to achieve, they never seem to tire of trying.

The leader that has grown through this fear of chaos has usually tried command and control in earlier times. This person's experiences, though, have taught her or him of the futility in striving to exercise too much control. This person has learned that a plan that is too rigid stifles creative expression, and tends to eliminate the nice surprises that often occur when people have more freedom to pick their own approach to the work ahead. This individual has learned to relax and accept a certain amount of chaos and uncertainty as natural, perhaps even healthy. In fact, chaos is a precondition to creativity. The leader who has come to embrace chaos in the workplace has learned to allow a certain amount of ambiguity in work processes and to be patient in allowing a more creative solution to emerge. If this approach fails, one can always revert to command and control methods and grind out a routine solution. Under the gentle hands of this leader, this alternative is rarely necessary.

The Denial of Death

Leaders who project this shadow are afraid of negative evaluation or public failure and will strive to keep their department, position, or project alive well beyond the end of its useful life. The people working within this shadow thus are engaged in a charade to keep the signs of life visible long after all meaning and vitality have left their endeavor. By definition, the productivity in an organization that is infected with this shadow is essentially nil, since the time for meaningful work is past. The only choice that this leader offers, though, is to keep up the illusion of meaningful work. When the end finally comes, as it must eventually, any results from current efforts will most likely be discarded.

Leaders who are unaffected by this fear of death understand that the cycle of life—birth, growth, decline, death, and renewal—applies as well in business. They understand that, before renewal can occur, those things that have moved beyond their usefulness must end. In product innovation, a project that has ceased to make meaningful progress toward the introduction of a viable product must be canceled before the project team can move on and become engaged in the next exciting opportunity. The life to come can only be reached by enduring the death at hand. Delaying the inevitable only prolongs the agony. An enlightened leader strives to bring the end quickly and mercifully, while protecting the self-esteem of all involved. The well-managed cancellation of a new product effort that has ground to a halt generally creates a feeling of relief and gratitude among those who have been released to move on to their next assignment. In the words of John Gardner:[3]

> *[Good leaders] think in terms of renewal. . . . The leader or leader/manager seeks the revisions of process and structure required by ever-changing reality.*

➤ Fear Is the Common Enemy

The common thread among all five of Palmer's types of shadow is fear in the heart of leaders—that their insecurities may show, that someone may take advantage of them, that they may fail, or that someone may actually have knowledge or skills that are better than theirs. The fear of the leader in each case projects outward and creates a working environment in which employees are fearful as well. And an ambiance of fear in the workplace has a negative impact on business performance. It makes employees reluctant to offer creative ideas. It creates feelings of distrust between managers and subordinates, and between peers working together on a team effort. Fear isolates people and stifles the flow of information. Perhaps worst of all, fear tends to destroy intellectual honesty. Fearful people become unwilling to speak the full truth in

---

[3] Gardner, John W. *On Leadership.* New York: Free Press, 1993 (p. 4).

a difficult situation, and instead say what they think others want to hear.

In contrast, leaders at the visionary companies studied by Collins and Porras seem to enlist a full measure of energy and creativity from each employee.[4] These companies move farther and faster than others because everyone pulls hard in the same direction. The knowledge that is available in these firms is more likely to be distilled from the collective wisdom and insight of everyone, not just a few select leaders at the top. Employees feel more free to speak their mind, and leaders listen more often to what is being said. The best ideas are used, regardless of their source. As Gardner states it:[5]

> The large-scale organization must ask a great deal of its lower-level people. It needs their local knowledge, their initiative, their problem-solving skills, their intimate grasp of realities on the firing line.

Leading companies are successful in unleashing the full capabilities of their workforce described by Gardner. On the other hand, an atmosphere infected with fear can so stifle the initiative and creativity of individual employees that it effectively cripples a business enterprise. Instead of exercising initiative and doing what makes sense, employees, hold back and wait to be told what to do. They protect themselves by staying out of sight and by avoiding any work that might put them on the critical path of their project. In effect, then, the energy of each employee becomes focused on avoiding the most important work that needs to be done. The impact on business results is devastating.

➤ The Competence Inversion Phenomenon

In a healthy company, part of the natural order is that competent people develop over time and rise to higher levels of responsibility in the organization. One of the duties that managers are expected to carry out is to develop the skills of their employees and to prepare the most able among them for higher positions in the organization. This process goes on at each level so that the most

---

[4] Collins, James C., and Porras, Jerry I. *Built to Last: Successful Habits of Visionary Companies.* New York: Harper Business, 1994.
[5] Gardner. *On Leadership,* p. 90.

competent people systematically grow and develop in their capabilities and periodically move up into positions of higher and
higher responsibility. In a stable company that has been operating
this way for some time, one would thus expect to find higher levels
of competence—greater knowledge, broader perspective, more wisdom, more insight, greater maturity, stronger character, more self-
confidence, and stronger management skills—at the higher levels
of management.

This healthy state of affairs is depicted in Figure 11.2a. Management level is represented by the vertical axis with a higher
value representing positions closer to the top leadership position.
Some generalized notion of competence is represented by the horizontal axis, with greater competence at positions toward the right.
A person who starts at A grows in competence through training
and experience until they reach A'. When a position at the next
level opens up, they are promoted to B because they are the most
qualified, and the next cycle of growth and promotion begins. Ideally, this process continues until they reach a position that utilizes
their fullest potential, and their upward progress tapers off.

Occasionally, though, an inversion in this pattern blocks the
upward flow of competence in a firm in much the same way that
a temperature inversion in the atmosphere blocks the upward
mobility of a cell of warmer than normal air. Consider the graphical

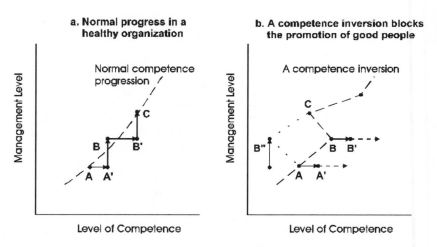

Figure 11.2 The competence inversion phenomenon.

representation in Figure 11.2b. The manager at C has been promoted beyond his level of competence. He knows this and is deeply insecure about his current position. If C's manager ever learns how competent B has become, it will be all over for C, who must therefore keep B hidden from view from above at all costs. As long as C is in control, B does not have a chance of being promoted, no matter how competent she becomes. So the career path for B is probably sideways for a while and then out of the organization. In the meantime, A is growing in capability and expecting to be promoted sometime soon.

B eventually gets fed up and leaves, creating a promotion opportunity for someone at A's level. Of course, A applies for the job, but doesn't realize that he has no chance of getting the promotion. C recognizes that A is just a younger version of B and is inherently more confident and more competent than C himself. Managing B cost C a lot, in terms of personal economics. On occasion, B asked tough questions, and put C on the spot. Keeping B hidden from high-level managers was also an ongoing concern. C's personal economics will thus be better off if someone less competent takes over B's position. So, instead, C picks a less competent peer of A's. This moves the competence inversion one level further down in the ranks.

Initially, A is bewildered by this outcome. Eventually, though, A will learn how this system works. Perhaps he will have to be passed over for promotion a second time, and see another of his less competent peers selected instead. In the end, though, it will most likely be sideways and out for A as well. It seems that the best people are never afraid to look for new opportunities elsewhere, while those with less self-confidence cling to their jobs no matter what comes. So a company infected with shadows and competence inversions drives out the very people it needs in leadership positions.

Once established in an organization, competence inversions can become quite stable. Managers who are promoted to positions beyond their inherent level of competence often become adept at hiding their insecurities. To survive, they must learn to appear solid and capable to higher-level managers, who are often too busy to look very closely. Those who work for them, on the other hand, always see their darker side and have to live in the shadow that they cast. The symptoms of a competence inversion are easy to detect if a high-level manager simply applies due diligence. A review of archived data on employee terminations will usually reveal an unusually high turnover rate among top performing lower-level employees. If the exit interview process promotes intellectual honesty, the reasons given for leaving will paint a clear picture of the problem. A little MBWA among individuals from one to three management levels below the inquisitive high-level manager will be informative as well. A cup of coffee in the hand and a smile help makes this exercise less threatening to lower-level employees and promotes candor. Careful listening to perspectives offered by several lower-level employees on the work situation will usually turn up enough clues to reveal the problem.

■ DISTRIBUTING LEADERSHIP TO LOWER LEVELS

One of the business objectives for the working environment highlighted early in this chapter was to encourage the most competitive work behavior from each individual and each team. These behaviors include:

➤ A feeling of ownership by individuals for the business impact of their work.

➤ The confidence to do what makes sense.

➤ Teamwork in achieving project goals.

➤ Intellectual honesty.

➤ Elevation of problems quickly and appropriately.

The working environment created by business leaders has a major influence in developing these desirable work patterns and attitudes. In particular, the likelihood of these behaviors is determined by whether leaders attempt to retain power and control at the top or distribute it throughout the workforce. Don Peterson, former president of Ford Motor Company,[6] has recommended:

[Push decisions] as far down in the organization as we think we possibly can, on the very sound principle that the farther down you get, the closer you're getting to where there's true knowledge about the issues.

The goal is to engage each employee more fully with the issues within his or her capacity to resolve, and to involve more people in

---

[6] Baily, Ronald, "Not Power But Empower," *Forbes,* May 30, 1988, pp. 120–123.

doing the most important work. Accomplishing this produces these beneficial results:

➤ The talents of each individual are more fully utilized.

➤ The work performed by each individual creates more value for the customer.

➤ People who are contributing to their fullest extent are happier and more motivated.

➤ Motivated employees work harder.

➤ Motivated employees are less susceptible to burnout.

➤ Motivated employees are less likely to leave the company.

➤ Methods for Moving Leadership Closer to the Work

Management by objective is a useful management technique in moving decisions and leadership out of the hands of a few, into the hands of many. The idea behind this technique is to entrust employees with objectives—clearly stated, finished results that need to be achieved—and to avoid giving task-level assignments. Ideally, employees will work together, and with their managers, in defining their own objectives. Once work objectives have been established, employees are free to pick their approach and define the individual steps to achieve the desired results. An objective might take a month or it might take a year or more, depending on the scope of the targeted results. Sometimes an individual will receive the services of other people who will help her or him achieve an objective. These people should work as a team to establish some number of subordinate objectives. Each team member then assumes ownership of some appropriate subset of these objectives and proceeds accordingly.

For example, a marketing manager in charge of introducing a new consumer product might be concerned about how to get a customer, who has never heard of this product, to pick it up from the store shelf and buy it. He could call one of his subordinates in and assign the following task:

➤ Design a cardboard floor display that depicts a full-size man holding our product and that communicates the attached list of product features. Begin with sketches and submit them for review.

Alternatively, he could ask this same employee to assume ownership with the following objective:

> ➤ Create a point-of-sale merchandising scheme that induces a customer, who has never heard of our product, to examine it and then buy it.

The task assignment limits the employee involvement to execution of a preconceived approach, and outlines the steps for implementing this approach. Assigning tasks keeps the higher-level manager in control, involved, and responsible for a successful outcome. On the other hand, assignment of an objective transfers ownership of the end result to the employee. To achieve an objective, this individual must first conceptualize the approach, and then plan and execute it. The objective assignment invites the employee to contribute at a much higher level and to take responsibility for the success of the approach. The high-level manager can still influence this process by periodically reviewing the employee's work, and offering appropriate guidance. Care must be taken during these reviews, though, not to exercise so much control that the employee loses ownership of the objective.

The fundamental principles that make objectives more effective than tasks in fully engaging individual energy and creativity with business objectives are, once again, connected to personal economics. When employees are assigned to accomplish a task, their self-esteem or sense of accomplishment may be associated with how well they accomplish the assigned work. But, since they had nothing to do with defining the approach that resulted in the task, they are less concerned with whether their work actually leads to a successful overall result. In fact, they may think that the whole approach is flawed, but since they were not involved in crafting it, they do not feel any personal ownership of those flaws. They are likely to keep quiet about the approach and simply do what they have been told to do.

For example, early in the career of one of the authors, he designed a plastic spool that was intended to act as a frame for a wire coil. He sent a detailed drawing to the machine shop and, in a few days, the parts came back in a little plastic bag. They bore no resemblance at all to the finely detailed drawing, for they appeared to be just wadded-up lumps of plastic. On closer inspection, though, the dimensions of each part proved to be precisely correct. The wall thickness had been specified so thin, though, that there was no structural rigidity left, and its own internal forces just curled the plastic up into a little ball. The amazing part was that the machinist had managed to work the plastic into those dimensions at all. The author sheepishly gathered up those embarrassing parts and went to congratulate the machinist, an old, weathered man with a twinkle in his eye. After a good laugh, they discussed the original objective and together worked out a design, using a different material that would work. The experience of the machinist was invaluable in designing a workable approach that could be effectively implemented. Once he had participated in designing the approach, the machinist became fully committed to seeing that his parts worked as intended. Before that, he had been more interested in highlighting the shortcomings of young engineers, and in demonstrating his skill to his peers by proving that he could machine some squishy plastic to ridiculous tolerances.

➤ Transferring Ownership

Distributing leadership and decisions to lower levels inherently means that high-level managers must learn to give up ownership and, to a large degree, relinquish control over the work that gets done. For many people in business leadership positions, this is a difficult and uncomfortable step. But business leaders cannot have it both ways. It is simply impossible to more fully engage people at lower levels in the organization, and still retain all power and control at the top. To do their best, employees need to assume ownership over their results. This means that they must have control over the approach and the implementation steps. It also means that they have full responsibility for the quality of the outcome. Transferring ownership requires that high-level managers give up control and trust lower level employees to do the job. To the degree that high-level managers try to exercise control after they have assigned an objective, they take back ownership of the results. The good news is that, as high-level managers learn to transfer ownership to their subordinates, (1) they make room in their agendas for more important, strategic issues, and (2) they accelerate the achievement of desired business results.

➤ Leadership Roles in Managing Objectives

Passing ownership of objectives to employees does not imply, however, that high-level managers become uninvolved. They need to fulfill several important roles to achieve each objective. These roles include clarifying objectives, removing obstacles, establishing and maintaining accountability, and recognizing good work. Once they have assigned an objective, high-level managers need to periodically review progress to make sure that each employee's efforts are focused on the right results. Clear communication of the objective will help ensure that supervisor and employees share a common mental model for the desired outcome. But nothing guarantees that this is true as well as clear progress in exactly the right direction. As work strays from the expected path, the high-level manager should raise the issue. Perhaps the high-level manager will guide the effort back on track, or possibly he or she will learn good reasons why the original objective was off track. Either way, management expectations and the work effort will become realigned. Progress reviews should occur often enough to keep them accordant.

As employees establish their approach and begin to implement their steps in achieving an objective, they often encounter obstacles. High-level managers can play an instrumental role in either circumventing or removing these obstacles. The role here, though, is one of coaching, not redefining the approach. Again, care must be exercised to avoid taking ownership of objectives away from employees.

A creative work environment, to be most effective from a business perspective, should include a strong sense of urgency and a high degree of accountability—two forms of stress that can be very constructive. A key role of high-level managers is to ensure that these two elements of the environment are in place. As work on assigned objectives is reviewed with employees, the urgency of the solution should be highlighted, and employees should be reminded (1) of the importance of their work to the desired business outcome, and (2) that other people are counting on them to fulfill their commitment.

Finally, high-level managers play an important role in recognizing the creativity and excellent efforts of employees. Appropriate recognition of desired work behavior is the most effective way for business leaders to ensure that they will see more of the same. As discussed earlier, appropriate recognition may vary with the culture; but if it is delivered in a form that an employee's peers might envy and also want, then it is probably appropriate for the circumstances.

On the other hand, poor performance encountered during progress reviews should be dealt with professionally, and in private. The goal in managing poor performers should always be to improve overall business results. In dealing with this issue, high-level managers should consider that blame and punishment have little or no business value. Certainly, an employee needs to receive clear feedback on disappointing performance. But the emphasis should be on desired work behavior and how to move the employee in that direction. If effectively handled, this feedback will influence the employee's personal economics to encourage his or her investment in improving performance. For example, performance improvement might be connected with improved self-esteem and thus offer a better overall state of personal economics. Vehement actions by a high-level manager to blame or to punish the employee run the risk of creating resentment. And this reaction will likely alter the employee's personal economic in a way that completely eliminates all motivation to improve.

Often employees who are working on an objective will come to their manager for advice or guidance. The manager needs to assess these requests carefully and decide whether the employee is raising a legitimate issue. If this is true and is beyond the employee's capacity to resolve, then immediate help is in order. If the issue is within the employee's span of control, the manager needs to handle the situation differently. If not effectively managed, these interactions can result in a subtle but steady transfer of ownership of the objective back to the manager. "What do you think that I should do in this situation?" can quickly lead to "Well, I tried what you said, and it didn't work. What do you think I should do now?" And the manager is back in the loop handing out task assignments. A better response by the manager to the initial query may be something like, "I'm not sure what you should do in that situation. You are closer to the problem than I am. Why don't you figure out what makes sense and do it. I'll back you up on whatever you decide." Encouraging employees to do what makes sense leaves ownership with them and empowers them to use their own judgment. Making decisions and acting on them helps employees to develop both judgment and self-confidence. If they make a bad decision, there is always an opportunity to guide them onto a better path at the next progress review.

➤ A Useful Conceptual Measure of Success

Moving decisions and leadership lower in the organization should produce important, measurable business results. The rate of progress toward business goals should improve—goals such as the introduction of a new product, or the implementation of an improved method or capability. Eventually business parameters such as revenues, profits, and market share should also improve. But these can be immensely lagging indicators of success. These measures will move visibly only long after a project effort has succeeded or failed. Leaders need more responsive measures of progress that give a real-time view of progress. Such measures are often qualitative or conceptual in nature.

Organization velocity is an example of a useful conceptual measure:

$$\text{Organizational Velocity} = \frac{\text{Actual work done to deliver value to the customer}}{\text{Total capacity to create value for the customer}}$$

In this equation, the denominator is the sum over the total workforce of the fullest potential of each individual to create value for the end customer. An ideal value for organizational velocity of 1.0 means that each person in the organization is contributing at the highest possible rate. Moving responsibility and decisions down to the lowest reasonable level more fully engages each employee in the workforce with the important jobs that need to be done, and moves the value of this performance indicator toward its ideal value.

This measure provides an intellectual framework for high-level managers in evaluating how well they are currently distributing both decisions and leadership to lower levels. As they sample the lower level work environment, either through formal reviews or informal wandering around, they should ask themselves as they encounter people, "What is this individual working on and how does that activity compare with this person's full potential for contribution?" Further, they can assess where people are spending their time and compare this result to alternative ways that they might use their time that would accumulate value for the customer faster. As they find opportunities for improvement in this exercise, they should ask themselves, "How is the work environment that I have helped to create aggravating this misuse of time and energy?" Another important question is, "How can I modify circumstances to encourage these people to apply their time and energy more effectively?"

In one work situation, a review such as this revealed that the typical meeting workload for managers, first level and higher, was over 35 hours per week. Sampling a few of these meetings determined that almost half of the attendees had little or no business reason for being there. People were attending these meetings out of fear of being reprimanded by high-level managers for not being there. On average, almost 20 hours out of every manager's 40-hour work week were being wasted in nonessential meetings. Even the necessary meetings were poorly managed and made little contribution to customer value. So, for these managers, organizational velocity was reduced to 20 percent or less by performance issues strictly related to meetings. A serious consideration by high-level managers of the elements of organizational velocity in this situation might have caused them to reassess their own actions. For one thing, berating people who failed to attend nonessential meetings might have stopped.

■ PERSONAL ECONOMICS AND THE WORKING ENVIRONMENT

In this chapter, we have examined the exaggerated effect of high-level managers on the working environment as well as the value of moving decisions and the ownership of work results lower in the organization. The key idea is that the muscle required to create business success resides in the large population of people who work at lower levels in a company. To perform among the leaders in its industry then, a business enterprise must effectively engage these people and bring their full energy and creativity to bear on the work of the business. But the working environment has a major impact on the behavior of these individuals, and if it is not right, it can thwart the efforts of business leaders to improve the utilization of their workforce.

Chapter 9 introduced the notion of personal economics: each employee is adept at adjusting his or her behavior to optimize personal well-being in any given situation. And the employee's sense of well-being at any moment is the result of a kind of mental economic equation that he or she evaluates. This economic equation assesses costs and benefits in terms of a particular set of personal currencies that are important to that individual. This section explores relationships between the personal economics of employees and the work environment in which they "live and move and have their being."

➤ The Work Environment as an Infrastructure

The work environment sets the context in which each individual works their personal economic equation. The costs and benefits of the behaviors and actions that they can make at any given time are, at least in part, established by this environment. In many ways, the work environment influences the choices of employees in the same way that the general economic infrastructure affects the financial choices that a family makes. The economic infrastructure establishes ground rules such as laws of ownership, contract law, and the rules of ethics. In addition, it includes the current economic conditions. For example, a family may decide to take out a loan to buy a new car, based on current conditions in the infrastructure. The health of the economy, the likelihood of losing one's job, and the terms and current interest rates of the loan will all influence this decision. The cost of ownership, including luxury taxes, annual registration fees, the cost of insurance, and anticipated operating costs will also affect the family's decision.

In a similar fashion, the work environment establishes ground rules that influence work-related choices of employees. The deeply held values and beliefs prevalent in the organization, established attitudes and practices of high-level managers, and formal policies all contribute to the social underpinnings in a company that affect the behavior of each employee. The choice to take a work-related risk is influenced by the current working environment in much the same way as the family's decision to take a financial risk is swayed by the current economic situation. The costs and risks associated with the decision will be weighed against perceived benefits in making a rational choice. Only in this case, the currencies used in the economic equation will be the personal currencies, discussed in Chapter 9, that the employee values most highly.

A seasoned engineer might weigh a decision to exercise initiative in crafting a new approach to the design of a subsystem important to a new product. The new approach might offer significant performance advantages that would improve the product's competitive position. Furthermore, since the approach would emphasize a new, more highly integrated circuit chip set, it would reduce product cost. But there are risks. The approach might be more difficult to implement than anticipated. The announced introduction date for the new chips may slip and cause project delays. What are the likely benefits—sense of achievement, improved self-esteem, professional growth, a raise, recognition from high-level management, perhaps even a stock option? What are the potential costs—extra hours when the crunch comes, embarrassment if the approach fails, unwanted attention from bad-tempered, high-level managers if the design gets on the critical path and puts the project behind schedule? The answers depend on the work environment and the existing infrastructure that it has created for personal economics. And these answers will determine the engineer's decision, and will significantly impact the business outcome.

An Employee's "Bill of Rights"

In the United States, at least, the legal system and, in particular, the Bill of Rights are important elements of the infrastructure. The infrastructure thus guarantees certain rights to each individual and family. These same rights extend into the work environment as well. In addition, however, some business enterprises bestow additional rights to employees that are either formally specified as policy, or de facto. These additional rights are often associated with the deeply held values and beliefs discussed in Chapter 10.

For example, at HP one of the HP Way values is respect for individuals. Associated with this value is an enterprisewide open-door policy that has existed since the company was founded. The open-door policy is one element in what might be called an HP employee's Bill of Rights. The idea behind this policy is that, because of HP's respect for individuals, any employee who feels the need to discuss an issue with a high-level manager has the right to do so. The physical manifestation of this policy is that there are no doors on managers' offices at HP. Even the office of chairman and CEO, Lewis Platt, has no door. Over HP's history, there are innumerable cases of low-level employees using this policy to discuss problems and concerns with high-level HP executives, including Bill Hewlett, the late Dave Packard, John Young, and Lew Platt. High-level executives in HP also respond promptly and in person to e-mail and phone calls. Respect goes both ways, though. Employees rarely abuse this privilege. They are inherently respectful of their leaders and generally only raise issues that are worthy of their attention.

An interesting test of a company's core ideology, as defined in Chapter 10, is whether an employee Bill of Rights is either explicitly stated or implied. If a statement of values has any serious meaning or commitment behind it, then it should imply some set of rights, privileges, or expectations for each and every employee. Establishing and communicating the ramifications of established values is thus a key step in extending the influence of the core ideology and establishing the strange attractor.

In a healthy corporate culture, these rights will be so strongly ingrained that any employee can feel confident in raising the issue if a co-worker violates one of these rights, regardless of the relative management rank of the two parties. Occasionally, a high-level manager may endorse a particular set of values one day, and then violate one of the implied rights the next, either through words or actions. When this happens, a lower-level employee should be able to point out the inconsistency without fear of reprisal. An effective working environment depends on both this lack of fear and a high degree of intellectual honesty. Instant and spontaneous feedback on behavior that is disallowed by the value system is essential in keeping all employees, regardless of rank, well aligned with the prevalent culture, and keeping the value system vital.

Alignment between Workplace Values and Off-the-Job Values

Each employee, in general, has one system of values that they exercise at home and in their community, and another that they adhere to at work. The alignment between these two value systems, to some degree, determines the work-related stress that an employee will experience. In extreme cases, misalignment of these value systems can severely hamper an employee's performance. For example, an individual who is deeply religious and scrupulously honest at home, can have a great deal of difficulty coping in a work environment in which most of her peers are routinely profane and treat customers dishonestly. Likewise, if someone is a rugged individualist away from work, he can have trouble fitting into a team environment at work and working closely with others all day.

Performance is improved if employees are selected both for their work-related talents, and for the degree of alignment between their personal values and those prevalent in the workplace. As misalignment occurs, managers must be willing to manage the friction that inevitably occurs. Just as a society can thrive with diverse cultures, a company can thrive with diversity in the workforce by implementing policies of mutual respect and tolerance.

➤ Creativity and the Social Climate

Research performed by Synectics, Incorporated, in Cambridge, Massachusetts, has established a direct correlation between the quality and productivity of creative problem-solving efforts and the social climate in which they occur.[7] The Synectics research has uncovered a range of specific principles that apply to product innovation, and has produced an excellent methodology for creative problem solving. The aspect of their work described here provides an excellent example of personal economics at work.

The Synectics research has revealed that small groups, on the order of seven people, that are focused on generating creative solutions for a given problem, are most productive. Observation of such groups over several decades has shown that each person who participates in a creative problem-solving session apparently brings with him or her one common but hidden agenda item. Each person comes into the session with a goal of leaving the group with at least as much self-esteem as at the beginning. As the dynamics of the creative problem-solving activity unfold, events occur that might reduce an individual's self-esteem—a criticism of their half-formed idea, or perhaps a pointed question from another member of the group. When this occurs, the affected individual immediately diverts his or her attention away from problem solving and begins to work on regaining self-esteem. Furthermore, other members of the group are sensitive to apparent risks to their own self-esteem that are inherent in the environment of the problem-solving session. Criticism and questions from other members of the group directed at emerging thoughts and ideas can create a threatening environment that gradually suppresses participation by members of the group until the productivity, in terms of new and creative ideas, drops to nil. To counteract this effect, Synectics trains facilitators to

---

[7] This discussion and Figure 11.3 are provided with permission from Synectics, Incorporated, 20 University Road, Cambridge, MA 02138, Phone: (617) 868-6530.

control the social climate in a problem-solving session and keep it from becoming confrontive.

Figure 11.3 provides a graphical representation of the relationships at work here. To begin, each person coming into a problem-solving session has a personal comfort level for the mental energy that he or she is willing to invest. This is represented by the horizontal, dashed line in the graph. Second, each individual has a level of mental energy required to maintain self-esteem, and this level varies with the social climate in the room. Maintaining self-esteem in a confrontive environment requires a greater investment of energy than a supportive social climate. For each individual then, there exists an "S" curve like the one shown in Figure 11.3. When the environment in the room becomes too confrontive, more mental energy is required to maintain self-esteem than the person is comfortable delivering, and some degree of anxiety exists. On the other hand, if the environment is more supportive, the mental effort spent on protecting self-esteem drops sharply and the anxiety disappears. At the supportive end of the scale there is a margin of mental energy available for invest-

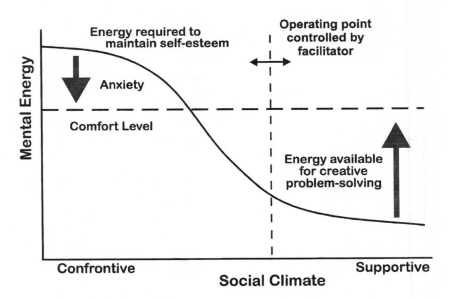

Figure 11.3 Influence of the social climate on creativity.

ment in creative work. A key role of the facilitator in a Synectics problem-solving session is thus to control the social climate in the room and keep it on the supportive side of the scale.

The Synectics research has shown that self-esteem is a very important personal currency, particularly during creative problem-solving activity. Their observations of thousands of creative problem-solving sessions indicate that the behavior of individuals is directly related to their level of concern with regard to this particular personal currency. As questions and criticism are allowed during a problem-solving session, the likely cost of offering an idea goes up. A half-formed idea might draw criticism or questions that are embarrassing to the one who offered the idea. As each person in the room sees this happen, they adjust their assessment of the evolving infrastructure in the room that sets the context for their own personal economic equation. As the cost of offering an idea goes up and the apparent benefits go down, each individual alters his or her behavior in a way that withholds all but the most bulletproof ideas.

On the other hand, when the environment in a creative problem-solving session gets supportive, the cost of offering a half-formed idea goes down. Instead of shooting it full of holes, someone in the group is more likely to respond with something rewarding like, "I like this creative aspect of that idea, and would like to offer the following embellishment. What if . . ." Now the one who offers a creative thought is likely to be rewarded with recognition, a sense of accomplishment, and, of course, improved self-esteem. As people in the group see this happen, they rush to offer their own ideas like investors swarming to buy a hot new stock—and the productivity of the group skyrockets. The promise of an attractive return-on-investment apparently works for personal economics as well. It seems then that the notion of personal economics is completely consistent with and supportive of the wisdom gained in the Synectics research.

Results from the Synectics research underscore the points made earlier about the impact of fear on the willingness of individuals to engage with and participate wholeheartedly in the achievement of business objectives. The fearfulness of employees is directly related to the costs that they consider in their personal economic equations. As the level of fear in the environment goes up, the likelihood of severe cost, in terms of important personal currencies, increases. Available benefits pale in comparison so individual behavior becomes guarded and defensive as people attempt to minimize their exposure.

■ THE BUSINESS VALUE OF LOVE

There is a definition of love that offers profound insight into the key elements of the work environment that separates a leading company from its less capable peers in the marketplace:[8]

> *Love is this—that two solitudes border, protect, salute one another.*

While love is not usually an acceptable topic in a discussion of business matters, this definition provides a broader meaning that applies not only to two people who are romantically involved, but to athletic teams, to product innovation teams, and to the general business workplace as well. After due consideration, love of the sort described by Palmer seems to be an essential element to almost every winning team effort, including business teams.

Palmer's definition first recognizes that people are solitudes. By our very nature, we are each one isolated from the other, and different. Almost by definition then, what is right for one will never be exactly right for another. So a constructive, loving relationship starts by acknowledging our separateness and honoring it. It seems that the very definition of love begins with acceptance (1) of the distance that must exist between individuals, and (2) of the inherent differences between them.

Even though we are each one a solitude, and therefore separated from each other by an inevitable distance, we can border one another. This means that we can touch at our boundaries, communicate, and keep each other company. We can surround each other and keep each other from being isolated and alone. We can smile at one another, and acknowledge each other's presence. We can see and acknowledge the joy and the pain in each other. And these are all elements of a loving relationship.

Solitudes that border each other can also protect one another. Even though we are solitudes, we can shield each other from harm. We can strike back at those who might attack the individuals we border—the members of our team, for instance. We can protect each other from self-attack or self-recrimination by reflecting back to each other the true beauty that we each radiate. For in our darkest

---

[8] Palmer, p. 19. Palmer paraphrases a similar definition by German poet, Rainer Maria Rilke.

moments, it is hard to remember sometimes that we ourselves are both capable and beautiful.

Finally, solitudes that border and protect each other may also salute one another. The *Random House Dictionary* provides the following definition of the word *salute:* "to express respect or praise for; honor; commend."

The third element then in a loving relationship between people—solitudes—is an inherent feeling of respect or honor for one another. This respect originates from an understanding of, and appreciation for the other individual's inherent qualities—his or her values, goals, intentions, intelligence, strength, courage, skills, or integrity. As we understand those we border and protect more fully, we often find reasons to respect and honor them. And this provides us with the third and final element in a loving relationship.

➤ A Manly Example

Imagine yourself with a bunch of friends on a Sunday afternoon, watching professional football on television. Your team has just scored another touchdown against an opponent who was favored to win. Now 13 points in the lead, your guys are celebrating in the end zone. There is head-butting and chest-slamming going on and one of the blocking backs is carrying the guy who made the score around in a vicelike bear hug.

A football team is a bunch of solitudes who border, protect, and salute one another. On the best football teams, the love is so thick that you can cut it with a knife. All this slamming and butting after a touchdown is simply a manly show of bordering behavior, along with some honor and respect. Those guys have learned to border each other through thick and thin. They have learned to protect each other—both on and off the field. And they salute each other. Each one is there because they are all really good at what they do. And they honor and respect that in each other. On a well-managed football team that is on its way to the Super Bowl, strife and hostility between players has been largely resolved. Even rivals for a single position honor and respect one another. You may hear of acrimony—between players, and between players and their coaches—on other teams, but generally not among those who will play in the Super Bowl.

Love—as Palmer defined it—is an essential ingredient to a winning football team. It creates an environment in which each player has the confidence to take risks and strive to deliver his best effort. The players know that, if their best attempt fails on one play, they can try just as hard again on the next, for they have no fear of criticism from their teammates. And their teammates will protect them; from excessive self-recrimination, and from attack by others. The long months of practicing and playing together—bordering one another—teach each player what to expect from his teammates. They learn to think with almost one mind. Those incredible passes that thread the needle and end up in the hands of a receiver who only at the last second looks for the ball, can happen only because the quarterback and the receiver know each other's moves so intimately. A winning football team is beautiful to watch, for it is a group of incredibly talented individuals who work together as a well-oiled machine that functions better than all others partly because it is steeped in team spirit—love.

➤ Love versus Fear

Palmer's definition of love consists largely of verbs, behaviors that we can choose to exhibit toward one another. If these behaviors—bordering, protecting, and saluting—have a positive influence on the performance of an athletic team, or perhaps a work group, then their opposites may provide some insight into working environments that inhibit excellent performance. Consider the following relationships:

Border	vs.	Isolate
Protect	vs.	Attack
Salute	vs.	Criticize
Love	**vs.**	**Fear**

According to a thesaurus, antonyms for *love* include words such as *hate, hatred, aversion, dislike,* and *disgust.* In the workplace, a person's reaction to a manager or co-worker who remains isolated as much as possible, who attacks others, and who criticizes the efforts of others may include these feelings, but it will very likely also include a large measure of fear. When someone attacks or criticizes us at work, our short-term reaction may be anger or even hatred, but these emotions take a lot of energy to maintain. Furthermore, these emotions need to be focused on someone, an individual, a group, or a general class of people. If these adverse conditions—isolation, and a propensity to attack and criticize one another—are pervasive throughout the work environment, then it becomes difficult to maintain feelings of anger and hatred, for they become defocused and directed at no one in particular. Over time, they usually dissipate and leave behind only the more durable emotion, a sense of fear.

This fear is a healthy reaction that is essential to survival in such a hostile environment. It reflects the knowledge that attack and criticism are likely and will probably occur when we are most vulnerable. So fear keeps us focused on the best strategy for optimizing personal economics in this environment—never do anything that makes us vulnerable.

The performance of each individual in a work environment is therefore strongly influenced by the ambiance that exists. We have built a fairly strong case that says a winning effort only occurs when each individual and each team involved is comfortable assuming ownership of important objectives, deciding on what makes sense, and working hard to achieve success. These behaviors, though, inherently require that people willingly make themselves vulnerable, so they are unlikely to occur in a work environment where fear dominates. A loving environment, as described, is required to enlist the highest levels of performance from each individual. An atmosphere where fear pervades suppresses initiative and leads to defensive, safe behaviors.

➤ Love Is a Choice

This important principle in healthy personal relationships applies as well in the workplace. The behaviors listed in Table 11.2 are all choices that we make, in both our personal lives and our work relationships. When we come to work, we choose whether to approach people, connect, and communicate, or to isolate ourselves. We choose to either protect them when they are vulnerable, or attack them. And we choose whether to look for attributes in our co-workers that are worthy of respect and praise, or to seek out flaws that can be criticized. No one is either all positive or all negative in behavior, but the most prevalent behavior that each person exhibits tends to establish how others view that person in the workplace. And these behaviors that our co-workers learn to expect from us are the result of our own choices. These choices are, in effect, our votes—for a loving work environment, or for one characterized by fear.

Given the disproportionate impact that leaders have on the work environment, as described earlier in this chapter, the choices that high-level managers make have a particularly strong influence. Their attitude toward subordinates, the way they deal with peers, and the way they treat their own managers are all choices that they make on a daily basis. And these choices provide behavioral role models for others. Their lack of corrective action toward a subordinate who performs at substandard levels is a choice. Also their tolerance of isolation, attacks, and criticism among subordinates is a choice. If they want to alter these behaviors in those who work for them, and move them toward the left side of Table 11.2, they can make that choice. Furthermore, they can choose to recognize and reward bordering, protecting, and saluting behaviors when they occur.

In a very real sense then, improving the work environment is simply a matter of deciding to make different choices. And, because of their stronger influence on the work environment, high-level managers need to lead the way.

➤ The Matter of Style

All this talk of love undoubtedly makes some readers uncomfortable. It is just not very "professional." We may seem to be advocating an ideal work environment that is reminiscent of a 1960s' hippy commune where everyone wears flowers in their hair. But, as our football team example illustrates, one loving environment can look vastly different from another. People can border, protect, and salute one another in many ways. Head-butting and chest-slamming work for football players, but it wouldn't have been appropriate in the work environment that the authors knew at HP. When asked by a young engineer why one should seek a job at HP, the late Barney Oliver, then vice president of R&D for HP, answered, "It's a chance to do great work with your friends." That pretty much summed up the engineering work environment in HP at that time. A lot of bordering, protecting, and saluting went on there, but in the friendly collaborative style characteristic of HP.

In another company, the style might be much more confrontive, but nonetheless loving. The French have a saying that, when translated, means something like, "In the clash of ideas the truth will out." Some work environments are like this. People argue constantly, attacking each other's ideas, but not each other. And in their confrontive way, they move the collective thinking forward, toward a desired business result. If the environment is truly healthy, though, each individual remains protective of the self-esteem of others, and manages to slip in some respect and admiration along the way. Bordering, protecting, and saluting is alive and well, it just looks different.

Many styles can serve as a suitable vehicle for bordering, protecting, and saluting behaviors. An elite, military commando unit might create a particular environment in which people routinely border, protect, and respect one another, and achieve the highest levels of individual and group performance. A group of nuns in a convent may create their own characteristic environment to support these loving, trusting relationships within their group. An all-male construction crew might take on a completely different ambiance that is socially acceptable to its participants, but that nonetheless supports the three loving behaviors outlined in Table 11.2.

A work environment then is a little like a suit of clothes. Each suit has its particular fashion and style. There are feminine styles, and masculine attire, formal dress and work clothes. All are appropriate in their own time and place. But each garment must satisfy some fundamental requirements for warmth, protection, and modesty. And each garment should be pleasing to the aesthetic tastes of the one who wears it. Each work environment too should be pleasing to those who are immersed in it. And each environment should also satisfy the same fundamental business purposes:

➤ To encourage and support the most competitive behavior from each individual and each team.

➤ To help attract and retain the best available talent.

■ APPLYING CHANGE-MANAGEMENT PRINCIPLE TO THE ENVIRONMENT

For a working environment to become and remain healthy, each individual must be willing to work toward this goal. All of us have, sometime in our career, have experienced a co-worker who influenced our working environment dramatically, either in a positive or a negative way. In particular, though, an individual who decides to impose on others in a work group can have a devastating and long-term effect on the mental well-being and productivity of the entire group, unless the person is somehow brought into line. The change management principles outlined in Chapter 9—high-level endorsement, grassroots involvement, metrics, and enviable recognition—can provide useful tools for dealing with such situations and for enlisting the efforts of everyone in creating and protecting the desired working environment.

To begin, the high-level manager who has span of control over the environment should (1) communicate a clear vision of the working environment that is desired, (2) outline how this environment relates to the deeply held values and beliefs of the firm, (3) describe the business advantage of establishing the target environment, and (4) endorse the required changes. As discussed earlier, including an implied bill of rights in the description might be useful. The endorsement can be formal, such as formal policies or training programs, or informal through comments and conversation. The goal is to convey throughout the workforce a clear vision of the desired working environment and a sense of its importance. Once launched, the endorsement should be communicated widely and often by all members of the management staff.

Next, grassroots involvement should be encouraged. Employees need to have opportunities to compare the realities of their current situation with the working environment that is desired. Every employee will have "war stories" about difficulties that affected his or her performance or resulted in feelings of mistreatment. There should be a safe setting in which employees can tell their stories, express pent-up feelings, and make suggestions. They should help identify "symptoms of health" for the desired environment—what are the visible and outward signs that it is in place and working? These indicators will make visible the progress toward establishing the desired environment. Finally, employees should be instructed in constructive ways for dealing with work environment issues—what steps they can take on their own and when to enlist the help of higher-level managers. Most importantly, they should be empowered with acceptable ways of providing feedback to high-level managers on their own deviations from acceptable behavior.

Once these initial steps are complete, high-level managers need to play three key ongoing roles:

1. Ongoing endorsement of the desired work environment.
2. Tracking the symptoms of health.
3. Providing enviable recognition of role model behaviors.

Occasionally, managers will have to deal with employees who exhibit adverse behavior as well. In particular, employees who are chronically and openly critical of others probably need an attitude adjustment. These actions should be taken in private, but should be strong and clear enough to leave no doubt about management's intent and commitment to a healthy work environment. The goal of these steps is to alter the personal economics of each employee in ways that induce them to help establish and support the desired working environment.

■ CONCLUSION

This chapter has focused on the work environment and its influence on individual performance in the business enterprise. The goal for business leaders in managing the environment should be to enlist the full energy, power, and creativity of each individual in the company. This chapter has described how a healthy work environment creates an infrastructure that is essential to this desired result. Conversely, the discussion has also shown how an unhealthy environment can arise, and how it inhibits desired behaviors, and adversely affects the level of individual performance. The concept of personal economics introduced in Chapter 9 is useful in explaining key relationships between the work environment and an individual's on-the-job behavior and level of performance.

The need for a safe environment that keeps each individual free from fear was emphasized, and the roles and responsibilities of business leaders in establishing these conditions were outlined. But gaining the greatest performance from each individual requires constructive tension as well. Techniques for getting each individual personally committed to specific work objectives were discussed and the roles of high-level managers in transferring ownership of these objectives and in creating the necessary sense of importance and accountability were also discussed.

Responsibility for managing the environment is squarely in the hands of high-level managers, for they have a disproportionate degree of power to create the ambiance in which others "must live and move and have their being," to echo Palmer one last time. In fact, "cones of shadow" in the work environment were described that can arise from personal, even unconscious, attributes of high-level managers. These shadows can debilitate the workforce that resides within them, but are often obscure from the vantage point of business leaders higher in the organizational structure. To guard against the development of shadows, high-level managers need to wander around and sample conditions throughout their organization, especially at levels significantly below their own. Without due diligence from the top of the organization, these shadows can become permanent handicaps to a company that seriously degrade its ability to perform at competitive levels.

A definition of love was offered outlining desirable behaviors that are crucial to an effective work environment. These behaviors were contrasted with their opposites to show that love and fear occupy opposites ends of a spectrum of behaviors commonly found in the workplace. Pertinent research was cited that establishes a solid connection between the prevalent social climate and the creative behavior of individuals. This discussion established an intellectual framework that high-level managers can use in evaluating conditions in their own workplace. Finally, techniques were outlined for actively managing the work environment and systematically improving it.

One task remains to complete the commitment made in Chapter 1 of this book. Chapter 12, in Part V, describes principles and practices for measuring the success of product innovation efforts in a business enterprise. This information will enable the reader to design effective measurement techniques for first diagnosing the innovation engine to determine areas of focus for improvement efforts, and then for tracking the progress in performance, once improvements are made.

Desired Upper Management Behaviors:
Leadership and the Creative Environment

➤ Look for symptoms of fear at all levels in your organization. Work to remove sources of fear and reduce its impact on personal economics.

➤ Wander around and look for shadows in the environment. Take corrective action.

➤ Identify the ideal environment for your organization—values, style, bill of rights. Assume ownership of making it happen.

➤ Encourage employees (1) to assume ownership of their work objectives, and (2) to do what makes sense.

➤ Encourage bordering, protecting, and saluting behaviors.

Part V

Measures of Success

Chapter 12

Measuring Product Innovation Performance

When you can measure what you are speaking about, and express it in numbers, you know something about it; but when you cannot measure it, when you cannot express it in numbers, your knowledge is of a meager and unsatisfactory kind.

Lord Kelvin
British mathematician, physicist,
President of the British Royal Society
of Science, 1824–1907

Heavier-than-air flying machines are impossible.

Lord Kelvin,
circa 1895

The first quotation for this chapter was coined in the era when deterministic, pseudoscientific models of business management were evolving. And, in fact, the distrust of information that is unsubstantiated by numbers is still reflected in the attitudes of some business leaders today. Lord Kelvin's message has merit, though, particularly in the field of science. Theoretical models in science are not of much use if they cannot be used to predict quantitative results. However, attempting to impose this philosophy too rigorously on business matters can be distracting and expensive. It can also lead to delayed and inferior business decisions.

This chapter will discuss both numeric and qualitative measures of product innovation performance. The viewpoint here is very much opposed to the notion that all knowledge that cannot be expressed in numbers is "of a meager and unsatisfactory kind." As the second chapter quote indicates, Lord Kelvin was sometimes fallible in his pearls of wisdom, as are most of us. Qualitative and intuitive measures of performance can lead to significant and timely management insights. In fact, much of the knowledge that high-level managers use to make difficult and timely business decisions cannot be quantified. The possession of this intuitive and qualitative knowledge, though, is often a key differentiator between competitors in today's dynamic marketplaces.

This discussion begins with a description of fundamental principles for designing effective performance measures. Appropriate roles of effective performance measures are outlined and some pitfalls that can occur with inappropriate application of performance measures are noted. Next, these design principles are applied to the product innovation process, with specific examples of interesting performance measures. Corporatewide measures that attempt to quantify the performance of the entire innovation engine as a system are discussed first. Following this, indicators of effective performance in product portfolio management are outlined. Measures of performance for the key elements in this process are covered, including knowledge base development, strategic and portfolio planning, and project tracking. Several measures that highlight overall process performance at the portfolio level are then discussed. Symptoms of health for an effective product innovation environment are described next. In the final section, measures are proposed for highlighting the performance of business leaders in their efforts to manage product innovation efforts in their enterprise.

■ DESIGN PRINCIPLES FOR PERFORMANCE MEASUREMENT

This section outlines some fundamental principles for the successful design and application of product innovation performance measures. To begin, a discussion of appropriate uses of performance measures describes both possible benefits and pitfalls. Next, desirable attributes of good performance measures are outlined. A methodology for designing and verifying performance measures is described that begins with identifying desired work-related behaviors. The final part of this section examines in detail those behaviors that characterize successful product innovation activities.

➤ Appropriate Uses of Product Innovation Performance Measures

Product innovation performance measures can serve several valid business purposes, and some that are less appropriate. In general, performance measures are useful in establishing performance baselines for current work processes in a given business unit. These baselines are useful in several ways. First, they calibrate the expectations for project performance, and establish a realistic framework for performance estimates on all projects. Second, they serve as a standard against which performance improvement efforts can be measured. Another beneficial application of performance measures is to provide a uniform and consistent means for evaluating the progress of all projects in a new product portfolio. A well-thought-out set of project performance measures provides a common vocabulary and an intellectual framework for both portfolio managers and project managers. This commonly understood framework greatly streamlines the project review process.

Product innovation performance measures are useful as well for tracking the impact of performance improvement efforts. Well-planned improvement initiatives should include a specified set of performance metrics that will accurately reflect changes in work processes and related employee behaviors as they occur. Examples might include the percentage of project teams that adopt a new method or tool in their work. Further, measures of the impact of these new methods and tools on the productivity and quality of work performed by each development team are useful. These indicators provide high-level managers with assurance that their investment in each improvement initiative is having the desired effect. If movement of these measures does not occur in the direction or the degree anticipated, this information enables the improvement initiative team to take timely corrective action.

In companies with multiple business units, corporate-level executives are sometimes tempted to establish common performance goals for all business units. Performance targets for revenue growth and profit level are familiar examples. Common financial targets may be appropriate, for they may be interpreted as the hurdle rate that is required to make each business unit financially interesting. Occasionally, though, these corporate goals are aimed deeper into the work processes of each business. The authors have seen attempts to apply corporatewide goals for time-to-market or project ROI. The level of performance of each business unit on these measures is then compared with the others. But as the technology, market, and customer focus vary between business units, the specific performance of product innovation processes may vary as well. Comparing the measures of performance of various business units at the detailed process level may thus lead to undue pressure, and bad business decisions. This use of performance measures is not recommended. Instead, each business unit should be free to manage its internal processes as needed to meet the common financial targets.

Often executive salary increases and bonuses are tied to revenue or profit growth performance. There are two major problems with this practice. First, current growth performance is often a delayed result of good decisions and investments made earlier, as described in Chapters 2 and 4. Turnover in the executive staff can thus mean that the compensation of the current executive staff may, at least in part, be due to the performance of their predecessors. Secondly, executives may be induced by this system of rewards to take actions that cause short-term increases in revenue and profit. Such actions may include expense cuts and accounting decisions that can injure the firm's competitive capability and sacrifice future business results. Instead, executive compensation should ideally be driven by the quality of recent decisions and investments that these individuals have influenced, and that will determine future business growth. Such compensation programs are more difficult to define and manage, but they tie rewards more closely to desired executive behaviors.

➤ Performance Measures Can Be a Double-Edged Sword

In medieval times, the knight who wielded the double-edged sword was a more lethal combatant for he could cut both ways, with both sides of the blade. But, if he was careless, he could do himself considerable damage as well with his own blade. Product innovation performance measures are like that double-edged sword. They can focus attention on important issues and make people's performance visible for all to see. They can help create a strong sense of accountability that keeps people moving in the right direction. They can, however, also cause adverse behaviors that are sometimes quite unexpected, and that can be detrimental to overall business results. The rule is that if a particular aspect of performance is made both visible and important, it will improve, one way or another. Performance measures must therefore be applied very carefully to make sure that they affect work behavior only in the manner that was intended.

In an integrated circuit company, top-level management decided that time-to-market (TTM) was the key to improved revenue growth. They established a common definition for TTM that applied to all business units, and attached the salary increases and bonuses received by key managers to TTM performance improvements. Each business unit's TTM performance was now both visible and important. The manager in charge of technical product documentation in one business unit came up with a scheme—an adverse reaction to this method of rewarding performance. Since he had control over new product model numbers, he decided to simply create new model numbers and specification sheets for existing products. While the product innovation process remained basically unchanged and continued to introduce new products at the same rate as before, additional new model numbers were generated that were simply attached to existing products. This scheme created the appearance of steadily improving TTM for this business unit. While other groups struggled to improve TTM the hard way, the managers in this business received kudos for their apparently excellent performance, and enjoyed exceptional salary growth and bonuses. Eventually though, when revenues and profits failed to respond to the improved TTM, a closer look by corporate management revealed the scam. Those responsible were promptly "de-cruited."

The message in this story is that performance measures can have a powerful impact on work-related behavior. Making some aspect of performance both visible and important will cause it to change. High-level managers must first understand the fundamental principles at play, however, to design measures that will reliably support the desired improvements in business performance.

➤ Properties of Effective Measures

An effective set of product innovation performance measures should exhibit several key attributes to be effective. This section outlines these attributes and provides a brief description of each.

Relevance

First, the information provided by performance measures should be pertinent to important business performance issues. The measures imposed by upper management should be clearly focused on the performance issues of concern. People will be reluctant to accept and support a performance measure whose relationship to important matters at hand is not inherently obvious.

Timeliness

The information provided by a performance measure should, as much as possible, reflect the current state of processes and performance. Decisions and actions need to be based on two key kinds of information: (1) mental models that accurately reflect how the real world works, and (2) an accurate understanding of what is currently true about the real world. Thus, performance measures should ideally provide an accurate and nearly real-time view of the state of the system being measured.

Product innovation performance measures fall into three categories with regard to timeliness. Measures of results are generally lagging indicators of process performance. Current revenue and profit performance are generally good indicators of how well the innovation engine was working when it created the products that are presently in the company catalog. Today's revenue and profits provide no information at all, however, about how the innovation engine is currently working.

Measures such as those examined at gate reviews of projects in the new product portfolio provide current information about the operation of the innovation engine. Engineering workforce assignments, project schedules, prototype test results, and the rate of progress of each project toward its objectives are all examples of current performance indicators.

Leading indicators of product innovation performance provide insight on how competitive innovation engine performance will be in the future. Progress measures for current product innovation improvement efforts are examples of such leading indicators. Also, the current success rate in hiring good engineers and the current attrition rate among top performing product innovators are good leading indicators for the future competitiveness of new products efforts.

Completeness

Performance measures should make visible all important aspects of the system being measured. Furthermore, the set performance measures used should place a balanced emphasis on all performance characteristics that are essential to the desired business results. Product innovation managers are adept at making trade-offs and will tend to optimize whatever is being measured. For example, if unit manufacturing cost (UMC) and product reliability are measured, more time and money can be invested in the design, and in production tooling. Or perhaps UMC and reliability goals can be achieved more quickly by leaving out product features. If these other aspects of the product innovation effort are important, then the set of performance measurements used should make them visible as well.

Elegance

The goal of performance measures is to create insight and an awareness of current conditions that will lead to better decisions and actions. Elegant performance measures create maximum insight and information with minimum data gathering and analysis. Every performance measure that is imposed on a work group comes with a cost—the time and energy required to gather and analyze the data, and then to report the measurement. The only benefit from this effort is the insight and useful information that the performance measure provides. Elegance is thus a qualitative benefit-to-cost ratio for a given performance measurement.

In one particularly inelegant example, a product innovation manager decided to use measurements to improve the performance of his new product efforts. He came up with a list of over 50 measurements for his people to support. Basically everything that moved during normal operations got measured. The hope was that reviewing all this data would provide some insight into how to the system worked and how to improve its performance. This approach was exactly backward. Effective mental models for system performance that delineate critical success factors should exist before the designing of performance measures. The measures are then used to determine exactly how this system is working so that improvements can be made. In this example, the measurements imposed were so burdensome and revealed so little insight that they quickly fell into disuse.

In another example, an engineering laboratory attempted to infuse automated engineering tools into the product development process. They conceived an elaborate scheme to measure the effectiveness of these tools. This approach involved characterizing each mechanical design in terms of its complexity and then gathering data on the design complexity handled by each engineer per unit of time. After considerable effort was spent trying to perfect this measure and gather meaningful data, it became obvious that engineers were not using the new tools to any extensive degree anyway.

Eventually this automated design system was scrapped and replaced by another. This time the performance measurement applied was simple and elegant. At the time this second system was acquired, the engineering laboratory contained 121 drafting tables. If engineers adopted the new tools, these tables would no longer be required. So the discard rate for drafting tables became the new measure of success. As engineers became familiar with the new tools, they found that they could achieve productivity and quality in their designs that were never before possible. One by one, their drafting tables began showing up on the obsolete equipment list. After one year, only two drafting tables were left in the lab, and success was declared. This elegant measure of performance provided managers with all they needed to know about the acceptance rate for the new tools.

Signal-to-Noise Considerations

Performance measures are attempts to obtain accurate information about the operation of a business process. Like the signal from a radio that is tuned to a distant station, though, a good deal of unwanted "noise" tends to obscure the useful information. Whether the incoming message on the radio can be understood depends on something that communication engineers call the "signal-to-noise" ratio. Managers need to evaluate the information that they receive and assess the sources of noise that can influence it. Noisy sources of information should not be ignored, they simply should be used with care. Their usefulness will depend on the signal-to-noise ratio that exists.

The price of a company's stock is an example of such noisy information. The value of this common financial indicator reflects a firm's overall value and business performance. In fact, in Part I, we described the link between the performance of the innovation engine and shareholder value. The stock price, however, also reflects the mood of the market and the general overall health of the economy. As a result, stock prices can fluctuate dramatically while, back at the company, it is simply business as usual—nothing at all has changed to vary the shareholder value of the enterprise. Business leaders, though, are often beleaguered by shareholders, market analysts, and even their own board of directors when their stock price fails to move steadily upward, and instead responds to erratic market fluctuations. In some cases, executive compensation is tied to the price of the company stock. This can make business leaders unduly sensitive to these capricious outside influences and distract them from effectively managing the long-term success of the enterprise.

➤ Methodology for Designing Performance Measures

The design of an effective set of product innovation performance measures begins with a clear understanding of the desired on-the-job behaviors that will lead to business success. The behaviors of interest will, in turn, depend upon the detailed workings of the product innovation system and the aspects of its performance that are to be tracked. The discussion in Chapter 5 and a system framework for the reader's product innovation process, comparable to the one described in Chapter 6, provide invaluable underprintings to the design of effective performance measures. As a starting point in the design process, this information should be used to outline as completely as possible those behaviors and practice that are essential to a successful business outcome.

Figure 12.1 provides a schematic representation of a design methodology for performance measures. It begins with the set of desired behaviors defined above. Candidate performance measures are then designed to highlight the level of performance on each of these behaviors. Attention is paid to the relevance and timeliness of the information provided by each candidate measure. Consideration is also given to the work involved in gathering needed data for each measure, and the goal of elegance is constantly sought.

As each measure is conceived, it should be tested for adverse behaviors. If this were the only measure used, how might devious people attempt to make their performance look good without adopting the desired practices? Uncovering such weaknesses in a performance measure should trigger a loop back through the design process to reduce the susceptibility of the measure to being gamed. If a single measure cannot prevent adverse behaviors, perhaps adding measures to the set can suppress them.

Once a fairly robust set of candidate measures has been defined, it should next be tested for completeness. Does this set highlight all the important business-related behaviors? How might

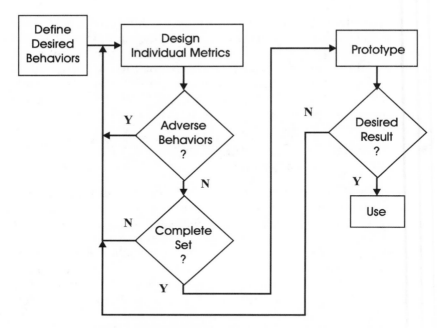

Figure 12.1 A design method for performance measures.

devious people sacrifice performance in other important areas to make their performance with regard to these measures look good? If holes are detected in the span of visibility created by the candidate set, additional measures should be defined to fill these gaps. The design of a set of measures should iterate through the adverse behavior and completeness loops until it appears ready to use.

Like any new product, performance measures should be tested somehow before being widely deployed. One way is to prototype these measures in a limited situation for a period of time and see how well they work. Do they deliver the desired information about current performance? Do they trigger adverse behaviors? Do they encourage emphasis of the desired work-related behaviors? Are they burdensome or costly to support? If problems are detected, then a loop back to the design phase is indicated.

Actual prototyping of performance measures can take a considerable length of time. Another technique that has worked well is to present the candidate set of performance measures to a selected group of expert practitioners and gather their reactions. This can be done fairly quickly in a workshop setting. Once the group understands the measurement set, they should be led through an exercise in which they attempt to game the proposed system of measures by identifying ways in which an individual or a team can apparently perform well without adopting the desired behaviors. Once the flaws in the candidate measurement set are listed, the group can then suggest how to make the measurement set more elegant and robust.

This alternative not only results in an improved and verified set of measures, it engages thought leaders throughout the organization in making the resultant measurement set better. Once these people have done this, they tend to assume ownership of the improved outcome. When the measures are then introduced into general practice, these influential individuals are more likely to support their use. Their influence will, in effect, lower the overall level of resistance to the new measures. This approach can materially improve acceptance of the performance measures throughout the organization.

➤ Desired Behaviors in Product Innovation

The first step in a discussion of performance measures for product innovation should be a description of desired behaviors. While this description may vary somewhat from one business enterprise to the next, a generic list of key behaviors appears in Table 12.1. The meaning and implications of the behaviors listed here should be fairly obvious, so only a few words of amplification will be included here.

Table 12.1   Key Behaviors in Product Innovation

➤ Generating creative new product concepts.

➤ Selecting new product investments well.

➤ Linking development activities to customer needs.

➤ Making competitive commitments.

➤ Planning and managing projects effectively.

➤ Maintaining high-quality development processes.

➤ Motivating the product innovation workforce.

➤ Transferring products smoothly into manufacturing.

➤ Contributing to business strategies.

➤ Maintaining a sense of urgency.

Product innovation success starts with a firm's ability to generate creative new product concepts. In Chapter 6, we described the "fuzzy front-end" of the product innovation process. The level of performance for this part of the process depends, to a large degree, on how well a company is able to engage its full range of insight and imagination in creating product concepts that will delight the customer. Ideally, these concepts not only will be focused on what the customer wants, but also will anticipate what the customer will come to want by the time the new product is introduced.

After selecting an exciting new product concept for investment, the firm should make competitive commitments for this product. This means first of all that the product feature set should be competitive enough to offer a significant performance advantage over competing products in the marketplace. The time-to-market must be considered relative to the rate of performance progress in the particular marketplace to determine the likely levels of performance that will available to the customer at the time of introduction. A competitive commitment thus includes initial product specifications that are aggressive enough to provide significant performance margins over the competition at the time of introduction.

Another element of a competitive commitment is the project schedule and development cost. Project teams should be willing to commit to aggressive schedules and development budgets that outperform those that their competitors are likely to put in place. If product innovators want to be the best in the world, then they should strive to perform that way. Budgets and schedules should be realistic and achievable, but they should encourage product innovation teams to stretch.

Finally, a competitive commitment includes the willingness of high-level managers to invest at a level that ensures the project team can achieve product performance commitments and get the product to market as quickly as possible. If the product is one of a family that is needed to dominate a particular market niche, then a competitive commitment includes the willingness to invest in the other new product efforts that are required to take and hold the high ground in this marketplace.

The connection between product innovation efforts and strategic business processes should be a two-way link. The organizational vision and business strategy should obviously influence the focus and direction of new product activities. Likewise, product innovation efforts inevitably create new learning with regard to customer needs, competition, and new technology. As this learning occurs, it should somehow be able to influence the business strategy of the enterprise. High-level managers are responsible for making sure that this linkage is in place.

Finally, a sense of urgency should be pervasive throughout all product innovation activities at all levels in the firm. This sense of urgency should be generated not by fear, but instead by a genuine desire to excel, and a feeling of accountability for commitments that have been made.

If a business enterprise has all of these behaviors solidly installed, its innovation engine will be in pretty good shape.

Desired Behaviors for High-Level Managers

Chapters 2 through 11 each end with a table of desired behaviors for high-level managers implied by the chapter discussion. Collectively, these tables offer a comprehensive perspective on the nature of the business leader who successfully manages product innovation. Effective performance measures for high-level managers should thus encourage the listed desirable behaviors. In particular, bonuses and other forms of compensation will be more successful incentives for creating business success if they are somehow tied to these behaviors outlined earlier in this book.

The design methodology for performance measures previously described, must be carefully applied. The adverse behaviors of some business leaders in optimizing their wealth under poorly designed compensation schemes have had a devastating effect on the long-term business performance of the firms that hired them. Some of these business leaders have, in fact, become famous, both for getting rich quick and for leaving wreckage in their wake as they move through the business world.

■ INNOVATION ENGINE PERFORMANCE MEASURES

Figure 12.2 provides a cash-flow model for the innovation engine, similar to the one used in Chapter 2, that serves as a framework for identifying enterprisewide measures of product innovation performance. In this model, the shipment of value to the customer—in the form of new products, mature products, services, and consumable

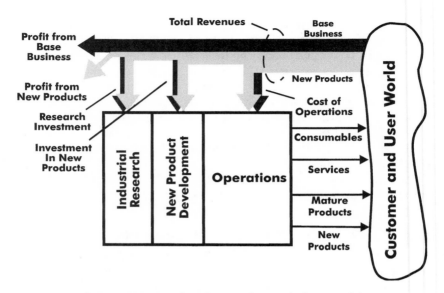

Figure 12.2 Product innovation cash flow model.

materials—results in a flow of revenue to the business enterprise. This revenue is divided into income associated with new products and services and income created by older products and services. Each enterprise needs to decide on its own definition of what the phrase "new product" means. For the purposes of this discussion, it is defined to mean a product or service that has been on the market for two years or less.

The cost of operations in this model includes not only the cost-of-goods-sold (GOGS), but all operating expenses as well, except the funds invested in industrial research and the creation of new products. As shown, both new and mature products and services pay their fair share of these costs. Operating profit is shown exiting to the left of the diagram after the funding for product innovation activities has been removed from the revenue stream. This profit stream is shown in two parts, profits from the older, base business of the enterprise, and those from new products. A desired behavior for this model is that product innovation activities cause substantial and sustained growth in both revenues and profits. Another desired behavior is that product innovation activities generate enough new revenue so that, after their part of the cost of operations is paid, they generate enough excess income (1) to cover the cost of all product innovation investments, and (2) to provide a net positive contribution to the profit from operations.

➤ Revenue Growth Drivers

The first set of performance measures suggested for the innovation engine are associated with the new product vintage chart described first in Chapter 2, and reproduced as Figure 12.3. This chart not only shows historic revenue growth, but also makes both the vintage-year revenue dynamic and new product revenue gain performance of the enterprise visible in graphical form. The new product revenue ratio (NPRR) is visible on this chart as well as the fraction of total revenues in a given year that is included in the top two segments of that year's bar. The data used to create this chart are also useful for constructing an up-to-date assessment of the key revenue growth drivers described in Chapter 2 so that a revenue growth table for the enterprise can be created and kept current, using the methodology described in the Appendix. This growth table provides a useful tool for high-level managers in managing

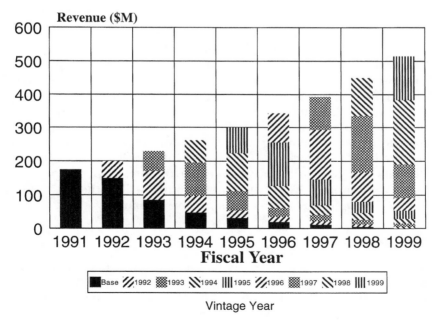

Figure 12.3 A new product vintage chart.

their new product investment rate, and in setting appropriate financial performance targets for new product efforts.

Each of these performance measures, however—revenue history, NPRR, vintage-year revenue dynamic, and new product revenue gain—is based on historic results from the innovation engine, and is thus a lagging indicator of the performance of that business process. The latter two of these four were identified in Chapter 2 as key drivers for revenue growth. A secondary set of measures is needed to make visible the aspects of business performance that determine the level of achievement for these growth drivers—the drivers for the growth drivers, so to speak.

Vintage-Year Revenue Dynamic

The attributes of a desirable revenue dynamic have not yet been discussed. In fact, further work is being done by one of the authors in this area that is not yet ready for publication. The fundamental principle, though, that connects the shape of the revenue bow wave created by a new product to revenue growth rate seems to be simply that receiving revenue earlier creates greater growth rates. For a given revenue gain then, a vintage-year revenue dynamic that has a steeper initial ramp will create more growth.

Performance measures that look at the planning and execution of the market introduction of each new product are thus indicated. The gracefulness of the introduction of new products into the manufacturing process is also important. Performance measures that test the links between engineering and manufacturing, and that examine the design and implementation of manufacturing processes are needed. Do sales build to mature volumes as quickly as possible? Is the manufacturing ramp-up to mature volumes steep and trouble-free? Each business enterprise will have its own leading indicators and performance measures for these parts of the product innovation process. These measures, though, will be the precursors to good vintage-year revenue dynamic performance.

New Product Revenue Gain

The drivers for this growth driver include the value proposition that each new product offers to its customers and the effectiveness of sales and distribution efforts. Ideally, each new product offers such compelling value that every customer will buy it once he or she becomes aware of the product. A sales and distribution effort that brings information about the product to every potential customer and then makes the product readily available will then ensure 100 percent market penetration and the highest possible revenue gain. Performance measures that examine these aspects of the product innovation processes will provide current information related to the new product revenue gain that will eventually occur.

Once again, each enterprise will have its own measures for value proposition performance, and for sales and distribution. In general, though, the value proposition begins with the business strategy of the enterprise, and the new product and new technology road maps. Excellent opportunity scanning and an effective product definition and planning process for each specific product are also crucial. Measuring the effectiveness of sales efforts is also important. The design, structure, and staffing of this part of the enterprise should be a focus of ongoing scrutiny. Finally, the performance of product distribution efforts should be subjected to periodic review. Measures that examine these aspects of the innovation engine in each enterprise will provide current information about eventual new product revenue gain performance.

New Product Investment Rate

The new product investment rate, the fraction of total revenues that is currently invested in product innovation, is inherently a leading indicator of future revenue growth. This performance measure is an important driver for revenue growth, and its current value foreshadows revenue growth—on the order of one product innovation cycle into the future.

➤ Innovation Effectiveness Index

Figure 12.4 identifies how common financial indicators are represented graphically in the cash flow model, and highlights another interesting product innovation performance measurement. An approximate calculation of the return-on-investment (ROI) for the innovation engine can be made by adapting an approach that was published in the *Journal of Product Innovation Management* in 1994.[1] The investment part of this calculation—the denominator—

---

[1] McGrath, Michael E., and Romeri, Michael, N. "The R&D Effectiveness Index: A Metric for Product Development Performance," *Journal of Product Innovation Management*, 1994, pp. 213–220.

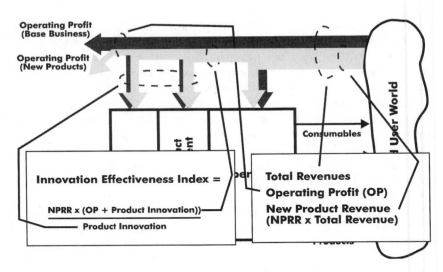

Figure 12.4 Measures of product innovation impact.

is straightforward. It is simply the sum of all cash spent each year on industrial research, and on getting new products to market. Usually the R&D expense listed each year in a company's annual report makes up a significant part of this expenditure. But other new product-related expenses such as product marketing, manufacturing engineering, and production tooling should be included as well.

The excess cash generated each year by new products can be approximated by first calculating the cash flow left over after operating costs are funded. This part of the cash-flow stream is easily seen in Figure 12.2 to be simply the sum of operating profit and all money spent on product innovation. The part of this cash flow that is created by new products can be estimated by multiplying the total cash flow at this point by the NPRR. The Innovation Effectiveness Index (IEI) is then defined as the ratio of this estimate of excess cash generated by new products to the product innovation investment, as represented by the equation in Figure 12.4.

When the cash generated by new products exactly equals the total investment in product innovation, the value of the IEI is 1.0, and there is exactly zero balance left over for the new product contribution to operating profit. If the value of the IEI is greater than 1.0, then new products make a net positive contribution to the operating profit. If the value of the IEI is less than 1.0, then operation of the innovation engine takes money away from operating profits.

A true ROI calculation, though, would use the actual investment that created the return. Because of the time lag inherent in the innovation engine, cash flow from new products in the current year is largely the result of investments made some time ago. A more accurate approximation is thus achieved if the denominator represents product innovation investments that occurred at some point in the past, say one product innovation cycle time into the past.

Several significant problems exist with the IEI analysis. First of all, it is based on historic results. At best, IEI might be calculated for the fiscal year most recently ended. It is thus a severely lagging indicator of innovation engine performance. To manage current new product activities with such a performance measure is a bit like steering your sailboat by the distant wake. It is a practice that is likely to put you on the rocks. Second, the calculation of IEI presumes that an enterprise tracks the fraction of revenues created by new products. HP is one of only a very few companies doing this. In our opinion, though, NPRR is an important product innovation performance measure, and routinely tracking it is a highly recommended best practice.

➤ HP Innovation Effectiveness Index Performance History

Even though it is a lagging indicator of performance, IEI has something to teach us. An analysis of the IEI over time for HP provides an interesting picture of that company's transformation from an instrument company into the world's second largest computer company. It illustrates dramatically the long-term financial impact of John Young's decisions in the late 1970s, and of his tenacity in pursuing his vision for the corporation over a dozen or more years. An analysis of IEI performance for Hewlett-Packard thus provides an important addition to the mental models developed so far in this book and tends to validate many of the concepts and principles that we have advocated.

An analysis of HP vintage charts published in the company's annual reports over the years provides the NPRR data plotted in Figure 12.5. As the company shifted away from electronic instruments, the average market life of a product declined. This, along with high annual revenue growth rates that were consistently in the range of

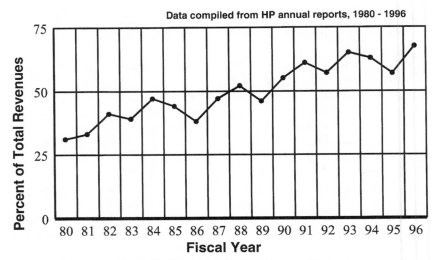

Figure 12.5 New product revenue ratio (NPRR) for HP.
(A new product is defined as one that has been
on the market for two years or less.)

20 percent to 30 percent per year, tended to increase the fraction of revenues generated by new products. Over a 16-year period this fraction grew from under 30 percent to almost 70 percent.

Like most other companies, HP does not report total product innovation expenditures in their annual report, only those invested in R&D activities. Other product-innovation-related expenditures are assumed here to be a relatively small and constant fraction of the R&D budget. The R&D expense reported each fiscal year in the annual reports is thus used as a surrogate for total product innovation expenses. The IEI data plotted in Figure 12.6 is therefore only a reasonable approximation of actual performance.

Two versions of the IEI are plotted in Figure 12.6. One uses the R&D expense for the current year (i = 0) as a denominator and the other uses the R&D expense reported two years earlier (i = 2) for a denominator. The presumption for this second curve is that a typical new product development cycle might take two years; so, on average, the investment that caused current new product revenues occurred about two years before current time. This time shift, in general, makes the denominator smaller and thus increases the

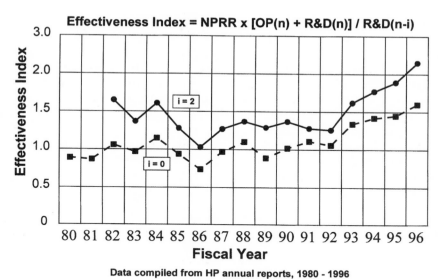

Figure 12.6 HP's innovation effectiveness index performance.

magnitude of the apparent IEI. In addition, though, it produces higher values for IEI in the early 1980s that seem to decline as the years pass.

Using the "i = 2" curve for discussion then, the IEI data seem to show performance declining as the electronic instrument business continues to weaken in the early 1980s. HP at this time had not yet learned to compete with much success in the computer marketplace. Investments in both toner and thermal ink jet printing technologies were underway, but HP's main impact on the office and personal printer businesses was yet to come. IEI performance remained relatively flat until 1992. Then the index began to increase dramatically, almost doubling in four years.

John Young retired from his position as CEO at the end of fiscal year 1992. A facetious person might be tempted to remark, "Well, that sure points out the problem. Once we got rid of him, performance really improved." The authors left HP in 1993, so we were at least partially responsible for holding down HP's performance as well.

The real reason for HP's success at this time was that the hard work and investment over the previous decade had finally come together to create a successful computer business. HP had undergone a transformation. Since 1980 almost everything had changed—the customer focus, the organization, core competencies, technologies, sales and distribution methods, and individual skills. During this period, many new approaches were tried and most were discarded. Those that made sense, though, were retained and became part of a new foundation for doing business. John Young's tenacity and un-wavering focus on the bold objective of turning HP into a successful computer company had finally paid off. In 1992, HP entered a time of excellent revenue growth and truly outstanding growth in profit, as shown in Figure 12.7. They had become the second largest com-puter company in the world and, at least for the next several years, enjoyed the strongest earnings in the industry.

■ PORTFOLIO MANAGEMENT PERFORMANCE MEASURES

Most of the desired product innovation behaviors listed in Table 12.1 can be established by those individuals in each enter-prise who lead the new product portfolio process. This is also the best level from which these behaviors can be observed and mea-sured. Understanding the current state of the innovation engine

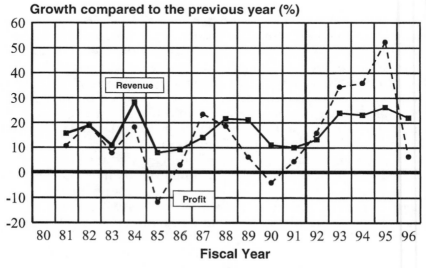

Data compiled from HP annual reports, 1980 - 1996

Figure 12.7 HP revenue and profit growth history.

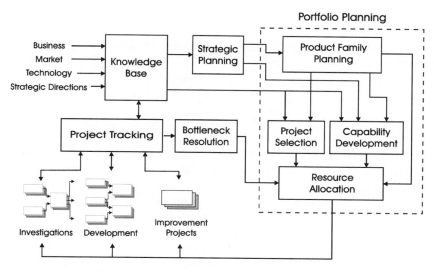

Figure 12.8   The product portfolio leadership process.

thus requires an effective set of portfolio management perfor-mance measures. That will be the focus of this section. As a frame-work for this discussion, the product portfolio leadership process diagram from Chapter 8 has been reproduced here as Figure 12.8.

➤ Knowledge Base

At the core of every successful business is the knowledge that it possesses. To repeat the words of Arie P. de Geus:[2]

> *The ability to learn faster than your competitors may be the only sustainable competitive advantage*

An important element in the current state of the innovation engine is thus the level of knowledge that it contains, and more importantly, the rate at which that knowledge base is increasing. Designing quantitative indicators for knowledge level, however, is beyond the skill and experience of the authors, so other, less spe-cific measures will have to do.

---

[2] de Geus, Arie P. "Planning as Learning," *Harvard Business Review,* March–April, 1988, pp. 70–74.

Perhaps the best one can do in measuring knowledge growth is to assess the nature and intensity of activities that should produce learning, and then to qualitatively assess the level of imagination, insight, and judgment that is applied to product innovation. Chapter 8 discussed the knowledge base required to run a competitive business. It includes an imaginative understanding of customers and their needs, knowledge of pertinent technologies and trends, and a general sense of conditions in the marketplace and in the world at large.

A useful set of performance measures that at least measures the symptoms of knowledge accumulation is focused on the activities of those business leaders who are responsible for managing the new product portfolio. Are they routinely involved in activities that might lead to the accumulation of this knowledge? Furthermore, what is the SEI level of process maturity for these activities, as defined in Chapter 5? If they are done in an ad hoc or reactive manner, they are at Level 1. If, on the other hand, they are a matter of routine and are done in much the same way each time, they are at Level 2 on the SEI scale. A Level 2 SEI rating for these activities is usually quite competitive.

For example, an imaginative understanding of customer needs requires routine interaction with customers from all important market segments, and these interactions cannot simply be through sales support efforts. Business leaders need to learn answers to important questions such as:

➤ Who is my customer's customer?

➤ What value is my customer trying to deliver to his or her customer?

➤ What is my customers vision for a successful future?

➤ How might the capabilities provided by my company help our customers achieve their own vision?

➤ What decision criteria does my customer use in selecting a product?

➤ Why has this customer in the past refused the value proposition offered by my products?

➤ What obstacles keep my customers from serving their own customers more effectively?

➤ What obstacles keep my customer from having a happier, more fulfilling life?

➤ How might we innovate new solutions to these issues?

➤ What other services or products might my company offer that would more effectively satisfy this customer?

This kind of information is not routinely discussed during a sales call. Instead, special effort is required to create situations in which these conversations can take place.

A first stab at measuring the accumulation of this crucial knowledge is to determine how many customer visits of this nature are conducted by business leaders each month. Second, how often do these leaders meet to compare notes on their findings and build a common knowledge base?

With regard to technology awareness, the means by which business leaders learn about new product and manufacturing technologies should be cataloged. Then the effectiveness of each of these learning methods should be assessed. Do these efforts seem to add up to a competitive influx of information on new technologies and important trends? What other methods might be more effective? How often do business leaders meet to discuss these technology issues and build a common knowledge base?

The impact of these learning efforts can be at least partially seen by evaluating the interactions that go on between business leaders and product innovation project teams during project reviews. What is the nature of the information that flows from business leaders to the project team, and from the project team to business leaders? Which group seems to have the broadest perspective, and the most judgment about the business matters at hand? Who is coaching whom? Are project team members compelled by the wisdom and insight offered by business leaders to alter their approach to project issues? Do business leaders add value in these meetings? Are business leaders in the lead?

➤ Strategic and Portfolio Planning

Strategic plans for the business unit and product family plans are other areas in which quantitative performance measures are difficult. The discussion that follows will, instead, offer some qualitative measures of performance in these areas.

Strategic Planning

The first measure of a strategic plan is its very existence. Has one been done? Is it current? The second measure of performance in this area is the degree of relevance of the strategic plan. Has it simply been written and then filed? Or is it a dog-eared document that is actively referred to as a guide for plans and activities as they unfold? The relevance of a strategic plan, to a large degree, reflects the quality of its thought and information. A third measure of a strategic planning effort is the degree of process maturity with which it is executed. Levels 1 through 3 of the SEI scale are generally applicable to this activity. Level 1 implies that strategic planning is sporadic, often done as a reaction to outside forces. Level 2 means that it is done in a repetitive fashion, usually once per year, and is done in much the same way each time. Level 3 implies that there is an established strategic planning process that follows documented guidelines.

Table 12.2 elaborates the sample contents for a business unit strategic plan from Chapter 8. This time it is offered as a checklist for assessing the quality and completeness of strategic planning efforts. If all the elements in this table are executed with diligence, the result should be a relevant document that reflects best practices in organizational vision and portfolio management outlined in earlier chapters. As an example of best practice in this area, HP has developed a strategic planning process that includes many of the elements shown in Table 12.2. During the time the authors were with HP, this process was executed by each business unit throughout the company on an annual basis. HP's planning process operated at the third level of SEI maturity.

One of the outcomes of effective strategic and portfolio planning efforts is the realization of how the capabilities of the business unit must change over time. These changes may be required to exploit new market opportunities, or simply to remain competitive in existing markets. The changes may include adding new capability, evolving capabilities that already exist, or eliminating capabilities that have become noncompetitive and burdensome to maintain. In general, five areas need to be considered in identifying needed changes in capability: (1) core competencies, (2) strategic partnerships, (3) technologies, (4) processes and tools, and (5) workforce.

Measurements of planning performance level in this area begin with the quality and clarity of thought that links required changes in capability to other parts of the strategic plan. Changes in capability should be clearly driven by new market opportunities or customer needs from Item 3 in Table 12.2, or by changes in the competitive picture identified in Item 4. They should be essential to support the required products and services outlined in Item 5. Finally, they should align with and support the purpose of

Table 12.2 Contents for a Business Unit Strategic Plan

1. Purpose statement for the business unit
2. Long-range objectives
   Bold objective for the business unit
   Capability development and adjustment objectives
   Other objectives
3. Analysis of markets and customers
4. Analysis of competition
5. Required products and services
6. Required capability development and adjustment
   Core competencies
   Strategic partnerships
   Technologies
   Processes and tools
   Workforce
7. Financial analysis
   Long-range financial projections
   Outline of major expenditures
   Long-range budgets for functional areas
8. Assumptions and recommendations
   Interdependencies
   Potential problems
9. Plans for the coming year
   Work breakdown structure
   Schedules
   Major milestones
   Resource expenditures

the business unit stated in Item 1. When the specifics of required capability development and adjustments have been defined in Item 6, they should result in one or more objectives that are included in Item 2.

Product Family Planning

The first level of performance for product family planning efforts is the mere existence of a product road map. Once this level is achieved, performance measurement focuses on the quality of thought that has gone into the road map and the strength of the rationale behind the particular set of included products. The degree of imaginative understanding of customer needs embodied in the plan is a useful qualitative measure of performance. The degree of alignment with indicated directions from the strategic plan is an important performance measure. The financial value of the opportunities addressed is a quantitative measure that should be compared with revenue growth and new product revenue gain targets derived from innovation engine performance measurements. The diligence applied in substantiating these financial estimates is a revealing qualitative performance measure.

The existence of a corresponding technology road map is a valuable measure. Beyond mere existence, a high-quality technology road map will reflect substantial knowledge of technical developments and trends, and insightfully connect this information to customer needs and market trends.

The level of process maturity that exists in the processes that create the product and technology road maps is a significant measure. Again, SEI Levels 1 through 3 seem appropriate. A Level 1 process will in general be ad hoc and reactive. Activity at Level 1 is generally event driven. A competitor will introduce a new product or technology and the company will scramble to figure out how to respond. Or perhaps a major development project will be completed, freeing up a large engineering workforce. What should we do with all these people? At Level 2, current road maps exist and are routinely updated. As long as the same people do this work each time, the process used stays generally the same. At Level 3, the creation of each road map is guided by a documented process. The design embodies available understanding of best practices so that, in general, the quality and business value of the result is higher with a Level 3 process.

Of primary importance to the performance level of product family planning efforts is the quantity and quality of available market- and technology-specific information. An astute portfolio leadership team will routinely launch market and technology investigations to gather and develop this information. The results from these efforts will have a significant and ongoing impact on both the product and technology road maps. The skill with which portfolio leaders launch, manage, and use these investigations is a critical area of product family planning performance measurement. Initial performance levels again begin with existence. Are formal investigations used at all? Beyond this, the clarity of their objectives and the sense of urgency and accountability that investigators feel are important qualitative indicators of performance level. The rigor and process by which these investigations are tracked and coached are also indicators of performance level. Finally, the degree that portfolio leaders learn from these efforts and utilize this new knowledge is a qualitative measure of performance.

Capability Development

The projects included in capability development will vary widely with the specific business circumstances of each company. Some will be developing new core competencies. Others may be eliminating noncompetitive capabilities and restructuring operations around a smaller set of competencies. Still others may be searching for and developing critical strategic partnerships. Most will have competitive issues to address that involve work processes, tools, or perhaps weaknesses in the workforce. Almost all companies will be concerned with acquiring new talent, and developing new skills in their product innovation workforce. A key measure of performance is how well portfolio leaders have converged these activities onto a limited, affordable set of well-defined projects.

Performance measures in this area are, in general, simply those of good management practices. Capability development efforts should be well aligned with the direction established by the strategic plan. They should be well-funded and well-staffed activities that are focused on clear objectives. Ownership for each of these activities should assigned to a capable manager, and they should be tracked by portfolio leaders in the same way as any other investment. The ongoing concern in each case should be, "Is this investment producing the desired business result?"

Project Selection

Perhaps the first performance measure to apply to the project selection process is the SEI level of process maturity. Levels 1 through 3 seem to make sense for this process. Level 1 implies that project are launched in an ad hoc fashion, usually as a reaction to a recent customer input, or to a creative idea in either engineering or product marketing. A process maturity of Level 2 means that projects are all launched the same way through a repeatable process. Usually portfolio leaders will gather to consider a project proposal and then, after some discussion, either approve or reject the proposal. The same people are usually involved each time so the selection process remains fairly consistent. A Level 3 selection process has been designed and documented. It includes a large measure of both industry best practice and local wisdom. Both portfolio leaders and those who propose new projects follow published guidelines, including a list of accepted project selection criteria.

The ultimate measure of the level of performance in the project selection process is the business value of the current product innovation project portfolio. As depicted in Figure 12.9, if this process sets high standards for project proposals and examines each proposal with due diligence, then the business value of those projects that are allowed into the portfolio will be exceptional. This level of performance in project selection also puts pressure on the early phases of product innovation. Published project selection standards should set high expectations; for an imaginative understanding of customer needs, for innovative technology, and for a clear focus on a substantial financial opportunity. These high standards will raise performance levels in market and technology investigations and in product definition and planning activities as well. Good results from these processes coupled with an excellent

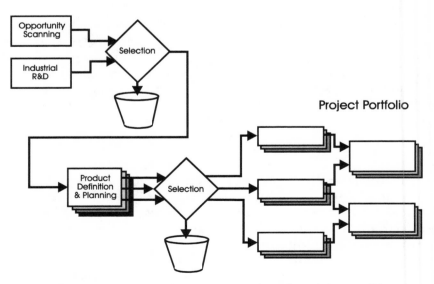

Figure 12.9 Front-end processes set the value of the portfolio.

selection process ensure that the business value of the project portfolio will be as high as possible.

Resource Allocation

Three performance measures will be highlighted for resource allocation. The first is the degree to which each project in the portfolio is staffed to achieve desired business results in the minimum amount of time. Whether a new product effort or a capability improvement effort, each project has been created to achieve a particular business return. The "market window" for that return begins only when the effort is complete. Each effort will thus create the greatest return for the enterprise if it is finished sooner rather than later.

A second measure of performance is the degree of knowledge possessed by portfolio leaders of the total capacity of their product innovation system to do projects and the current work loading in that system. If they approve the next project proposal, does the company have the capacity to support the required effort? The level of performance in this aspect of resource allocation is directly related to the ability of portfolio leaders to answer this question with confidence. The availability of engineers and other resources for the project team is only one aspect of this issue. In addition, other departments, such as the model shop, technical publications, manufacturing engineering, and test engineering, must have sufficient excess capacity to support the project.

The third measure of effective resource allocation is the availability of resources to address bottlenecks. A painful lesson learned in manufacturing is that loading all resources at 100 percent of capacity guarantees that a bottleneck anywhere in the operation will have a devastating impact on schedules. The same is true in product innovation. Bottlenecks will always occur, so some margin of available resources should be invested in less time-critical work so that they can be applied to bottlenecks wherever they may occur on other projects. A best practice is thus to invest about 10 percent of the engineering workforce in investigations and other non-critical-path activities.

➤ Project Tracking

Once projects have been launched, portfolio leaders must be able to effectively measure their progress and direction to ensure that, as business investments, they continue to make sense. These measures are gathered through formal gate reviews, through periodic reporting, and by wandering around and talking to people.

This discussion begins with an outline of performance measures applied to the product innovation process. Measures for the front-end processes are described first. Next, useful measures for development efforts are outlined. This is followed by measures applicable to the introduction phase. Finally, performance measures appropriate to capability development efforts are described.

Tracking the Performance of Front-End Efforts

Figure 12.9 provides a framework for outlining performance measures for the front-end of the product innovation process. The ultimate purpose of these early processes is to work together to present portfolio leaders with frequent new product proposals that (1) address exciting business opportunities, (2) embody an imaginative understanding of customer needs, (3) employ the latest and most appropriate technologies, and (4) promise substantial financial growth for the company. These processes need to work so well that portfolio leaders are faced with more excellent project proposals than they can afford so that some pretty good offerings have to be discarded. An excellent overall measure of performance for the front-end process is thus the degree of anguish caused by new product proposals that have to be turned down. If some excellent offerings end up in the discard bucket in Figure 12.9, then the ones that become projects in the portfolio must be truly great.

The purpose of the opportunity scanning process is to create a prioritized queue of exciting business opportunities that are aligned with the business strategy and organizational vision of the firm. Measures of success include, first of all, that such a list exists. Opportunity scanning should go on all the time as a background process. As people learn about their customers, markets, and applicable technologies, new product opportunities should emerge from time to time to form the list. A measure of the success of this process is that the best of these ideas should be so compelling that they sell themselves throughout the organization. Portfolio leaders should be anxious for the next product to be introduced so that the development team can be redirected to one of the opportunities at the top of the list. Another measure of the success of this process is the amount of delay between the time when a new product effort is finished and the point where the people on that development team are gainfully employed on other important work—the so-called project team changeover delay. With good opportunities readily at hand, changeover delay should be nil. A final performance measure for the opportunity scanning process is that more good business opportunities are found than the enterprise can pursue. When this happens, some good opportunities again end up in the discard bucket accompanied by considerable anguish.

A primary purpose of industrial research is to find and verify applicable new technologies. The output of this process is both knowledge about new levels of performance that are made possible by each new technology, and pertinent design rules that will enable development engineers to apply that technology with confidence in their design. Once again, if this process is working well, it will discover and verify more new technology than development projects can assimilate, so that some good technology will end up in the discard bucket. As before, the quality of that which is discarded is a reliable performance measure. Other measures of success, although lagging indicators, are that (1) no competitor ever gets to market faster with a significant new technology, and (2) the firm routinely introduces products employing new technology in ways that delight the customer. The company thus has a reputation among customers as the one that brings new technology to bear on their needs faster and better than other firms.

The purpose of the product definition and planning process is to transform an assigned business opportunity into a compelling new product proposal. This proposal should, in general, include (1) a clear definition of a competitive product that addresses the opportunity, (2) a business case for that new product including analyses of both the investment required and the return expected, and (3) a project plan that includes both a proposed schedule and resource requirements. To create such a credible proposal, investigation teams will generally have had to verify the market opportunity, specific needs of the customer, and any new technologies that will be used in the product.

The primary measure of success for the product definition and planning process should be a formal gate review at which portfolio leaders decide whether to launch the project. As discussed earlier, this formal review should be designed around a published list of project selection criteria (see Table 8.3), and specified deliverables that are required to launch the project. These deliverables will usually include some form of product specification, a project plan, and a business case. While every effort should be made to eliminate unnecessary paperwork, these three deliverables, at least, should be documented in accordance with standard content and format requirements.

Another measure of the success of this process is the level of enthusiasm generated by the outcome of the product definition and planning process. This enthusiasm should be readily apparent at the gate review. Elements of the new product proposal that contribute to this positive reaction include both the size of the projected financial return and a sense that the product will delight the customer. People should anticipate that it will be easy to sell this product. In addition, new products that are likely to surprise the competition and create an inherently sustainable competitive advantage tend to generate a great deal of enthusiasm.

A final measure of success for this essential element in the product innovation process is its maturity level on the SEI scale. A Level 1 characterizes an ad hoc process. Product definition and planning activities will not follow any prescribed flow or pattern. Instead, members of the team define processes individually as they go. Whether or not their efforts add up to a good result depends strictly on the level of perspective, insight, and judgment of each member of the team, and of the project manager. Often Level 1 activities fail to take advantage of best practice and prior organizational learning. A Level 2 version of this process follows work flow and methods that have evolved over time in the organization. A work process at this level usually performs fairly well and embodies at least some organizational learning. A Level 3 process has generally been designed and documented with careful attention to industry best practices, and to the lessons learned by the organization through earlier experience. A product definition and planning effort operating at this level of maturity usually creates more business value than less mature processes.

Tracking Projects in the Development Phase

Performance measures for new product development team efforts should include a combination of formal reviews, periodic reporting, and informal wandering around. Each enterprise needs some form of institutionalized phase-gate process, as discussed in Chapter 7, that outlines the activities, objectives, and deliverables that are pertinent in each phase of the product innovation process. This process provides portfolio leaders with specific opportunities, called gate reviews, to formally measure the performance and progress of each project. It also provides guidance to project managers on what needs to happen to get a new product out on schedule. The process provides a useful framework for the general flow of work and information during a new product effort, and highlights key interdependencies. Phase-gate process documentation should guide both project managers and portfolio leaders in preparing for gate reviews. Portfolio leaders should then attend each gate review armed with a checklist of pertinent deliverables and questions, and ready to apply due diligence on their investment.

In an enterprise that supports several new product efforts at any one time, portfolio leaders can spend a significant fraction of their time reviewing product innovation projects and attending gate reviews. A standardized presentation of key information on each project facilitates this work. This information should be reported monthly as well as reviewed along with other information at gate reviews. Much like the instrument panel in an airplane, this display of project information should enable portfolio leaders to quickly discern the state of a project, identify areas that need attention, provide needed corrections, and make important decisions regarding their business investments.

Just as an aircraft instrument panel provides a standardized display of attitude, airspeed, altitude, direction of flight, and position, certain types of information should be displayed on the portfolio manager's "instrument panel." Portfolio managers need to quickly visualize project progress relative to schedule, project expenditures relative to the budget, measured product performance and cost relative to plan, and planned product financial return relative to initial estimates. In addition, reviewing managers need to quickly understand changes to plans and commitments in all these categories. As changes to plans and commitments occur, the reasons for these changes need to be clearly described and readily available. Finally, at the launch of every new product effort there are usually assumptions and constraints that affect the business case for the product and the commitments that the project team makes. As the project unfolds, portfolio leaders must learn of any changes to these conditions that might invalidate the business case. The following paragraphs describe information tools that may have value for the portfolio leaders' instrument panel.

Gantt Chart Figure 12.10 provides an example of a Gantt chart representation of a project schedule. The work breakdown

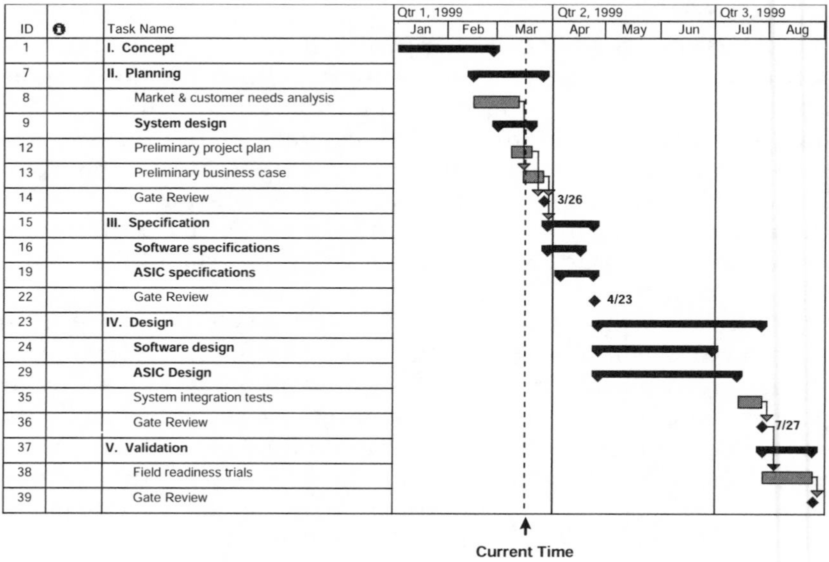

ID	❶	Task Name	Qtr 1, 1999			Qtr 2, 1999			Qtr 3, 1999	
			Jan	Feb	Mar	Apr	May	Jun	Jul	Aug
1		I. Concept								
7		II. Planning								
8		Market & customer needs analysis								
9		System design								
12		Preliminary project plan								
13		Preliminary business case								
14		Gate Review			3/26					
15		III. Specification								
16		Software specifications								
19		ASIC specifications								
22		Gate Review				4/23				
23		IV. Design								
24		Software design								
29		ASIC Design								
35		System integration tests								
36		Gate Review							7/27	
37		V. Validation								
38		Field readiness trials								
39		Gate Review								

Current Time

Figure 12.10 A project Gantt chart.

structure of the project is listed in outline form on the vertical axis, while the horizontal axis shows calendar time. A vertical line drawn at the current time quickly orients the reader with regard to current project activity, tasks that have just been finished, and work that lies ahead. This chart is useful for showing the full scope and multifunctional nature of the project. It can also show when completion of certain tasks falls behind schedule, and it can be used to highlight the critical path of the project. The critical path is the subset of interdependent tasks that determines the ultimate time to completion for the project. This information tool is useful for communicating the overall nature and state of a project, and for recording schedule slips at the task level.

Software tools are available for project planning that create Gantt charts as one of the standard project representation formats. The example in Figure 12.10 was created with Microsoft Project 98.

The Brunner-Gram Another unique, and creative method for visualizing project progress was used widely in HP during the 1960s and 1970s. This device enables a high-level manager to review results from many projects in a very short time and immediately identify the few that are in need of help. While it has not been widely used outside HP, this tool is so valuable for reviewing projects at the portfolio leader's level that it will be described here in some detail.

In the late 1960s, HP was getting big enough that high-level managers were having trouble keeping track of the large number of new product efforts. More and more projects were in need of help, but HP's business leaders were beginning to have difficulty just knowing where to focus their attention. The late Dave Packard appointed Bob Brunner, now retired, as corporate engineering manager and asked him to figure out how to give these engineering teams some help. As a first assignment, Dave asked Bob to design a method for tracking project progress that would, in Packard's words, ". . . tell us what we need to know about a project. Make it so the answers jump quick." The graph that Bob designed to satisfy this challenge became affectionately known as the "Brunner-gram." Over the years, thousands of product development projects have been tracked using this reporting device.

A sample Brunner-gram is presented in Figure 12.11. The vertical axis measures project expenditures and calendar time is

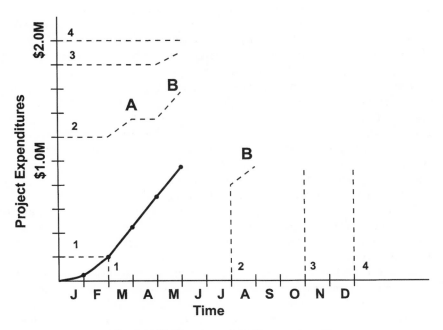

Figure 12.11 A project Brunner-gram.

represented on the horizontal axis, beginning with the project start date. The solid line is simply a plot of actual project expenditures versus time, typically with one data point added every month. The Brunner-gram is created early in the project, usually at the end of the first month. At that time, vertical dashed lines are drawn upward from the x-axis at the estimated times at which each key milestone will be completed. In this example, four milestones are shown. Four horizontal lines are drawn outward from the y-axis at the estimated total expenditures at each milestone. The height of the vertical lines matches the last y-value of the solid line, and the horizontal lines are drawn outward to the date of the last entry on the project expenditure curve. As the project progresses, expenditures move upward and to the right and the plotted milestone estimates converge with the plot of actual expenditures.

If a milestone is reached on schedule and on budget, the three lines simply converge over time and come together at that point. On the other hand, if the estimated schedule or budget for a milestone changes, the new estimates are plotted the next time that the Brunner-gram is updated. An estimated increase in budget for a milestone, for instance, causes the corresponding horizontal line to jog upward. A change in schedule causes the corresponding vertical line to jog left or right in time. As the graph continues its monthly updates, a historical record of estimate changes is created along with a record of actual project expenditures over time. Each time an estimate changes, the change should be annotated with a corresponding letter that refers to an explanation for the change, usually included on the back of the Brunner-gram.

In Figure 12.11, reference letter A denotes a change in the estimated budget for milestone 2 that occurred at the end of March. At the end of May the budget estimate for milestone 2 was again increased, and the estimated completion date was moved out one month. Since the same explanation applies to both of these adjustments, they are marked with the same reference letter, B.

A Brunner-gram can provide significant insight into the state of health of a project. In Figure 12.11, note that two changes have been made in the budget for milestone 2, and one in the budget for milestone 3. The budget for milestone 4, though, is still shown at its original value. How does the project plan to pull that off? Likewise, at the end of May, the schedule for milestone 2 was pushed out a month, but milestones 3 and 4 are still shown on their original schedule. Is that realistic? How will they accelerate the work that occurs between milestones 2 and 3? These questions are easily formulated at the time the updated Brunner-gram is received. Asking good questions at the right time helps portfolio leaders learn where to focus their efforts.

All Brunner-grams look pretty much the same at the beginning of a project. As a project unfolds, however, its Brunner-gram assumes a unique shape and gets more interesting. A couple of examples are provided in Figure 12.12. When a project alters its estimates of budget or schedule, its credibility is called into question. Each time, high-level managers listen to the reasons and judge whether to accept them as sound. The history of schedule changes on a project is a key piece of information that helps high-level managers assess the state of health of that project, and the credibility of the new estimates. When a project develops a history of frequent estimate changes, such as the example illustrated in Figure 12.12b, the project should be closely examined by portfolio leaders and given appropriate help. The project depicted in Figure 12.12b is clearly having trouble making progress toward milestone 3. Portfolio leaders should dig for the underlying root cause for this and either fix the problem or cancel the project. The historical record in the graph indicates that the project team is unlikely to make further progress on their own.

The P-Chart One of the few leading indicators available, a P-chart—presumably "P" stands for "Progress"—provides an early warning that a project schedule is in trouble. To construct a

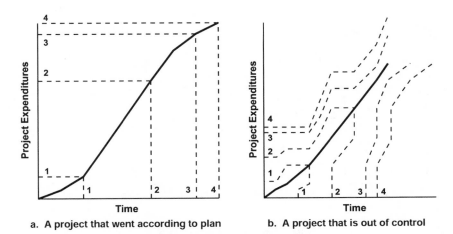

a. A project that went according to plan

b. A project that is out of control

Figure 12.12 Examples of project Brunner-grams.

P-chart, the project managers asks each engineer on the project to count the tasks that they have remaining and estimate how much time they need to complete the work for reaching the next major milestone. The project manager adds up all the engineer-months of work and divides by the number of engineers on the project to get the estimated time to completion. As shown in Figure 12.13, a dashed line is drawn between the total work to be done, as estimated at the start of the current project phase, and the predicted completion date. Each month this exercise is repeated, only now the result is plotted as a new data point on the solid curve. As the solid curve diverges from the dashed line, an error in the estimated time of completion is indicated. Over time, trend lines can be used, as shown, to create new estimates for the milestone completion. Alternatively, the latest estimate can be used to determine how many more people will be needed to finish the milestone on time.

One of the reasons that so-called "bottoms up" estimates, where each engineer estimates the size of the job that lies ahead, are inaccurate is that people cannot anticipate the unforeseen work that will emerge as they get into a task. Their estimates are thus almost always too optimistic. The P-chart captures the effect of this additional work almost as soon as an engineer becomes aware of it. Portfolio leaders can ask project managers to construct a P-chart for their team, and report the results each month as part of their standard project status report.

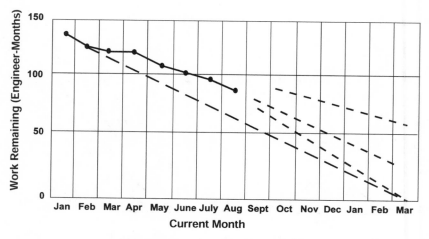

Figure 12.13 A project P-chart.

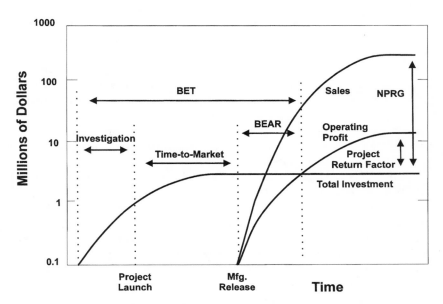

Figure 12.14 A project return map.

Project Return Map Another useful project tracking device that was invented at HP is the project return map.[3] This technique emphasizes the concurrent management of time-to-market, total development cost, and profitability. Central to this technique is the concept of breakeven time (BET) which is the time between project start and when the profits returned by the new product have just paid off the total cost of getting it to market, as shown in the example provided in Figure 12.14. The vertical axis of this sample return map is accumulated total dollars, either for product innovation expenditures, profits, or sales. Note that the vertical scale is calibrated logarithmically to facilitate display of the wide range of financial numbers involved. The horizontal scale is calendar time beginning at the start of the project. Other features of this graph noted in the figure include BEAR, which stands for breakeven after release, and the project return factor, which is the ratio of accumulated profits to accumulated total product innovation cost. Also shown is the new product revenue gain (NPRG) for the project.

---

[3] House, Charles H., and Price, Raymond L. "The Return Map: Tracking Product Teams," *Harvard Business Review* (January–February, 1991), pp. 92–100.

The return map should be created at the time the proposal for a new product effort is considered for approval. It is an important element in the business case to justify the product. Providing this exercise at this early time ensures that engineering, manufacturing, and product marketing people have all discussed trade-offs in product cost, development cost, time-to-market, and profitability. Furthermore, it requires that product marketing create a preliminary forecast of both sales and profits. The decision to launch the product will be partly based on the desirable project return depicted by the return map.

An updated return map should then be included in each periodic report and milestone review after project launch. The original curves, however, should not be removed from the graph. These original estimates remain on the graph as a reminder of the financial basis for the decision to launch this project. As each new version of the return map graph is generated, the new data for actual development cost, estimated future development costs, the sales ramp, and the profit curve should all be drawn on top of the original data and distinguished by line patterns or colors. As each new graph is issued, portfolio leaders can see how the real world has affected the financial basis for the project since the launch decision. After product introduction, these curves should continue to be updated showing actual sales and profits, at least until the BET has occurred.

As the project unfolds, trade-off decisions between product features, development time, development cost, and unit manufacturing cost should all be assessed for their impact on BET. Anything that shortens BET is generally a good business decision. Using BET as a backdrop for day-to-day project decisions encourages just the right behaviors among all members of the multifunction product innovation team.

HP's use of the return map in this manner is the only instance, in the authors' experience, where sales and profit estimates are made visible and tracked throughout a product innovation project. This practice stimulates rapid learning and improvement in this product marketing skill.

One caveat should be added regarding the use of the return map. This technique is useful for those products where a single product model number is created by a single product innovation project team. This allows development costs, sales, and profits to be linked and tracked over the life of the product, from concept to obsolescence. On the other hand, with products such as a computer server, the product in the market may be the result of the efforts of multiple project teams, working in different locations, and at different times. Trying to associate the ultimate profit stream back individually to each of these project efforts has proven to be an intractable problem. The calculation of BET for each project thus becomes at least very complicated, if not impossible. The return map is therefore not recommended for complicated product lines.

Business Case Assumptions and Success Criteria The return map covers some important elements of the business case for a new product, but not all. Along with an up-to-date Gantt chart, a Brunner-gram, and an updated return map, portfolio leaders also need to review the other important aspects of the business case to ensure that continued investment in a particular new product effort still makes sense. The initial business case should list the assumptions and success criteria that are essential to the success of the new product. This list, along with indicators for the status of each item, should become a final item on the portfolio leaders' "instrument panel." Simple red, yellow, and green markers at the end of each item on the list may suffice. Notes of explanation for red and yellow status indicators should be included. This status indicator focuses the attention of portfolio leaders on the most important issues and invites them to pursue further any issues of concern.

Product Introduction Performance Measures

Measures of performance for the product innovation process in the introduction phase are generally associated with the steepness of the sales ramp and manufacturing volume ramp, and the level of hassle, ambiguity, and rework that occurs after manufacturing release. From a philosophical point of view, the ramp-up to maturity of both sales and manufacturing volumes for a new product should be limited only by the learning curve of customers, and perhaps dynamic effects that are inherent to the particular market. If market introduction plans are as effective as possible, the customer learning curve should be steep indeed. Usually, though, uncertainties and rework occur after manufacturing release that also affect the rate at which orders and shipments approach their mature values.

In Chapter 5, the product innovation process was described as an information assembly line, a system for creating knowledge about a new product. If this system works perfectly then, at manufacturing release, perfect knowledge should exist within the business enterprise that describes how to sell, how to manufacture, and how to support the new product. The only people lacking knowledge about the product at this point should be the customers.

If there is an internal shortage of knowledge at product introduction, however, it is reflected in the internal learning that occurs after manufacturing release. Measures of a knowledge gap at introduction therefore might include the number of changes made after manufacturing release of the product, such as (1) engineering change orders, (2) manufacturing tooling or process changes, or (3) revisions and corrections to technical publications. Initial rework of assemblies on the manufacturing line is another useful measure. Quality flaws, product performance problems in early production runs, or vendor parts that have to be returned or reworked are other indicators. Finally, any lack of confidence in manufacturing that compels people to ramp initial manufacturing volumes up slowly reflects this shortfall in product knowledge.

The speed and efficiency of market introduction activities is another area for performance measurement in this phase. These activities, as quickly and effectively as possible, should get customers in the target market to consider the value proposition that the new product offers, and to make their buy decision. Once customers have decided to buy the product, this part of the innovation process should focus on getting the product to them quickly and in good shape. If marketers could gain access to the information, customer awareness versus time would be a relevant measure of product innovation performance. Once customers have received the sales introduction message, the steepness of the order rate will be determined partly by those market dynamics mentioned earlier, but more importantly, by the impact that the product value proposition has on them. The speed and effectiveness of distribution channels in getting the product in the hands of the customer are also pertinent performance measurements. A final area that could provide critical information is an assessment of the reasons some customers who have considered the product value proposition say, "No."

Tracking Capability Development Projects

An effective capability development effort begins with the goals and priorities set by product portfolio leaders, so measurement of performance should start there. The qualitative measurement effort offered here is simply a list of questions:

➤ Are goals and priorities clear and do they align with and effectively support the organizational vision and existing strategic plans?

➤ Are business leaders aware of the current issues with product innovation performance that have the greatest impact on the firm's ability to compete effectively? Have they addressed these issues in their goals and priorities?

➤ Have their goals and priorities been translated into effective project objectives and has ownership of each objective been assigned to a capable person?

➤ Has each objective owner received the necessary resources to succeed?

➤ Have business leaders insisted on a good project plan for each capability development initiative and are they tracking the progress of these investments with due diligence?

While they are only a qualitative assessment, honest answers to these questions will indicate the overall effectiveness of a capability development effort and highlight areas for possible improvement.

Another aspect of capability development is hiring and retaining good people. Performance measures in this area include the degree to which a business enterprise is considered the employer of choice within the professional communities of practice with which it is involved. If it is low on the "employer of choice" scale, the root causes for this lack of stature then provide an important focus for performance measurement and improvement.

A related performance measurement is the rate of attrition among top performers in all product innovation job categories, especially among those individuals who occupy industry-critical positions. In some industries, individuals who possess a particular product marketing perspective, or perhaps system-level technical expertise, become highly sought after among competing companies. These individuals are critical to the development of an imaginative understanding of customer needs, and the defining of new product lines that will determine the future of the industry. Business growth can sometimes become constrained by the ability to find, hire, and retain people with these critical talents. Because of their disproportionate value to business success, they are often courted by competitors. Hiring such people and keeping them happy and gainfully employed is a vital aspect of a firm's efforts to build capability.

➤ Portfolio-Level Performance Measures

The preceding paragraphs have described performance measures for individual projects. This section offers several interesting measures of process performance at the overall portfolio level. Each is a lagging indicator of current process performance but, nonetheless, is useful in demonstrating the impact of existing process improvement efforts and in identifying opportunities for future improvement.

Portfolio Progress Rate

The progress of projects in the portfolio toward their current milestones is an important overall performance measure for the product innovation process. This can be measured each month on each project by looking at the time remaining to current milestones. If the milestone date remains unchanged, then one month of progress was made in a month of effort. The progress rate for that project is thus 1.0. On the other hand, if the milestone slips a month, then it is just as far away as it was at the end of the previous month. Zero progress was made. If a two-month slip is declared during the month, then the milestone is a month further away than before and the progress rate is −1.0. Overall progress for the portfolio can then be estimated by calculating an average for all projects that is weighted by the amount of effort invested in each project during the month. Figure 12.15 provides an example of a portfolio progress rate graph.

Schedule Change Pareto Chart

As schedule changes occur on individual projects, the reasons for those changes should be recorded. Over time, the reasons for schedule slips inevitably fall into discrete categories, usually less than a dozen in number. A product innovation process performance measure is then constructed by summing the impact of these schedule slips across the entire new product portfolio, categorized by the reason for change. The impact of a slip is the length of the delay caused by the slip that has occurred times the number of people involved with that effort. This summation should be made over a moving window in time, say over the past year. The Pareto chart in Figure 12.16 provides a convenient format for displaying this information.

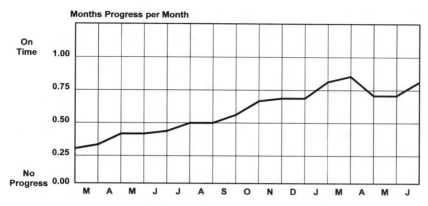

Figure 12.15   Portfolio progress rate chart.

This chart builds a picture of chronic weaknesses in the product innovation process. Improvement efforts should be focused on the top few categories that impact schedules the most, probing first for root causes, and then implementing solutions. As these solutions impact performance, this graph will change and other categories will move to the top of the chart.

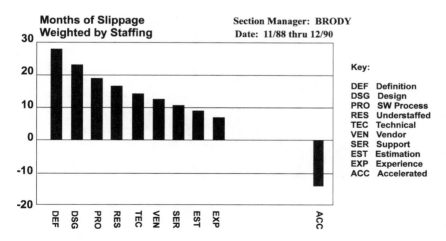

Figure 12.16   Schedule-change Pareto chart.

Product Innovation Inventory

As discussed in Chapter 10, managing product innovation as if it were an investment in inventory leads to better business decisions. A means is needed for displaying and tracking this intellectual property inventory, and the occasional "scrap" that occurs. Figure 12.17 illustrates a useful format for presenting this information.

The vertical axis measures the percentage of total product innovation resources that are invested in each category in a given quarter, and the horizontal axis shows time, usually by fiscal quarter. Five categories are recorded in a stacked bar chart format, two representing intellectual property inventory that has been released to manufacturing, two that denote canceled project efforts, and one that shows intellectual work-in-process (WIP). Both canceled and released inventory categories make a distinction between inventory whose status has changed in the current quarter,

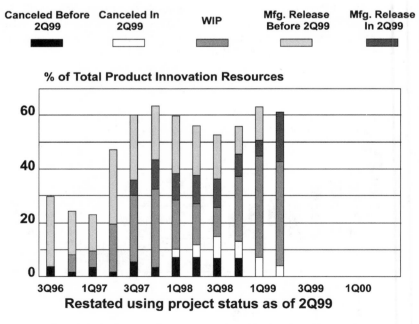

Figure 12.17 Product innovation inventory assessment.

and that which has accumulated due to actions taken in prior quarters. In a quarter in which a new product is introduced, all of the WIP inventory associated over time with that effort gets restated as intellectual property released in the current quarter. In the following quarter, this same block of effort will move to the other category of "shipped" intellectual property and will be added to that which has already accumulated in this category.

Using this chart to assess and manage product innovation inventory evokes many of the same thought patterns and issues that have long been familiar to manufacturing managers. In many businesses, the only significant differences are that the investments represented by the numbers shown on this graph will dwarf their counterparts in the manufacturing department, and the time scale is longer. Because of the increased time scale, the time value of money is a much more important consideration in managing intellectual property inventories.

First of all, finishing projects in a timely fashion is seen from this perspective as moving sunk costs out of WIP and converting this investment into a means for revenue and profit generation. The more quickly this can be done, the lower the net present value of the investment. Second, manufacturing managers become concerned with old inventory. "Does it still have value? How long will it be until this stuff becomes scrap?" The same concerns should bother product innovation managers: "That project has been going on far too long. I wonder if it still makes sense for the intended customer."

The right level of scrap in product innovation, though, is not generally zero. In HP, we used to have words of consolation for the engineer who had just made a costly mistake, "If you are not generating some scrap, you are probably not moving fast enough." A version of this advice applies to product innovation projects as well. If a business enterprise does not cancel a new product effort now and then, it is probably not being aggressive enough.

Some companies, though, are as ad hoc and vague about canceling projects as they are about starting them. No formal process or clear decisions are apparent. Engineers are gradually moved on to other work so that a project that was fully staffed one month will have almost no one working on it two months later. Eventually no one works on it and its memory simply fades over time. The investment in these abandoned projects simply lays there in the WIP category much like obsolete inventory that sometimes takes up space in the factory. The graphical technique shown in Figure 12.17, highlights such forgotten investments, sometimes showing them as isolated islands of WIP on the graph. Making intellectual property inventory visible in this fashion encourages more effective management behaviors.

Best practice with regard to project cancellations is to make clear decisions that are broadly communicated. The act of project cancellation can send important signals throughout the product innovation community in a business enterprise. An understanding of the pitfalls that can bring a project to a halt provides important guidance and motivation for other projects. Product innovators need to be reminded from time to time that their task is not just about elegant new technology; it is also about making money through judicious investment in an effective business process. It helps keep product innovators on the right track when they know that the same thing could happen to their project if it stops making business sense to high-level managers.

■ MEASURES OF AN EFFECTIVE ENVIRONMENT

Measures of the product innovation environment should focus on those working conditions that tip the economic equation of individual product innovators in favor of remaining with the company and investing themselves wholeheartedly in their work. They should thus assess aspects of the infrastructure that relate to personal currencies such as freedom from fear, professional growth, sense of accomplishment, financial rewards, and self-esteem. The performance measures that relate to these issues will largely be qualitative in nature.

A couple of useful measures in assessing both the level of fear in the environment and the level of intellectual honesty that exists will be offered first. The frequency with which product innovators initiate conversations with high-level managers two or three management levels above their own position is one such measure. In many businesses, this is equivalent to an individual contributor, such as a design engineer, feeling comfortable in starting a conversation with the VP of engineering, or perhaps even the CEO. A second measure is the apparent willingness of individuals at all levels to raise important work-related issues in a public forum. A new engineer may point out a flaw in the design approach that was established before he or she arrived on the project. Or a product marketer may raise an issue concerning the suitability of the current product definition for a particular market segment. This measure is focused on the willingness of people such as these to risk saying exactly what is on their mind. If the actions described in these qualitative measures occur often, then the levels of vertical information flow and intellectual honesty in the firm are usually fairly healthy. Furthermore, the personal economics of individual product innovators will be concerned with more constructive currencies than freedom from fear.

The degree of management by wandering around (MBWA) that takes place is another measure of a healthy working environment. In companies that compete effectively in product innovation, business leaders are unlikely to manage by "remote control," with undue reliance on memos and other formal interactions. If they are concerned about something, they are more likely to take a walk and talk to the right individual. One HP human resources manager, who wanted to reemphasize MBWA as a management practice, invented a creative way to put a number on it. Special wooden coins were issued to people throughout each department. Each coin was inscribed, "Good for 10 minutes of quality MBWA." All managers were given a special transparent glass mug with a scale marked on the side. Throughout the week, managers carried their MBWA mugs around begging for coins. All they had to do to get one was have a conversation with an employee who had one. Every Friday the human resources manager visited each manager and recorded the level of coins in his or her mug. The coins were collected and redistributed for the coming week. The MBWA performance data was reviewed with the general manager at staff meetings. Not only was a manager's level of MBWA now visible, it was also important. The general manager, by the way, also had a mug and got a score each week.

Table 10.1 described some relevant performance measures that will be repeated here. Although these measures are qualitative, high-level managers who apply them know the right results when they see them.

➤ *The "Parking Lot" Metric* Does the parking lot for the cars of your product innovation people fill up early each day and empty out late? Do you see people going home early? Or do they sometimes have to be chased out with a stick to get them to go home at all?

➤ *The "Monday Morning" Metric* When a product innovator comes in early on Monday morning, before the supervisor gets there, what does this individual do? Does this person know what work needs to be done, and does he or she want to do it?

➤ *The "Grandparents" Metric* Can each employee explain, with pride and in simple terms that someone disconnected from the work situation can understand, (i.e., their grandparents) what the company does, and why their own job is important?

➤ *Attrition Rate and Exit Interviews* The level of attrition among product innovators, particularly the top performers, is an excellent performance measure for the working environment. Superior employees are generally more mobile and less bound to their current job. They can always find a job with another firm so they are less fearful of leaving. Consequently, if they stay, they do so because they like their job and the work environment. Increased attrition among employees at this level may indicate growing problems with that environment. Information gathered in exit interviews can thus be valuable in identifying needed improvements.

■ PERFORMANCE MEASURES FOR BUSINESS LEADERS

This discussion of performance measures for business leaders assumes the point of view of either the board of directors, in the case of a small-to-midsize firm, or the corporate executive staff, in the case of a large company with multiple business units. The important questions from this perspective are:

➤ What behaviors do we want from our business leadership team with regard to product innovation?

➤ What measures will make these desirable behaviors visible?

➤ How can these measures best be used to encourage the desired behaviors?

At the highest level, the goal should be to encourage behaviors that cause shareholder value to increase. As discussed in Chapter 2, shareholder value is the present value of cash flow from operations, discounted at the cost of capital for the firm.[4] The present value of cash flow can be divided into two terms: (1) the present value of cash flow from operations throughout the current forecast period, and, (2) a residual value, the present value of cash flow that is expected to occur beyond the current forecast. The second term is heavily influenced by the competitive position of the firm or business unit at the end of its forecast period. So the behaviors that we are looking for from our business leaders are those that will create good cash flow during our forecast period while, at the same time, ensuring a strong competitive position at the end of this period.

How business leaders affect product innovation efforts can have a great impact on both of these components to shareholder value. Management of the innovation engine revenue growth drivers, discussed in Chapter 2, impacts both forecasted cash flow, and the long-term competitive position of the firm. Cash flow throughout the forecast period depends on current products and services that the enterprise already has in the market, but is also heavily influenced by those that are currently under development in the new product portfolio. The influence that business leaders have on the timely and effective conclusion of these current new product activities will thus impact shareholder value. The competitive position of the firm at the end of the forecast period will depend on what markets and competitors do, but it will also be determined by the decisions and actions of business leaders as they manage the innovation engine in their business. Their efforts to increase their own knowledge, their business strategies, the creativity that is applied in long-range new product and technology planning, and their insightful leadership in building capability will all contribute to the future competitive position of the enterprise.

The required performance measures then must encourage business leaders to balance their efforts between three areas of focus: (1) effectively managing the innovation engine, (2) executing current new product efforts successfully, (3) and building competitive capability for the future. A fourth performance measurement is required, though, that will encourage business

---

[4] Rappaport, Alfred. *Creating Shareholder Value: The New Standard for Business Performance.* New York: Free Press, 1986 (chap. 3).

leaders to grow in their own ability to perform more competitively in these areas of focus. A comprehensive overview of the desired behaviors that form the basis for this set of performance measures is provided by the tables included at the end of Chapters 2 through 11.

Management of the Innovation Engine

Measures of performance for business leaders should assess how well they manage the innovation engine described in Chapter 2. To begin, they must manage the growth drivers to the innovation engine. They have direct control over new product investment rate (IR), but also must manage the other two drivers, vintage year revenue dynamic and new product revenue gain. This includes both understanding historical performance in these other drivers, and setting targets for improved performance. Before they can make an intelligent decision on the right level for IR, though, they need to understand the relationships between IR and revenue growth that are established by the other two drivers. So good performance in this area begins with an understanding and effective application of some sort of growth model that is appropriate to the enterprise.

Understanding of the Growth Model

Measures of performance for business leaders in this area should highlight how well they establish and manage a model for revenue growth that is appropriate to their business. The methodology for creating growth models offered in Chapter 2 works well for some businesses, but is only a starting point for others. For example, an enterprise that develops components that engineers at other companies design into their own products will also have a revenue model that depends on growth drivers. As with the model presented in Chapter 2, these drivers will include investment rate, some form of new product revenue gain, and some form of revenue dynamic. The latter two drivers, though, will differ from their counterparts described in Chapter 2. The method used to derive growth relationships between IR and these other two drivers will also be different from the one demonstrated in Chapter 2. Regardless, the business leaders in each enterprise must strive to understand their own growth model well enough to make intelligent decisions in setting IR to achieve desired revenue growth rates. The performance measures applied to their efforts should make visible their level of success in doing this.

Management of Growth Drivers

Performance measures for business leaders should also assess how well they manage the growth drivers to their innovation engine. In setting their new product investment rate, they must balance the use of current income between (1) investments in future revenue growth and competitive capability, and (2) current operating profits. The value they pick for IR, though, will determine the level of overall revenue gain that must be achieved. A low value of IR that makes profits look good simply raises the revenue gain performance required from the innovation engine to achieve growth targets.

Business leaders must also establish, assign, and manage targets for both revenue gain performance and new product revenue dynamics. The overall revenue gain target for the innovation engine must be translated into specific performance criteria for individual product innovation projects. Business leaders must then see that each product innovation project being launched meets these criteria. Managers of the innovation engine must also set performance targets for the vintage year revenue dynamic. This involves understanding the underlying relationships that have created historical performance in revenue dynamics, determining how this performance can be changed to create increased revenue growth rates, and then setting appropriate targets for these performance improvements.

Portfolio Strategy and Business Case

Another performance measure that can display the level of leadership being applied to the innovation engine is a business case for the new product portfolio. This might take the form of an annual report with a semiannual update. These reports should be in written form with in-person presentations. The contents of the business case should include perhaps the first five sections of the strategic plan outlined in Table 12.2 plus the current new product and technology road maps for the enterprise.

The quality of the new product and technology road maps is a key measure of business leadership performance. The business rationale that supports the particular set of entries in the product road map should be sound. The underlying philosophy for balancing the portfolio—between short- and long-term investments, between market segments, and perhaps between existing and new markets—should make sense. The degree to which these road maps reflect an imaginative understanding of both existing and emerging customer needs is of particular importance in measuring the quality of the business case. Each product and technology effort included in the portfolio should be compelling in that it addresses a substantial business opportunity, promises an excellent financial return, and helps move the firm toward its strategic goals. The portfolio should also include at least one new product offering or technology that promises to destabilize current markets and trigger explosive growth in some new direction. Overall, the new product and technology road maps should provide leadership for the customer base that anticipates what they will come to want, and that will provide them with surprise and delight throughout the period. Finally, the new product road map should be aggressive relative to what is known about competitive efforts, so that it will likely keep competitors off balance and behind.

Finally, there should be a financial analysis of the present value of the current portfolio over the forecast period, along with projections of revenue and profit growth. A forecasted new product vintage chart should be included. These growth estimates should predict increasingly positive cash flow for the business over the forecast period. Furthermore, the product and technology road maps should support a strong competitive position at the end of the forecast period. A good portfolio strategy and business case will thus portend excellent growth in shareholder value.

➤ Management of Current Projects

Measures of performance for business leaders should also make visible the quality of their efforts to help near and midterm project efforts succeed. These efforts may include applying due diligence to current investments, guiding and coaching project teams, providing support resources, and initiating improvements to work processes and tools.

Another aspect of managing current new product efforts is the establishment of the work environment. As discussed in Chapter 8, intellectual honesty is the lifeblood of successful product innovation. High-quality, freely available information is the raw material that supplies the information assembly line and keeps it running smoothly. It is the stuff from which new products are conceived and then described. The environment that business leaders establish is essential in supporting candor and honesty.

Due Diligence on Current Investments

The documents that business leaders use to track new product efforts can also serve as a performance measure for their portfolio management efforts. A portfolio tracking notebook, a simple three-ring binder with one or two pages dedicated to each project, can highlight the status of the entire project portfolio as well as the efforts of portfolio leaders to keep these projects on track. The first section in this notebook might include portfolio summary information, such as that presented in Figures 12.15 through 12.17, along with a short summary of current portfolio issues and actions. In the project section, information for each project would ideally include the project name, a Brunner-gram (Figure 12.11), a current return map (Figure 12.14), the name of the project leader, a brief summary of the resources dedicated to the project, a summary description of the product, unit manufacturing cost targets, a list of key customers, and a list of key competitors. The data for each project should also briefly describe the reasons for any changes in budget or schedule that have occurred since the beginning of the project. Project sheets for improvement efforts should be included in the binder, too. The format of these sheets may vary somewhat from that used for new product efforts.

Support Resources, Processes, and Tools

The performance of business leaders in providing effective support resources for product innovation projects should be evaluated. These support resources might include model shop facilities, environmental test resources, or materials and component engineering support. A technical library and patent search services are other examples. The purpose of these support resources is to ensure that individuals working on a new product effort have all the parts, materials, and information that they need, just when they when they need them. Furthermore, effective support resources ensure that members of a new product team can spend all their time and effort working effectively on their assigned objectives. A useful measure of performance in this area might be the fraction of total work time that individual contributors spend at nonessential tasks that distract them from their central focus, and that someone else could probably do more effectively. The business leaders of an enterprise in which individual design engineers spend a third of their time supporting their own computer systems, for example, get a particularly low score in this area.

The performance of business leaders in addressing the competitive performance of product innovation work processes and tools should be assessed. A test for effective performance in this area is to ask for a description of the most critical few issues that impair the ability of current product innovation projects to perform at competitive levels. How have these issues been determined to be the most critical? Then ask for a description of the efforts that are underway to resolve each issue. Has ownership been clearly assigned to a capable individual? Is the level of resources invested in each issue appropriate? Are effective progress measures being tracked? The responses to these questions should be evaluated to establish the quality of leadership.

Creation of an Effective Environment

Performance measures that assess how business leaders affect the working environment include periodic employee surveys and MBWA.

An annual employee survey can provide important information about the effectiveness of business leaders in creating a positive working environment. Survey questions can probe for information that relates to aspects of the environment important to product innovation, such as intellectual honesty or freedom from fear. Analysis of the data with regard to the level from which it is collected can both indicate problems that may exist in the working environment at each level, and provide information about the likely sources of those problems.

Opportunities for members of the board or corporate executives to interact one-on-one with product innovators can be created; they are a useful source of information in evaluating the health of new product efforts, and hence the performance of business leaders. The agenda for an annual on-site review of business operations might call for a dinner that includes employees at the level of first line supervisors and higher. Seating arrangements could ensure that local managers sit at table with members of the reviewing team. The list of invitees would include all project managers of new product efforts. Presentations of selected new product efforts could be part of the formal review on the following day. Live demonstrations of product prototypes are memorable and would stimulate discussion. Ideally, visitors would form small groups for presentations. This promotes more questions and interaction with members of each project team. The review agenda should provide an opportunity for the visiting review team to discuss confidentially among themselves what they have seen and heard.

➤ Development of Competitive Capability

Measures for the performance of business leaders in their efforts to establish the future competitive stature of the firm are associated with the business directions that they set and their efforts to build future capability. Objectives in setting directions for the future should be to steer the enterprise to opportunities and markets that (1) support excellent growth, and (2) present a tractable competitive situation. The first objective for building future capability is to forge and reshape the capabilities of the enterprise to support the business as it is envisioned. These capabilities include the skills, core competencies, and strategic partnerships that will be needed by the end of the forecast period. The other objective in building future capability is to ensure that the capacity of the enterprise to create new products is second to none by the end of the forecast period.

Strategic Direction

Direction setting begins with the organizational vision. Measuring the core ideology of the enterprise, the capstone of the organizational vision, might include assessing its clarity, appropriateness, and authenticity. Reviewing the efforts that have been made to communicate it might also be helpful. Authenticity can be evaluated both through personal interaction with business leaders, and through the multilevel surveys described earlier. A few questions can be included in these surveys that probe the attitudes of people at each level in the enterprise to issues related to the core ideology. Do business leaders "walk their talk" with regard to stated values? Does the purpose statement for the firm make sense? Does it matter? Do day-to-day activities align well with the stated purpose and values of the firm?

The bold objective set by business leaders can be reviewed in a similar fashion. First of all, does one exist? If so, does it align well with the core ideology and is it a necessary and sufficient response to the current business situation? Is it likely to have a dramatic impact on the ability of the firm to serve its customers and grow revenues? How well has it been communicated throughout the organization? Is it having the desired influence on action at all levels? Once again, the multilevel survey can be a useful source of information, as can MBWA.

Another step in measuring the direction-setting performance of business leaders is to carefully assess their strategic plan. It should contain the elements outlined in Figure 12.2 and be both current and relevant to existing business concerns. It should provide a specific action plan that includes steps that will be taken by the business to achieve a more successful and competitive future. As business leaders manage the enterprise on a day-to-day basis, their decisions and actions should reflect and align with the guidelines laid down in the current strategic plan.

Implementation of Future Capability

The first measurement of performance that relates to building capability is to assess the quality of strategic plans for building new capability (see Item 6 in Table 12.2). First of all, do such strategic plans exist? Second, do they create a coherent and compelling vision for the future of the enterprise? Do the plans for creating new capability move far enough and fast enough in the right direction? Do they include getting rid of capabilities that will be unneeded in the future as well as adding new capabilities? Do these plans reflect an imaginative understanding of how the needs of customers and the marketplace will evolve?

The next performance measurement in this area is the effectiveness of management action taken to implement these plans. Are there specific objectives and a timeline? Has each objective been assigned to a capable person? Is the enterprise investing appropriately in these capability development activities? Are these activities well managed and making progress? Are these activities likely to create a strong competitive position for the firm at the end of its forecast period?

➤ Leadership Capability

The skill and wisdom that business leaders exhibit as they track and coach new product efforts is an important area focus for performance measures. This skill level includes their overall management abilities and their knowledge of general business matters. It should also include, however, their knowledge of those fundamentals specific to their own business. Their understanding of the mental models that apply and their skill in using these models in exercising management control are all key elements to performance. This understanding includes both an awareness of important cause-and-effect relationships, and a sense of the response times that are typical of their business processes.

Another area of focus in assessing the capabilities of business leaders is the rate of growth in their operating knowledge. Is their understanding of customers growing fast enough? Are they keeping abreast of technology developments that apply to their business? Are they up to date on their competition? Are they in touch with performance issues and working conditions in their own enterprise? Perhaps the question most important to shareholder value: Are they learning faster than their competitors?

A final area for performance assessment that relates to leadership capability is the ability of business leaders to set appropriate performance targets for their product innovation teams, and then manage and coach these teams toward achieving these expectations. This aspect of performance includes effective involvement by portfolio leaders in the early phases of each new product effort, ensuring that each project gets launched in the best direction with a sound business case, a good product definition, and a solid project plan. Related to this aspect of performance is the time that business leaders seem to spend fighting fires late in the product innovation cycle. The more effort that high-level managers invest in the early project phases, the less hassle and turbulence occurs late in the project. Where business leaders spend the most time in the innovation cycle is thus a good indicator of the leadership capability that is in place.

➤ The Business Leaders' Product Innovation Report Card

The qualitative performance measures discussed in this section need to be reduced to a quantitative assessment tool for evaluating the performance of high-level managers in their efforts to lead and manage product innovation. Such a tool might be useful to the board of directors of a small- to-midsize company for setting performance objectives for their business leadership team, and then later evaluating the quality of their results. It might also be a useful checklist in evaluating candidates for a high-level position. As a self-evaluation tool, it might help business leadership teams answer these questions:

➤ How are we doing?
➤ Where should we focus our improvement efforts?

The performance measures discussed in this section are mostly subjective and difficult to express in numbers. In fact, they are about as subjective as "How is little Johnnie doing in school?" So how about a product innovation report card for business leaders?

Table 12.3 shows a sample report card, based on the headings in this section of Chapter 12, for evaluating the performance of the business leadership team in managing product innovation activities. Each element in this report card is described in detail in the previous paragraphs, and each implies objectives and actions that, when accomplished well, will help improve shareholder value.

The traditional grading scale is recommended for this report card, with a grade of "A" corresponding to excellent performance and an "F" signifying failure. Following are more specific criteria suggested for each level of performance:

A—Performance is a clear competitive advantage, equivalent to that of world leaders.
B—Performance is equal to that of other dominant participants in the marketplace.
C—Level of performance is even with marketplace norms. No competitive advantage.
D—Performance level is a competitive disadvantage, a source of concern.
F—Level of performance threatens long-term survival of the enterprise.

Testing this report card against the design methodology in Figure 12.1 indicates that it may be a fairly robust measure of portfolio leadership performance. The design of the set of measures contained in this report card began with an exhaustive attempt to define desired portfolio leadership behavior—Chapters 2 through 11 of this book. The tables at the end of these chapters summarized desired behaviors for high-level managers implied by the material discussed in each chapter. Collectively, the line items listed in the report card span the set desired behaviors listed in these tables.

Table 12.3 Business Leaders' Product Innovation Report Card

Activity	Grade	Overall Grade
I. Management of the innovation engine		B -
Understanding of the growth model	A	
Management of growth drivers Investment vs. profit Revenue gain performance Revenue dynamic performance	C	
Portfolio strategy and business case Product & technology strategies Creativity & excitement Financial performance	C	
II. Management of current projects		B -
Due diligence on current investments	B	
Support resources, processes and tools	C	
Creation of an effective environment	B	
III. Development of competitive capability		C
Strategic direction	C	
Implementation of future capability	C -	
IV. Leadership capability		B
Knowledge of fundamentals	B	
Learning rate	B -	
Management skills	B	

Leaving out any of these desired behaviors will, in general, reduce a corresponding grade on the report card. So the report card includes a relatively complete set of measures spanning all desired behaviors. The authors have not been able to imagine adverse behaviors that could game this report card. Nor have we been able to come up with ways in which portfolio leaders can raise their scores by sacrificing an important resource not measured by the report card. However, it has not been prototyped, or reviewed yet by a group of expert practitioners, so it probably contains some flaws.

The quality of this report card as an evaluation tool, though, can only be as good as (1) the information available to those who apply it, and (2) the insight and judgment that they can bring to bear when applying it. Ideally, those who might rate the performance of a portfolio leadership team would have access to the portfolio strategy and business case, the portfolio tracking notebook, and multilevel survey information. They would also have had an opportunity to visit the business, interact with people in the product innovation community, and attend new product project reviews. Their insight and judgment would come from long business experience with companies that have a strong track record for successful product innovation. Given these conditions, the report card might be a useful evaluation tool.

One business situation has occurred repeatedly in recent years where a report card such as this might have made a difference. A number of companies over the past 10 years have hired so-called turnaround experts to manage their companies out of current financial troubles. On occasion, these individuals have applied a heavy hand in cutting costs and expenses. At times, they have not only cut fat out of the budget, they have discarded large chunks of muscle and bone as well. The result has been serious damage to the core competencies of the firm, and to its product innovation capacity. The results have been dramatic improvements in profitability and return on assets, at least for the short term, and usually an initial dramatic rise in the stock price. In the long term, however, revenue growth and profitability have suffered and the stock price has plummeted. This is reminiscent of Scenario A in Chapter 4. If the boards of directors of these firms had applied a report card such as the one offered in Table 12.3, either in screening candidates for CEO, or in overseeing this individual's leadership efforts, they might have been able to detect and correct the errors before they inflicted serious damage.

■ CONCLUSION

This chapter has outlined some important principles for the design and application of performance measures for product innovation. Along with these principles, a cautionary note was sounded.

Performance measures can do more harm than good if they are misused. A clear understanding of those desired behaviors that will create improved business performance was shown to be central to the successful application of performance measures. A design methodology was offered for creating sets of performance measures that avoid potential pitfalls and encourage only the desired product innovation behaviors.

Next, these principles were applied to the business of product innovation at various levels. First, system-level performance measures for the entire innovation engine were discussed. Following this, measures of performance for each element in the product portfolio leadership process were outlined. Quantitative performance measures that have been gathered from experience and industry best practice were assembled into a portfolio manager's instrument panel for tracking the progress of individual projects in the portfolio. A set of qualitative measures were offered to assess the quality of the ambiance in the working environment. In each case, the measures were aimed at highlighting behaviors that contribute to the business success of product innovation efforts.

Finally, measures were proposed to examine the behavior of business leaders themselves in their efforts to manage the innovation engine as a business process. This set of measures took the form of a report card that could be used either in self-appraisal or, perhaps, as an evaluation tool by corporate executives or a board of directors.

A paraphrase of the initial chapter quote by Lord Kelvin might correct its initial deficiencies, at least for business management applications, and provide a suitable closing thought:

> *When you can measure what you are speaking about, and express it in terms of desired behaviors, you know something about it; but when you cannot measure it, when you cannot express it as desired behaviors, your knowledge is of a meager and unsatisfactory kind.*

This chapter has attempted to summarize, in terms of measurements, the elements of the innovation engine discussed in earlier chapters. These measures, in each case, present performance in a way that encourages constructive behaviors. These efforts to measure performance make our knowledge of product innovation more substantial, and more satisfying.

Chapter 13

Conclusion

What is the HP Way? I feel that, in general terms, it is the policies and actions that flow from the belief that men and women want to do a good job, a creative job, and that if provided the proper environment they will do so.

Bill Hewlett
HP Cofounder

This book has described product innovation as an enterprisewide system that not only involves coordinated effort among the members of each product innovation team, but also promotes a vertical teamwork linking business leaders to the efforts of individual product innovators. The long-term success of a business enterprise depends on how well the elements in this business process perform and how well they work together as an integrated program. Throughout, this work has emphasized important roles and responsibilities that only the business leadership team can fulfill. The factors that inhibit healthy growth in a business are often associated with the performance of high-level managers as they execute these critical functions. The preceding chapters have provided a comprehensive description of this enterprisewide system and described fundamental principles, best practices, and mental models to help readers provide the leadership that their own product innovation efforts need.

This discussion began with an outline of the essential relationships between the product innovation system and business growth. Key parameters of the innovation engine were described that drive exponential growth in the revenue stream. The critical success factors for single product innovation projects were also discussed, and the time response product innovation as a system was demonstrated.

This early work provided a set of mental models for the product innovation system that would allow readers to make effective management decisions even though the results of those decisions might occur well beyond their own learning horizon. Another purpose of developing this view of product innovation was to provide readers with the perspective needed to fully understand product innovation as a business process, and to enable them to begin a system-level assessment of their own new product efforts.

Next, three critical areas of focus were addressed in depth: work processes, leadership roles, and the creative environment. These discussions emphasized general principles that apply broadly across diverse business situations, industries, and technologies. These discussions had a twofold purpose. First, they provided the reader with sufficient information to more completely understand their own product innovation efforts, and to begin a detailed assessment of their strengths and weaknesses. Second, these discussions provided a vision of successful work performance in each of these areas to guide the future efforts of business leaders.

Finally, the issue of measuring performance was addressed. Some fundamental attributes of effective measures were described first, and then a methodology was outlined for designing successful performance measures. Next, both qualitative and quantitative measures for the product innovation system were discussed. The performance measures outlined here focused on the areas of responsibility owned by product portfolio leaders. Finally, a report card was proposed for assessing the overall performance of business leaders in their efforts to manage product innovation.

The perspective on product innovation that has been presented is both broad and deep. Where should the reader start? What are the next steps? To succeed, does the reader's company have to accomplish with perfection everything in this book? Of course not. Ideas for simple, quick improvements to current performance ("low-hanging fruit") can sometimes produce profoundly better results. This is a good place to start. Highlighting these opportunities and implementing solutions quickly both produces an early payback and sends strong signals throughout the enterprise that performance in product innovation is important. The techniques outlined in Chapter 9 might be useful here.

Beyond the low-hanging fruit, though, a comprehensive system-level diagnosis of current product innovation activities may be needed. For product innovation efforts to achieve their full potential, each element in the system must perform competitively, and all the elements must work together well as an integrated system. If this is not the case, an investigation should be launched to determine where and how the system is broken. Improvement efforts should then focus on these specific areas of weak performance.

Having this diagnosis performed by an experienced team from outside the company often leads to better results. A group such as this can view the entire enterprise with a fresh perspective and will often see opportunities for improvement that are not apparent to those working within the system. Furthermore, individual employees often talk more freely with experienced outsiders about performance issues because these visitors are not part of the internal power structure. An outside agency is thus often able to build a better picture of reality. Regardless of the means used for the diagnosis, the quality of the information gathered is critical to the success of subsequent improvement efforts.

Once the business leadership team is empowered with accurate information about the performance issues affecting product innovation efforts, they can define and invest in specific performance improvement projects. The techniques covered in Chapter 9 can be applied to guide the work forward from this point.

The authors have several aspirations for this work. First, we hope it will enable readers to more tightly link their new product efforts to their business needs in ways that dramatically improve the growth and financial performance of their businesses. The preceding chapters have described product innovation as a key business process that drives financial growth. Specific and useful information in this work will enable readers to make substantial improvements in the financial performance of their own company.

Second, the material covered should help readers align their product innovation efforts with a meaningful organizational vision that focuses the energies of their enterprise on fruitful, long-term market opportunities, and allows it to effectively serve its customers in new and important ways. Business enterprises are one of the most powerful influences for change in the world. In their pursuit of profit, they focus immense amounts of capital and human energy on selected opportunities. Ultimately they succeed because they satisfy customers. So customers who vote with their dollars wield the ultimate power, but business enterprises—with their creativity, their new technology, and their core competencies—provide these customers with the attractive choices that can make their lives better in various ways. This symbiosis between businesses and their customers is a strong and potentially positive force in the world.

Finally, we hope that, over time, the material presented here will help improve the personal well-being of individual product innovators everywhere and amplify the contribution they can make to the world with their unique skills. High-level managers are responsible for ongoing evaluation of the state of a business, both external and internal to the company, and for setting the strategy and direction for the enterprise. Individual product innovators, however, provide much of the "bone and muscle" of the firm that moves it into its future. Product innovators, by applying their extraordinary talents, invent new technologies, create new solutions, and bring new products into existence. And these new products both drive revenue growth and create progress toward the strategic objectives set by business leaders.

Often the efforts of these product innovators change our world in important ways. If automobiles of the future are to be powered by highly efficient, low-pollution fuel cells instead of internal combustion engines, it is product innovators who will make this happen. If homes of the future are to be built from alternative materials such as recycled plastics, it is product innovators who will show the way. If humankind is to somehow learn how to live on its planet in a sustainable fashion, then product innovators will play essential roles in bringing the required changes into being. And, to take a fair look at the other side of the coin, if our world is someday destroyed in a nuclear holocaust, it will be product innovators who bring these weapons of destruction into existence. The power of product innovators is like that double-edged sword mentioned in Chapter 12. The combined diligence of business leaders, customers, and political systems is required to see that this power creates consistent, positive change in the world.

The power of product innovators is greatly affected by a company's ambiance. And this working environment can vary wildly between companies. The authors have personally encountered a wide spectrum of product innovation environments. Some routinely produce happiness, pride, and joy among product innovators, and others create fear, frustration, and tears on a daily basis. And the long-term business success of each enterprise seems to vary almost directly with the mood that is prevalent throughout its product innovation community. In general, product innovators who understand and believe in the business direction that their employer is pursuing, and who have the support and freedom they need to do a good job, will completely invest themselves in their work, and take pride and joy in doing so. This was certainly true at HP, as reflected in the chapter opening quotation by Bill Hewlett.

If this book in some way improves the sense of pride and accomplishment that product innovators take in their work, then it will have met its objectives.

Appendix

A Mathematical Link between New Product Investment and Revenue Growth

This appendix provides a derivation of the mathematics that relate revenue growth to the rate of investment in new product operations, the new product revenue gain, and the vintage-year dynamics of the revenue stream, as discussed in Chapter 2.

Figure A.1 is used here as a prototypical vintage-year representation of annual revenues for a company. The total revenues for each year are a summation of contributions from products introduced in that year plus products introduced in some number of earlier years. How many years contribute to the revenues for a given year is a function of the vintage-year revenue dynamic. A key assumption is that the revenue dynamic is the same for all vintage years. In other words, the distribution of revenues into the future for products introduced in any vintage year can be represented by the same constant vector with fractional elements.

The following row vector, α, is an example for a business with an 11-year revenue life for each vintage year. Figure A.1 is derived using α as the revenue dynamic. Each element in the vector represents the fraction of total revenues for that vintage year that will occur for a given year after product introduction. The sum of all elements of α therefore must be 1.0. The elements of the vector are designated symbolically, from left to right, as a_0 through a_n.

$$\alpha = (.05\ 0.1\ 0.1\ 0.1\ 0.1\ 0.1\ 0.1\ 0.1\ 0.1\ 0.1\ .05) \quad (1)$$

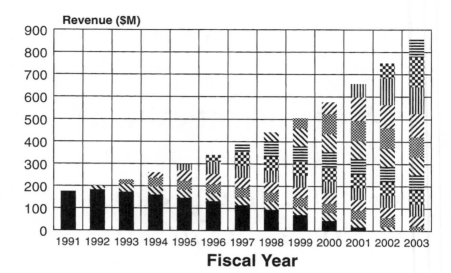

Figure A.1 A prototypical vintage chart.

The perspective assumed here is that new products *cause* revenue to happen. The total amount of revenue that a vintage year causes over the full life of its products is given by

$$\text{Revenue}_{\text{Total}}(k) = G_{RD} \times RD(k) \tag{2}$$

Where G_{RD} is a revenue gain factor (\$ Revenue/\$ R&D) and $RD(k)$ is the investment made in new products in year k.

The revenue gain factor, G_{RD}, depends on the opportunities selected for new product investment and on the productivity of the people, processes, and tools involved in the effort. While G_{RD} may change over time as business conditions vary, for the purposes of this derivation it is assumed to be nonvarying over the time span of interest.

The vector, α, describes how $\text{Revenue}_{\text{Total}}$ will be distributed forward in time. In year k, products from vintage-year k will cause:

$$\text{Rev}_0(k) = a_0 \, G_{RD} RD(k) \tag{3}$$

In year k + i, products from vintage-year k will cause:

$$\text{Rev}_i(k + i) = a_i \, G_{RD} RD(k) \tag{4}$$

Revenue caused by vintage-year k will continue in this manner through year $k + n$ and then stop because the full value of Revenue$_{\text{Total}}$ will have been distributed..

Shifting the perspective to a single fiscal year, year k, the total revenues for that year can now be calculated by summing up the contributions from each of the relevant vintage years. In Figure A.1, refer to fiscal year 2002, which is the first year in the graph that is made up totally from contributions from vintage years that are all covered by the graph. Mathematically, total revenues for fiscal year k are given by:

$$Rev(k) = a_0 \, G_{RD} \, RD(k) + a_1 \, G_{RD} \, RD(k-1) + \ldots .$$
$$+ \, a_n \, G_{RD} \, RD(k-n) \tag{5}$$

The investment in new products for a given year is given by:

$$RD(k) = RD\%(k) \, Rev(k) \tag{6}$$

For simplicity, the percentage of revenues invested in new products will be assumed to remain constant from year to year at a value represented symbolically as RD%. This is approximately true in most companies and is a reasonable approximation, in particular, for the Hewlett-Packard Company.

The revenues from year to year are related by the fractional growth term, g, such that:

$$Rev(k) = Rev(k-1) \, (1 + g) \tag{7}$$

Since revenue growth is caused by new products, g will be determined as a function of investments in new product activity and the revenue gain factor, G_{RD}. Again for simplicity, g will be assumed to be constant from year to year. Applying equations (6) and (7) to equation (5):

$$Rev(k) = a_0 \, G_{RD} \, RD\% \, Rev(k) + a_1 \, G_{RD} \, RD\% \, Rev(k) \, (1 + g)^{-1}$$
$$+ \ldots . + a_n \, G_{RD} \, RD\% \, Rev(k) \, (1 + g)^{-n} \tag{8}$$

Let

$$K = G_{RD} \, RD\% \tag{9}$$

and

$$x = 1 + g \tag{10}$$

Applying these relationships to equation (8) and gathering terms on one side of resulting equation yields:

$$\text{Rev}(k)[1 - a_0 K - a_1 K x^{-1} - \ldots - a_n K x^{-n}] = 0 \qquad (11)$$

Finally, dividing both sides by Rev(k) and multiplying both sides by x^n gives:

$$(1 - a_0 K) x^n - K [a_1 x^{n-1} + a_2 x^{n-2} + \ldots + a_n] = 0 \qquad (12)$$

The relationships between RD%, GRD and the revenue growth term, g, are established by solving for the roots of equation (12). Specifying a value for RD% and estimating the value of G_{RD} allows calculation of a value for K. Evaluating the revenue time dynamic, either by averaging historical vintage-year performance or by estimating future revenue performance, provides values for a_0 through a_n. Once these factors are all specified, equation (12) can be solved through either closed-form or approximation techniques to determine the root values for x which is, of course, equal to $1 + g$. In general, there will be n different values for x that satisfy equation (12) so care must be taken to choose the one that is realistic for the business case. For typical values of RD%, G_{RD}, and α, this will usually be the first real and positive value for x that satisfies equation (12).

Many different values of G_{RD} and RD% can be combined to yield a given value for K. Equation (12) needs only to be solved for a particular value of K. That solution for x then works for any combination of G_{RD} and RD% that yields the value of K used in the solution.

The revenue growth tables in Chapters 2 and 4 were derived using Mathcad 7™ worksheets to systematically solve equation (12) for different values of RD% and G_{RD}.[1] Each growth table utilizes a different vector, α, characteristic to the given business. For example, Figure 2.3 gives the values of a_0 through a_7, characteristic to HP, that were used to derive Table 2.3.

---

[1] Mathcad 7 is a product of MathSoft Corporation of Cambridge, Massachusetts.

About the Authors

Marvin L. Patterson is cofounder and president of Innovation Resultants International (IRI), a firm dedicated to helping client companies achieve greater business success through more effective product innovation. Since founding IRI in 1993, Marv and his colleagues have helped dozens of companies improve their new product efforts. IRI has developed a unique perspective on the key success factors for competitive product innovation that has proven useful in a wide range of industries from office products to heavy equipment to telecommunications to integrated circuits.

Before establishing IRI, Marv enjoyed a 20-year career at Hewlett-Packard Company where, most recently, he served as the Director of R&D Operations. Before that, he was Director of HP's Corporate Engineering group, whose mission is to improve the productivity and competitiveness of companywide new product development efforts. Under Marv's leadership, Corporate Engineering launched several successful initiatives that addressed critical areas of the product innovation process including improved methods and tools for software development—EE and ME design—project management, and product portfolio management.

Marv joined HP in 1973 as a development engineer at the San Diego division. He was responsible for bringing the grit wheel plotting technology, invented by HP Laboratories, to the marketplace. This launched a generation of revolutionary new plotters which were extremely successful. Prior to joining HP, Marv worked as a development engineer and engineering manager in the areas of telemetry systems, microwave structures, and target drone control systems for the U.S. Navy at Pt. Mugu, California.

Marv is the author of the highly regarded book, *Accelerating Innovation: Improving the Process of Product Development* (New York: John Wiley & Sons, 1997), as well as many technical papers. He holds three U.S. patents and has been on the Board of Trustees for the National Technological University and the Board of Directors of the American National Standards Institute. Marv received his BSEE and MSEE from the University of Washington and is a graduate of the University of Michigan Executive Program.

E-mail: MarvPatrsn@aol.com

John A. Fenoglio is cofounder and vice-president of IRI. Since founding IRI with his colleagues in 1993, John has helped dozens of companies improve their new product efforts. His work at IRI has provided hands-on experience in diagnosing new-product-related performance issues and developed an ability to define and implement effective corrective measures.

Before establishing IRI, John enjoyed a 21-year career at the Hewlett-Packard Company where he served in various positions related to product innovation. Early in his career he worked as a development engineer, product marketing manager, and development engineering manager at HP's San Diego division. In 1989 John joined the Corporate Engineering group in Palo Alto, California, to help improve companywide new product processes and tools. In his work there, John was responsible for HP's efforts to improve product development management methods throughout the company. He also managed HP's interaction with other companies in benchmarking new product practices.

John received his Bachelor degree from California Polytechnic University in Pomona and his Masters degree in electrical engineering from San Diego State University. He is an accomplished speaker on diverse topics related to product innovation and has participated as copresenter in dozens of IRI executive seminars.

E-mail: JohnFenoglio@home.com

Index